THE COMPUTER ENTREPRENEURS

Other books by
Robert Levering, Michael Katz, Milton Moskowitz

► The 100 Best Companies to Work for in America

► Everybody's Business Scoreboard
  Corporate America's Winners, Losers, and Also-Rans

► Everybody's Business: An Almanac
  The Irreverent Guide to Corporate America

THE COMPUTER ENTREPRENEURS

*Who's Making It Big
and How
in America's Upstart Industry*

BY
ROBERT LEVERING
MICHAEL KATZ
MILTON MOSKOWITZ

NAL BOOKS

NEW AMERICAN LIBRARY

NEW YORK AND SCARBOROUGH, ONTARIO

To Florence, a precomputer mother
To Susan and Reuben
To Jane

Copyright © 1984 by Robert Levering, Michael Katz, Milton Moskowitz

For information address New American Library

Library of Congress Cataloging in Publication Data

Levering, Robert, 1944
    The computer entrepreneurs

    "NAL books."
       1. Computer industry—United States—Biography.
2. Computer service industry—United States—Biography.
3. Computer industry—United States. 4. Computer
service industry—United States. I. Katz, Michael,
1945. II. Moskowitz, Milton. III. Title.
HD9696.C63U5215 1984 338.7'6100164'0922 [B] 84-19057
ISBN 0-453-00477-6

SIGNET, SIGNET CLASSIC, MENTOR, PLUME, MERIDIAN,
and NAL BOOKS are published *in the United States* by
New American Library, 1633 Broadway, New York, New York 10019,
in Canada by The New American Library of Canada Limited,
81 Mack Avenue, Scarborough, Ontario, M1L 1M8.

First Printing, November, 1984
1 2 3 4 5 6 7 8 9
PRINTED IN THE UNITED STATES OF AMERICA

► *Research Director & Technical Editor*
HARRY STRHARSKY

Senior Writers
SUSAN SHEPARD
LINDA HESS

Contributing Writer
KRISTIN ANUNDSEN

Editorial Assistant
JANE HIRSHFIELD

Research Assistant
CAROL TOWNSEND

► *Project Manager*
JILL FOX

Production Editor
CHERYL COLLINS

Designer
THOMAS INGALLS + ASSOCIATES

Typographer
ON LINE TYPOGRAPHY

► *Illustrator*
BOB JOHNSON

INTRODUCTION

This book tells the stories of 65 men and women who personify the 1980s version of the American Dream. They are rich, for the most part, some inconceivably so. They are independent: most run companies they founded. They are powerful: most employ hundreds, if not thousands, of workers. They are associated with the glamour industry of the decade—computers. And some are famous: two (Arthur Rock and Bill Gates) have been on the cover of *Time,* while another (Steve Jobs) has the media status of a rock star.

We did not set out to write a book about individuals. We wanted to profile an industry—the personal computer industry—which had grown up overnight. We discovered it was an industry of entrepreneurs. It barely existed when we wrote an earlier book, *Everybody's Business: An Almanac,* describing 317 of America's largest corporations. But in the course of a few short years, the personal computer ushered in a Gold Rush unlike any other in the history of American business. Companies were formed—and fortunes created—with incredible speed. Apple Computer made the *Fortune* 500 roster less than five years after its birth in a Silicon Valley garage. No company had ever achieved that before. Another young venture, Compaq, became the first firm to do more than $100 million in sales its first year out of the starting gate. And while it took McDonald's 15 years to get to the $1 billion sales mark, ComputerLand stores accomplished it in only 8.

As we began our research, we realized that we were presented with a unique opportunity. We could take a snapshot of an industry-in-the-making—a group portrait of the people who would change, with their new technology, the way we live. No one, we noticed, appears to have done a similar survey of the only comparable period in American business history—the early stages of the automobile industry. Dozens, even hundreds, of people tinkered in their barns, trying to forge, weld, and bolt together the contraptions they hoped would secure them fortunes. Everyone knows the story of the most successful tinkerer—Henry Ford. But little is known about most of the other automobile pioneers—who they were, what products they made, and how they started their businesses. We realize that all but a charmed handful of our computer entrepreneurs are similarly destined for oblivion, and we don't care to offer predictions as to who will survive. The richest man in this book—William Millard, reputed to be a billionaire—took his previous venture into bankruptcy only five years ago. We've tried to catch the computer entrepreneurs now, before the industry "shakes out," while they are still willing to offer a glimpse of their backgrounds, motivations, and dreams.

In innumerable magazine articles during recent months, entrepreneurs have been called our next cultural heroes. They have been hailed as the embodiment of a new business spirit that has arrived in the nick of time to pull us out of our economic malaise. A veritable cult of entrepreneurship proclaims that out of this group will arise the innovation and new jobs that will save the American way of life. Indeed, the cult aspect has become so strong that one of the largest companies in the U.S. economy, IBM, has tried to recreate an entrepreneurial mode within its corporate walls, and a new term, "intrapreneurship," has even been coined to describe big-company efforts to encourage individual initiative.

We spent the better part of a year tracking down computer entrepreneurs. We met with them in their offices and factories. We visited them in their homes (or, in some cases, mansions). We squeezed in interviews during trade shows amidst the bustle and clamor that epitomize the excitement of their industry. We caught up with them on the run, in their hotel rooms, in restaurants, and in bars. In all, we talked to nearly 100 computer entrepreneurs.

We found them to be an amazing bunch. We were struck again and again by their diversity, energy, intensity, and, in some instances, pure charisma. It is impossible to shoehorn these people into a simple mold. In background they range from an Oklahoma farm girl whose first job was bringing in the cows, to a Korean street urchin who used to shine shoes and sell pencils on the sidewalks of Seoul, to a California teen-aged tire thief. Their roads to success were equally varied: some came through decades of employment in America's largest corporations; others turned their backs on a whole series of promising career starts.

We tried to see if we could invent a typology, to find categories into which these computer entrepreneurs could be placed. It's not a perfect fit, but here are seven recognizable types:

—Survivors: Those who, like Jack Tramiel and Philip Hwang, endured harrowing experiences as children, but emerged with a relentless drive that has served them in good stead in the American business world.

—Popeyes: People who spent 10 years or more inside big companies before they "had all's they could stand," ate their spinach, and went out on their own. IBM, for instance, spawned a half-dozen of these entrepreneurs.

—Entreprenerds: Gary Kildall and Bill Gates have made fortunes because of their smarts; their curiosity and drive have created key pieces of the technology.

—Visionaries: Men like Steve Jobs, Dustin Heuston, and Regis McKenna are intoxicated by the technology itself and see computers as a way to a better world.

—"Me Too's": Those who were patiently working in and around the computer world and saw others get wealthy by setting up their own shops; they, too, determined to take part in the Gold Rush. One, Porter Hurt, developed this feeling while driving nails into buildings for Silicon Valley start-ups.

—Compulsive Business Starters: They love starting new businesses. When they fail, men like Sheldon Adelson and William von Meister simply start another. For them, incorporating is a way of life.

—Lucky Ducks: Stumbling upon an opportunity, these entrepreneurs (Lorraine Mecca, William Millard, Robert Leff, and Dave Wagman) realized they were at the right place at the right time, and seized their chance.

We also found patterns in the stories of their personal lives. Many of the computer entrepreneurs come from humble backgrounds—very few were born rich. A handful experienced real poverty. Many were the first in their families to enter the "professional" class. There is a pattern of broken families and divorces; some call it part of the price of starting a business. They are all extremely hard-working, if not outright workaholics.

As for motivation, some, notably Jerry Sanders and Ken Williams, told us frankly that theirs is simple: they want to make a lot of money. Yet no one should think that because these people got rich quickly, it could have been done without a lot of groundwork. Most spent years becoming familiar with the technology, or getting their experience through the hard knocks of launching enterprises that failed. We found it notable that many of these businessmen and women have a strong social conscience; their explanations of what drives them have a '60s ring—they want to make the whole culture change.

The computer entrepreneurs are conscious of being on the leading edge of a new technology. They are at ease explaining what they are doing in intellectual terms. But while several of them have doctorates, a surprising number have dropped out of school and never bothered to get a degree. And there are a great many Democrats in this group, unlike in a sampling of traditional business leaders. There are also more women than one might expect; three of the companies in this book are headed by women. That's only one out of 20, but it's a quantum leap from the proportion of women among the general business elite.

So this is clearly a different group of business types—and it's their diversity, their off-the-wall character, that made it fascinating to talk with them, and to hear them tell their stories. To a great extent, you will find here the world as they see it. It's not always a pretty picture. You will see arrogance here. You will see jealousy. You will see people who covet Rolls-Royces. You will, above all, see people with colossal egos who tend to believe the world revolves around them. It's a reminder that despite the new technology, these folks have not created a new world. As far as business goes, they are operating, for the most part, with the old patterns. But there are exceptions, of course, and we found it a hopeful sign that a number of the entrepreneurs were paying attention to both the quality and the integrity of their products and to providing a good place for people to work. Two of them head firms we selected in our last book, *The 100 Best Companies to Work for in America.*

The founder of one of the largest companies in this book

told us that, in all the time he had spent with reporters, no one had ever asked him about himself. We hope that the profiles in this book will be of interest, serve as guideposts and cautionary markers, and amuse. But we also hope this book will help readers see the side of business that is often hidden: that the attitudes, hopes, and intentions of individuals are responsible for the kind of culture we share.

ACKNOWLEDGMENTS

The page listing the contributors to our book only begins to express the debt we owe to those who have helped make this book a reality. First and foremost, we cannot say enough about Harry Strharsky, whom we nominate as the best corporate researcher in the business. He spent countless hours in libraries and behind his computer hooked up to various on-line data bases, getting every scrap of published information on these entrepreneurs and their companies. Nor can we overpraise Jill Fox and Cheryl Collins: Jill, for her incredible organizing skills that kept the project together from the beginning and got the book to press on time, and Cheryl, for her patience in transcribing dozens of hours of taped interviews and her sharp proofreading eye that was always focused on quality.

We also would like to express our appreciation to journalist John Dvorak and other industry insiders who prefer to remain anonymous for offering hours of behind-the-scenes insight. Finally, we would like to thank Joe Esposito, our editor at NAL, who knew when to stay out of our hair and when to jump into the fire.

We welcome comments from our readers. Our address is: Everybody's Business Almanac, 1537 Franklin Street, San Francisco, California 94109.

Robert Levering
Michael Katz
Milton Moskowitz
September 1984

CONTENTS

CHAPTER 1

MACHINE MAKERS

Nolan Bushnell

"Live entertainers are expensive. You don't have to pay robots"

▶ **BEST-KNOWN VENTURE:** Atari

OTHER VENTURES: Syzygy, Catalyst Technologies, Pizza Time Theaters, Sente Technology, Lion & Compass, Androbot

BORN: 1943

RAISED: Clearfield, Utah

FATHER'S OCCUPATION: Mason

SCHOOLING: B.S., engineering, University of Utah

ORIGINAL FINANCING: $500

PERSONAL NET WORTH: $70 million

HOME: Woodside, California

FAMILY: Divorced; remarried; two daughters from first marriage, three sons from second marriage

PERSONAL TRANSPORTATION: Rolls-Royce, Mercedes, Peugeot (among others)

⅃⅄ATARI

ATARI: Pioneers of video games and makers of home computers.

▶ **BEST-KNOWN PRODUCTS:** *Pac Man, Pong, Space Invaders,* VCS 2600 game machine, *Asteroids, Missile Command*

YEAR FOUNDED: 1972

EMPLOYEES: 250 and falling (August 1984)

HEADQUARTERS: Sunnyvale, California

SALES: $2 billion (1982); $1 billion (1983)

LOSSES: $500 million

OWNERSHIP: Jack Tramiel

Nolan Bushnell is the man who rejected the idea of a personal computer when Steve Jobs proposed it to him. Jobs was then working for Bushnell's company, Atari. That was in 1976. At the same time, Steve Wozniak was making an identical proposal to his superiors at Hewlett-Packard. They also rejected it. So the two Steves left to found Apple Computer. Seven years later, reflecting on the short shrift he'd given Jobs, Bushnell remarked, "See, I never said we were perfect."

The six-foot, four-inch, bearded Bushnell is the entrepreneur born and reborn and reborn. Much of what he has started has gone down in flames. He admits he has trouble running companies. But he's still out there, smoking his pipe, looking for ideas, and enjoying his reputation as one of the early wizards of Silicon Valley. Not too long after he turned down Jobs's idea, Bushnell sold his company, Atari, to Warner Communications. There was a messy lawsuit with his wife, who contested his title to the stock; and then there was a problem involving a newspaper picture of Bushnell in a hot tub with a lady friend; but he did become a millionaire at age 33 by selling the company he started.

When we saw him in the summer of 1984, Bushnell was happily ensconced behind a *Star Wars*-type desk in Sunnyvale, not far from where he scored his initial big success in Silicon Valley with *Pong*. The huge, plastic-laminated desk has two built-in video terminals. At the edge of the desk is a video console with a one line display that allows his secretary to communicate with him without talking directly to him or buzzing the phone. Behind his desk is a six-foot-high TV screen. Nolan Bushnell is a gadget freak.

The Nolan Bushnell story began in Utah during World War II. Nolan was born into a Mormon family in Clearfield, which is near Ogden. He was the second of four children and the only boy. Bushnell's father was an independent contractor, a mason who expected Nolan to work. And work. And work he did. He operated the proverbial lemonade stand. He sold strawberries. He helped his father. Nolan showed an early mechanical aptitude. By the time he was 10 years old, he was a ham radio operator, and the attitude around the Bushnell home was: "That stuff costs money. If you want to spend it, you have to earn it."

To say that young Bushnell worked his way through the University of Utah would be an understatement. He started with selling the campus blotter, which was a schedule of events surrounded on all sides by advertising. "The best way to save your money," he points out, "is to get a second job." And so Bushnell worked nights—and summers—at the Lagoon amusement park. He started out as a regular employee. By the time he was out of school, he was running the games at the park and had 100 young kids working for him. Meanwhile, he was introduced to computers. Naturally, he played games on them. He received his engineering degree, but he didn't graduate with honors. In fact, he figures he must have been 197th in a class of 197. His UU days were notable for one other development: he met and married his wife there.

Nolan Bushnell knew what he wanted to do with his degree: work for Walt Disney. With his amusement park background, it seemed to be a natural transition. He applied to Disney, but was turned down. So he took a research job in Northern California at Ampex, the company best known for its development of videotape. Ampex was based in Redwood City, on the edge of what we know today as Silicon Valley.

The Bushnells—they had two daughters—settled into a tract home in Santa Clara. Bushnell would come home from his boring job at Ampex to tinker with his old love, games. He began designing video games, eventually moving his younger daughter out of her room so that he could have some work space.

Bushnell wasn't the only computer whiz trying to come up with video games. Credit for the first video game usually goes to an MIT student who had written *Space War* in the early 1960s. It was a sophisticated shoot-'em-up that had become a kind of underground classic played on mainframes in the wee hours of the morning by computer programmers all over the country. As time went on, some of those programmers began trying to write commercial versions of *Space War* and its offshoots. But before Nolan Bushnell, no one was able to make a video game that fit into a box that could be put in an arcade.

Although Bushnell's first game, *Computer Space*, showed some promise, it flopped commercially. But his next one, *Pong*, turned out to be a barn burner.

Pong allowed two people to sit before a TV screen and play a form of electronic table tennis. The story of how he market-tested *Pong* has been told in the computer trade many times. He designed *Pong* as a coin-operated game—one play for a quarter—and had it installed in Andy Capp's Tavern in Sunnyvale. He soon got a call from the tavern owner saying that the game had broken down and would Bushnell please come around and take it away. However, when Bushnell went to pick up his machine, he found it hadn't broken down—it was just so stuffed with quarters that the mechanism had jammed. He knew he had a winner.

So in 1972 Bushnell resigned his job at Ampex to start Atari, a term used in the Japanese game *go* that means "I'm going to attack you." The 29-year-old Bushnell bootstrapped the company without the benefit of outside financing, which took confidence and guts. He went to suppliers and ordered thousands of dollars worth of parts needed to make *Pong*. He had 30 days to pay these bills. Then he turned around, made the machines as quickly as possible, and put them in the hands of distributors, asking for immediate payment so that he could pay his suppliers. It worked. Bushnell told us that in its first year Atari turned over its inventory 28 times. Atari shipped its first *Pong* game in November 1972. In 1973 the company sold 10,000 games at $1,200 apiece. In 1975 Atari started selling a home version of its games. Sears alone bought 100,000 cartridges.

Nolan Bushnell, who had always been in love with games, had invented the successor to the pinball machine. Soon kids all over the country were pumping quarters into video games. Atari rode the wave, although it quickly had plenty of competition. Bushnell seems to remember those early years of making it with some affection, even though he was divorced from his wife in 1975. Everyone who has ever written about those days of Atari describe them as a "loose" time—a period marked by playfulness, when everyone wore jeans and T-shirts to work. Bushnell was called "King Pong" in the press and had a large stuffed bear in his office and beer on tap. *Fortune* once described three-day brainstorming sessions at a vacation retreat on the California coast where company executives smoked dope and drank beer.

Bushnell particularly liked the give-and-take sessions with engineers. Larry Kaplan, one of the early Atari game designers, once characterized Bushnell as follows: "He loves games. If you did a good game, Nolan would come down and say, 'God, I really enjoyed your new game.' Nolan understands engineers; they like working for him."

The jury is still out on whether Nolan Bushnell can—or wants to—run an organization. He once said, "I like to develop the strategy, not work on it." Atari's sales had bounded past the $20-million mark by 1976 but Bushnell had not taken much money out; it mostly went back into the business. He decided to sell because it seemed time "to consolidate your win." His favorite company, Walt Disney, took a look but declined the opportunity. Warner Communications, the house of rock music records and *Mad* magazine, accepted, paying

$28 million, of which Bushnell himself pocketed $15 million.

Bushnell stayed on for two years after Warner took over, but then left to pursue his own ventures. Warner moved in its own people. John Hubner and William F. Kistner Jr. did a superlative article on "what went wrong at Atari" for the November 6, 1983, issue of *West,* the magazine supplement of the Sunday *San Jose Mercury News.* Bushnell told them that Warner wanted to demote him from chairman to vice chairman. "I thought vice chairman was a horseshit title," Bushnell said. "I didn't want it. I want to be in the thick of things." The man Warner installed to run Atari was Raymond Kassar, who presided first over an incredible boom—and then over just as incredible a bust. Kassar spent 25 years with Burlington Industries, the nation's top textile manufacturer. "When he made Kassar chairman," Bushnell told Hubner and Kistner, "I told Manny [Warner honcho Emanuel Gerard] he was the wrong man. I didn't think Kassar could get along with engineers. He couldn't get down on the floor with them. Unless you can do that, you're not going to get along with them. An engineer doesn't always come in a body that can talk. But they're not shitheads. You've got to have enough faith in them to say, 'I don't know what you're talking about; here's some money, go show me."

Bushnell's perception proved to be deadly accurate. Hubner and Kistner described a meeting in 1979 between Kassar and four of Atari's top game designers: Larry Kaplan, Dave Crane, Al Miller and Bob Whitehead:

"The designers found Kassar at his desk, wearing a well-tailored suit. They were, as usual, in jeans. The four had a lot on their minds. They wanted Atari to treat them the way Warner treats recording artists. They felt their games had played a large role in the company's success, and they asked Kassar for royalties on them. They wanted recognition, too. Musicians got their names and pictures on record albums; why couldn't theirs be put on game cartridges?"

"Kassar called us 'towel designers,'" Kaplan recalls. "He said, 'I've dealt with your kind before. You're a dime a dozen. You're not unique. Anybody can do a cartridge.'"

Five months later Crane, Miller, and Whitehead left to form

Activision. Other former Atari engineers later formed Imagic, another major Atari competitor.

Out on his own, Bushnell launched a slew of new ventures. It's clearly what he likes to do. He conceded to us that he gets easily distracted and that he becomes very unhappy when he finds that he's spending more than 25 percent of his time with lawyers and accountants. He also thinks that he becomes too friendly with the people he does business with. "If I have a fault," he said, "it's that I hire well but I don't fire well."

There's not much that Nolan Bushnell hasn't done. He helped start a computer camp, TimberTech, and a computer store, Exec-Tech. He put $2 million into a vain attempt to rescue Advent, the company that tried to make it as a maker of large-screen projection TV equipment. He started Pizza Time Theatre, a combination pizza hall, video arcade, and electronic classroom presided over by an animated robot, Chuck E. Cheese.

Bushnell went to Washington, D.C., in 1982 to promote Pizza Time. Interviewed by the *Washington Post,* he depicted these pizza restaurants as places where children could learn about computers. "Woe to those parents who deliberately restrict their children from playing with these new games," he said. "They will be handicapping their children. Ask them, is the computer here to stay? Does a child need to learn word processing to succeed in college? And where is he going to learn it?" In early 1984, however, Pizza Time entered Chapter 11 bankruptcy proceedings.

Another Bushnell venture that was having a hard time getting off the ground is his robot company, Androbot. It lost $3 million in its first five months of operation and had to cancel a planned public offering of stock. According to *Business Week,* Bushnell put up $2.2 million to buy Videa Inc., a software game company started by other ex-Atari engineers. Games are still important to this man, who said: "The fun business is as important as smokestack America."

Bushnell has his own venture company, Catalyst Technology, set up in 1982 to fund interesting new ideas. In pure Bushnell, he doesn't just fund. It's a hands-on game for him. He still considers himself an engineer. Visiting his sleek new office building in Sunnyvale, in the heart of Silicon Valley, you see a long roster of high-tech sounding companies as you enter, including: ACTV; Androbot; Bally-Sente; ByVideo; Cinemavision; Etak; I'ro; Lion & Compass; Magnum Microwave; and Vistar.

Bushnell is chairman of the board at six of the companies, including Bally-Sente, which is a division of the big slot machine maker, Bally.

Perhaps the most successful of these ventures is the Lion & Compass, an upscale, white-tablecloth restaurant that Bushnell opened in 1982 just off the Bayshore Freeway in Sunnyvale, not far from his office. Silicon Valley, for all its *nouveau* residents, is a wasteland of fast-food joints—and so Bushnell started the Lion & Compass as a fine dining establishment and as a place that would stock his favorite British beers, John Courage and Watney's. The Lion & Compass has become *the* gathering place for Silicon Valley heavies. The restaurant has a Bronx-born chef, Steven Goodwin, and is operated by Bushnell's second wife, Nancy, and her family.

Bushnell may have worn jeans when he started Atari, but no more. He dresses in shirt and tie and finely tailored suits. He is no longer a practicing Mormon. He drives a Rolls-Royce and, by his own estimate, is worth $70 million. He describes himself as a "conservative Republican," having found, he said, that those "bleeding heart policies don't work when you're running a company." He dismisses liberal Democrats such as Regis McKenna and William Hambrecht as "limousine liberals. They've never been in the trenches." By that he means running a company. He recalls that when he started Atari he used to bus workers in from Oakland. He claims half of them would usually fail to show up and he had to work hard even to get paychecks to those that did. According to Bushnell, he beat back a union-organizing drive at Atari, 80 to 20, with the 20 percent in favor of the union consisting of incompetents whom he hadn't had the courage to fire.

Nolan Bushnell is a patriotic entrepreneur—that is, he believes entrepreneurship is what will save America and provide all the future jobs. He is quite irritated at the term "Atari Democrats," referring to Gary Hart-types who look for economic salvation through high technology and a national industrial policy. He also sneers at the term "industrial policy." If we had an industrial policy, he told us, "the last thing that would be targeted by these planners are companies like Atari and Apple. You know which industries would be targeted? Steel, corn, automobiles. Because they have political constituencies."

Regis McKenna, when told he had been depicted as a limousine liberal by Bushnell, said: "At least my company is still surviving and making money. His isn't."

OVERNIGHT MILLIONAIRES

The Crop of 1983

K. Philip Hwang	TeleVideo Systems	$610 million
Andrew Kay	Kaypro	$245 million
Lorraine Mecca	Micro D	$ 59 million
Mitch Kapor	Lotus	$ 56 million
Hal Lashlee	Ashton-Tate	$ 49 million
George Tate	Ashton-Tate	$ 48 million
James Toreson	Xebec	$ 44 million
Dustin Heuston	Wicat	$ 31 million
Terry Johnson	Miniscribe	$ 31 million
Gary Friedman	Fortune Systems	$ 31 million

*(Value of their personal stock the morning after their
initial public offerings)*

John Ellenby

"I got married about the same time I got interested in computers. My wife was one of the first computer widows"

► **BEST-KNOWN VENTURE:** GRiD Systems

BORN: 1941

RAISED: Newcastle-On-Tyne, England

PARENTS' OCCUPATION: Professors of zoology

FIRST POUND EARNED: Scavenging bombed-out buildings after World War II

SCHOOLING: Accounting degree, University College, London, England

ORIGINAL FINANCING: Savings and friend/investors

PERSONAL NET WORTH: "Around 10 percent of GRiD Systems"

HOME: Palo Alto, California

FAMILY: Married; two sons

PERSONAL TRANSPORTATION: Audi 5000

GRiD SYSTEMS CORPORATION: Makers of the high-end portable computer for people in high places.

▶ **BEST-KNOWN PRODUCTS:** The GRiD Compass

YEAR FOUNDED: 1979

EMPLOYEES: 252

HEADQUARTERS: Mountain View, California

SALES: $22 million (1983)

OWNERSHIP: Private, jointly owned by founder, several institution venture capital firms, and an employee stock plan

The U.S. power elite has fallen in love with John Ellenby's pint-sized computer, the GRiD Compass. Every member of the 40-person entourage that went to China with President Reagan in 1984 carried one. A specially shielded Compass invaded Grenada with the U.S. Army Airborne Division. NASA crews aboard the space shuttles have grown so fond of the Compass on the dash that they've nicknamed it "Spock."

The Compass is the most sophisticated and expensive computer ever to fit in a briefcase, and its creator's impeccable credentials undoubtedly add to his product's appeal to customers in high places.

Born and raised in England, Ellenby is the son of two scientists. Although he liked the science courses at his Quaker boarding school in Yorkshire (he recalls creating rare explosives with particular fondness), he felt that "with two prestigious zoologists in the family already, I should do something else."

The London School of Economics was so impressed with him that they urged him to go straight for a Ph.D. in accounting without stopping for a master's degree. Then suddenly, in 1966, the course of his life changed. While testing his thesis that energy consumption could predict the direction of the entire economy, he called up IBM's United Kingdom office to ask for help with his elaborate computations. After taking a two-week course in the use of IBM's equipment, Ellenby did in two months what would otherwise have taken him five years. He was hooked.

He dropped his pursuit of the doctorate and soon started consulting for a civil engineering group and a big oil firm. Before long he moved to Scotland to teach in Edinburgh University's computer science department while also helping to design a family of minicomputers for Ferranti Electronics. His wife Gillian, a Scottish sculptress, became, in his words, "one of the first computer widows."

Both his academic and consulting jobs involved travel, and one of the places Ellenby visited was California. In 1973, after he'd given a lunchtime seminar for Xerox, they offered him a job at their computer science laboratory in Palo Alto. He accepted.

Under the protective wing of Xerox, Ellenby had his first warm-up for becoming an entrepreneur. He proposed a Special Programs Group to design advanced products for internal company use, and Xerox let him build his own organization in El Segundo, outside Los Angeles. The SPG's first product was the Alto II (for Palo Alto), a streamlined version of a futuristic personal work station that had been the brainchild of another Xerox employee, Bob Metcalf. Xerox was pleased; building the Alto II took half the time and half the money they'd budgeted.

Besides making the Alto II, the SPG built Dover laser printers and spearheaded several software developments. At its height the SPG numbered around 200 people.

In 1977 Ellenby got an opportunity to lead another sexy project. He produced a one-day extravaganza in Boca Raton, Florida, to demonstrate to Xerox executives what the future would be like for users of advanced Xerox technology. This presentation so excited the top brass that Xerox started an Advanced Systems Department with Ellenby in charge of two hardware and two software groups. "We had customers all over the world, including the White House and Boeing Corporation," recalls Ellenby.

Ellenby was riding high at Xerox, but if he thought that Xerox would support any idea he came up with, he was wrong. Top-level executives balked at his proposal for volume production of some of his advanced prototype machines. Very disappointed and frustrated, Ellenby began to wonder if his ideas would ever reach the world beyond Xerox. At this juncture he almost accepted a long-standing offer to set up a new entrepreneurial division on the West Coast for a "very major company" he refuses to identify. Then he said to himself: "If they have enough faith in me to do this for them, why don't I have a similar amount of faith and do it myself?"

Ellenby isn't the impulsive type. He decided to wait until the end of 1979 so he could get his profit-sharing check from Xerox. Then—unlike many renegades who set up their own small companies while still working for big ones—he politely informed Xerox of his impending departure before he had made up his mind what he was going to do on his own.

He had earlier sought advice from Gene Amdahl, who left IBM to found Amdahl, and was perplexed at Amdahl's response: helpful, but not encouraging. When Ellenby finally called to say he had given Xerox notice, Amdahl's tone changed. "'This is the best day in the whole of your life, John. Come over and see me right away,' relates Ellenby. "I said, 'Gene, I'm scared shitless, actually,' and he said 'If you were not anxious about this I'd worry about you, because you'll *use* that anxiety.'"

John left Xerox on his 39th birthday, a mid-week day in January, which "annoyed personnel immensely," but was "a nice, symbolic act."

Out of a job, Ellenby now had to decide what his new company, which he was calling GRiD, would do. He had several ideas in mind, including making a laser printer. While methodically considering his options for the new venture, he kept coming back to a conversation he'd had with a Xerox customer. "He really liked the Alto," Ellenby recalls, "but said he wasn't going to use it. I asked him why, and he said, 'Well, if I start using it I'll become dependent on it. And then I'll be trapped in the office because it can't go with me. What I really want is the power of the Alto in a briefcase.' We had a big laugh about it because at that time a lot of the technology, the components [for such a small computer], just weren't there."

In early 1980 Ellenby was no longer laughing. Supported only by his own money, he worked for seven months developing a business plan and working through the major technical problems in creating such a machine. He invited members of the computer aristocracy, venture capitalists, and prospective suppliers to stop by and sip tea with him in the little guest house under an oak tree in his backyard. "If you have a good idea and can reach these people, they are very keen to speak to you," Ellenby says.

Ellenby's impressive reputation enabled him to recruit an equally impressive group of supportive investors, including Gene Amdahl (who now sits on GRiD's board), Sam Wiegand (an ex- Honeywell executive who had helped establish Tandem Computers), an attorney, Larry Sonsini, and Ray Williams (also from Amdahl). Among them, they came up with $170,000 in seed money to rent an office and start a payroll.

By the end of the year, Ellenby had raised $2.6 million in venture capital from institutional investors like Citicorp Venture Capital and the Mayfield Fund. He hired several top-notch engineers from Apple, Hewlett-Packard, and Xerox to develop his tiny computer.

When the Compass made its debut in the spring of 1982, *Business Week* described it as "a Porsche for top executives," noting that it was on the frontier of technology not only in hardware, but also software and office system networks. It didn't just fit into a briefcase, it left room to spare, and weighed under 10 pounds with a six-inch, state-of-the-art, flat-panel screen. It also had a built-in, high-speed modem for easy connection to other computers by phone, and an advanced bubble memory.

The Compass was introduced at a propitious time. Its forward-looking technology and well-thought-out business plan appealed to the investment community, which, in late 1982 and early 1983, was anxious to jump on the personal computer bandwagon. Ellenby took advantage of the moment and raised a total of $34 million for his privately held company—one of the highest amounts ever raised by any new computer firm.

At $8,150, the Compass was certainly not for everyone. But it wasn't supposed to be. It was designed for the Rolls-Royce (not Porsche) set: top managers of Fortune 1000 companies. GRiD didn't succeed in this market as well as it had hoped, but another lucrative client emerged, the federal government—especially the military and the CIA. When GRiD introduced its $12,500 espionage-proof version—specially shielded from electronic bugging—the Department of Defense loved it. Almost one-third of the company's business goes through its Washington, D.C., office, and GRiD's ads now describe the Compass as a "weapon" rather than a "tool" for management. In mid-1984 Ellenby refused to confirm an earlier report of a $100-million contract with the Army, but admitted that GRiD's current defense contracts could easily exceed that amount of business "if we perform and they perform."

Ellenby seems comfortable dealing with this world of high-tech spooks and military brass. When we visited him in his office in an ordinary-looking Silicon Valley plant/office building, he invited us to his private "lair." To get there we had to pass through a series of doors that opened only when Ellenby held up his notebook, which apparently contained some device that triggered a mechanism in the doors. After this preamble we expected to be ushered into something like Dr. No's inner sanctum, but Ellenby's private room was quite small and plain. Work benches along two walls were bare except for a single GRiD Compass, the only other furniture was a coffee table and two chairs; a poster on the wall announced an exhibit of Gillian Ellenby's sculptures.

Ellenby has entrusted the running of the company to Sam Wiegand. He sees himself as a research-and-development person, who also knows a lot about finance but not much about sales or marketing. And he says that if he ever loses his imagination, his ability to identify with his customers' needs, he'll hand over that end of the company to someone else, too.

His lifestyle has changed little. He and Gillian live in the same Palo Alto house they bought when they came to America, and, when he can, he enjoys the same hobbies—photography, scuba diving, theater, music, and "a lot of reading." When we talked with him, he had just completed reading the complete works of Mark Twain. Unlike many people in computer hardware, Ellenby is at ease talking about subjects outside his field. He speaks rapidly and articulately, coming to the point more directly than you might expect from a British ex-professor. Though his accent is still unmistakable, many Americanisms have crept into his conversation.

Gillian still does mixed media sculptures, using plastic, metal, and acrylic. She sometimes uses junked materials she picks up at GRiD's shipping dock.

Ellenby's days begin around six o'clock, with some exercise and three newspapers before breakfast; his workday is over around 7:30 in the evening, with half-days on weekends. He does drive an Audi now, because his old white Dodge van "occasionally embarrassed" the bankers and investors he was carrying around.

LARGEST EMPLOYERS

Company	Employees
Jerry Sanders (Advanced Micro Devices)	13,000
Don Estridge (IBM Entry Systems Division)	9,500
Steve Jobs (Apple Computer)	4,850
Jugi Tandon (Tandon Corp.)	3,550
Terry Johnson (Miniscribe)	1,650
Pat McGovern (International Data Group)	1,400
William Millard (ComputerLand)	1,100

SMALLEST EMPLOYERS

Company	Employees
Arthur Rock (Arthur Rock & Co.)	1
Sat Tara Singh Khalsa (Kriya Systems)	9
Tom Perkins (Kleiner Perkins Caufield & Byers)	9

Don Estridge

"If you're competing against people who started in a garage, you have to start in a garage"

▶ **BEST-KNOWN VENTURE:** IBM Entry Systems Division

BORN: 1938

RAISED: Jacksonville, Florida

FATHER'S OCCUPATION: Professional photographer

FIRST DOLLAR EARNED: Apprentice to an electrician

SCHOOLING: B.S., electrical engineering, University of Florida

ORIGINAL FINANCING: IBM

HOME: Boca Raton, Florida

FAMILY: Married; four daughters

PERSONAL TRANSPORTATION: Wouldn't say

IBM®

IBM ENTRY SYSTEMS DIVISION: Makers of the best-selling personal computers.

▶ **BEST-KNOWN PRODUCTS:** IBM personal computer, PC XT, PCjr, PC portable, PC AT

YEAR FOUNDED: 1980

EMPLOYEES: 9,500

HEADQUARTERS: Boca Raton, Florida

SALES: $4 billion (1983 estimate)

OWNERSHIP: A division of International Business Machines (IBM) Corporation

What's an established behemoth like IBM doing in a book devoted to entrepreneurs? It was founded in 1911. Its annual sales exceed $40 billion. In 1983 it made more profits than any other corporation in the world. It's almost the polar opposite of entrepreneurship.

The short answer is that IBM decided in 1980 that if it was going to make a personal computer, it had better act like an entrepreneur. So it set up a new unit that was relatively unencumbered by IBM bureaucracy. "If you're competing against people who started in a garage, you have to start in a garage," explained Philip D. (for Don) Estridge, the veteran IBMer who was placed in charge of the new independent business unit (IBU). Frank T. Cary, former chairman of IBM, described the new unit as the company's answer to the question: "How do you make an elephant dance?"

Don Estridge, the dance master, was 42 years old when he embarked on this entrepreneurial venture inside the IBM walls. His profile fits the IBM mold: he's a tall, soft-spoken electrical engineer who wears wire-rimmed glasses and dresses conservatively. He was born and raised in Jacksonville, where his father was a self-employed professional photographer, and has spent most of his life in Florida. He took his first job when he was a teenager as an apprentice to an electrician. He also worked for a while in a civil engineering firm.

Estridge went to the University of Florida at Gainesville and graduated in 1959 with a degree in electrical engineering. IBM was one of the companies that interviewed him on campus. He took his father's advice and went with them, and he has never worked for another company since.

IBM had him report to Kingston, New York. Accompanying him was his bride, the former Mary Ann Hellier, whom he had married the summer before his senior year. In Kingston, Estridge worked in a Federal Systems unit that supplied the Air Force with an early-warning radar system called SAGE (Semi-Automatic Ground Environment). After four years, he was transferred to Washington, D.C., to do programming for the Goddard Space Flight Center. Then, in 1969, he returned to his native state, where IBM was just beginning to establish a presence in Boca Raton. It built a plant on swampland there in 1968. Today, with a payroll nearing 10,000, IBM is the largest employer in South Florida after Eastern Airlines.

Boca Raton suited IBM in many ways, according to Emilia Askari, business writer for the *Miami Herald*. She wrote:

"It's a place where you *must* mow your lawn after it grows beyond twelve inches in height. And where the City Council spells out just how skimpy your bikini top can be: no less than three inches of material, which must be centered on each nipple.

"To outsiders, these rules may seem peculiar. But to IBM, they are the sort of details that make Boca Raton and its stellar employer a good match."

On the other hand, Don Estridge pointed out to us that "the purpose of Boca Raton has always been to develop lower and lower cost computers. And so the people in Boca Raton were experimentalists in terms of introducing new products" and also entering areas where IBM had no previous experience.

Boca Raton, then, was the logical place for the IBM brass to raise the question: Do we want to build a personal computer? Estridge described the process to us. A group of engineers, manufacturing people, planners, and the laboratory director, William Lowe, worked for a month to come up with a business plan for a personal computer project. The plan was submitted to Armonk (IBM headquarters in New York), which raised other questions. The team then worked for another month before coming up with a final plan that won a corporate go-ahead.

The approval came in the early part of August 1980; it was only then that Estridge entered the picture. We asked him how that came about, and he replied: "Well, I was in Boca and when I got wind of the project—I had always been fascinated by personal computers—I said, 'That's something I want to work on.' Eventually, it turned out that I did." Just prior to this assignment, Estridge had been heading up product development on the Series/1, an IBM general purpose minicomputer.

Estridge was named manager of the new IBM department, Entry Level Systems—Small Systems; it was responsible, as IBM put it, "for the development of small microprocessor-based systems for tiny business and personal use." It's unlikely that any entrepreneurial start-up has ever had as tight and thorough a plan as Estridge's did. The timetable called for shipping personal computers in a year; a budget specified how much money would be supplied to get IBM into the business. The timetable was met—and Estridge said he never had to ask for more funds than were earmarked in the budget. To ensure that he had a free hand in moving the project forward, Estridge headed an integrated unit. "I had reporting to me," he explained, "R&D [research and development], the developers of activities for both programming and engineering, all of marketing, all advertising, all sales, manufacturing, and finance. So any decision we wanted to make was made at my level or below it."

Does this mean that the IBM people at the top didn't know what Estridge was doing? Not at all. Built into the process was a review and evaluation every six to eight weeks. And between those periods other parts of IBM had a chance to review what was going on at Boca Raton and contribute their thoughts. In this way, said Estridge, "we were able to act in an entrepreneurial way in establishing what we wanted to do, and yet at the same time, stay close enough to the needs of the rest of the business so that we didn't create an ongoing stream of activities that were fundamentally at odds with the way IBM could operate over time."

The reviews, Estridge emphasized, were always done "at the top of the business"—meaning at the highest corporate level—to avoid the logjams of endless committees. "When we met with the top of the business," related Estridge, "we said, 'Here's the way we want to do business.' And they said, 'Yeah.' And that was it. We didn't have to continue to discuss it within the company."

In short, it was the best of all possible worlds. The Estridge team had the latitude to set its own course but it had support from the central body. It was entrepreneurship inside the corporate compound. This special mixture also operated in the risk-and-rewards equation. In the typical entrepreneurial start-up, if the founders hit it big, they stand to make a lot of money from their equity. That obviously wasn't possible here, but Estridge pointed out to us that IBMers have motivations beyond pay and advancement—they also appreciate "being able to contribute to a breakthrough and provide leadership to the rest of the business," opportunities that were present in this project. And, Estridge was quick to observe, "if the project were to fall apart, these people can work somewhere else in IBM. And that is not true in a real entrepreneurial environment. If you own your own company and it falls apart, you're out on the street. That safety net is important to a lot of people. So this was a way to be risk-taking without the pain of failure being quite so severe as if you were on the outside. And I think people understand that and appreciate it and substitute that safety net for what might otherwise be equity."

Estridge estimated that in the first year of the personal computer project, he recruited between two-thirds and three-quarters of his staff from within IBM. "We went around to various locations," he said, and "explained the project. We said it was really risky and we didn't know if we were going to be allowed to introduce the product even if we did the project successfully because other things could have a bearing on that. And the people who responded were fundamentally high risk-takers. In the first part of 1982, I had a study done of the makeup of the group and found that the vast majority of people came from field sales or field service or from the Federal Systems Division, which are, if you know IBM, the three places that tend to have the risk-takers in the sense of having to manage your own affairs where you don't have any clear guidance on what's the right answer or not. You know, you have to sort of make it up as you go along."

The success of the project—IBM sold 750,000 personal computers by the end of 1983—well ahead of its business plan projections—is reflected in the burgeoning employee population under Estridge's command. It was lucky such success was not predicted, Estridge told us, because "it probably would have frightened us and we wouldn't have done it." He started with a group of 12 people in August 1980, which grew to 135 in January 1981, 330 in January 1982, 3,300 in January 1983, and 9,500 in August 1984. IBM's Entry Systems Division—its name today—therefore employs more than twice as many people as Apple. (The IBM PC, by itself, generated $2.5 billion in sales for IBM in 1983.)

For Don Estridge, the gestation period of the personal computer was exciting in more ways than one. Three of his four daughters married over the course of the presumably frantic year preceding the introduction of the PC.

Since the debut of the PC and its rocket-like takeoff, Estridge has attracted a fair amount of media attention, a rather unusual occurrence for anyone in the IBM ranks. His picture appeared in *Business Week* (talking with Apple's Steve Jobs), *Time,* and other publications. Doug Clapp, columnist for *InfoWorld,* dubbed him "the Cary Grant of micros." His achievement has also not gone unnoticed by his employer: in January 1984 he was promoted to corporate vice president, no small achievement at IBM. And while he has been clearly buoyed by the entrepreneurial venture of the personal computer, he remains very much the IBM man, showing a high regard for the company's culture. In the middle of 1983, *Time* did a cover story on IBM, which included a mini-profile of chairman John Opel that reported he drove "a six-year-old car whose make he will not divulge." When we asked Don Estridge what kind of car he drives, he said: "Oh, no, I don't want to get into that. You don't need to know that."

The chip that powers the IBM personal computer was made by Intel. The operating system came from Microsoft. Most of the disk drives were made by Tandon. SCI Systems supplied the circuit boards. Epson made the printer. Estridge and his staff opted for what is called an "open architecture" instead of a closed proprietary system. Estridge explained why: "In terms of the technology of the chips, we didn't have that technology. So creating the chips was out of the question. In terms of the programming, there was no reason to believe we could do it any better than was being done by people like Microsoft. And what they were doing is widely accepted. And thirdly, from the standpoint of the people in the stores selling the product, if we went in and were unfamiliar and new-looking, we created a learning curve ahead of the sales that was unnecessary. So it was just a better strategy to fit than not fit."

That's why when the early critics of the IBM PC said it had nothing that was technologically new, Estridge's response was: "Great! That was the best news we could have had. We actually had done what we had set out to do."

In working with outside suppliers, IBM imposed conditions of speed and high security. Bill Gates, head of Microsoft, said the timetable presented to him "basically proved we were three months behind schedule before we started." The Microsoft people told Paul Freiberger and Michael Swaine, authors of *Fire in the Valley,* how tight IBM was about secrecy: "IBM sent its own file locks, and when Gates had trouble installing them IBM sent its own installer. The room [where the project was based] had no windows and no ventilation, and IBM required that the door be kept constantly closed. IBM conducted several security checks to make sure Microsoft followed orders."

IBM is not entirely pleased with the many laudatory reports that have appeared depicting it as a new hotbed of entrepreneurship. Although it has set up a dozen other independent business units to pursue different projects, the company reacted testily to a 1984 inquiry from *Inc.,* a magazine whose *raison d'etre* is entrepreneurship. Stephen Quigley, senior information specialist at IBM, told reporter Eugene Linden that there's nothing new about the IBUs and that they represent not a way to reward budding talent but a normal business response to market conditions. IBM, Quigley emphasized, "is not concerned with entrepreneurs not getting their share of opportunity." Linden interviewed others—Thomas Peters and Robert Waterman, co-authors of *In Search of Excellence,* and venture capitalist L.J. Sevin—who agreed that envy is the central problem of the corporate entrepreneurial relationship. People inside the company see others getting rich and they wonder: why not me? It's a tough issue to manage. Sevin said: "Briefly, a part of IBM was entrepreneurial, and it was breathtaking to behold. But it looks like it was a temporary phenomenon."

Gary Friedman

"I think it's very difficult for someone that's run a company of any substance or significance to work for somebody else. I think you basically become unemployable"

▶ **BEST-KNOWN VENTURE:** Fortune Systems

OTHER VENTURE: Itel

BORN: 1934

RAISED: San Francisco, California

FATHER'S OCCUPATION: Owner of a forklift truck manufacturing business

FIRST DOLLAR EARNED: Waiter at the Bohemian Club

SCHOOLING: B.A., business and public administration, University of Arizona (on a football scholarship)

ORIGINAL FINANCING: $8.5-million venture capital package

PERSONAL NET WORTH: Made $8 million on Fortune's initial offering; still owns 6 percent of the company

HOME: Hillsborough, California

FAMILY: Divorced; remarried; three children

PERSONAL TRANSPORTATION: Mercedes

FORTUNE SYSTEMS

FORTUNE SYSTEMS CORPORATION: Manufactures a "super micro" desktop computer system that allows several users to process a number of different jobs at the same time.

▶ **BEST-KNOWN PRODUCT:** Fortune 32:16

YEAR FOUNDED: 1980

EMPLOYEES: 600

HEADQUARTERS: Redwood City, California

SALES: $54 million (1983)

LOSSES: $15 million (1983)

OWNERSHIP: Public (1983); largest stockholder is the French company, Thomson-CSF; Gary Friedman holds 6 percent

There are two points of view about Gary Friedman. One: He's an overconfident, fast-talking supersalesman, full of hype and always after a quick buck. Like many entrepreneurs, he's great at starting enterprises but lousy at managing. Worse, he's too egocentric to know when to step aside and let someone else take over. For good reasons he was thrown out of the two companies he co-founded, Itel Corporation and Fortune Systems. Itel went bankrupt and Fortune had a lot of red ink on its ledgers, despite plenty of cash in the bank.

Two: Besides having a lot of personal charm, he's a genius at starting companies—especially at raising venture capital—and he knows how to staff them. Itel had a blue-chip personnel roster and lasted more than 12 years before it went into bankruptcy. Friedman had little to do with its demise, since he'd been shunted aside by his co-founder long before. As for Fortune, it suffered from unfair comparisons with other companies as well as being haunted by the ghost of Itel, but it's making a comeback.

There's truth in both of these seemingly contradictory perspectives. But one thing everyone would agree on is that Gary Friedman is no shrinking violet. "High profile" is how he's described in the trade. And he does things his own way, which is not always the way other people do them.

For example, consider how he joined IBM. In his senior year at the University of Arizona, Friedman heard that a friend of his had gone to an interview with IBM and been turned down. This intrigued him, so he went for an interview, too. At the time, Friedman had a football scholarship (he still has the physique of a football star), but he also graduated with academic honors. According to Friedman, IBM offered him a job almost on the spot. Friedman declined, saying, "I don't even know what you guys do." When the manager of the Phoenix office called urging him to join the IBM team, he replied that he'd like three months to think about it.

He did deign to join the company shortly after he graduated in 1956. But six months later it turned out the Army wanted him too, and Uncle Sam had more clout than IBM. "They sent me to Fort Knox, Kentucky, and I stood in the snow and rain for three months learning how to drive a tank," he recalls. Friedman had his own solution: "I said, 'this isn't for me.' So I wrote to the general of the U.S. Army to tell him they were making a terrible mistake."

Realizing the error of its ways, the Army sent him to Camp Irwin in California, which had just received some IBM equipment that nobody knew how to run. "I spent about eighteen months setting up and running an IBM installation in the Army," says Friedman. "It was excellent experience and a lot of fun."

Released from his military duty, he returned to IBM and rose rapidly in the marketing field. In 1965, when he was 31, he was promoted to branch manager in San Francisco, where he'd been born and raised.

It was a good setup. But as much as he liked IBM, Gary Friedman had bigger and better things in mind. In December 1967 he co-founded a computer-leasing company—Itel—with

Pete Redfield, a Transamerica executive introduced to him by a mutual friend.

Leaving IBM after 11 years didn't cause him even a pang of anxiety. "It's a question of personal confidence," he says, "and of having an opportunity to expand at an exponential rate." The confidence seemed well justified. "In the first fifteen months," says Friedman, "Pete and I raised 75 million dollars, went out and bought 100 million dollars worth of computers, got some more money, and bought another 100 million dollars worth."

Itel was a fast-growing company, with a reputation for a flashy lifestyle. *Fortune* magazine, for instance, once described "the glory days" at Itel in these terms: "Handsome, young M.B.A.s trod rare Persian rugs in their San Francisco offices, zipped around in Porsches and Mercedes, and struck deals earning them 150 thousand dollars a year and up. On a 2.8 million-dollar Itel junket, one Young Turk resided pasha-like in Howard Hughes's old suite at the Acapulco Princess. 'It was a fabulous whirl on a roller coaster,' he says, savoring the memory." Friedman says that reputation was overblown. "People were saying there was Perrier in the water faucets," he recalls. "Quite frankly, a lot of people were jealous of the company."

Friedman's personal life was on the move, too. "I bought a house in Atherton in '64, then I bought another one in '66 or '67, and then in 1972, I got divorced and moved to Tiburon. In 1974, I got remarried and moved to Hillsborough." (All are wealthy suburbs of San Francisco.)

Itel collapsed in 1980 (the actual bankruptcy was declared in January 1981) when IBM's new 4300 mainframe pushed Itel's inferior computers out of the leasing marketplace. Both Redfield and Friedman left under duress. But well before that, *InfoWorld* reported, "the running of Itel had been taken over by a group of cronies headed by Pete Redfield. In a bold political move, Redfield had gotten Friedman out of the chain of command and out of the day-to-day business. Friedman's job was negotiating leases in some corner."

Still, a court-appointed examiner in the bankruptcy proceedings recommended that Itel sue several managers, including Friedman, for "breaching their fiduciary duty" to the company. Itel declined to sue.

Friedman, who was to receive some $1.5 million from Itel as a golden parachute, didn't let it get him down. In 1980 he got together with two other Itel alumni, Homer Dunn and Dave Van Den Berg, and founded Fortune Systems. "We were not equal founders," reports Friedman. "I had 30 percent more stock than the others and I was president and chairman of the board." That was because, he says, the others didn't know how to put their ideas into action.

For three months, 14 hours a day, the three sat in Friedman's San Francisco office, figuring out what markets to go after with what product and writing the business plan. Dunn and Van Den Berg wrote the technical part, Friedman the business part.

The product they came up with was the Fortune 32:16, a machine that offered the computing capability of minicomputers with the price—$5,000 for the cheapest version—and ease of use of a micro. (It was called 32:16 because it combined an advanced 32-bit processor with a 16-bit "data bus," the link between the memory and the rest of the computer.) It could act like a dedicated word processor, a powerful computer, and a professional communicating work station.

Once again, Friedman had no problem raising the financing. He boasts, "Here we were, three guys who had never built anything, in an industry that was new, using an operating system that had never been used commercially before and a chip that people said wouldn't work—and we went out and raised 8.5-million dollars in the first round of financing. We raised 12 million dollars in the second round. The first round took about nine months; the second round took a couple of weeks."

Fortune had acquired the most venture capital ever raised by a personal computer maker. Investors included both domestic and foreign corporations, investment firms, and banks; the largest stockholder is still the French electronics company, Thomson-CSF. When Fortune went public in 1983, it was one of the largest initial public offerings by a start-up firm on record. The cashier's check—for $90,420,000 from Security Pacific National Bank—hangs framed on Friedman's wall.

At first, the Fortune 32:16 appeared to justify all the enthusiasm that had been whipped up. When the prototype made its debut at the 1981 COMDEX show, it won the highest raves. The first year of business, 1982, Fortune shipped about $65-million worth.

But problems began to surface. Although the computer was supposed to handle several users and applications simultaneously, it responded sluggishly when more than three users were on it. Deliveries were late and there were bugs in the system.

Fortune stock dropped the day after it was issued, and continued downward as revenues declined and losses mounted. Four stockholder suits—still unresolved—charged that Friedman and others had withheld negative information at the time the company went public.

According to Friedman, "Some of the technical people were, let's say, overly optimistic in terms of what they felt they could do in that time period." He adds that the product suffered from a perception problem: "How many systems at that time had three or more users? Less than five percent. So what we had wasn't a problem." In other words, expectations were too high. Opinions differ as to who raised them.

After Fortune had lost $9.1 million on sales of $9.1 million in the third quarter of 1983, the board of directors ousted Friedman and began searching for a new president. Both Friedman and the board attributed the separation to differences about "management style." Perceptions again, says Friedman. "When things weren't going the way they were supposed to, people said, 'Oh God, it's Itel all over again.'"

The company endured more top-management shifts and began fixing up its product line. It hired as president and CEO James S. Campbell, formerly head of Shugart Associates, a Xerox subsidiary. In mid-1984 Wall Street analysts were giving mixed reviews over the fortunes of Fortune: the company had a lot of money in the bank—more than $50 million as of first quarter 1984, but sales were off.

Friedman emerged from Fortune with 6 percent of the firm's stock plan plus cash. When we visited him a few months after his ouster from Fortune, he seemed somber, but far from defeated. He was working on his own in an office in a building in the San Francisco suburb of San Mateo. On his desk was a stack of governmental studies related to waste management. Gary Friedman was onto his next venture: a microcomputer-controlled process for converting solid waste to electricity.

We asked why, after his two apparently stunning defeats as an entrepreneur, he had decided to try again. Friedman had a quick answer: "I'll always be an entrepreneur. It's very difficult for someone who's run a company of any substance or significance to work for somebody else," he says. "You basically become unemployable."

GET IT IN CASH

Fairs and exhibitions are very important in the computer business—they are where entrepreneurs display their wares and meet their customers. One of the oldest of these shows is the West Coast Computer Faire, founded in San Francisco in 1977 by Jim Warren. Warren tells this story about Jim Egan, booth decorator, who worked the first Faire:

"So," says Warren, "these two bearded, hippie, pony-tailed kids in Levis come up to the counter . . . and here's this old, white-haired guy that's been on the show trail for 20 years, right? Every shuck-and-jive hype artist in the world has come up at one time or another. So these two kids come up and say, 'Hey! You know, we'd like to set up some of these really nice chrome displays to make our stuff look flashy.' And Egan says, 'Fine, I rent them.' And the kids say, 'Yeah, but we're sort of short of loot. Instead of giving you money, could we maybe give you stock in our company? It's called Apple Computer.' And Egan pounds on the table and says, 'Apple Computer? Hell no, man, I deal in hard cash here. You want the displays, you pay the cash.'"

Steve Jobs and Steve Wozniak went ahead and fixed up their own exhibit, and Jim Egan is still in the booth decorating business.

Harry Garland and Roger Melen

► **BEST-KNOWN VENTURE:** Cromemco

BORN: Garland—1947; Melen—1946

RAISED: Garland—Detroit, Michigan; Melen—Chico, California

SCHOOLING: Garland—undergraduate degree, mathematics, Kalamazoo College; Ph.D., biophysics, Stanford University; Melen—B.S., California State University at Chico; M.S. and Ph.D., electrical engineering, Stanford University

ORIGINAL FINANCING: $5,000 in personal savings

PERSONAL NET WORTH: 42.5 percent of Cromemco each

HOMES: Both live in Los Altos, California

FAMILIES: Garland—married; two children; Melen— married; one child

PERSONAL TRANSPORTATION: Garland—Cadillac, Cessna 210; Melen—Mercedes

Cromemco

CROMEMCO INC.: A pioneer in the personal computer industry, it now makes computers for industrial and engineering uses.

▶ **BEST-KNOWN PRODUCTS:** C-10 personal computers, D-series expandable desktop systems

YEAR FOUNDED: 1975

EMPLOYEES: 400

HEADQUARTERS: Mountain View, California

SALES: $50 million (1983)

OWNERSHIP: Privately held by Harry Garland and Roger Melen, 15 percent reserved for profit-sharing

Harry Garland and Roger Melen met in 1969 when they lived in the same dormitory at Stanford. The name of the dorm was Crothers Memorial Hall. When they formed a company several years later, they named it Cromemco, to honor their old dorm.

Although the two men came from different parts of the country (Garland from Michigan, Melen from northern California) and were pursuing Ph.D.s in different areas (Garland in biophysics, Melen in electrical engineering), they had so many things in common that it was inevitable their paths would cross.

For one thing, both of their fathers were entrepreneurs. Garland's started out as an auto mechanic in Detroit and ended up founding several companies of his own. Melen's has two businesses: a hardwood floor contracting company and an almond farm. "Roger and I grew up in an environment where it was natural to work for yourself," comments Garland.

The second thing the two had in common was ham radio, and a third was engineering, which was Melen's major field and Garland's minor. Both of them had little labs set up in their dorm rooms along with their ham radio sets. The two tinkerers gravitated toward each other, discussing such hobbies as building "simple little" electrocardiographs and ham radio devices. Eventually they collaborated on an article for *Popular Electronics,* then the preeminent journal for hobbyists across the country. Heady with the excitement of selling the article and receiving a $300 check that amounted to "a whole month's stipend," they went on to write several more.

Meanwhile, upon graduation in 1972, they were both invited to join the faculty of Stanford's electrical engineering department, and their paths continued along parallel courses. Married shortly after graduating, Garland moved from the dorm to an apartment building in Palo Alto. Shortly thereafter, Melen moved into the same building, so once again the two had labs down the hall from one another. About a year later, Garland moved to a house, and Melen followed suit. Finally, they bought houses in Los Altos within a few minutes of each other.

The two Stanford professors and neighbors continued to tinker in their spare time, as well as to contribute articles to *Popular Electronics.* Soon a business partnership began in response to the articles. They would put together the gadgets they described in their articles and offer them for sale to the magazine's readers. It was a decidedly small business, something that hobbyists/tinkerers like Melen and Garland could easily do in their spare time. And it might have remained such if *Popular Electronics* had not decided to place one of their inventions, the Cyclops Camera (which enabled hobbyists to project their own faces onto the tubes of their oscilloscopes), on its February 1975 cover. Melen went to New York to talk with the editor, Les Solomon. While in the magazine's offices, Melen's eyes happened to fall on the subject of the cover of the January issue: the MITS Altair computer.

Melen was so taken with the Altair that he changed his return reservation and stopped off in Albuquerque to see the president of MITS, Ed Roberts. The two talked into the wee hours of the morning, ideas flashing back and forth. When he returned to California, Melen found Garland totally receptive to his ideas of developing electronic devices for the Altair. The two would simply expand their tiny gadget business. They would have done this in the proverbial garage, but the garage was too messy, so they commandeered the dining and living rooms of Garland's house.

The first device Cromemco sold under its own name for the Altair was called Dazzler, which permitted the Altair to hook up to a color TV set and produce graphics. While displaying the Dazzler at a meeting of the Homebrew Computer Club—one of the earliest computer clubs—around the end of 1975, Garland noticed what he recalls as a "scruffy sort of kid" who was "very aggressive, asking a lot of questions." That kid turned out to be Steve Jobs, and Garland asserts that the Dazzler design was the basis for the Apple computer.

Garland remembers having a discussion with Jobs at that time that reflected the path Cromemco would take. While Jobs argued that these small personal computers could be bought by hobbyists and others for use in the home, Garland insisted the primary market would be for businesses. And over the years Garland and Melen have carefully carved out a niche for their business machines. Cromemco offers state-of-the-art products to an industrial and professional clientele that includes Delta Airlines (for weather projections) and over 50 percent of television weather forecasters. Its reputation is for quality rather than price; the owners have been known to say that "if it's cheap, it's not a Cromemco."

Mindful of its original aim—making add-on products to personalize and expand the usefulness of a computer—the firm subscribes to the philosophy that all its products should be interrelated. "Most of our systems are bus-oriented, so you can configure them to your needs," states a company brochure. "You can expand memory, add peripherals, network systems, add graphics, and connect to phone lines. You can set up a personal work station or a network of hundreds of work stations; interface to large data bases or build your own."

From the beginning, Cromemco's revenue growth has been impressive. In 1975, before it was even incorporated, it made $50,000. There's been substantial sales growth every year (to over $50 million as of early 1984), and the company's goal is

$250 million in revenue by the end of the decade. There has been little turnover among employees, particularly in key areas such as R&D and marketing. One reason for this apparent loyalty may be the company's profit-sharing plan, which is open to all employees. Each person's share is based on a percentage of his or her salary. Employees own 15 percent of the company's stock. Melen and Garland share the rest.

Until a few years ago, management was vested in only two officers, Garland and Melen. "I worried about today's business," says Garland, "and Roger worried about tomorrow's products." Finally, and somewhat reluctantly, the two brought in some functional managers to keep up with expanding business and increasingly complex decisions.

Garland drives a Cadillac, Melen a Mercedes; the names identifying their reserved parking spaces at Cromemco are preceded by "Dr." Garland does own a Cessna 210, but he's been flying since his teens—one of his father's businesses was a flying school. His other extra-curricular activity is playing the organ he and his wife assembled from a kit 15 years ago.

Cromemco's financial structure is a prime example of the Garland/Melen conservatism. The company has never accepted a penny of venture capital or incurred any long-term debt. Its first credit line, from Bank of America, was for $250,000, and Cromemco never used it all. B of A by now has upped the credit line to $10 million, and the company still doesn't use it all. Even the bank considers the Cromemco approach reserved. Outside business guidance has come from a CPA, whose only directive from the owners is that their progress be totally self-financed. Cromemco's 200,000-square-foot plant in Mountain View is rented, not owned, because owning would incur long-term debt—a Cromemco no-no.

EGGHEADS

Marty Alpert, M.D. (Tecmar)

Harry Garland, Ph.D. (Cromemco)

Dustin Heuston, Ph.D. (Wicat)

Portia Isaacson, Ph.D. (Future Computing)

James Johnson, Ph.D. (Human Edge Software)

Gary Kildall, Ph.D. (Digital Research)

Roger Melen, Ph.D. (Cromemco)

Adam Osborne, Ph.D. (Osborne Computer)

James Toreson* (Xebec)

Jim Warren** (West Coast Computer Faire)

Honorary doctorates:

William Godbout (CompuPro)

K. Philip Hwang (TeleVideo)

* Doctoral course work completed, dissertation pending

** Earned three master's degrees

William Godbout

"As far as the entrepreneurial thing is concerned, I didn't know I couldn't do it. I grew up with it"

▶ **BEST-KNOWN VENTURE:** CompuPro

OTHER VENTURES: William J. Godbout Co. Inc. (includes Godbout Electronics and an airplane-leasing firm)

BORN: 1939

RAISED: Warwick, Rhode Island

FIRST DOLLAR EARNED: Repairing televisions and radios while in junior high school

SCHOOLING: Massachusetts Institute of Technology (no degree); D.Sc. (honorary degree), Providence College

ORIGINAL FINANCING: Sale of his electronics counterintelligence company

PERSONAL NET WORTH: Over 90 percent of William J. Godbout Co. Inc.

HOME: Hayward, California, and Warwick, Rhode Island

FAMILY: Wouldn't say

PERSONAL TRANSPORTATION: Cadillac, four small airplanes

A *GODBOUT* COMPANY

COMPUPRO: One of the oldest personal computer companies; maker of quality components and high-performance, multi-user business systems that receive top critical ratings.

▶ **BEST-KNOWN PRODUCTS:** CompuPro 10 multi-user, multi-processor business computer; System 816 family of business, industrial, and scientific computers

YEAR FOUNDED: 1973

EMPLOYEES: 115

HEADQUARTERS: Hayward, California

SALES: $40 million (1983)

OWNERSHIP: Private, held by William J. Godbout Co. Inc. (a holding company)

William Godbout is a hard man to pigeonhole. He founded and heads CompuPro, one of the oldest and most-respected computer companies in the business, but he refuses to act the part of the dignified laureate. He has referred to the industry that made his fortune as "a business that's known for charlatanry." He also likes to project an air of cynicism. He told *InfoWorld*, "If mavericks are selling this year, then I'm going to be a maverick."

Despite his often prickly personality, Godbout inspires intense loyalty from his employees, and he rewards them for it with generous profit-sharing plans. He attacks the government as inept, but he is also a flag-waving patriot who demands that his managers drive American cars.

In the casual polo shirts that he routinely wears to work, and in his blunt speaking style, Godbout gives the appearance of down-to-earth openness. In fact, he is curiously secretive, a trait he may have learned as a maker of electronic spy devices.

He rarely grants interviews; when he does, he frequently refuses to answer questions about himself. For a man whose business success has put him in the public eye, Godbout strives surprisingly hard for anonymity.

Godbout describes his career up to the founding of Compu-Pro as "horribly mundane," and he does his best to make it sound that way. But most people wouldn't consider his background in military intelligence to be mundane. After his discharge from the Army in 1967, Godbout actually ran a counterintelligence operation where he made radio-jamming equipment and the like—a business successful enough to provide the capital to start CompuPro (under the name CompuKit) in 1973. Godbout, however, refuses to be more specific.

He also ducks questions about his studies at MIT. Education, for Godbout, was "something distasteful to be gotten out of the way as rapidly as possible." As a schoolboy in Warwick, Rhode Island, Godbout remembers he was a "so-so student who tried to skate and do the absolute minimum." He was far from idle, however. Instead of cracking open hated history books, Godbout pried apart discarded radios he found in sidewalk trash cans and at the dump. He bicycled regularly to the General Electric plant's garbage heap—a treasure trove for a self-confessed electronics dump picker.

Godbout again uses the phrase "horribly mundane" when he describes a childhood of crystal radio sets, electronic Heathkits, erector sets, microscopes, Cub Scouts, and paper routes. "I'm sorry I can't give you a great, wonderful Horatio Alger type thing," he apologizes.

It is true that Godbout did not grow up a poor orphan, but an upper-middle-class kid who lived in an "umpteen room Victorian" with his parents and a brother and sister. His father, a structural engineer, was an entrepreneur who started out in the depression as a heavy construction carpenter. He developed an avocation for electronics and the Godbouts bought one of the first television sets.

At that time, the early '50s, electronics enthusiasts congregated at TV repair shops. William rearranged his paper route so that he finished up at the TV shop where he could "peer over the repairman's shoulders and ask a whole list full of questions." Soon, Godbout jettisoned the paper route entirely and worked at the TV repair shop part-time while he was still in junior high. He opened his own TV repair business in high school, complete with printed business cards.

The TV repairman and his father taught him his entrepreneurial skills, Godbout believes, but he knew many men who had their own businesses. "It was almost as if I didn't know that you didn't go off and start your own business," he says.

Throughout MIT, IBM, and the U.S. Army, Godbout never lost his fond feelings for dump picking, fiddling around with electronic components, and building kits. All those childhood delights surfaced in 1973 with CompuKit.

But before that, he learned a number of important skills at a variety of jobs. As a design engineer at IBM, Godbout worked on the 704, 705, 709, and "stretch" computers. He also learned management techniques at IBM that would be valuable to him later on. Godbout, an Army reservist, was recalled to active duty in 1960 at the start of the Berlin Wall crisis. He began the counterintelligence business in the service and then sold it within a few years of his discharge in 1967. Next, Godbout took a two-year job as the crisis manager of a troubled company near San Francisco.

In the early '70s, Godbout again became a dump picker of a sophisticated sort in business. With the money from his counterintelligence business, he started a mail-order company that sold surplus electronic parts. He located the business at the Oakland airport where he had (and still has) an air-charter service with four planes. The company is not only a tax write-off, it's a hobby, as well as a business. Godbout has had a pilot's license since his teens and he is a member of an aircraft historical society. Another business under the William J. Godbout Co. umbrella is Godbout Electronics, a wholesaler of printed circuit boards and components for such companies as Digital Equipment and Hewlett-Packard.

Godbout was having a good time and making money, too. One business allowed him to fly and one business allowed him to pick through the "Arab bazaar atmosphere of wholesale electronics mail order." His customers were people like him: hackers, hobbyists, and ham radio operators who wanted anything from microwave transistors to diodes and counter chips used in ham radios. After the advent of the microprocessor in 1971, Godbout rekindled another childhood hobby—kits—in 1973.

CompuKits did not contain a full computer, but were more like a "memory kit, a power supply, and some logic stuff"—parts for people who were building their own computers. Godbout advertised in radio electronics magazines before the Altair appeared. Because both CompuKits and Altair sold well, Godbout realized the market could take a complete system. That's when CompuKit evolved into CompuPro.

As the business of selling the "unkits" (that only needed minimal soldering) increased, Godbout phased out the mail order business and sold off small divisions like MusicKit, a computer music modifier. Godbout and his friend George Morrow (who is also profiled in this book) had designed the 16-bit S-100, but CompuPro didn't produce its first fully assembled computer until November 1982—the System 816.

Godbout's companies have never run up losses. A libertarian distrust of government creeps into his talk of business. "I thought you ran a business for fun and profit. I thought only the government ran at losses," he remarks. He refers to venture capital as "vulture capital." (Obviously, he doesn't have such capital invested in his business; he did not incorporate until 1983.) Godbout claims that "starting companies is easy. The biggest impediment to doing business is that there's lawyers in Washington making work for other lawyers."

Godbout is cagey about his company's profits. He'll only say that the Godbout holding company is, "totally, privately held and we don't talk about it." Of course, he's perfectly willing to mention stock options for his 115 employees, as well as the 80,000 square feet in four buildings in Hayward, just south of Oakland, California, which CompuPro moved into in 1983 (one of which was formerly occupied by Osborne Computer).

He'll also talk at length about his new computers and their market. CompuPro aims its business computers not at giant corporations, but at the nine million businesses in the country with revenues between $1 and $25 million. He remains committed to his policy of S-100 computers and components that are flexible, modular, and expandable. CompuPro has already sold over 10,000 816 Systems that allow their user access to both eight- and 16-bit programs. An 816 System did the computer effects for the popular movie *War Games*.

In 1983—after ten years in the computer component business, and a personal electronics career that spans the vacuum tubes of 1959 through transistors and chips—Godbout introduced the CompuPro 10, a multi-user business computer with close to a million characters of main memory, for $4,995. With his focus on small- to medium-size business users and the high marks for quality the S-100 and CompuPro 10 machines receive, CompuPro hopes to increase its 1.3 percent share of the market. CompuPro also offers a full-year's warranty, unlike the 90-day warranty of most computer companies.

At age 44, Godbout is living the hobbies of his youth on a monumental scale. His ties to that childhood in Rhode Island remain strong. He divides his time between an apartment in Hayward and a home in Rhode Island, where he still votes in town meetings. Perhaps he even drives by the old GE dump now and then. But that would be too mundane to tell.

Dustin Heuston

"I struck out. I lived on the road. I hardly ever saw my family. I was constantly on the edge of collapsing from bankruptcy. But I managed to keep this thing limping along"

▶ **BEST-KNOWN VENTURE:** Wicat Systems

BORN: 1932

RAISED: The Bronx, New York

FATHER'S OCCUPATION: Advertising executive

FIRST DOLLAR EARNED: Camp counselor in Maine

SCHOOLING: B.A., English, Hamilton College;
   M.A., English, Stanford University;
   Ph.D., New York University

ORIGINAL FINANCING: Between $100,000 and $200,000 from
   foundations and individuals

PERSONAL NET WORTH: $30 million (1983)

HOME: Orem, Utah

FAMILY: Married; five daughters, one son

PERSONAL TRANSPORTATION: Mercury station wagon

WICATsystems

WICAT SYSTEMS INC.: Innovators in computer-assisted instruction.

▶ **BEST-KNOWN PRODUCTS:** Wicat super microcomputers and video-disk training systems

YEAR FOUNDED: 1980

EMPLOYEES: 500

HEADQUARTERS: Orem, Utah

SALES: $23 million (1984)

LOSSES: $13 million (1984)

OWNERSHIP: Public (1983); Dustin and Nancy Heuston own 8.3 percent (1.7 million shares); Wicat Education Institute, 21 percent; Kleinwort, Benson, 10 percent

D ustin Heuston may be one of the most rejected men in America. In his quest for financial backing for what has become Wicat, Heuston was turned down over 600 times in three years. IBM said no 14 times. From January to September 1980, 26 venture capitalists gave Heuston the thumbs down.

Heuston told us about a typical interview at the time: "It would be one of those hysterically funny conversations like:

'I want to help children.'

'What are you doing now?'

'Well, I run a nonprofit.'

'What was your last job?'

'A private girls' school.'

'What did you do before that?'

'I was an English teacher with a Ph.D., specializing in women's education.'

"And at this point they would go out the window."

None of these hardened business people seemed to understand that Dustin Heuston was a man with a mission: to give all children a computerized education. Heuston believes education with computers is not only superior to the classroom, but it's better than a private tutor. "I've become an entrepreneur in order to do that," he says. "I was a reluctant entrepreneur because I had not wanted to get involved in the whole business of making money. But now it's absolutely fundamental to the success of the whole thing." By way of explanation for his evangelical zeal about computers in education, Heuston asks, "If you found yourself in the position to change the history of education, wouldn't it excite you?"

It obviously excites Heuston. After years as a teacher and school administrator, Heuston grew increasingly concerned about studies showing that a child received only six-and-a-half days of individual instruction or personal attention over his or her life in the average school system. "The computer can just blow that wide open. It's like having the finest psychologists and the finest tutoring experts available for private tutorials. The educational delivery system has functionally gone unchanged for five centuries," Heuston argues. "Only the computer starts to force the learner into some kind of active role."

Heuston himself received the kind of good, traditional education that an upper-middle-class boy receives on the East Coast. He attended schools in his native Bronx until his father, an advertising man, sent him to a boarding school in Massachusetts (Mount Herman) at the age of 14. He later received a scholarship to Hamilton College, which Heuston calls, "a very old, eastern liberal arts college," in upstate New York, where he majored in English.

The three years Heuston served in the Navy following college were notable for his conversion from the Episcopalian to the Mormon church. He subsequently got a job teaching English at Brigham Young University in Provo, Utah, where at the age of 27, in 1959, Heuston married a 17-year-old freshman. "Shortly after that," Heuston deadpans, "she started dropping babies around the landscape"—six babies to be exact.

Even though Heuston was a God-fearing, reproducing Mormon, he found BYU a bit too right-wing for his moderate sensibilities. On the other hand, his next job at Pine Manor, a women's junior college near Boston, was too liberal. "I went from being a communist to being a fascist by just an airplane flight," Heuston jokes.

There were other problems as well. Like earning only $6,500 a year when he had a growing family. "I now had a house with just beds in it. Nothing else." So he moved from the classroom into administration. "I changed careers simply and purely for economic reasons," he explains.

Heuston said there was another reason for getting out of teaching. While at Pine Manor, he was completing his Ph.D. dissertation on Theodore Dreiser. He said his degree was held up for two years because he refused to write a Freudian interpretation of the American writer. That angered Heuston: "I didn't want to write about Dreiser's search for a father figure. I wanted to write what I found." Heuston's frustration turned him against the scholarly life of teaching and research. So, when he left teaching at Pine Manor, "I started running things." For the next eight years—1969 to '77—Heuston ran the Spence School, an exclusive New York City school for girls. It was there Dustin Heuston discovered computers.

A few college-bound students expressed the desire to work with computers. From that initial suggestion, Heuston became so convinced of the efficacy of computers that, as the school's headmaster, he talked the board into buying a $200,000 computer system—a large DEC computer with 55 terminals for the students. That was the start of Heuston's mission. He began to develop his ideas about computer-assisted education in papers like, "An English Teacher's Conversion to Technology." He crisscrossed the country for five years from 1972 to '77 on a Sloan Foundation grant to examine education and computer research. He worked 18 hours a day to train himself in programming and electronics.

The Mission. Heuston "had a dream": a stable research organization to develop new computer-assisted instruction and a model school to put that research into practice. In 1977 Heuston quit Spence and moved to Utah to take advantage of researchers at Brigham Young, especially Victor Bunderson and Robert Mendenhall (now president of Wicat).

Heuston raised between $100,000 and $200,000 from foundations and individuals (his own daughter gave the first $10), but "in general," Heuston says of his nonprofit fundraising, "I struck out. I lived on the road. I hardly ever saw my family. I was constantly on the edge of collapsing from bankruptcy. But I managed to keep this thing limping along." In 1980 Heuston gave up trying to see his vision realized with a nonprofit organization, and formed Wicat as a profit-making company.

The Money. Heuston thought Wicat (World Institute for Computer-Assisted Teaching) Systems could make money three ways: (1) Manufacture computer hardware; (2) Offer computers and software for industrial and military training; and (3) Heuston's baby, develop software programs for world literacy and education.

A large English merchant bank, Kleinwort, Benson, bought the plan and invested early. In the next two years, Heuston raised $100 million, $60 million of which came from going public in 1983.

Heuston started making his own computers because he wasn't satisfied with what others were making for the classroom. Wicat was the first producer of powerful, 16-bit microcomputers based on the Motorola 68000 chip for use by businesses and school systems. The Hydra, a computer with 30 terminals that fit in a classroom and sells for $80,000, is one such school computer. Wicat also makes video-disk training systems, such as "Diagnostic Challenges in Gastroenterology," which was made for SmithKline Beckman (the medical company). Other commercial customers include AT&T, American Express, and the U.S. Department of Defense.

Some personal computer software companies sell "educational software," meaning they may offer one program to teach multiplication or another to teach typing. Such programs may be run on a computer at home. That's not what Wicat means by educational software. Wicat emphasizes a full-scale, kindergarten-through-twelfth grade computerized curriculum. In a September 1984 full-page ad in *Time,* Wicat boasted of the results seen in two math classes in a junior high school in Port Heuneme, California. Each had the same teacher, textbooks,

and academic history. One spent one hour per week with the Wicat system; the other did not. At the end of the semester, 90 percent of those who received the Wicat instruction passed the state's objective mastery test, as opposed to only 64 percent of the others.

Heuston has plowed much of the money the company has raised into a massive research effort. Wicat has spent $25 million on research in educational software, and employs three dozen Ph.D. researchers. The company even has its own laboratory—the Waterford School, a model computer-oriented school in Provo, Utah. At one point, 3,000 children had applied for the 275 places in the private, free school. The school is a family affair: Heuston's wife, Nancy, runs the school and the two youngest Heuston children are students there.

Heuston is the chief executive officer of Wicat Systems, but still insists, "I'm trying to spend my time on education." On the job, "Dusty," as his more than 500 employees call him, is not your buttoned-down, buttoned-up executive. One employee told us that there aren't many companies like Wicat where "the janitor dresses better than the CEO." Informal to Dusty does not mean designer jeans, but garage-style work pants. Heuston's Wicat stock was worth over $30 million when the company went public in 1983 (though it was worth about $5 million in mid-1984 because of the beating Wicat stock had taken on Wall Street). Despite his multimillionaire status, Heuston continues to drive a station wagon and live in a "normal house" in Orem, Utah. He continues a lifelong hobby of nature photography. He says that the only difference the money has made in his life is that he can "pay tuitions for his children." Two of his daughters went to Harvard, another to Yale, and a fourth is at Brigham Young.

In 1983, during a business meeting in New York City, Heuston felt a very sharp pain. Within hours he was undergoing emergency surgery for a perforated intestine. "I damn near wiped out," he says grimly. But that hasn't slowed him down. Heuston rises at 5:30 a.m. and works 12 hours "as a rule."

Heuston is willing to work constantly because, he says, "I'm serious. There isn't any way to avoid the implication that if what I do succeeds, I can help a few billion children."

Steve Jobs

"I'm just a guy who should have been a semitalented poet on the Left Bank. I got sidetracked here"

▶ **BEST-KNOWN VENTURE:** Apple Computer

BORN: 1955

RAISED: Los Altos, California

FATHER'S OCCUPATION: Machinist

FIRST DOLLAR EARNED: Repairing stereos

SCHOOLING: Reed College (one semester, no degree)

ORIGINAL FINANCING: His Volkswagen bus and Steve Wozniak's two calculators

PERSONAL NET WORTH: $200 million

HOME: Los Gatos, California

FAMILY: Single

PERSONAL TRANSPORTATION: Mercedes

apple computer

APPLE COMPUTER INC.: The company that started it all.

▶ BEST-KNOWN PRODUCTS: Apple II, Lisa, Macintosh

YEAR FOUNDED: 1977

EMPLOYEES: 4,500

HEADQUARTERS: Cupertino, California

SALES: $1 billion (1983)

PROFITS: $77 million (1983)

OWNERSHIP: Public (1980), Steve Jobs holds 11.6 percent, Mike Markkula holds 10.2 percent

When he was 13 years old and a student at Homestead High School in Los Altos, the heart of California's Silicon Valley, Steve Jobs tackled, as a class project, the building of a frequency counter, a device to measure the speed of electronic impulses. He called up William Hewlett, the president of Hewlett-Packard, and said, "I'm Steve Jobs and I was wondering whether you had any spare parts I could build a frequency counter out of." Hewlett-Packard was in nearby Palo Alto, but distance didn't faze Jobs. He also picked up the phone and called Burroughs, collect, in Detroit to ask for spare parts. Brash and determined—that was Steve Jobs from the start. And effective: Bill Hewlett was taken aback by the call, but Jobs got his parts. And the following summer Hewlett arranged for Jobs to work in a H-P factory.

The computer industry seems too young to have a mythology but Steve Jobs already qualifies as a mythic hero. He and his high school chum, Steve Wozniak, ushered in the era of the personal computer. From parts they "liberated" from Atari and Hewlett-Packard (where they were working in the mid-'70s, Jobs at Atari, Wozniak at H-P) and with a $20 microprocessor, they built their own computer in the garage of Jobs's parents' home in Los Altos. That was the Apple I.

The two friends began assembling computers for their friends at the Homebrew Computer Club, an informal group of computer enthusiasts who met regularly at Stanford University. They then built 50 of them for one of the nation's first computer stores, the Byte Shop in Mountain View. To finance their garage enterprise, Jobs sold his Volkswagen bus and Wozniak sold his two H-P calculators.

It was Jobs who wanted to start a business. Woz, as he's always called, is the brilliant scientist type who admits he's not competitive. Jobs, on the other hand, is competitive from the word go. If it was Woz who created the first computer to bear the Apple name, it was Jobs who created the company to go with it. Jobs took care of the business details. He dealt with suppliers, customers, and public relations and advertising people, and eventually with the venture capitalists who advanced the seed money that launched Apple Computer. There were other personal computer makers before Apple—notably MITS and IMSAI—but it was Apple that made it come off, thanks in great part to the messianic persistence of Steve Jobs.

When Apple Computer went public in 1980, one of the lead underwriters was Wall Street's Morgan Stanley. If Jobs had shown up at Morgan Stanley in 1976, when he and Wozniak were first assembling their computer, he probably would not have made it past the receptionist. He looked like the archetypal counterculture kid in those days, with hair down to his shoulders, a scraggly beard, and dirty blue jeans. He was often barefoot—and often unwashed. Don Valentine, a Silicon Valley venture capitalist, went to see him at the suggestion of public relations wizard Regis McKenna, and his first reaction was: "Why did you send me to this renegade from the human race?"

But California venture capitalists are not put off by appearances. Valentine sent A.C. "Mike" Markkula to the Jobs garage, and this veteran of Fairchild Semiconductor and Intel, then a retired millionaire at age 38, saw the promise in what the two Steves were doing. Markkula threw in with the two kids, putting up his own money, raising other money, and coming out of retirement to work full-time for Apple.

In 1976, when Apple Computer was about to be formed, Steve Jobs was all of 21 years old. He had been adopted as a baby by Paul and Clara Jobs, and grew up in Silicon Valley surrounded by kids from more affluent families. His father worked as a machinist at Spectra-Physics. As a youngster, Steve was serious and intense and is remembered by teachers as a loner. He also showed an early aptitude for commerce, making money at Homestead High by fixing stereos and selling them to classmates.

He forged a friendship and business partnership with Wozniak, who was five years older. Their bond was pranks. They went into the "blue box" business, the field pioneered by the legendary Captain Crunch (John Draper). A blue box enabled the holder to break into telephone lines and call for free to anywhere in the world. A great practical joker, Woz loved doing things like calling the Vatican to wake up the Pope. Jobs did, too, but he was also intent on selling the devices to kids who wanted to outwit the phone company.

Jobs entered Reed College in Portland, Oregon, in 1972. It was the perfect place for him. He wanted to go to a school where "nobody knew what they were going to do. They were trying to find out about life." At Reed, Jobs became interested in Eastern religion. And vegetarianism. And LSD. And *I Ching*. He dropped out of school after one semester but continued to live on campus. Wozniak used to come up from Berkeley to visit with him on weekends. Woz dropped out of the University of California at Berkeley after his junior year to take a job with Hewlett-Packard. Jobs returned from Reed to take a job with Atari, saved his money and went off to India with a friend, Dan Kottke, searching for the famous spiritual leader, Neem Karoli. He wandered around the Indian subcontinent for several months before returning to Silicon Valley, where he went back to work at Atari and recontacted his friend Woz at H-P.

Atari was, of course, the company Nolan Bushnell started to market his video game, *Pong*. Wozniak, ever the brilliant practical joker (he scored 800 on the SAT mathematics test), designed his own game, which he demonstrated to Atari. It wasn't quite marketable. When the player missed the targeted blip, the screen would flash, "OH SHIT." Atari offered Woz a job but he preferred to stay with H-P, although his friend Jobs dragooned him into working nights to design a new game that he, Jobs, had promised Bushnell he would deliver in four days. He did, thanks to Woz.

It seemed that it was always the same drill: Jobs pushing Wozniak to design and create. He had to argue long and hard in the end to get Woz to quit his job at Hewlett-Packard and join Apple Computer in its new offices in Cupertino, just two miles from their old high school. Wozniak went back later to get his degree at Berkeley. He also dropped out of Apple for a while to stage two "US" music festivals in Southern California to engender the idea that the '80s should be an "us" period in contrast to the "me" era of the '70s. He reportedly gave away as much as $25 million in these ventures. Steve Jobs never left Apple once it was started. And he never even tried for a college degree.

Apple Computer, by almost any measure, has been a raging success. The Apple II, designed by Wozniak in late 1976, ignited the personal computer revolution. It weighed 12 pounds, it was easy to use, and it inspired dozens of competitors, including the industry giant, IBM, which entered the personal computer market in 1981 with a machine that was soon outselling the Apple. The folks at Apple struck back in early 1984 with the Macintosh, a computer introduced with a strident anti-IBM theme. In its initial year, 1977, Apple Computer registered sales of $800,000. In its eighth year, 1984, it was a cinch to hit $1.5 billion. It made the *Fortune* 500 roster in five years; no company had ever done that in such a short time.

Outsiders got a close look at the fortunes to be made in a successful start-up when Apple Computer sold 4.6 million shares to the public in December 1980. The shares were sold at $22 apiece, and since that represented only 8 percent of the company, Apple Computer was then valued in the marketplace at $1.3 billion—less than four years from its founding. Jobs and Wozniak became instant millionaires, at least on paper. Wozniak's holdings were worth $88 million, Jobs's $165 million. Markkula's stake was worth $154 million. Arthur Rock, a San Francisco venture capitalist, had bought 640,000 shares of Apple at nine cents a share in 1978; that $57,600 investment turned into $14 million.

Steve Jobs underwent a face-lift in his new role as corporate executive. He's clean shaven. He wears shoes. His hair is fashionably long—and styled. And he dresses in business suits, though he often comes to the office in designer jeans. He's not without some flair. He likes to wear bow ties and has been known to wear suspenders.

He has seemingly also been able to avoid the pitfalls of the entrepreneur who wants to do everything. While Jobs doesn't win high marks for his humility, he has been willing to accept Markkula's judgment that he may not know how to run a company. The first president of Apple was Michael Scott, whom Markkula recruited from National Semiconductor. Scott departed in 1981 and Markkula himself assumed the role of chief executive officer. Then, in 1983, Apple recruited John Sculley, president of Pepsi-Cola, to become its new chief, agreeing to pay him a cash bonus of $2 million to make the transcontinental and transcendental move from soft drinks and corn chips to computers.

By no means, however, has Steve Jobs taken a back seat in the company he founded. He's the chairman of the board—and a very active one. He's still the largest stockholder in Apple Computer, owning close to 12 percent of all the shares. He represents the company in sessions with reporters, security analysts, and congressional committees. When *Time* designated the computer as its "Man of the Year" in 1983, its story was mostly about Jobs, describing him as someone whose blind faith in the computer "would have been the envy of the early Christian martyrs."

Jobs's abrasive style in dealing with employees was also touched on in the *Time* article and in other stories. Jeff Raskin, a former publications manager at Apple, was quoted as saying this about Jobs: "He would have made an excellent King of France." Paul Ciotti, who wrote one of the seminal pieces on Apple in the July 1982 issue of *California* magazine, said that Jobs is known for walking into a laboratory, looking at something people have been slaving over for weeks, and pronouncing, "This is a piece of shit."

Intensity is Steve Jobs's trademark. He's extremely ambitious—and likes to link the growth of Apple Computer with a vast social revolution in which the computer will help to liberate people from menial tasks. He's a prime architect of the "Apple Values," which declare that the company expects "to make this world a better place to live" and that "we recognize that rewards must be psychological as well as financial." Apple is one of the few companies in the nation to extend stock options to all employees. In 1982, in celebration of the company doing more than $100 million in sales in a single quarter, Apple gave an extra week's paid vacation to all employees.

Just shy of 30 in 1984, Steve Jobs seems to be almost the last person in the world who would want to take an extra week's vacation. He extols the virtue of work. He lives in a Tudor home in Los Gatos, a 20-minute drive in his Mercedes from Apple headquarters, but he has not furnished it lavishly. And while he has bought a Central Park duplex in Manhattan and hired I.M. Pei to design it, he is not known as a sybarite. Jobs has never been married but he had, according to the January 3, 1983, cover story in *Time*, a stormy relationship with a woman who had a baby girl in 1978, claiming Jobs to be the father. Jobs denied the paternity, insisting that "28 percent of the male population of the United States could be the father," but a blood test indicated a strong probability that he was the father and the court ordered him to pay $385 a month for child support. In 1983, when Apple introduced its new computer for office use, it carried the name, Lisa—the name of the baby whose paternity he denied.

Jobs has sold hardly any of his Apple stock. As a result, his fortune is still largely tied up in the company. At one point in 1983, when the price of Apple's stock soared to over $60, he was worth more than $400 million on paper. Then the stock skidded to $20, which meant he lost more than a quarter of a billion dollars in one year. Asked how he felt about that, he said: "It's very character-building." The clearest expression of how he feels about work and money came in an interview he had in 1984 with reporter Tom Zito, which appeared in *Access*, a *Newsweek* publication. Asked by Zito whether he considered himself "the new astronaut," Jobs replied:

"No, no, no. I'm just a guy who probably should have been a semitalented poet on the Left Bank. I got sort of sidetracked here. The space guys, the astronauts, were techies to start with. John Glenn didn't read Rimbaud, you know; but you talk to some of the people in the computer business now and they're very well grounded in the philosophical traditions of the last hundred years and sociological traditions of the sixties. There's something going on here, there's something that's changing the world and this is the epicenter."

Jobs said in this interview that he didn't think the Silicon Valley people started these companies just to make a buck. They did it, he explained, to pioneer something significant. In addition, Jobs said the "right company" concept was important. "Remember," he told Zito, "the role models were Hewlett and Packard. Their main achievement was that they built a company. Nobody remembers their first frequency-counter, their first audio oscillator. But what does symbolize Hewlett-Packard is a revolutionary attitude toward people, a belief that people should be treated fairly, that the differentiation between labor and management should go away. And they built a company and they lived that philosophy for thirty-five or forty years and that's why they're heroes. Hewlett and Packard started what became the Valley."

The Jobs philosophy has worked its way into Apple literature. In their 1983 report to shareholders, Sculley and Jobs depicted Apple Computer as "nothing less than a great American company," one whose essential character sets it "apart from the rest of our industry and the rest of corporate America."

Jobs went to Boston in early 1984 to introduce the Macintosh computer. At a press conference he told reporters: "We are looking at what will be a 40-billion-dollar [personal computer] market by the end of the decade. I honestly believe that once the smoke clears, only two companies will be competing for that market. We expect to be a 10-billion-dollar entity by the time that happens."

Joseph P. Kahn, associate editor of *Inc.*, who was at the press conference, commented:

"Those are big expectations. But the kid talks big."

Andrew Kay

"I'm afraid of ignorance. If someone is willing to spend 3,000 dollars for an Apple that will do the same thing as a Kaypro for 1,500 dollars, I'm afraid of that"

▶ **BEST-KNOWN VENTURE:** Kaypro

OTHER VENTURE: Non-Linear Systems

BORN: 1919

RAISED: Clifton, New Jersey

FATHER'S OCCUPATION: Textile weaver

FIRST DOLLAR EARNED: Picking fruit

SCHOOLING: B.S., electrical engineering, Massachusetts Institute of Technology

ORIGINAL FINANCING: Raised $1 million through real estate deals to get into computer manufacturing

PERSONAL NET WORTH: $245 million at the time of the public offering

HOME: Del Mar, California

FAMILY: Married; two sons, one daughter

PERSONAL TRANSPORTATION: Mercedes diesel

CORPORATION

KAYPRO CORPORATION: Mom-and-pop manufacturers of personal computers.

▶ **BEST-KNOWN PRODUCTS:** Kaypro II and 4 portable computers, Kaypro 10 hard disk version

YEAR FOUNDED: 1953

EMPLOYEES: 572

HEADQUARTERS: Solana Beach, California

SALES: $75 million (1983); $165 million (1984 projection)

PROFITS: $12.9 million (1983); $22.7 million (1984 projection)

OWNERSHIP: Public (1983), the Kay family owns 86 percent of all outstanding shares

I f you were motoring up the California Coast from San Diego, you wouldn't think that Solana Beach is the home base for an aggressive company that has battled its way into fourth place in the personal computer market. Located 25 miles north of San Diego, between the beach towns of Del Mar and Cardiff-by-the-Sea, Solana Beach looks like a typical Southern California surfer's paradise. Kaypro is there because in 1953 (before anyone had even thought of a personal computer) Andrew Kay, for whom the company is named, had a falling out with his former boss over whether it was a good idea to tie one's fortunes to the Pentagon.

The son of an immigrant from an obscure region of what is now Poland, Andrew's name was originally Kopischiansky. His original language was Lemko, the region's native tongue. Since no one ever called him Kopischiansky at the various places he worked, as it was a difficult name to pronounce, Andrew officially changed his name to Kay in 1947.

As a kid growing up in New Jersey, Andrew was always interested in science. He inherited the trait from his father, who though a textile weaver by profession, pursued electronic hobbies, fixing the neighbors' radios and TVs and keeping up with whatever new inventions were on the horizon.

With a high school friend, Andrew built a chemical lab, a physics lab, a biology lab, and a machine shop in the friend's basement. There the two experimenters spent their time on such endeavors as X-raying small animals and building little rockets. "We had a 50,000-volt X-ray machine," Kay recalls. "It's a wonder we didn't kill ourselves." He later gravitated toward engineering, receiving his degree from MIT in 1940.

After that, Kay moved around to various jobs on the East Coast. It was wartime, and most of these jobs were related to the air defense effort. In Philadelphia, where he was married, he worked for an aviation firm. In New York, he taught people how to repair aircraft instruments. Then he settled down for a time in Cleveland, where he supervised test engineering for Jack & Heintz, which made automatic pilots. The company was noted for high productivity levels and team spirit.

It was at Jack & Heintz that Kay first conceived the idea of a digital voltmeter—a tool for testing electronics components and systems. But he had no time to develop it, since many of the firm's employees had gone off to war and the remaining staff was working 12-hour days just to keep up. "I had no one to work with but women and cripples," says Kay, adding, "I was one of them." Because of a knee injury incurred while wrestling, he was 4-F.

Kay left Jack & Heintz to move to California, where he joined Jet Propulsion Laboratories (JPL) in Pasadena, making controls for guided missiles. But in 1949, after less than two years at JPL, he departed to team up once again with Bill Jack of Jack & Heintz. Jack had set up a plant in Solana Beach that was devoted largely to designing and producing aerial reconaissance systems. "I was the first man on the payroll," Kay recalls, "and my title was vice president in charge of engineering."

This time, though, the relationship between Jack and Kay didn't work so well. Kay wanted to emphasize engineering; Jack was more concerned with production. "He really didn't understand the engineering business," grumbles Kay. Finally, a political—not engineering—argument between the two propelled Kay out on his own.

Kay wasn't sorry to become an entrepreneur. Years earlier, back in Cleveland, he had entertained fantasies of designing and producing such products as controls for steam heaters. And now he had an idea to pursue that had been on the back burner for a decade: the digital voltmeter.

His new company, Non-Linear Systems, made all sorts of voltmeters. In the late '60s, says Kay, "we put minicomputers on them and gathered data from a thousand different points." Sales rose to $6.7 million, dropped to $1.67 million, and rose again to $4 million. Around 1980, Kay noticed that "computers constituted 90 percent of the electronics business, and I was in the other 10 percent—and a very tiny fraction of that 10 percent." Also, the aerospace business (a major client) was dwindling, and Kay felt that no matter how hard he worked, he wasn't really getting anywhere. So he decided that Non-Linear Systems should go into the personal computer business, and he set up a team (whose principal member was Bill MacDonald) to work on the design. He believed his computer would fill a totally unmet need: it would be a complete package—including disk drives, keyboard, and a substantial amount of software in the basic price—and it would be portable.

In 1981, the first full-feature portable computer made its debut at the West Coast Computer Faire. Unfortunately for Kay, it was not manufactured by Non-Linear Systems, but by Osborne Computer. However, Non-Linear was hot on Osborne's tail, and introduced the Kaycomp II at the same show exactly one year later. It looked much like the Osborne portable computer, but had several advantages, including a nine-inch screen (Osborne's was a five-inch). And it sold for the same price: $1,795 including the software.

Despite Osborne's early dash out of the starting gate, the Kaycomp II rapidly began closing the gap. Then Osborne stumbled and fell, and Kaypro—as the company was now called—rushed in to take over the niche.

Originally, the Kays thought they'd sell their computer mostly to engineers—the market they were used to dealing with. Wrong. It soon became a favorite with small business people, especially writers, who appreciated the affordable price (now down five hundred dollars) and the choice of two word processing systems that came in the package.

Since the introduction of the Kaycomp II, Kaypro has grown to be the fourth-largest seller of desktop computers in the $1,000 to $3,000 price range, behind IBM, Apple, and Tandy/Radio Shack. Some thought it would nose out Radio Shack by the end of 1984. A February 1984 print ad proclaimed, "In the past fiscal year, Kaypro sales grew 1,400 percent." Prudential Bache, the brokerage house that took Kaypro public, estimated sales at $150 to $175 million for the fiscal year ending August 31, 1984.

In the 1983 initial public stock offering, Andrew sold 600,000 shares worth $6 million, retaining another 64 percent of the 37 million shares outstanding, worth a whopping $245 million. Andrew's sons, David and Alan, each own 5.4 percent of the outstanding shares. So the Kays are not poor, even though the stock price dropped from $10 a share at the offering to a low of under $3 in mid-1984. After paying off some mortgages on personal real estate holdings, Andrew was able to buy himself a slightly larger house with an indoor pool.

Kaypro, says David, has grown quickly by sticking to its basic policy of selling a complete package and by manufacturing all its components in the Solana Beach plant, which helps keep prices down. Another cost-cutting technique is the elimination of the distribution middleman; Kaypro works directly with its dealers. It also insists that they pay COD, which makes for better cash flow but causes some retailers (such as Entre and ComputerLand) to shun the Kaypro line.

Management may be another factor in Kaypro's success. "Jack & Heintz had a big impact on me—I saw how it was possible to manage a large organization with very few managers," Andrew recalls. So when he started Non-Linear Systems, he introduced a form of participative management, replacing the traditional assembly line with teams. "The people assembling the boards are putting in all sorts of components and walking around—moving all the time, like people should, from computer to computer. It makes for a more interesting and varied atmosphere." The teams teach new members, so "I don't need any industrial engineers."

The original Kaycomp II is now known as the Kaypro II, and there are also Kaypros 4 and 10 (each has additional disk storage capacity). Kaypro also announced a "notebook" (lap-size) portable, which can use programs sold for the IBM PC (when connected to its desktop base station); and makes a small desktop micro called the Robie (because, David says, "some people thought it looked like a robot in the early stages").

The lap-size computer is produced in conjunction with Mitsui, a Japanese trading company. The Kays hope to enter into more deals with the Japanese, who, David believes, will soon produce products that "can do twice as much for half the money and better reliability" than those produced in the United States.

It remains to be seen whether the Kays can build an on-going company. Despite their "participative management" structure, the Kays still run the show. Kaypro is a sort of mom-and-pop operation. In fact, mom, pop, sons, grandpop, brother, and daughter all work there—it's enough to give nepotism a good name. Founder Andrew Kay is the patriarch of the clan. His son, David, a former windmill salesman, is vice president of marketing; his other son, Alan—also a vice president—heads the administrative staff. His wife is secretary of the corporation; his father superintends the maintenance staff; his brother runs the company print shop; and his daughter, who owns an architectural firm, is a consultant. Occasionally, the family's influence shows up in odd ways. For example, the menu at the company cafeteria consists of fruit juices and salads—Andrew and David are both vegetarians.

Wall Street analysts have complained that the company needs a more professional management. The Kays moved in that direction at the end of 1983, bringing in a new team of managers, including Blair Newman as director of marketing and strategic planning, Michael Dortch as a special consultant, and Sandy Kutik as head of project management. On February 21, 1984, Kaypro even had Newman speak before the New York Society of Security Analysts, where he cited the new management team members and summed up the company's approach as follows: "Kaypro's new strategy can be summed up by how the label on one of our future products might read: 'Designed in the U.S. by top independent technical talents, made in Japan by robots, and sold world-wide by Kaypro.'"

Two weeks later, the *San Diego Union* reported that Newman, Dortch, and Kutik were all fired. At the same time, five of Kaypro's 13 regional sales managers and 10 other support staffers left the company to join Seequa Computer Corp. in Annapolis, Maryland. A frustrated Blair Newman, who came to Kaypro from the Yankee Group, told *Business Week:* "There are too many Kays and not enough pros."

Analysts do not expect Kaypro to go the way of Osborne, but some predict hard challenges ahead. They're concerned about an overly large inventory of Kaypro 10s and about the Kays' refusal to adapt to the needs of the large chains.

Andrew himself, who is mounting an aggressive campaign against IBM, is afraid of nothing but ignorance. Some people, he sniffs, are willing to spend $3,000 for a machine that will do the same thing as a $1,500 Kaypro. "We don't sell half a computer and call it a computer and then ask a person to come back and buy the rest of it later. It's like selling an automobile without wheels or seats and saying, 'Those are options.' IBM, Apple, and Tandy play that kind of game. But we don't."

AIRBORNE DIVISION

Pilots

Harry Garland (Cromemco)	Cessna 210
Fred Gibbons (Software Publishing)	Cessna 210
William Godbout (CompuPro)	Four small planes
Ken Grant (Synapse)	Piper Seneca, Cessna
Sat Tara Singh Khalsa (Kriya Systems)	Cessna Skyline
Gary Kildall (Digital Research)	PITS Biplane

Ham Radio Operators

Nolan Bushnell (Atari)	Roger Melen (Cromemco)
Harry Garland (Cromemco)	Seymour Rubinstein (MicroPro)
William Godbout (CompuPro)	Ken Williams (Sierra On-Line)
William von Meister (Source Telecomputing)	

Allen Michels

"We encourage people to take risks and just go for it. I've always believed that people are more apt to do well than do badly"

▶ **BEST-KNOWN VENTURE:** Convergent Technologies

BORN: 1940

RAISED: Chicago, Illinois

FATHER'S OCCUPATION: Shoe store owner

FIRST DOLLAR EARNED: Selling shoes

SCHOOLING: B.S., mathematics, University of Illinois (academic scholarship); M.S., mathematics, Illinois Institute of Technology

ORIGINAL FINANCING: $2.5 million—$700,000 from a friend; the balance from two of his friend's friends

PERSONAL NET WORTH: $30 million

HOME: San Francisco, California

FAMILY: Divorced; remarried; four children

PERSONAL TRANSPORTATION: Mercedes 500 SEL

Convergent Technologies, Inc.

CONVERGENT TECHNOLOGIES INC.: Manufacturers of computers, which they sell to original equipment manufacturers (e.g., large computer makers), who adapt and market them under their own names.

▶ **BEST-KNOWN PRODUCTS:** Small computers sold by Burroughs, NCR, AT&T

YEAR FOUNDED: 1979

EMPLOYEES: 1,800

HEADQUARTERS: Santa Clara, California

SALES: $140 million (1984 projection)

PROFITS: $14.9 million (1983)

OWNERSHIP: Public (May 1982); founder retains 2.5 percent

Anyone who thinks that Silicon Valley is a workers' paradise of beer busts, swimming pools, flexible work hours, and lavish bonuses hasn't seen Convergent Technologies in Santa Clara. Convergent's founder/president, Allen Michels, describes his firm as "the Marine Corps of the computer industry."

Eighty-hour work weeks are not uncommon for executives there, and everyone felt the effects of a cost-cutting binge in September 1983. Besides urging employees to watch overtime, expense account meals, photocopy usage, and so forth, the company also deferred employee bonuses and raises, cut back overtime and hiring, slashed the pay of six top officers, and reduced advertising.

There are no frills at Convergent, because Michels doesn't believe in mixing work and play. He himself sets the example, typically working from 7 a.m. to 11 p.m. six days a week, lunching at his desk, and talking about "austerity" as though it were a positive force.

Maybe it's because austerity was the keynote of his early life. Born in Chicago in 1940, the son of a small shoe store owner, he remembers dining on "stuffing sandwiches" because that's all there was to eat. "I'm fat now because of that—I'm certain of it," he says, peering at us across his cluttered desk through a cloud of cigar smoke. Young Allen was also no stranger to hard work. He'd go to school until 3 p.m., attend Hebrew school from 3 to 5, practice the violin (as his mother demanded) from 5 to 6, eat from 6 to 6:20, and then work in his father's shop, or—if time permitted—do his homework until bedtime.

So Michels is used to a stiff regimen. But how does he manage to maintain the skilled, experienced work force that customers consider to be one of the company's greatest strengths?

The incentive for many is freedom—including the freedom to fail. "I'm very good at trusting," says Michels. "We encourage people to take risks and just go for it. I've always believed that people are more apt to do well than do badly. Just trust them and let them know that whatever happens, you're with them. And I love the people who work here. I trust them."

Curiously, the hard-driving, cigar-smoking Michels was forced into many of his career choices by women. He initially wanted to be an archeologist, not a technologist. But the mother of his high school sweetheart and intended bride warned him, "You'll never marry my daughter if you're going to be an archeologist."

So, with the aid of a scholarship, he entered the University of Illinois with the intention of becoming a CPA and then going on to law school. But he discovered that he was "incredibly bored" with accounting. And a law aptitude test "said that I ought to be wrapping fish at a fish market but certainly not studying law."

He switched to engineering because he loved math, and continued his education at the Illinois Institute of Technology. His first job after graduation was with a division of North American Philips, based in upstate New York. He worked first in engineering, then in marketing. After a business trip to Holland, he came back to find his wife and children gone. His wife, who hated upstate New York, had left him a note: she'd moved back to Chicago and asked him to join her as soon as possible.

Reluctantly, he followed her to Chicago but had to give up his job. Soon he got an offer from a company called Mechtronics Nuclear, which made high-speed instruments for measuring atomic reactions. Digital Equipment hired him away from there in 1968, and he ended up working for DEC in sales, marketing, and business development for 10 years—first in Chicago, then in California, and finally in Massachusetts.

Then once again, he was forced to leave a job he enjoyed, this time because his wife didn't like Massachusetts. She moved back to California, and Allen followed. "I should have known," he groans.

Once again he landed on his feet, going to work for Intel, a major manufacturer of silicon chips. In 1979, after a year and a half there, he got tired of working for what he considered to be "inferior people" and figured that "I couldn't work any harder than I was working, so why not do it for myself?"

He had an idea for an office work station. It would combine all the functions and capacity of a file cabinet-size minicomputer yet fit on a desk. And the individual machines could be networked together, so different users could share information. As he told us proudly, "It did just about everything but make toast." And it was the first machine of its kind. He asked a friend, Bill Rollnick, head of an equipment leasing firm which had been his biggest customer at Intel, for "about a million-and-a-half," to start a company.

"You knucklehead—you can't do anything on a million-and-a-half," was the response. "You'll need two-and-a-half million, at least, to get started. Now tell me what it is you want to do."

"I drew it on a napkin," Michels recalls. "In fact, that napkin was on our annual report one year."

Rollnick came up with around $700,000 and introduced him to two other investors who pitched in the rest of the $2.5 million within a few days. Michels recruited an engineer and a marketing person and launched Convergent Technologies.

When the first integrated work station rolled out the door

in October 1980, Michels was ecstatic. "I observed the birth of one of my children, too, and I can't tell you which was more exciting to me," he says.

This successful birth was followed by other products, including a supermicro called Megaframe, and NGen, a desktop computer that's completely modular, with mix-and-match components. You never see Convergent's name on these machines because Convergent sells them to other manufacturers, such as Burroughs, NCR, Thomson-CSF (the French company), Prime Computer, Datapoint, and AT&T. These customers then adapt the basic Convergent unit to fit their needs—adding hardware and/or software—and sell them to businesses under their own name.

"Our idea was to get large fast, because either you're a major player and have major purchasing capabilities for raw materials or you're a nonentity in the business," Michels says. And the best way to get large fast was to team up with manufacturers who would provide market knowledge, resources to develop software, and sales and support staffs.

What Convergent's customers get, according to Michels, is "more than an extension of their manufacturing capabilities. What they look for and depend on in us is the innovative vision of what tomorrow's product requirements are going to look like and what will sell." He carefully cultivates his relationships with these large firms, giving some of them large stock options in Convergent stock. Burroughs, for instance, accounted for 36 percent of Convergent's revenues in mid-1984; NCR accounts for 10 percent. Burroughs holds options to buy up to 15 percent of Convergent's stock.

"I'd say that marriages in general need to be constantly nurtured," says Michels, referring to his company's partnerships with these firms. His personal marriage died from lack of nurturing. He's on good terms with his ex-wife and has married again, but when he's asked about his nonwork life, he announces gruffly, "This company *is* my life!" Still, he may be mellowing. He recently bought a house on San Francisco's Russian Hill, farther away from the office, because "the distinction between the man and the company has become very blurred."

Convergent's product development strategy is summed

up in a maxim that appears on plaques in senior executives' offices: "Think small: focus, make decisions, take risks, make it happen." Think small? In a company that wanted to get large fast? Michels hastens to explain that it means "think that you're in a small company where you can get things done. Think of being responsible for yourself and for what you do. Don't identify and acknowledge inhibitions, just go out and do it."

He fosters this small-company image by throwing executives out of the corporate nest to form their own entrepreneurial "strike forces." These groups operate on their own—supported only by money—to bring new products to the marketplace quickly. Michels stays in the background and worries.

Raising money for his company has never been one of his worries, though. Altogether, about $170 million has been raised from venture capitalists and public offerings. The company went public in 1982, with Michels's shares valued at $30 million. Michels immediately went into a post-partum depression. At the suggestion of his friend Sandy Kurtzig (founder of Ask Computers), he went out and bought a Mercedes to make himself feel better. Now he enjoys being at the helm of a public company, arbitrating the "tug of war between operating management, legal concerns, and the auditors." His reasons? "I've always been a student of history and of human behavior. I've always had a sense of the ironic and the absurd."

He's also willing to laugh at himself. With candid delight, he showed us a large and elaborately mounted Marine combat boot with a gory bullet hole in it, explaining that it was presented to him by his sales organization. Reminiscent of a similar trophy President Reagan presented to former Secretary of the Interior James Watt, it signified a time when Convergent had shot itself in the foot. Production of Convergent's NGen had been delayed because the NGen used an Intel chip that wasn't delivered on time. Michels doesn't blame Intel—"we rushed the engineering and production to a degree that we simply stumbled on ourselves," he says.

However, that didn't stop him from needling Intel's president. On bended knee, he handed him a Cookie Monster doll with a note taped to its middle: "Give me chips!"

Michels also acknowledges an actual product failure. This was the Workslate, a lap-size portable computer that's part spreadsheet (number-cruncher), part telephone modem, part tape recorder, part calendar, part address book, and part calculator. It does everything but word processing. Michels himself is in love with this brainchild of his—he owns 10 Workslates—and that may have been part of the problem: "You should never fall in love with products."

It did not do well. Michels admits that it was too expensive—the price was raised from $895 to $1,195, for which he blames his own management laxity. Another reason it didn't catch on, Michels suggests, is that it was ahead of its time. Since it was sold through retail channels under Convergent's own name, its failure didn't do the company image any good. In a lengthy article detailing the Workslate's demise, *Business Week* cited the "manufacturing and management misjudgments" including an "excessively hasty design" and no market research being done on the original Workslate concept. The magazine also pointed a finger at Michels's belief that "good products sell themselves," which meant he was extremely reluctant to spend money on sales and marketing, hiring only one sales executive for the entire United States.

In July 1984, Convergent stopped making the Workslate, after losing over $10 million on the machine. Some key people who were involved in its development have left. But Michels remains optimistic. "You know," he reflects, "we've had problems from the day we started the company. But you jump on them, you beat the shit out of them, you spit them out in little pieces. We're not going to let a failure alter our behavioral style."

Convergent's revenues have been growing every year ($163.5 million in 1983), and a recent deal with AT&T, Michels told *Business Week*, will probably earn the company $300 million in 1985 and '86. But in mid-1984, analysts were lukewarm regarding Convergent's future. Its stock had not recovered from a 1983 drop. It's a volatile industry, and there's a lot of competition in the office automation business, from such big names as IBM, Apple, Wang, and Hewlett-Packard.

So Michels continues to worry, think hard, and work hard, trying out all the competition's products "because I want to know what people are doing that's better than ours." He also adheres—and insists that his subordinates adhere—to another plaque-enshrined company maxim, this one composed by chief operating officer Ben Wegbreit: "Work hard, stick together, improve every day, and always ask the question, 'How badly do I want it?'"

George Morrow

"I'm not a pioneer. I was out in the middle of the desert, the train came along and stopped. The guy said, 'You want to get on?' And I got on."

▶ **BEST-KNOWN VENTURE:** Morrow Designs

OTHER VENTURES: Morrow's Micro Stuff, Thinker Toys

BORN: 1934

RAISED: San Francisco and Redwood City, California

PARENTS' OCCUPATION: Luncheonette owners

FIRST DOLLAR EARNED: Dishwasher

SCHOOLING: B.S., physics, Stanford University; M.S., mathematics, University of Oklahoma

ORIGINAL FINANCING: $6,000 from family savings

HOME: Berkeley, California

FAMILY: Married; three children

PERSONAL TRANSPORTATION: Audi 5000

MORROW

MORROW DESIGNS INC.: The low-cost leader in desktop business systems. Sets price first, before production, unlike most who build the machine, calculate costs, and then add profit.

▶ **BEST-KNOWN PRODUCTS:** Morrow Micro Decision line of eight-bit personal computers

YEAR FOUNDED: 1976

EMPLOYEES: 104

HEADQUARTERS: San Leandro, California

SALES: $22.6 million (1983); $40 million (1984 projection)

PROFITS: $1.6 million (1983)

OWNERSHIP: Private, 72 percent held by George and Michiko Morrow

D on't judge a book by its cover—or George Morrow by the computer he makes. The Morrow Micro Decision is usually described in the most workaday terms. It is efficient, functional, reliable, and admirable in engineering and price. Morrow, the man, is caustic, comical, histrionic, and undiplomatic; he flaps his arms to simulate wings, clutches his heart and writhes on the floor (in mock horror at a supplier's raised prices), speaks to reporters in a stage whisper, and passes vivid, abrupt judgments.

"Venture capitalists don't have the slightest idea what the ingredients of success are.

"If I had a business which relied on kids sticking quarters in a machine, I couldn't sleep at night. I equate that with being a drug dealer."

Morrow is also streetwise and philosophical. As a small boy he stood on a milk crate to wash dishes in his uncle's luncheonette. Later he learned to make sodas, scoop ice cream, and dish up burgers and egg salad sandwiches at his father's drive-in restaurant in Redwood City, south of San Francisco. With teenage friends he entered the "used white-wall tire business," which translates to stealing tires around the Bay Area and selling them in Southern California. Some of his partners are derelicts now, he says, in and out of prison. At the height of his antisocial period, he recalls, he received 37 moving violations in one 18-month period.

In 1950 no one would have bet a nickel on George Morrow's future. He was 16, a high school junior, his class record riddled with Ds and Fs. Allying himself with the dean of boys against his parents, he finally succeeded in getting ejected from school. In the next few years he had a hundred jobs, doing "virtually everything under the sun."

Morrow's tire-stealing escapades finally landed him in court, where a judge let him choose between spending a year in jail and joining the Army. He reached Korea in April 1953, a month before the truce. There, for the first time, he encountered a system he couldn't manipulate. Until then he had artfully played his parents off against one another, maneuvered his way out of school, flaunted the law, and never suffered anything worse than a suspended driver's license. But in the Army they'd seen every trick before. His gestures of defiance escalated until one day he realized that if he had another run-in with authority, he'd blow up and face the stockade or desertion. As he sat cleaning a rifle, he saw how his attempts to gain more freedom were backfiring. He made the decision he now sees as the beginning of his maturity—to compromise and adapt.

During more than two years in the Far East (16 months as a soldier, the rest doing civilian jobs in Korea, Hong Kong, and Saigon), Morrow taught himself to read Japanese and speak Korean. Back in the States, he worked as a restaurant cook—the same short orders over and over. After two or three years of that he felt as if he might go crazy. Out of "sheer desperation," he tried school again.

He was 27 and had dropped out 11 years earlier. "Oh boy, my head hurt," he remarks as he remembers trying to get through algebra. He worked his way up from C-minuses to As at Foothill Junior College, then transferred to Stanford on the GI Bill. His grades fell to Cs again. All the while he was supporting himself as a cook.

Two friendly suggestions from his mother had a great impact on him in school and long afterward. "George, don't worry about grades. Just learn how to think." And, "George, you should have fun in your life." Ten years older than most of his peers and worldly wise, George had fun as a student. He wasn't intimidated by professors, didn't cram for exams, and concentrated on understanding things day after day.

Though he was beginning to look like a model citizen, Morrow's rebel side wasn't far beneath the surface. A mechanical engineering major, he took his one required course in modern physics and realized he still didn't know anything about it. "I need more physics," he told his advisor.

"You need to finish your major and get out of school, so you can start earning money," said the advisor. "You're thirty years old. You're an old man." Then he added, "If I see any more physics courses on your card, I won't sign it."

"The hell with you," was Morrow's retort. He promptly changed his major to physics.

After a while it struck him that you can't do good physics if you don't really understand math. So he did graduate work in mathematics, first at the University of Oklahoma, then at the University of California at Berkeley, where he taught calculus to undergraduates.

But there came a point when teaching offered no more surprises. Morrow had left the food business promising himself that whatever he did now would be worthwhile and exciting, calling forth every bit of his potential energy and enthusiasm. Teaching calculus over and over, he faced the same questions and the same answers. It was egg salad sandwiches again.

He was pushing 35. He and his wife Michiko (a second-generation Japanese-American he had met at Stanford) had recently had a baby. Morrow panicked. Seven years of college, and all he could do was cook and teach calculus.

It was 1968. Morrow took some computer courses and got a summer job as a programmer at UC Berkeley. "That summer I walked on water," he says, remembering how he quickly solved a problem that had stumped three hapless assistant professors who were bidding for tenure. For most of the next seven years Morrow worked at the business school's Center for Research and Management Science, making models for computerized problem analysis and eventually learning hardware design. His co-workers included Rodnay Zaks (now president of Sybex Computer Books), and Chuck Grant and Mark Greenberg (co-founders of North Star Computers).

By 1975 Morrow was ready to move on. With $6,000 in the bank, he gave himself a year to figure out the next step. He tried consulting, but soon discovered that he didn't like solving problems somebody else had set. "You would walk into a room where a guy had painted himself into a corner, and he expected you to go in and make him fly."

Morrow tried designing a 16-bit computer kit with Bill Godbout, who had an electronics company that sold personal computer kits by mail order. The collaboration fell through, but Godbout began to market a Morrow-designed memory board, with Morrow receiving royalties. Morrow continued to design boards for Godbout Electronics, but it didn't take long for a familiar problem to arise: Memory boards, memory boards, like egg salad sandwiches. "Damn it, Bill, let's do some other products!" But no, Bill wanted only memory boards. George wanted to lower prices, Bill didn't. Though he liked and respected Godbout (now president of CompuPro), Morrow's frustration was mounting. Sitting with Michiko one day, Morrow exclaimed, "What's the difference between doing these products for somebody else and doing them for ourselves? Just an ad in a magazine!"

The magazine was *Byte*. The ad cost $500, and it brought in $5,000 worth of orders. The little company, christened Morrow's Micro Stuff, had sales of $50,000 between March and December 1976. But Morrow was still searching for the perfect name. Eventually, he found it: Thinker Toys.

"It took me a year to think of that name. It said everything about what I thought the business should be. The fun part and the serious part, even in the right order. You should think and you should have fun. Also, it expresses my idea about the way computers should be put together. Just as easy as putting together Tinker Toys."

But CBS dealt a cruel blow to Morrow's enthusiasm by suing him for infringement of its Tinker Toy trademark. In 1979, after three years and several levels of court decisions, CBS won. Thinker Toys died and out of the ashes rose Morrow Designs, Inc.

For the first two years of operation Morrow worked at home, designing in the dining room, making prototypes in the bathroom (where caustic solutions were less likely to destroy anything), and assembling in the garage. In 1978, the year that sales reached $600,000, he rented an office and hired his first employee.

After four years in the components business, Morrow put all the pieces together in the form of his own computer, the Micro Decision. In mid-1982, three months before Morrow introduced his first computer, his annual sales of components reached $8.6 million. The next year sales rose to $22.6 million, and the company had moved into a large building near the Oakland airport. In 1984, the Micro Decision line includes standard, hard disk and multi-user, and portable models. Morrow makes printers, modems, and other computer peripherals as well, sells through a network of 500 dealers, and provides service through its dealers and Xerox.

George Morrow is known for his ability to keep prices down; it is a keystone of his self-image as a computer maker. He compares himself to Henry Ford, who decided to set a price for a car that the masses could afford, then found ways of producing the car to meet the price. Morrow insists that parts be common, nothing esoteric ("wild horses wouldn't get me to design for a bubble memory"), and never allows more than a six-month gap between conception and production (the market changes too quickly). "I know the price of every component we use," he affirms, "every damn one of them! I never forget a number. I don't just put parts into my computers; each one is lovingly caressed, massaged into place."

For the last 25 years the former tire thief has had a clear and pragmatic sense of the necessity of honesty. He remembers, in the days of Morrow's Micro Stuff, returning thousands of dollars in checks to people when he couldn't deliver what they'd ordered promptly. He identifies with the Yankee ethic in which "your word is your bond," and says that integrity is essential to survival. "There is only one way I can expect you to be fair with me. I have to be fair with you."

The company's development has been paid for almost entirely from profits. There was no outside investment until 1983, when eight British venture capital firms put in $3.5 million. Morrow's blunt way of talking about money, bankers, and investors hasn't exactly endeared him to financiers. After one meeting with a prospective banker, Michiko—Morrow Designs' chief financial officer—got a call from New York. "Thanks, you were so gracious, and your husband was very honest. Perhaps too honest." They found another bank.

While most company presidents in the computer industry keep feverish schedules, rarely seeing their families, Morrow does about 85 percent of his work at home. In fact, he's not president anymore, having turned that job over to Robert Dilworth in mid-1983 ("I had already proved myself incompetent"). Morrow is chairman of the board and chief designer.

In 1983, the company prepared to make a public offering, while hoping that the depressed high-tech market would improve. It didn't, and the offering was withdrawn. Another unstated reason for staying private may be Morrow's position in the industry. It is a small company battling for a market niche against the growing trend toward such big-name companies as IBM and Apple and it will take all of Morrow's ingenuity to keep his computers in the stores. He himself admits, "Survival is a real issue."

Is George Morrow rich? "I've got this company that's doing 35 million dollars a year. That's worth a lot of money, right? But it's not a lot if you can't spend it." He likens the entrepreneurial world to a big casino. "So we put 6,000 dollars on the table [referring to the money with which he and his wife began the company]. We move it around, change the debt. Now there's this large stack of chips."

Continuing, George Morrow says what many others might if they had his candor: "Here it is, this wonderful stack of chips, and I can't get it off the table. All I can do is move it around. Fair to say it's driving me crazy."

WHO PAYS THE BILLS?

Finance According to George Morrow
"When you're a little guy, you've got to pay your own bills. When you become a little bit more successful, you go to the bank and get a line of credit and the bank pays your bills. You become more successful and you start using one or two products at a fairly good run rate and you are now an important customer for two or three suppliers, and your business is growing faster than your profits can sustain your growth. Then you start stringing out your suppliers. That means that they start paying your bills. When you become even more successful you put together a business plan and make some presentations to venture capitalists, who invest money. Then the venture capitalists start paying your bills. Now after you mine those successes and do a public offering, the public starts paying your bills. Finally you reach the epitome of success like Penn Central or Chrysler. You become so successful that you can't be allowed to go broke and the government starts paying your bills. That's socialism for the businessman."

Reprinted with permission from *In Business*, February 1984.

Adam Osborne

"I've been cured of a lot of my altruism about the way you run a company"

▶ **BEST-KNOWN VENTURE:** Osborne Computer

OTHER VENTURES: Osborne and Associates, Paperback Software International

BORN: 1939

RAISED: Bangkok, Thailand; Madras, India; and Warwickshire, England

PARENTS' OCCUPATIONS: Worked for a maharishi

SCHOOLING: B.S., chemical engineering, Birmingham University (England); M.S. and Ph.D., University of Delaware

ORIGINAL FINANCING: $100,000 from sale of Osborne and Associates to McGraw-Hill, $40,000 from investment fund controlled by Jack Melchor

FAMILY: Divorced; remarried; three children

PERSONAL TRANSPORTATION: Mercedes (totaled on August 28, 1984—driver unhurt)

OSBORNE COMPUTER COMPANY: Makers of the first portable computer.

▶ **BEST-KNOWN PRODUCTS:** Osborne 1, Executive

YEAR FOUNDED: 1981

EMPLOYEES: 35

HEADQUARTERS: Hayward, California

SALES: $93 million (1983)

LOSSES: $12 million (bankruptcy filing: September 1983)

OWNERSHIP: Jurisdiction of federal bankruptcy courts

B orn in Bangkok to an English father and a Polish mother, raised in India and England, educated in England and the United States, Adam Osborne has navigated a careening, charismatic course through the computer industry. His quirky independence helped him to score two major breakthroughs in the industry— and as 1984 dawned he was about to go for a third. Anyone who considers doing business with Adam Osborne should also know that if something goes wrong, Adam is likely to end up writing a book about it.

Writing has been Osborne's ticket to fame and fortune. He happens to be that rare bird: an engineer who can write. Besides, as he likes to tell people, "I come from a family of writers." Osborne's father was teaching history at the University of Bangkok when his middle child, Adam, was born in 1939, just as war was about to break out in Europe. Shortly after the Japanese bombed Pearl Harbor the Osbornes, still in Thailand, went to vacation in Kashmir. Invading Japanese armies quickly brought the war to all of Southeast Asia, leaving the Osbornes stranded. Adam's father returned to Bangkok to clean up his affairs—and was unable to get out again until the war was over. Adam and his mother spent the war years in a small village in South India just outside Madras. His father rejoined the family after the war.

The selection of this village was not by chance. Osborne's parents had become deeply involved in Eastern religion, and they became followers of a maharishi who practiced there. Adam describes the maharishi as one of the "old school": the lifestyle was ascetic, the politics fascist. Stories about Osborne have usually described his parents as "counter-missionaries," people who tried to convert Christians to Eastern religion. We asked Osborne about that. He said, "Well, they spent their time trying to persuade Christians to become human beings. At least that's my interpretation."

At age 11 Osborne was sent to England to live with friends and go through the English school system—not the upper-class system known as the "public schools," but the less prestigious government school system. He went to school in Warwickshire and then graduated from Birmingham University as a chemical engineer. That was in 1961.

Armed with his degree, he migrated to America, but not for career reasons. He had a girlfriend whose family had moved to the United States, and he followed and eventually married her. Osborne then began the first of a series of disastrous experiences working for industrial companies, disastrous in that he hated it. His first job was with a company called Scanco in Bethlehem, Pennsylvania, which made steam traps. He was asked, he said, to figure out why they work—and when he did, they began to resent him. So he next took a job with M.W. Kellogg, a fairly large engineering company, in their New York City office. The Osborne family lived in Elmhurst, a middle-class section of Queens. Osborne was a junior engineer at Kellogg, and he describes his experience as follows: "My personality was not too well suited for that kind of environment."

Osborne—or his wife—realized he would never get ahead unless he had a higher degree, and so, helped by a scholarship and money saved from his job, he enrolled at the University of Delaware. He received first a master's degree and then a Ph.D. in chemical engineering, graduating in 1968.

In 1968 a chemical engineer with a Ph.D. had no difficulty finding a job. He took one with Shell Oil in Emeryville, California, across the Bay from San Francisco. Osborne had worked with computers while completing his Ph.D. thesis, and at Shell he did mathematical modeling on computers. The Osbornes and their two children moved into an apartment in San Francisco's Marina section.

Osborne hung in with Shell for three years. Apparently they were less than fun. "It was hell," he told us. "Absolute hell! I spent far too much time wondering about the politics of the people around me and not nearly enough time getting the job done. The social implications of a large corporation I found quite nauseating." Osborne was appalled to find people just putting in their time, even in the research wing, forced to flatter superiors they didn't respect. It turned out Shell wasn't too happy with Osborne either. They told him his prospects there were not bright. And besides, in 1971 the company was moving its operations to Houston. So Adam Osborne struck out on his own.

Meanwhile, the Osbornes had moved across the Bay to Berkeley. He wanted to buy a house and found the prices in San Francisco too high. Osborne has lived in Berkeley ever since.

Left to his own resources, Osborne fell back on a skill he knew he had: writing. "I suddenly discovered technical writing was a very easy way to make money," he said. "Very low on the totem pole of prestige, but lucrative. I spent the next few years making a lot of money on technical writing—and losing it on programming." His big breakthrough came in 1972 when he made a cold call on General Automation, a Southern California minicomputer manufacturer. They desperately needed someone to write manuals their customers could understand. Osborne was hired to do all their technical documentation. By 1974 he had 15 people working for him. Then he lost the entire account as a result of a management upheaval.

One of the manuals he had produced for General Automation was a little book called *The Value of Power*—they used it as a giveaway to their customers. In 1975, Osborne expanded this manual into a longer book called *An Introduction to Microcomputers*, mainly, as he put it, because he wanted to distinguish himself from all the other consultants running around. Osborne claims it was the first book in the world to describe microcomputers. He sent the manuscript to John Wiley & Sons in New York. They rejected it, so he published it himself. Then, he got a phone call from Bruce Van Natta, a senior manager at IMS Associates, the California company that was building IMSAI microcomputer kits. He wanted to know how he could get a copy of *The Value of Power.* Osborne told him about *An Introduction to Microcomputers.* He ordered 10,000 copies at $4 apiece. By March of 1976 Osborne had sold 20,000 copies of his self-published book and it had been adopted as a textbook by 13 universities.

So Osborne, now 36 years old, regrouped. He gave up consulting to be a computer books publisher and a gossip columnist as well. He started a column that ran first in *Interface Age* and then in *InfoWorld.* It was called, "From the Fountainhead," which some people took as a perfect example of Osborne's colossal ego, although, as he explained with an air of injured innocence, all he meant was that the column was being written mostly about the doings in Silicon Valley, which was what "fountainhead" referred to. He does not mention a possible allusion to Ayn Rand.

Osborne used the column to do a bit of muckraking—and he became a familiar figure at all the early computer conferences. Osborne stood out from the crowd in a number of ways. He is tall, wears a moustache, and speaks with a British accent (he became a U.S. citizen in 1967). And he is known for his sharp tongue. Many believe him to be arrogant. In their book, *Fire in the Valley,* Paul Freiberger and Michael Swaine noted that Osborne was "never accused of toe-scraping humility." He has almost cultivated this reputation as the "industry brat," but a lot of it is probably an act. He is someone who enjoys his own press. Talking with a *Fortune* reporter about the column he wrote for five years, he said: "I specialized in scuttlebutt and frauds. I had a lovely time." Jim Warren, founder of the West Coast Computer Faire, who knows and likes Osborne, concedes that Osborne gives the impression of being arrogant, elitist, and sometimes smug, but says "all you have to do is just call him on it, 'Hey, you're being an arrogant ass again.' And then he'll respond, 'Right, but isn't it fun?' and become human again."

During this time period—the '60s—Osborne was unhappy with his marriage. How do we know? From Osborne's own mouth. Interviewed in 1983 by Robert Mamis of *Inc.*, Osborne said of this period, when he was devoting 95 percent of his time to work, "Business was an escape. I dreaded going home. I had a zero relationship with this woman who was my wife, and I *made* business overwhelming. I succeeded because I could control it, I could devote all my energies to it. Had my business been less successful I'd have gotten divorced much sooner." The Osbornes were divorced in 1981 after 19 years of marriage.

Osborne's company published some 40 books on computers in five years, 12 of which he wrote himself. In 1979, McGraw-Hill made him an offer that he "could not refuse," and so he sold his company. The purchase price has never been disclosed. One source said it was $3 million, another $10 million. Osborne took no end of pleasure in rejecting another suitor, John Wiley, the company that had turned down his first book on microcomputers. With the McGraw-Hill purchase came a three-year management contract for Adam Osborne. He lasted a year and a half before he reconfirmed that he was not made to work for others.

The next stage in Osborne's career was the much-celebrated Osborne Computer Corp. Here's his own description of how it came about:

"The idea was simple: no-frills computing. My no-frills concept hypothesized that most microcomputer owners do not begin to use the full capabilities of their computers and are therefore less impressed than they might be with new products that advertise 'more power' or 'more capabilities.' They tend to be far more impressed with lower prices and are amazingly accommodating to the inconveniences that can accompany low cost."

With this concept, Adam Osborne produced in a little over a year the low-cost personal computer that bore his name. He went first to Lee Felsenstein, whom he had met in the early days of the Homebrew Computer Club, to design his computer. Not only did Osborne know him well, but Felsenstein was easily accessible because he worked just a few blocks away from the Osborne/McGraw-Hill offices in Berkeley. Osborne agreed to pay Felsenstein meager wages along with 25 percent of the new company's stock. Before 1980 was out, Osborne had invested $100,000 of his own money and $40,000 from a venture capital fund controlled by Jack Melchor. In February and March 1981 he raised another $900,000— $300,000 from venture capital sources, the remaining amount from his friends and his own funds. "Those were the first days of working with an empty pain in the pit of my stomach as I added up 10,000 dollars here and 20,000 dollars there," recalls Osborne today.

When the Osborne computer was introduced at the West Coast Computer Faire in March 1981, its reception was sensational. What Osborne had done was to produce a computer with software bundled into it—*WordStar* and *SuperCalc*, for examples. And the *piece de resistance* was its portability—the computer was designed to fit under an airplane seat. It was priced to sell at $1,795, which guaranteed Osborne Computer Corp. an outrageous profit. Osborne wheeled and dealed to get his software programs and operating systems. He paid Digital Research a flat $55,000 to get the CP/M operating system. To get unlimited licenses to include the C-BASIC and M-BASIC language programs with each of his computers, Osborne gave each supplier 2,875 shares of stock, which at that time represented 2.5 percent of all the shares. He gave 4,000 shares to Sorcim, the supplier of *SuperCalc*. An even bigger chunk of stock went to Seymour Rubinstein at MicroPro International for *WordStar*, which turned the Osborne into a word processor. He estimated that the software added a total of only $10 in cash to the cost of each machine.

At the Computer Faire, Adam Osborne was his usual flamboyant self. He spent a good deal of his hard-raised money on a tall plexiglass booth that towered over the other exhibitors. And he regaled attendees by pointing out that an equivalent Apple II with the same amount of software would cost $3,000 and by declaring: "Do as I have done or perish." A newly hired Osborne employee was manning the booth when a call came from Steve Jobs of Apple. The message was: "Tell Adam he's an asshole." When the message was relayed to Osborne, he broke out in peals of laughter, much to the surprise of the employee. The next day Osborne repeated Jobs's message before an audience of 500 people at the Faire.

Osborne loved the jab from Jobs because it cast him in the role he likes to play: an upstart taking on the industry. It's the stance he habitually likes to take with journalists, having figured out that it's a way to get good press. In his own words, he knows how "to orchestrate the press." He once admitted lying to the press to get a story he wanted into print.

In any case, Osborne Computer took off like a rocket. It became one of the fastest-growing companies in the industry— and the country for that matter—moving from $6 million in sales in its first year to $70 million in the second. At its peak Osborne had 1,000 people on the payroll, sold 10,000 computers a month here and in Europe, and was competing well against the likes of Apple and Radio Shack. And in the portable market that it pioneered, Osborne was the dominant force.

With that kind of start, investors looking to make a quick buck were anxious to put money into Osborne. Some $34 to $40 million of capital was raised from private investors and the problem seemed to be that no one inside the company knew how to handle that kind of growth. Osborne describes it, "A big mistake I made at Osborne Computer Corporation was I just got cold feet. I found myself by August of 1982 with five hundred people on the payroll, and we were doing ten million dollars a month. And I thought, 'My God, here I am flying by the seat of my pants.' And I felt that professional managers of the highest caliber had to be brought in as quickly as possible." The man he finally selected to run the show was Robert Jaunich, who was president of a $6-billion company, Consolidated Foods of Chicago. Osborne claims he never liked Jaunich personally, but he still let him take over the company.

One usually doesn't get behind the scenes to see what happens inside a company. This time we do because as Osborne Computer went into bankruptcy in September 1983, with Jaunich blaming Osborne and Osborne blaming Jaunich, the two met and Jaunich told him that the last thing he, Osborne, should do is write a book about this affair. That was probably the wrong thing to tell Adam Osborne. Sitting down with John Dvorak, another celebrated chronicler of the computer industry, they churned out a book, *Hypergrowth*, to tell Adam Osborne's side of the story. Printed in the front, before the table of contents, is a copy of a letter that Jaunich's law firm, Petty, Andrews, Tufts & Jackson of San Francisco, wrote to Osborne on April 10, 1984, warning Osborne that Jaunich would be ready to sue him for libel. Osborne showed his book to a number of reputable East Coast publishers. They refused to publish it. So he self-published it under the name, Idethekkethan, which means "for this purpose" in a South Indian dialect. In the summer of 1984 he claimed that the first printing of 20,000 was sold out.

As could have been expected, *Hypergrowth*'s publication caused an immediate furor in computer circles. To support his charge that Jaunich was responsible for Osborne Computer going under, Osborne provides the following explanation: "By plunging the company into one more artificially created, temporary financial crisis for which he [Jaunich] could blame prior management... he could position himself as the 'white knight' who turned the company around." According to Osborne, this would enable Jaunich to make more money: "The contract he renegotiated for himself in the depths of the crisis would appear to be legitimate compensation for a corporate savior."

Osborne has received little support for his story blaming the firm's downfall on the man he hired. John Eckhouse, the respected technology correspondent of the *San Francisco Chronicle*, referred to Osborne's "white knight" theory as an "almost incoherent charge." Jaunich dismissed the book as the writings of a "third-rate novelist."

Adam Osborne has a great need to place himself as a loner. He has cutting things to say about many people, although much of it might be meant in jest. For example, the opening line of his book reads as follows: "The microcomputer industry has always been full of eccentric personalities. It seems to attract the misfits." And he told David Talbot of *Mother Jones:* "I admire the ability of Silicon Valley entrepreneuers to run their companies, but I find them as human beings to be in some world where we don't belong together. Those businessmen tend to be—although they don't realize it—idiot savants. They are brilliant at what they've trained themselves to do for their whole lives, but outside of that area, my god, they're nothing."

In the summer of 1983, shortly before Osborne Computer crashed, Adam Osborne said, in the *Inc.* interview with Bob Mamis, that he didn't know whether or not he would start another business, although he had been thinking of opening a San Francisco version of the Crazy Horse Saloon in Paris, and was also working on a third draft of a novel. If the novel were successful, Osborne told Mamis, "I would probably get as much satisfaction from it as I did starting Osborne Computer." Osborne's father and uncle were both academic writers. "Basically, I enjoy writing more than anything else," he said.

As it turned out, Adam Osborne did start a new company, Paperback Software International, in the spring of 1984. It was launched with $150,000 of his own capital and some $750,000 raised from venture capitalists.

Osborne's idea now is to revolutionize the software business by creating a company that will be a packager, distributor, and marketer for a stable of 25 to 30 small software companies. He wants to serve them the way Sunkist Growers, a cooperative, serves citrus growers. He plans to use the company to slash the price of software drastically and package it in such a way that consumers will just walk out of the store with it. And he is also aiming particularly at bookstores that don't know how to handle these new computer products. One of his first mailing pieces was a color brochure entitled, "How to Make Big Money Feeding Personal Computers"; inside, bookstore owners were informed: "Microcomputer software will be a 12-billion-dollar market by 1990. Bookshops will sell 80 percent of this software." (Not everyone in the industry would agree with the latter statement.)

Paperback Software set up offices in the industrial section of Berkeley. When we visited Osborne there, he was hard at work on a Compaq portable computer. In the summer of 1984, the new company had 15 employees.

The news release announcing Osborne's new venture was sent out by Barbara Burdick, who was one of the first employees of Osborne Computer in late 1980. In *Hypergrowth* Osborne describes her as "a charmer." In December 1982, Osborne and Burdick (18 years his junior) were married. They live in the Berkeley Hills, overlooking the University of California and San Francisco Bay.

The investors who put money in Osborne Computer obviously came up empty-handed. Some have sued, claiming they invested on the basis of misrepresentation by the company or selling shareholders. One who apparently bailed out in time was Adam's ex-wife, Cynthia. In December 1982, just as Adam and Barbara were getting married, she sold 66,000 shares of Osborne Computer for $1.1 million. She is a defendant in one of the suits filed by disgruntled investors.

As for the "new" Osborne Computer Company, when we called to ask how they were doing, we received a succinct reply: "We're trying."

ON THE RIGHT TRACK

Most Popular Schools

Massachusetts Institute of Technology	8
Harvard University	7
Stanford University	7
University of California	4
California State University	3
University of Michigan	3
University of Utah	3
University of Arizona	2
University of Illinois	2
Texas State University	2
University of San Francisco	2
State University of New York	2
University of Washington	2

Most Popular Professions

Engineers	20
M.B.A.s	9
Computer scientists	6
Educators	3

Chuck Peddle

"I am probably the least sophisticated user in my company. I used to say to people, 'How do you use this stuff?'"

▶ **BEST-KNOWN VENTURE:** Victor Technologies

OTHER VENTURES: Intelligent Terminal Systems, Sirius Systems Technology

BORN: 1937

RAISED: Bangor, Maine

FATHER'S OCCUPATION: Salesman

FIRST DOLLAR EARNED: Raising dogs with his brothers and sisters

SCHOOLING: B.S., engineering physics, University of Maine

ORIGINAL FINANCING: Severance pay from General Electric

PERSONAL NET WORTH: $3 million from sale of Victor stock; still owns 1.1 million shares of Victor

HOME: Scotts Valley, California

FAMILY: Married and divorced twice; four children

PERSONAL TRANSPORTATION: Porsche

VICT◉R

VICTOR TECHNOLOGIES INC.: Manufacturers of 16-bit personal computers, calculators, and electronic cash registers.

▶ **BEST-KNOWN PRODUCTS:** Victor 9000, Vickie

YEAR FOUNDED: 1980

EMPLOYEES: 235

HEADQUARTERS: Scotts Valley, California

SALES: $45 million (1982)

LOSSES: $48 million (1983)

OWNERSHIP: Public (1983); filed for bankruptcy on February 6, 1984; Datronic A.B. bought 90 percent in August 1984

C huck Peddle looks more like a Hollywood agent than the "father of the personal computer," as he sometimes calls himself. There's a Porsche in the garage of his condo in Scotts Valley, California, a small town near Silicon Valley. When we talked with him, Peddle was sporting tinted glasses, a jogging suit, gold chains, and a tan. The 47-year-old, twice-divorced Peddle flirted outrageously with two women who happened to stop by. His condo looks like the stereotypical bachelor pad with clothes and other belongings strewn chaotically over every available surface.

A psychohistory of Peddle might identify the childhood sources of his drive for fame, fortune, and flamboyance as poverty and a small-boy complex. Peddle was one of five children born in Bangor, Maine, to an uneducated, chronically unemployed salesman; three additional children often lived with his family. Of those times, Peddle says, "I was so poor I didn't know I was broke." To make matters worse, Peddle was a small, scrawny boy with a severe allergic reaction to poison ivy. Like the 98-pound weakling in the comic books who makes himself into a muscle-man after a bully kicks sand in his face, young Peddle pushed himself to gain weight, play sports, and eventually punch out the bully. "I didn't win my first fight until I was fifteen," he recalls, "but I haven't lost one since I was in high school."

His new-found strength got him a back-breaking job wielding a pick and shovel on a highway road crew. "The day I started, there were twenty-two guys in the morning. I was the only guy left working at the end of the day," Peddle says. "It really strengthened my resolve that I wasn't going to do that the rest of my life."

Peddle hungered for a life of glamour. To a poor, unsophisticated boy from Bangor, glamour meant radio announcers, who, Peddle believed, "had style and class." The hard-headed Peddle quickly discovered that he was a "no-talent guy. Not star class." But he'd learned enough about the field that he decided to study radio engineering at the University of Maine. After all, he reasoned, he had always been good at math.

Radio in any form turned out not to be fated for him. A course on the fundamental theories of computer science—binary arithmetic, Boolean algebra, and communications theory—"settled" his life on computers.

After college, Peddle looked for a job that would let him continue to work with computers and move to California, which he had visited in the Army Reserves. In 1959 he joined General Electric, determined to learn all he could in their training program and then get sent to the West Coast. Peddle worked happily for GE for over a decade in both engineering and management, although he ended up in Arizona instead of California.

GE even supplied the capital for Peddle's first entrepreneurial venture, by quitting the computer business in 1970 and laying him off. The 12 years' worth of benefits Peddle had accumulated allowed him to go into business, marketing computerized cash registers. Peddle claims that this business, Intelligent Terminal Systems, as well as a word processing firm that he started a couple of years later, failed for lack of sufficient financing, although their products were technically superior. "Too early," he told an interviewer from *Byte* magazine. He would later make the same claim about Victor.

Thwarted in these attempts to work for himself, Peddle next took jobs with a string of computer companies. At each of these firms, Peddle made tremendous technical contributions; and at each of them, he ended up quarreling with his superiors and leaving. At Motorola, for example, Peddle designed the successful 6800 chip before leaving over a "difference of opinion." At MOS Technology, he created the 6502 chip that sold for $25 and became the heart of both the Apple II and Commodore PET computers. MOS Technology was bought by Jack Tramiel of Commodore, and Peddle and the notoriously explosive Tramiel (now at Atari) "had a great love affair, and parting, a couple of times." One of those times, Peddle went off to join Apple, but "there was no chemistry there," either. Back to Commodore he went.

The tale of the 6502 chip Peddle designed is the tale of the early computer industry itself. While Steve Jobs and Steve Wozniak were assembling their Apple II in Woz's garage, Peddle was working frantically to beat them to market with the computer (which became known as the PET) he was designing for Commodore. Peddle even went over to the garage to convince the two Steves to let him use components from their Apple I in his PET, but Woz and Jobs turned him down. The PET was also, originally, being designed in collaboration with Radio Shack, but in the end that deal fell through, and Radio Shack built its own machine.

Peddle adamantly maintains that he won the race for "the first personal computer" when he demonstrated a prototype to Radio Shack in January 1976. *Byte* magazine seems to conclude it's a draw: "Apple shipped Apples first, but Commodore showed the PET first."

The PET reigned supreme for only a year before Wozniak put the first cheap floppy disk drive on an Apple. It was far superior to the cassette tape recorder used for information storage on the PET. "I always wanted to say, before I die, 'Wozniak's cheap disk really changed the industry,'" Peddle says magnanimously. But he goes on to complain, "The saddest thing was that I wanted to do it first, but I had so many other things to do, somebody else [at Commodore] was working on the disk. It didn't get out at that time. I really never forgave him for that." Since then, Peddle has been trying to recapture the fame and make the fortune that he feels would have been his, if not for Wozniak's disk drive.

But back at Commodore, Tramiel and Peddle continued their love-hate relationship. Finally, Peddle left for good when Tramiel moved Commodore's headquarters to Pennsylvania. There is some dispute (including a protracted lawsuit) about whether Peddle resigned or was forced out. Regardless, in 1980, Chuck Peddle decided to strike out on his own. He felt he had everything he needed to set up his own company. He had the idea: build a powerful desktop computer aimed at the office market. He had the experience: all his years as an engineer and manager. And, most important, he had the people: a talented team of designers who had worked with him at Commodore—Bill Seilor, Glenn Stark, and Bob Taylor.

Peddle was sure he could make a killing by making a machine tailored for office use. No one was then making such a machine—Apple and Commodore were busy selling computers to hobbyists, and it was still a year before IBM entered the personal computer fray. Peddle called his company Sirius Systems Technologies (after the star), and with his team of designers created the Sirius 1 (using a powerful 16-bit microprocessor). To improve their marketing clout, Peddle arranged a deal with a conglomerate, Kidde Inc., to merge Sirius with Victor Business Products, a Kidde subsidiary that had 50 branches and 700 dealers for its desktop calculators and cash registers. Peddle became president of the new company, named Victor Technologies.

The Victor 9000, as the Peddle team's machine was rechristened, was a smash. It received rave reviews and the moniker, "Mercedes of the Micros." The company advertised in the *Wall Street Journal* with full-page ads featuring a picture of Peddle and identifying him as the father of the personal computer concept. The Victor 9000 was especially hot in Europe, where it became the best-selling business personal computer. Peddle built new facilities in Scotts Valley, and the employment roster swelled to almost 3,000. By early 1983, Victor was ranked third, behind IBM and Digital Equipment, in the $3,000-to-$6,000 business computer market.

It looked as if Peddle would get real recognition at last. He had a quality machine, his own company—and big bucks. Even though Peddle describes poverty as something he knows is a "survivable condition," he had no desire to repeat the conditions of his childhood in Maine. When he started Sirius Systems, someone put up a photograph on the office wall that showed a courtyard in Germany full of Porsches. The caption scribbled underneath read: "Sirius parking lot." That was a main goal, Peddle recalls, everyone driving a Porsche. And after Victor went public, everyone on the design team bought a Porsche, including Peddle.

The euphoria was short-lived. A combination of management problems and an embarrassing shortage of disk drives for the Victor 9000 resulted in a loss of over $11 million in the summer of 1983. Peddle had to lay off half his work force, and by the fall, he had stepped down as president. The company filed for bankruptcy in February 1984. Six months later, Datatronic A.B., a Swedish microcomputer company, bought 90 percent of Victor for $28 million. Only 235 employees were still with Victor.

Peddle is not spending his time crying over the loss of Victor. Or if he is, he's crying all the way to the bank. The 182,500 shares of Victor stock Peddle sold in March 1983, when Victor went public earned him about $3 million. That's in addition to what he'd already made on the stock he owned in Commodore. (If Peddle wins his lawsuit against Jack Tramiel over the circumstances of Peddle's departure from Commodore, Peddle stands to win $10 million more in Commodore stock.)

Nor is he troubled over damage to his reputation. He shrugs off Victor's downfall by saying, "We got in a market space and didn't have enough money to pull off what we were trying to do. And we got clobbered. But I don't think you could identify a product error in our background."

Peddle gives a great deal of credit to his designers. He and they had already put together another company by the summer of 1984, with Bob Taylor as president. They call it NNA, short for "No Name Available."

Jack Tramiel

"I'm not in business to be loved. I'm here to make money"

▶ **BEST-KNOWN VENTURE:** Commodore International

OTHER VENTURE: Atari

BORN: 1927

RAISED: Lodz, Poland

FATHER'S OCCUPATION: Electrician

FIRST DOLLAR EARNED: Driving a cab in New York City

SCHOOLING: Completed fifth grade

ORIGINAL FINANCING: Profits from typewriter repair business

PERSONAL NET WORTH: $100 million

HOME: Saratoga, California

FAMILY: Married; three sons

PERSONAL TRANSPORTATION: Jaguar, Ferrari

 **commodore**

COMMODORE INTERNATIONAL: Dominates the low-end market for home computers.

▶ **BEST-KNOWN PRODUCTS:** PET, VIC-20, Commodore 64 computers

YEAR FOUNDED: 1954

EMPLOYEES: 2,500

HEADQUARTERS: Norristown, Pennsylvania

SALES: $1 billion (1983)

PROFITS: $100 million (1983)

OWNERSHIP: Public (since its 1962 start on the Toronto Stock Exchange)

In the summer of 1984, a group of survivors of the Jewish ghetto of Lodz, Poland, met at the Concord Hotel in upstate New York. Not among them was Jack Tramiel, who was born in Lodz in 1927. Tramiel was 12 years old when the Nazis invaded Poland in 1939. More than 200,000 Jews lived in Lodz at the outset of the war; when Lodz was liberated by the Red Army in January 1945, only 970 were still alive. Tramiel survived the attrition, remaining in Lodz until 1944. Then he passed through two concentration camps, Auschwitz and Bergen-Belsen. Once again he was a survivor, although he has disclosed that on the day before the camp was liberated, he had just about given up and resigned himself to die. In 1947, at age 20, he made his way to the United States.

While the Lodz survivors were meeting in the Catskills, Jack Tramiel was 3,000 miles away in California's Silicon Valley, trying to make sense out of Atari, a video game and home computer manufacturer started by Nolan Bushnell in 1972 and acquired by Warner Communications in 1976. Atari had nearly bled Warner to death, forcing its New York-based parent to report a whopping loss of $417 million for 1983—and who should know better than Jack Tramiel why Atari wasn't cutting it? Tramiel's company, Commodore International, had trounced Atari in the home computer market. Then, early in 1984, a week after introducing a new line of Commodore home computers at the Consumer Electronics Show in Las Vegas, Tramiel shocked the industry by resigning. Six months later he surfaced as Atari's new owner.

By now, nothing that Tramiel does should shock the industry. His reputation as an aggressive street fighter is well-established. He's close to few people outside his family, and is known as a taskmaster and ruthless scrutinizer of the expense side of the budget. And he's a tough bargainer. In 1983, when he was riding high at Commodore, having slaughtered the competition in the low end of the home computer field (the under-$500 market), Tramiel was profiled on the front page of the *Wall Street Journal*. Reporters Susan Chace and Michael W. Miller cited one of Tramiel's favorite maxims: "Business is not a sport. It's a war."

It is, of course, altogether too easy to speculate about how a man with Tramiel's background might develop such a worldview. Tramiel himself rarely mentions his formative years to business associates, and he has not talked with reporters about his early life in Poland. He refused to talk with us about it. We do know his formal education stopped in Poland at the end of the fifth grade. His first-known job in the United States was driving a cab in New York City. He's proud of that job experience. He then spent time in the U.S. Army, where he learned a useful skill: repairing typewriters. In 1954 Tramiel and another war refugee, Manny Kapp, started a typewriter repair business in The Bronx. They called their company Commodore Portable Typewriter.

In 1956 they relocated the business in Toronto, where Tramiel's wife, Helen, had relatives. In Canada, Tramiel was not satisfied with merely repairing old typewriters. He renamed the company Commodore Business Machines, started selling adding machines, and then gained the rights to market a Czech typewriter. But Tramiel's ambition exceeded his capital. To help finance his big plans for Commodore, Tramiel became involved with a shady promoter, C. Powell Morgan. Morgan's company, Atlantic Acceptance, financed Commodore and many other companies in a series of self-dealing manipulations that became the subject of an inquiry by a Canadian royal commission. As Kathryn M. Welling detailed in an exhaustive article in the March 2, 1981, issue of *Barron's*, the record was replete "with matter-of-fact accounts of stock manipulation, fraud and criminally creative accounting, pursued for the enrichment of Morgan and his colleagues." Among his colleagues was Jack Tramiel.

Tramiel is nothing if not a survivor. Atlantic Acceptance went belly-up in 1965. Morgan died of leukemia before he could be questioned or indicted. According to Welling's article, Tramiel was given immunity in exchange for testifying. He blamed the deceased Morgan for everything. And also according to Welling, who must have waded through a mountain of documents to come up with her narrative, Tramiel's company, Commodore, managed to avoid going down with Atlantic by the artful maneuver of shifting its debts to other companies with few or no assets.

But after Atlantic's collapse, Tramiel needed new financing; he secured it from another Canadian promoter, Irving Gould. In return for pumping money into Commodore, Gould acquired a controlling interest in Commodore and succeeded Morgan as chairman.

Gould had an interesting side as well. He was once convicted of perjury, and he had two brothers, Albert and Melville, who were not exactly on the side of the angels. Albert went to jail twice for various pieces of fraud. Melville died in 1977 amidst charges that he had taken kickbacks of $331,000 from a company that was a supplier to Interpool Ltd., a container-leasing firm headed by his brother Irving (Melville was also on board).

Meanwhile, Jack Tramiel marched on, as Gould allowed him to continue to run Commodore. And run it he did. He jettisoned the adding machines and, on a trip to Japan in 1968, hit upon the company's next product: the electronic calculator. In the early '70s Commodore became one of the major players in the booming market for hand-held calculators.

Tramiel moved back to the United States, and in May 1974, Commodore's stock was listed on the American Stock Exchange. It tripled in price that year. Disaster struck in 1975 when Texas Instruments, a supplier of calculator chips to Commodore, decided to get into the business, competing against its own customers. Chip prices plunged; calculators were soon selling for $9.95 instead of $100. Poor Jack Tramiel was stuck with a huge supply of $100 calculators in his warehouse, and Commodore lost $5 million that year on sales of $50 million. Tramiel vowed that he would never again put the company in such a dependent relationship: he would do his own manufacturing. Commodore bought one of its chip suppliers, MOS Technology of Norristown, Pennsylvania.

MOS Technology put Jack Tramiel and Commodore into the computer business. When Chuck Peddle, an engineer there, had an idea for a desktop computer, Tramiel went for it. He pushed Peddle to have a working model ready for the Consumer Electronics Show in Chicago in January 1977. Peddle worked three days and three nights before the show's opening to have it ready. That was Commodore's first computer, the PET, and it was a roaring success. Tramiel followed it up with more powerful models, the VIC-20 and the Commodore 64.

People at other companies may have thought they were more sophisticated than Tramiel, from both technological and marketing standpoints, but they didn't take his ferocious competitiveness into account. Tramiel let Apple and Radio Shack take the high end of the market; he went for the low end. "We sell to the masses, not the classes," is another Tramiel maxim. Making a high-quality product and supporting it with superior after-sales service were never priorities in Tramiel's book. He made computers as cheaply as he could and he got them out the door and into stores. The computer trade press was filled with stories about the horrendous failure rate of Commodore machines and the difficulties dealers had in getting stock or even finding where Commodore's head office was—it moved three times in six years.

From wherever he was sitting—Norristown or West Chester, Pennsylvania, or Palo Alto and Santa Clara, California—Tramiel ran Commodore the way you run a mom-and-pop grocery store: he watched the pennies. If a Commodore employee flew first class instead of tourist, the difference was deducted from his pay. Company cars had to be fuel-economy models. A manager who once worked for him told us, "Tramiel never took the time to learn management." Samuel Bernstein, who was Commodore's marketing vice president from 1971 to '79, said Tramiel practiced the "eyeball style of management," which meant that "if there's a single embarrassing document on your desk, sooner or later Jack will swoop in, pick it out of the pile, and then, look out!"

Under Tramiel there was not much thought given to building a permanent organization. Managers and suppliers came and went. Results were all that counted. During one period of a little over a year, Commodore had three different presidents. It went through four advertising agencies in three years. In 1983, when the company had the fastest-selling computer in the world, the Commodore 64, Tramiel fired all the independent sales representatives in the field and replaced them with an in-house sales force. Then, after three months, the in-house staff was disbanded. One former president, Jim Finke, said: "Remember Machiavelli? The strongest kingdom had the strongest barons and a strong king. There are no strong barons in Jack's kingdom. There is only a strong king." *Business Week* once found someone who said of Tramiel: "He is like a magnesium flare lit in a dark room. You may be left awed—but also choking because all of the oxygen was used up."

Those are all the kinds of comments reporters love to find, but no one can fault Tramiel on Commodore's market performance. Sensational would be an understatement. In 1982 Commodore sold more than one million computers—many of them in Europe, a market Tramiel was shrewd enough to pioneer ahead of his American competitors. In 1983 Commodore sold more than one million computers in the final three months of the year, and its share of the home computer market was put at 45 percent. Commodore's low prices drove Texas Instruments out of the home computer market—sweet revenge for Tramiel. It also drove Mattel out of the market, and Timex, too. And it nearly delivered the *coup de grace* to Atari.

Very few Harvard Business School managers ever achieve

what Jack Tramiel did at Commodore. From sales of $50 million in 1977, Commodore vaulted to over $1 billion in 1984 (its fiscal year ends June 30). Profits climbed from $3.4 million to over $100 million.

And what about Commodore's stock, which began trading on the New York Stock Exchange in 1981? If you had read every word of Welling's story in *Barron's* (a publication read avidly for stock tips) the last thing you may have wanted to do was to invest in Commodore. Too bad. You could have quintupled your money. And, of course, you would have done even better if you had bought Commodore stock after the PET computer was introduced in 1977. Every dollar invested then was worth $60 at one point in 1983. When Tramiel left the company in January 1984, the value of his stockholdings was estimated at $100 million.

"I'm not in business to be loved," Tramiel once told a reporter. "I'm here to make money."

Why Jack Tramiel left Commodore when he did was the subject of considerable speculation in the business press at the time. The stories indicated that Tramiel had been ousted by Commodore's chairman, Irving Gould, the Canadian promoter who rescued Tramiel in 1965. But Gould was careful not to openly criticize Tramiel, saying only that "Jack has been working unceasingly here, and he was just tired." For his part, Tramiel made himself unavailable to the press. To replace him, Gould brought in smooth-looking, silver-thatched Marshall F. Smith, an accountant by training who had once been a controller for U.S. Steel. The contrast with Jack Tramiel, who is short, stocky, jowly, with heavy eyelids, couldn't be sharper. Smith looks as if he has just walked out of a Brooks Brothers store to get his photograph taken by Bachrach.

If industry people were shocked by Tramiel's departure from Commodore, they were even more shocked when he surfaced as the new owner of Atari, which he purchased in exchange for $240 million in IOUs, no cash down. As soon as he assumed the command at Atari's headquarters in Sunnyvale, California, Tramiel put his characteristic stamp on the company. He fired 700 people and killed two lines, Atari's 7800 video game system and the $150 600XL home computer.

It didn't take long for Atari and Commodore to take up battle positions. Tramiel's three sons—Sam, Leonard and Garry—also left Commodore for Atari: Sam as president, Leonard as a software engineer and Garry in the corporate staff department. Leonard Schreiber, who was Commodore's general counsel, resigned to join Tramiel at Atari, as did four engineers. Commodore promptly sued the engineers, alleging they were stealing computer design secrets for Atari's benefit. In August, a month after Tramiel took over Atari, Commodore announced plans to acquire Amiga Corp., a Silicon Valley manufacturer of home computers. A week later Atari slapped Amiga with a $100 million lawsuit, charging that the company had broken a contract with Atari. Atari's suit asked the court to enjoin Amiga from delivering the chips to anyone else. The suit didn't mention Commodore but everyone took it as another shot in the Tramiel-Gould war.

But the crucial skirmishes will be in the marketplace, where Tramiel loves to fight. He promised that Atari would have a new array of products soon.

Tramiel and his wife, Helen, live in Saratoga, not far from Atari's headquarters in Sunnyvale. The Tramiels also own a ranch in Watsonville in Monterey County. And there's one report that Tramiel has become a legal resident of Hong Kong in order to do business there. People who see Jack Tramiel outside the office report that he is an affable host who likes to dine well. He dotes on his grandchildren, he sings opera arias, and he has been known to be a high roller at casinos around the world. Jaguars and Ferraris have been seen parked in his garage, but never a German-made car—not because of his feelings on the subject but because of his wife's. She, too, is a survivor of the Holocaust.

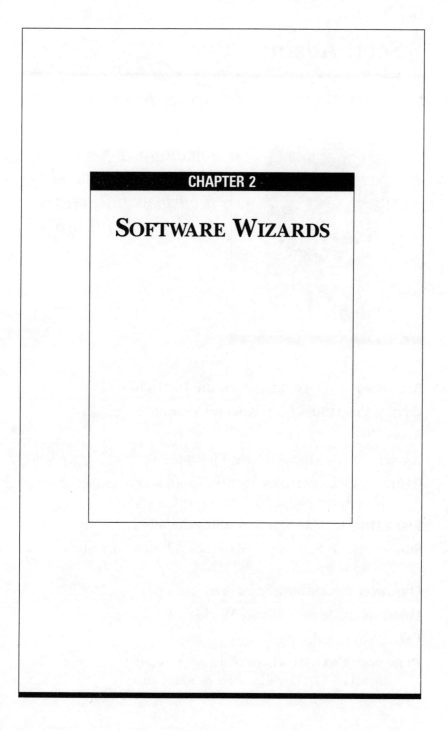

CHAPTER 2

SOFTWARE WIZARDS

Scott Adams

"Peter Pan is my hero. I don't feel like a grown-up. I feel like a kid, walking around in a business suit, getting to play with his toys"

▶ **BEST-KNOWN VENTURE:** Adventure International

OTHER VENTURES: Scott Adams Computers

BORN: 1952

RAISED: North Miami Beach, Florida

PARENTS' OCCUPATIONS: Father—pilot and manager of an aircraft company; mother—wrote poetry

FIRST DOLLAR EARNED: Wrestling alligators

SCHOOLING: B.S., computer science, Florida Institute of Technology

ORIGINAL FINANCING: Sales revenues

HOME: A castle near Disney World

FAMILY: Married; two daughters, one son

PERSONAL TRANSPORTATION: London Roadster (replica of an MG-TD), Cadillac Fleetwood, canoe

Adventure
INTERNATIONAL
A DIVISION OF SCOTT ADAMS, INC.

ADVENTURE INTERNATIONAL: Developed and sold the first text adventure game for personal computers.

▶ **BEST-KNOWN PRODUCTS:** *Adventure, Pirates Adventure, Commbat, Preppie I,* and *Preppie II*

YEAR FOUNDED: 1978

EMPLOYEES: 50

HEADQUARTERS: Orlando, Florida

SALES: Less than $10 million (1983)

OWNERSHIP: Private, controlled by Scott and Alexis Adams

Scott Adams's home is a castle. Literally. With moat and drawbridge, turrets and battlements, knights and dragons in stained glass, and a 2,000-acre "backyard" wilderness park teeming with bobcats, possum, deer, and large reptiles. Built near Disney World (which Adams has visited more than 100 times), it is the perfect setting for one of the computer games about fantastic perils, travels, and challenges that have made Adams a rich man.

Though he heads a multimillion-dollar enterprise, Adams looks out of place in a jacket and tie with his frizzy hair and scraggly beard. As he told us, "Peter Pan is my hero. I don't feel like a grown-up. I feel like a kid, walking around in a business suit, getting to play with his toys."

When he was eight years old, Scott Adams saw his first computer, a big old classic with twirling wheels and flashing lights with white-smocked technicians minding it. But the computer was behind glass doors; his visiting third-grade class wasn't allowed in. Scott said to himself, "Someday I'll get in there." He reckons his career choice happened then. Though a good student, Adams spent his childhood wrestling alligators in the Florida swamps or reading Marvel comics and science fiction books. He still reads a book a day, mostly science fiction.

Adams got his chance to join the white-smocked technicians at the Florida Institute of Technology, where he majored in computer programming. But it was on Ascension Island, a chunk of volcanic rock in equatorial Atlantic waters somewhere between Africa and South America, where Adams fell in love with computer games. RCA had a telecommunications station on the island and hired Adams to track radar signals there. But he remembers with greatest relish creating computer games during his off-duty hours. Technicians on Ascension Island are probably still playing his *Star Trek* game, beamed onto the screen of the radarscope.

After 18 months on Ascension Island, Adams completed school at FIT (graduating in 1976), spent nine more months with RCA in the West Indies, and finally returned to Florida where he got a series of programming jobs. Again his passion for games overshadowed his official job. He discovered the "adventure" game—an underground classic among mainframe programmers, in which a player tries to find a hidden treasure by searching for clues offered by the computer. Correct answers steer the player closer to the goal through a series of exotic locations, while wrong ones lead the player into perilous situations. Adams started coming to work early and leaving late till he solved the game (it took about a week).

The next logical step ultimately led to the creation of Adams' first commercial enterprise. Adams owned a Radio Shack TRS-80 Model I, one of the first personal computers on the market. He decided to program the game for his microcomputer. His programmer friends laughed. How could you transfer a program like that from a giant machine with megabytes of storage to a little toy like the TRS-80 Model I? Adams did it in about a year, completing the task the summer of 1978, but not without some fantastic perils at home.

Scott's wife, Alexis, got sick of his working on the *Adventureland* program from six o'clock in the morning till he left for work and again from the time he returned home till midnight. She was pregnant. One day she put all his disks, including the only copy of *Adventureland*, into the oven. His programming was over, she announced, until he spent some time with her. Luckily,

Scott reminisces, she had been so frantic that she'd forgotten to turn on the oven.

After demonstrating *Adventureland* at meetings of the local TRS-80 Users' Club (which may have been the first such club in the United States and was founded by Adams) his friends suggested he advertise the program in computer magazines. As the orders started coming in, Adventure International was born. By this time Alexis and Scott had ironed out their differences, and she has played a central role in their company since its inception. Before marrying Scott, Alexis had managed a chain of restaurants in Miami and had her own mail-order business selling cookbooks and recipes through ads in magazines and newspapers. Now, she collaborates in writing programs, manages business operations, travels with him to conferences throughout the world, and serves as vice president of the company.

To fill their first order from a dealer—for 50 cassettes—Scott and Alexis copied the tapes one by one and sent them off to the store in Chicago in plastic bags with business cards stapled on top. Getting the right kind of plastic bag was an early corporate crisis. Bag makers sold only in lots of thousands; Scott and Alexis needed a few dozen at a time. One day it hit him—baby bottle liners! Scott still remembers the looks he got at the supermarket checkout stand when he bought out the store's supply. "You've got a few kids, don't you?" "Oh yeah, we always wanted a big family."

Adventure International expanded quickly as distributors got excited, freelance programmers sent in their creations, and translations from the Radio Shack machine to the Apple became available. Adams helped the careers of other computer entrepreneurs. He gave Southern California distribution rights to his game to Ken Williams of Sierra On-Line. Bob Leff bought the rights and built Softsel. And one of Adams's first freelance programmers was Broderbund Software's Doug Carlston. Company headquarters moved from a 10 by 10 room in the Adams' home to a storefront to a small house to a three-story geodesic dome to a new building in an industrial park. They got into the retail computer business almost by accident while located at the storefront. The space suited their budget, so they decided to run a store in the front and software operations in the back. The Scott Adams Computers retail chain began in the fall of 1979; within four years there were seven stores in the Orlando area.

Both Scott and Alexis still love to put in time behind the counter and can often be seen at one of their stores on Saturday mornings. They believe one reason for Adventure's success has been their constant contact with the buying public.

They've made money, too. Each year business has been profitable, even the first one when revenue was only about $5,000. The second year it jumped to $50,000 and soon ballooned into the millions. How many millions? "It's still semi-proprietary," says Scott.

Adventure sends out nearly a half-million catalogs a year. The company sells about 200 different programs. Some of their programs are conventional arcade-style shoot-'em-up games like *Laser Ball* and *Fire Copter*. But the firm's best-sellers are their adventure games. The classic is Adams' first, *Adventureland*. The catalog describes it in these terms: "Wander through an enchanted realm and try to uncover the thirteen lost treasures. There are wild animals and magical beings to reckon with as well as many other perils and mysteries."

Scott and his three in-house programmers generate about half the games. When we caught up with him at a computer show in New Orleans in early 1984, he told us he's hoping to delegate some administrative duties, so he can spend more time doing what's most fun for him: programming on his TRS-80 Model I.

When we chatted with Adams he was still glowing with pride because of a deal he'd just made with Marvel comics, creators of The Hulk, Spiderman, Thor, and Captain America, among others. Marvel comics had come to *him* because of his reputation for adventure games, he beamed. When the talks were over, Adams' company had 10 years' exclusive rights to all the Marvel characters for use in micro games.

Not only that: Spiderman had recently come in person to his daughters' birthday party, a unique privilege associated with winning the Marvel license. That was a sweet fruit for a lifelong devotee of comics.

THE HIGH-TECH RABBI

For 14 years Rabbi Irving Rosenbaum watched over the congregation of the Loop Synagogue in Chicago. Now he runs the world's largest religious software company, Davka Corporation, whose name means "just because" in Hebrew. Rabbi Rosenbaum comes from a long line of orthodox Jews; his three sons are all rabbis and his daughter married one. But running throughout his distinguished career in education and civil rights has always been an element of "just because." He used to write a syndicated column for the *Chicago Sentinel* called "Rabbi At Random." A lifelong electronics tinkerer, he learned to program a Radio Shack TRS-80 around the time he turned 40, and was immediately struck by the possibility of using computers for religious instruction.

One example of Davka's products is *Bar-Mitzvah Compu-Tutor*, which, according to Rabbi Rosenbaum, allows the student preparing for a bar mitzvah to "progress at his own pace. The computer plays the Haftorah melody and a bouncing ball helps to follow every syllable." The program transliterates the Hebrew words, provides an English translation, and allows the user to vary the speed of the bouncing ball.

Davka also offers Bible adventure games such as *Philistine Ploy* and *Lion's Share,* but the company's most popular offering is a "Bible action game" called *Jewish IQ Baseball.*

Like other education and entertainment software publishers, Davka was disappointed by the performance of the marketplace in 1984. It is planning to add some more practical products to a line that already includes a word processor, *Hebrew Writer.* "We may do some synagogue management programs for the IBM," says Rabbi Rosenbaum. "We are in a vertical market, and that means you gotta keep climbing."

The rabbi says he is "ashamed to repeat" the number of hours he works at Davka, but assured us that they do not include the Sabbath.

Joel Berez

"It's clearly the most complicated, convoluted, disgusting piece of code that's ever been written"

▶ **BEST-KNOWN VENTURE:** Infocom

BORN: 1954

RAISED: Pittsburgh, Pennsylvania

FATHER'S OCCUPATION: President of Action Industries (plastic houseware and giftware marketing business)

FIRST DOLLAR EARNED: Working for his father's business

SCHOOLING: B.S., electrical engineering and computer science, and M.B.A., Massachusetts Institute of Technology

ORIGINAL FINANCING: Founding partners contributed $200,000 from savings

PERSONAL NET WORTH: 10 to 15 percent of Infocom

HOME: Waltham, Massachusetts

FAMILY: Single

PERSONAL TRANSPORTATION: Saab

INFOCOM

INFOCOM INC.: Creators of the best-selling piece of home entertainment software ever written, plus a dozen other interactive fiction games.

▶ **BEST-KNOWN PRODUCT:** The *Zork* trilogy

YEAR FOUNDED: 1979

EMPLOYEES: 50

HEADQUARTERS: Cambridge, Massachusetts

SALES: $6 million (1983)

PROFITS: $526,000 (1983)

OWNERSHIP: Privately held by partners, employees, and friends

The story of Infocom could be told as a piece of Infocom fiction: Once upon a time there was a strange galaxy called MIT. In the galaxy was a nebula called the Computer Science Lab, and in the nebula was a world-system known as the Programming and Technology Division. It was a long time ago, around the year 6 PCE (personal computer era). The inhabitants of this world-system had learned to travel through neuronic space on a mighty ship named the Mainframe. One day the Mainframe carried them to a place where they had never been before. It was called *Adventure*. It was a game.

If this were really an Infocom game, it would get interactive at this point. You would enter the nebula, find out all you could about it, have hair-raising skirmishes with creatures and forces, and through your choices determine the course of the story, which would have dozens of possible endings.

The Infocom story, since it actually happened, is less flexible (though not unwhimsical). When the MIT computer whizzes discovered *Adventure* in the circuitous guts of their mainframe in 1976, they were enchanted. That trailblazing game, created by a pair of earlier MIT graduates, offered a fantasy world with which the player could interact through simple verb-noun commands like "Take sword." But soon the young researchers felt a competitive itch. They knew they could create a game with many more complex options and a far more sophisticated text.

Three of them—Marc Blank, Dave Lebling, and Tim Anderson—started working nights on what was to become a cult: *Zork I*, which they initially set loose on the mainframe network in 1977, and which is now the first part of a *Zork* trilogy. Blank made up the nonsense name. With the help of MDL (pronounced Muddle), a powerful programming language previously developed at the lab by Blank and Anderson, *Zork* was several giant steps ahead of *Adventure*.

With *Zork*, you can type in a command like this: "Pick up the troll-wand and the rubber gerbil and give them to the Bog Monster. Then follow the magic chicken." When you find yourself facing the evil, axe-wielding troll in a gory grotto and decide to defend yourself by throwing a sack at him, you might get this shocking news: "The troll, who is remarkably coordinated, catches the brown sack and, not having the most discriminating taste, gleefully eats it. The flat of the troll's axe hits you on the head. I'm afraid you are dead."

Other members of the MIT programming research group were Joel Berez, Stuart Galley, Scott Cutler, and several others who would later become part of the Infocom inner circle. Credit for actually materializing the company goes to Albert Vezza, who was then the chief of their research group. He had long cherished the idea of channeling some of the talent at the lab into a commercial venture, and in 1979, Vezza brought together nine of the men who had worked with him at the lab a few years before.

Joel Berez was in Pittsburgh, where he was working for his father's company, Action Industries, and planning to go on to business school. Marc Blank had just finished medical school and was beginning an internship in Pittsburgh. When Vezza's invitation came to join him in Boston for the formation of Infocom, Berez quickly decided to attend MIT's Sloan

School of Management, and Blank dropped his two-week-old internship in order to go back to Massachusetts. Infocom was founded in June 1979, and Berez soon became its president and company spokesman.

Blank and Berez had been getting together for dinners when they were both in Pittsburgh. One of their favorite topics was *Zork*, which by then was quite a popular item among mainframe programmers. As Berez remembers it, they were at the Grand Conqueror restaurant, spooning up fish chowder, when a bright idea passed between them: Why not try to rewrite *Zork* for a personal computer and market it?

It was obvious why not. The program was immense, taking up a million characters of storage space on the mainframe; a floppy disk for a personal computer held about 100,000. But, in the next few days, both men became captivated by the idea, and they had the feeling they could do it. "It involved writing several new computer languages, a compiler, an assembler, and interpreters to run a lot of the machines," Berez told us, "but we thought it really was possible."

It was. They finished *Zork* in 1980, after recruiting former MIT comrades Michael Dornbrook, Stuart Galley, and Steve Meretsky as testers. A fledgling company called Personal Software took over the marketing and *Zork* quickly became a best-seller. Then, with the phenomenal success of its financial program, *VisiCalc*, Personal Software changed its name to Visi-Corp and divested itself of products that seemed to be beneath its newfound dignity. Naturally the grotto-and-monsters game had to go.

This was 1981, the year Berez graduated from MIT's business school and became Infocom's first full-time employee. Soon Blank also signed on full time, *Zork II* was released, and *Deadline*, their first mystery, was under development. In early 1982, sales trailed off, but when *Deadline* appeared in March, the charts soared and they've been soaring ever since. Sales in 1983 were $6 million, an increase of about 300 percent over 1982.

A *New York Times Book Review* writer described *Deadline* as "more like a genre of fiction than a game," declared that the narrative forms favored by Infocom have "archetypal power," and compared the *Zork* adventure to the Odyssey.

Most successful computer-related companies have a single star, or at most, two co-stars. Infocom is different. When newspapers and magazines write about the company, they favor group pictures: Berez, Blank, and Vezza; writers Galley, Meretsky, Lebling, and Michael Berlyn; Blank, Berez, and Dornbrook. They all have interesting stories. Berlyn, for instance, is the only non-MIT man in the leadership group. He was a recognized science fiction writer and head of a Colorado company called Sentient Software when he got hooked on *Zork I.* "I need more *Zork!*" he cried out, but there was no more. So he went to Boston and joined the group writing Infocom fiction, combining his skills as novelist and programmer. And when computer lab alumni Michael Dornbrook went to business school in Chicago, he initiated ZUG, the *Zork* Users Group, which he reckoned would take a few hours of his time each week. But when membership reached 20,000, he found himself obsessively producing maps, posters, T-shirt transfers, and bumper stickers. In 1983, he joined the company's management.

The fact that no single star outshines any other at Infocom must be due, at least in part, to the group's genesis in the MIT computer lab. The atmosphere of that lab—camaraderie, humor, intense intellectual effort that is both individual and collective—has carried over into the company. Ownership is fairly evenly distributed, with a number of people holding 10 to 15 percent of the stock and all employees receive stock options (which many have exercised).

Something else that has carried over is the emphasis on creating "state-of-the-art development tools" before plunging into specific applications. "If your tools are powerful enough," says Berez, "the applications drop out fairly easily." In the case of Infocom's interactive fiction, this means inventing the languages and codes needed to translate programs from the mainframe to more than two dozen personal computers. It also means developing and refining the parser—that special part of the program which makes complex sentences and interactions possible. Michael Berlyn says of Infocom's parser: "It's clearly the most complicated, convoluted, disgusting piece of code that's ever been written." Yet the company admits that its parser is still primitive compared to those that will make way for a truly sophisticated genre of interactive literature in the future.

Infocom claims to be the only major software company that writes its programs on a mainframe and then converts them into languages that can be understood by personal computers. To perform this esoteric act of translation, Marc Blanc and Joel Berez created ZIL (Zork Interactive Language). A rather idiosyncratic promotional story booklet called *Our Circuits, Ourselves!—The Heroic Struggle of Micro-Americans to be Free* likens this process to the dehydration of oats into oatmeal. A kind, archetypal old Infocom steward explains to the timorous hero, oatmeal company employee Delwood Bland, "Our Infokins do the same thing—taking the vast amount of information that goes into making up a world, then condensing it to a floppy disk you can slip into your Micro-American, without losing any of the 'goodness.'"

Infocom's mainframe is the DEC 2060, which a *Washington Post* writer describes as "the biggest byte-bender in Digital Equipment's fleet, compared to which your IBM PC is dumb as a toaster." The 2060 costs $750,000; the company bought its second one in mid-1984. With this machine, Infocom says its programmers can do in three months what might take three years on a personal computer.

But the makers of Floyd, Frobozz, and the cryogenically preserved hero of *Suspended* aren't satisfied. While $6 million may sound good by itself, it doesn't sound quite as good when compared to the sales figures of leading business software companies. The collapse of the arcade game industry in recent years has given all personal computer game makers cause to stop and reconsider; the Infocom team has lately been working hard— and secretly—on business programs. According to the *Wall Street Journal*, they will say only that they expect to produce something "more sophisticated than current data base managers." They also hint at the possibility of customizing the new programs for individual industries, and of adapting their games' conversational ability "to make business software less daunting." Naturally, they express confidence that they can make their way successfully into the already glutted business market.

Here again, as the relatively stable past gives way to the imaginary future, Infocom becomes a piece of fiction *in potentio*. Many times the dauntless crew has rushed across the universe in the mother ship Mainframe. Many times they have zipped in and out of the great ship's ports in their small and sporty micros. Long ago they left behind their home nebula, and now once again they are venturing into dangerous, uncharted worlds. There are scores of possible endings. Will there be a crash? Or will the VisiWizard and the Lotus Enchanter soon be trembling?

No one knows who writes the code for this story.

WHAT'S IN A NAME?

Ashton-Tate: The "Ashton" part of the name is a marketer's device to find a name that sounds nice with "Tate," the real name of the company's founder.

Atari: The equivalent of "check" in chess for the popular Eastern name, *go*.

Broderbund: The Swedish word for "brotherhood," a company run by two Carlston brothers and their sister.

dilithium: Name of the fuel crystals that energized the starship *USS Enterprise* in "Star Trek."

Epson: "Son of EP," the first electronic printer in this now-popular series of personal computer printers.

International Data Group: The first three cards company founder Pat McGovern pulled from a deck he had made of names with intentionally bland words.

Kriya: From the Sanskrit, meaning "completed action."

Lifetree: An amalgam of Lifeboat and Peachtree, two well-known corporate names when this company was formed.

Lotus: A yoga position.

MAD Computer: Modular advanced design.

Prelude Publishing: The Honda model that best-selling author Peter McWilliams drives.

Sorcim: Micros spelled backwards.

Tecmar: Shortened and reversed form of "Marty's Technology," named after company founder, Marty Alpert.

Daniel Bricklin

"The basic idea of what a spreadsheet would be came to me in the spring of 1978. The goal was that it had to be better than the back of an envelope"

▶ **BEST-KNOWN VENTURE:** Software Arts

BORN: 1951

RAISED: Philadelphia, Pennsylvania

PARENTS' OCCUPATIONS: Father—owner of a printing and graphic arts business; mother—high school science teacher

SCHOOLING: B.S., electrical engineering and computer science, Massachusetts Institute of Technology; M.B.A., Harvard Business School

FIRST DOLLAR EARNED: Ran his own photography business as a child

PERSONAL NET WORTH: Millions of dollars from one of the most generous royalty deals in the industry

HOME: Newton, Massachusetts

PERSONAL TRANSPORTATION: Honda Accord

Software Art.

SOFTWARE ARTS: Producers of the single best-selling piece of software for personal computers.

▶ **BEST-KNOWN PRODUCTS:** *VisiCalc, TK!Solver*

YEAR FOUNDED: 1979

EMPLOYEES: 65

HEADQUARTERS: Wellesley, Massachusetts

SALES: $10 million (1983)

OWNERSHIP: Private, majority owned by Daniel Bricklin and Robert Frankston, his partner

The story of *VisiCalc*'s creation has achieved the status of legend in the personal computer industry. A young Harvard Business School student gets tired of watching his professors put financial projections onto the blackboard. Every time they introduce a new element into the equation—a change in interest rates, for instance—they stand there and tediously erase and redo rows and columns of figures. "Why not do all these recalculations instantly on a small computer?" muses the student. He takes his idea to an ace programmer friend who writes what they later call *VisiCalc*, the first electronic spreadsheet. He then brings the program to another friend, who happens to be a hot-shot marketing graduate of Harvard. Within months, they create an industry and become extremely wealthy.

Unfortunately, this story does not have a happy ending. But let's start at the beginning, with Dan Bricklin, the enterprising young business student. He comes from a family of entrepreneurs. Bricklin's grandfather founded a printing and graphics company. The Bricklin automobile—a short-lived exotic sports car—was built by a distant relative. Bricklin followed the family tradition even as a child, setting up and running his own businesses. One he especially enjoyed was taking candid photographs of people and then selling them to the subjects.

Why did he need the money? To pay for his "electronics habit," he says. The young Dan Bricklin was fascinated by transistor circuits. He even tried to build his own primitive computer out of transistors and flip-flop switches while still in high school in Philadelphia. But it wasn't tinkering with equipment that engaged him. He discovered his true love when a cousin loaned him a book on Fortran, a sophisticated programming language. Bricklin devoured the book in one weekend. The next week his cousin took him to his Germantown High School and let him use a terminal linked to a mainframe computer. "I started typing out my own program," Bricklin recalls. "The first thing I typed in, of course, had a spelling error. I spelled 'dimension' wrong." This took place in the mid-'60s, before Bricklin could even drive a car.

Bricklin absolutely loved programming. He told us that his relatives like to remind him that he and his friends were so anxious to get at the high school's computer that they once broke in, dismantled a door, and got the key copied by a local locksmith. Bricklin also took a National Science Foundation summer course at the University of Pennsylvania, in a computer facility that, he points out, was "literally a stone's throw from where ENIAC [the first digital computer] was built [in the late 1940s]." Before he left high school, Bricklin worked afternoons helping Wharton Business School students learn Fortran, and even won an award from NASA for some programming work in Fortran.

Where does a young computer whiz go from there, even one who hopes to enter the business world one day? To MIT.

"The big thing at MIT is not that you go to the classes and learn. It's that you can also work in their labs as a student. If you get a job in the lab, either for credit or money—I did it for money—you're working with the top people in the world, as equals in many respects." Bricklin got a job at the MIT Laboratory for Computer Science with Professor Corbato, the father of computer time-sharing. Corbato also happened to be Bob Frankston's thesis advisor.

Frankston—who later programmed *VisiCalc* for Bricklin—graduated from MIT in 1970, when Bricklin was a freshman. For the next several years, Frankston continued to do graduate study and work in MIT's computer labs under Professor Corbato. Bricklin, Frankston, and others worked on Multics—a sophisticated operating system for programmers. Multics was a forerunner to UNIX, developed later by Bell Labs for use on mainframe computers. Much of the lab work took place at night, late at night. The Multics group often tumbled into Frankston's car at one or two o'clock in the morning to drive to some all-night eatery in Cambridge.

Bricklin and Frankston became close friends and kept in touch after both had left MIT—Frankston went to work as a program designer and consultant for Interactive Data Corporation and Bricklin became a software engineer for Digital Equipment Corporation (DEC). The two often talked about setting up their own software business long before microcomputers were around. But they never saw the right opportunity. Bricklin's interest in business eventually led him to enroll in Harvard Business School in September 1977, thinking he would eventually become an investment banker or financial analyst. Instead, his musings during the laborious blackboard computations of his professors brought him back to the world of computers.

Bricklin took his idea for an electronic spreadsheet to his old friend Frankston, who, after some prodding, agreed to do the programming. Bricklin also showed his idea to Dan Fylstra, a recent Harvard M.B.A. who was selling a computer game program called *MicroChess* out of his Boston-area apartment. Fylstra had an extra Apple II computer, and Frankston, still a night owl, used it during his all-night programming marathons. At three or four o'clock one morning in early 1979, Fylstra joined Frankston at one of his late-night breakfast haunts. On a napkin one of them wrote the name of the program Frankston was writing, *VisiCalc*, short for visible calculator.

The three felt they had a winner. Fylstra agreed to market the program through his company, VisiCorp (known originally as Personal Software), while Bricklin and Frankston concentrated on refining the program through their own company, Software Arts. The program's first break came when financial analyst Ben Rosen, in the July edition of the Morgan Stanley *Electronics Letter*, proclaimed *VisiCalc* to be the "software tail that might wag the personal computer dog."

Rosen was right. Thousands of people bought microcomputers because of *VisiCalc*. By mid-1984, more than 700,000 copies of *VisiCalc* had been sold, making it the most popular microcomputer software program ever. Software Arts received a royalty of between 36 and 50 percent on each copy sold by VisiCorp. By 1984 that amounted to over $22 million. Bricklin and Frankston plowed much of the money into their company, and in early 1980 they were hard at work on *TK!Solver* (TK stands for "tool kit"), a program to help engineers and scientists solve math problems. *TK!Solver* received rave reviews after being introduced to the press in May 1982. Sales were slow initially because Software Arts didn't even have a marketing department when it announced the program.

By the time Bricklin and Frankston were ready to sell *TK!Solver*, they weren't about to hand the program over to Dan Fylstra, who had moved west to Silicon Valley. The creators of *VisiCalc* were engaged in a bitter dispute with its marketers. Software Arts complained VisiCorp was trying to reduce their royalties; VisiCorp claimed Software Arts wasn't improving the program quickly enough. The battle eventually erupted publicly with both sides filing lawsuits. In early 1984, Software Arts announced it had terminated its marketing agreement with VisiCorp and began selling *VisiCalc* on its own.

Though not mentioned in the lawsuits, the personal styles of the principal antagonists could not be more dissimilar. Fylstra tends to dress in sharp business suits, presumably to impress dealers and bankers. Bricklin and Frankston usually wear blue jeans and T-shirts or flannel work shirts. They look and act very much like graduate students in mathematics, the sort of guys who, in the era before microcomputers, used to wear slide rules on their belts and plastic liners full of pens in their breast pockets.

Unfortunately, the battle between *VisiCalc*'s creators seems to be hurting both sides. One former VisiCorp employee told *Business Week*: "It's a battle of egos. It was a question of who got credit. The arrogance, egotism, and nonsense are equally shared." The war rages on though *VisiCalc* has apparently lost its popularity. In 1983, *VisiCalc* was selling 20,000 copies a month; a year later, only about 2,000 to 3,000 a month were being sold. Both companies were forced to drastic measures to keep from going under. During the summer of 1984, VisiCorp laid off 110 workers, with just 55 remaining; and Software Arts cut its work force in half, to 65 employees. Both sides were still talking a good game, though. Bricklin insisted the layoffs were the low point, and that a new, improved version of *VisiCalc* was imminent, which would put his firm back on track.

Bricklin is not one to simply take the ample amounts of money from his *VisiCalc* royalties and run. He seems sincerely committed to resurrecting his firm. "One of the reasons that we were able to do *VisiCalc* is that Bob [Frankston] and I were both living like students," Bricklin told us. "Our desires are relatively modest." He lives in a modest house in Newton, not far from the converted chocolate factory in Wellesley where Software Arts is headquartered. He drives a Honda Accord, explaining, "I may buy a BMW one of these days, but who needs it to commute for five minutes?"

Besides that, he said, "If you're an entrepreneur, you just don't spend it all. If you spend everything you've got, you can't take risks anymore. I guess, I'm an entrepreneur at heart. If I had all the money in the world, what I would have done is set up Software Arts."

John Brockman

"We're reasonably candid and low-key and, all the same, ruthless"

▶ **BEST-KNOWN VENTURE:** John Brockman Associates

OTHER VENTURES: *By the Late John Brockman, Afterwords* (and other books)

BORN: 1941

RAISED: Boston, Massachusetts

FATHER'S OCCUPATION: Flower wholesaler

FIRST DOLLAR EARNED: Delivered "Fruit of the Week" to women's colleges

SCHOOLING: B.S., Babson Institute; M.B.A., Columbia University

PERSONAL NET WORTH: "101 percent" of John Brockman Associates

HOME: New York City, New York

FAMILY: One son with his partner, Katinka Matson

PERSONAL TRANSPORTATION: Mercedes 380 SFL

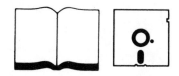

JOHN BROCKMAN ASSOCIATES INC.: The literary agent who put a floppy disk on his logo and panicked staid old Publisher's Row into a buying frenzy.

▶ **BEST-KNOWN CLIENTS:** *PC World, Whole Earth Software Catalog,* Lifetree Software, Human Edge Software

YEAR FOUNDED: 1973

EMPLOYEES: 16

CLIENTS: 200

HEADQUARTERS: New York City, New York

ANNUAL DEALS: $20 million (1983 estimate)

ANNUAL COMMISSIONS: $3 million (1983 estimate)

OWNERSHIP: Privately owned by founder

I'm not in business to help people. I'm not in business to make friends. I'm in business to make money." The persona John Brockman likes to present to the press (and the press has been very much interested in him lately) is one of relentless cynicism.

"I'm not in love with personal computers; I'm not in love with software. It's a business. We're doing it to make money, and we're making a fortune. When you have an opportunity like this you go flat out. Anyone who doesn't is an idiot."

Brockman earned his place in this book when he went flat out to create a new market—by selling the staid, New York publishers on computer books and software before they even knew what a floppy disk was. As the world's first software agent Brockman doesn't have to write, design, publish, distribute, or even look at the stuff (which is fortunate because he finds those tasks very boring). What he does for software producers is the same thing he used to do for his literary clients (including the three authors of this book): he picks up the phone and makes deals with publishers. In remuneration for this service, he keeps 15 percent of all proceeds.

By July 1984, John Brockman was making more money each month than he did in his entire first seven years as a literary agent.

So why do we have so much difficulty taking Brockman at face value—isn't he just another entrepreneur out to make as much money as possible? His previous personae have a lot to do with it. He was a first-rate literary agent, an avant-garde philosopher, a producer of multimedia performances, a promoter of experimental films.

When we interviewed him, he did his best to prove that his avarice is sincere. Speaking in his usual edgy and combative manner, he likened himself to his father: "He was the carnation king of America. He represented the major carnation growers in the Boston area, which at the time was the center for carnations. Basically he was an agent. He charged 15 percent commission, same as I do. The only difference between carnations and software authors is that carnations smell better and don't talk back. The similarity is that both businesses are fantastically profitable. My father, at various times, cornered the market on certain cut flowers like gladiolas and carnations. By controlling the supply, he could create the demand."

When we tried a joking question about growing up in a "flower environment," Brockman shook his head from side to side to relieve the tension in his neck. "It was a business environment. It wasn't about flowers; it was about making money."

Brockman went to college at the business-oriented Babson Institute and, in 1963, received an M.B.A. from Columbia University. With a classmate he started a company that leased multimillion-dollar equipment (printing presses and oil wells) to large corporations. But after six months he gave it up.

"I was in an office on Park Avenue all by myself. Every day I would go there in my elegant, post-business school clothes and be confronted with hundreds of pieces of paper. I was twenty-three and said to myself, 'Is this what I want to do the rest of my life? No way.' So I just walked away from it."

He walked away into a very different world inhabited by New York's mixed-media artists and underground filmmakers who were, in the mid-'60s, strongly influenced by LSD laced with Marshall McLuhan's theorizing on the nonlinear nature of reality.

In those days money was not important to him: "There are lots of things to do besides making money when you're young."

Brockman became manager of the Filmmakers' Cinematheque, New York's underground movie center. Being the only person in the milieu who understood business, he ran the commercial end of the enterprise. That led to a job running special projects for the uptown New York Film Festival which, in turn, led to Brockman's becoming a consultant on multimedia events.

"I was the person who brought intermedia to the public eye in '67-'68. I was partly responsible for two *Life* cover stories in one year—one on LSD art and one on mixed-media discotheques. With all the publicity, I was approached by a raft of people."

Over the next few years, Brockman's clients included Columbia Pictures, General Electric, the White House, the Pentagon, and Scott Paper. They all wanted him to represent their interests through multimedia presentations. There was even an anthropologist who wanted to plan an environment in which Lyndon Johnson would have his mind changed about the Vietnam War.

"The business was McLuhanesque consulting. We advised people on who they were and what they were doing, using cybernetic models, new ways of conveying information, where the channels themselves are the important thing."

In 1966 Brockman used to walk along Bank Street in Greenwich Village hoping for an opportunity to converse with a beautiful woman he knew lived nearby. One day it happened that both were carrying book manuscripts and Brockman took his chance. "What do you do?" he asked.

"I'm a literary agent," she said.

"I'm a writer," he declared.

Three days later he had a contract from Macmillan to do *The Book on Intermedia Theater*. The friendship with Katinka Matson eventually became a partnership, both at home and in the office. She is vice president of John Brockman Associates; their son Max was born in 1980.

The Book on Intermedia Theater, however, never got written. In 1967 Brockman went to Cape Cod with his co-author, an artist and poet, to write. The co-author brought along a woman 24 years his junior, and (except for functions necessary to sustain life) the two of them didn't emerge from the bedroom for four days. Lonely Brockman sat down and wrote what turned out to be a cult book of avant-garde epistemology, which he called *By the Late John Brockman*.

In 1968 Brockman, having made "a ton of money" from his consulting business, decided to close it down. "I bought a yellow Jaguar, had my phones taken out, and retired." He was 27, and for the next five years he studied and wrote while living on cash reserves. In 1973 his first two books were reprinted, along with a new work, under the title *Afterwords*. His books consist of a series of aphoristic messages printed on separate pages, with 50 to 95 percent of each page left blank. For example: "Reality is whatever the brain is doing. Time does not exist in the neural world. Information passes across the arbitrary boundaries of mankind as though they never existed." Brockman was trying to show that cybernetics presented a whole new reality, but nobody seemed to be paying attention.

Responses were varied. *The Whole Earth Catalog* praised the first book. *Vogue* called it a trashy specimen of the "newly prolific genre of electronic dada." A woman told Brockman her brother in a mental hospital had memorized it.

During his period as an "epistemologist," Brockman entered the circle of a brilliant and quirky array of scientists, mathematicians, philosophers, psychologists, and artists. In 1973 a group of them (including G. Spenser Brown, Gregory Bateson, Alan Watts, John Lilly, Heinz von Foerster, and Stewart Brand) spent a week together at Northern California's Esalen Institute. Brockman remembers it as "a very heady experience." They called it the AUM conference; the letters stood for American University of Masters and were also a play on the Hindu syllable *aum*, which is said to contain the essence of reality in its vibrations.

One morning two figures in hooded robes approached Brockman at the breakfast table. They were Watts (best known as an interpreter of Zen Buddhism) and Lilly (who did research on the intelligence of dolphins). Though their attire was mystical, their talk was practical. Nearly everyone there had written books, many of which had sold well. But none of these authors had particularly good deals with publishers. Brockman lived in New York and understood business. What did he think of the idea of being literary agent for the Masters?

He liked the idea, imagining that he could spend a couple of hours a day at it, continue his writing, and "make a fairly decent living in a painless way."

"I incorporated, got stationery, and did a proposal for John Lilly that I sold in two hours for 55 thousand dollars. What a way to start! From then on it was an oil well. I was riding on top of it and haven't come down since."

During the next 10 years Brockman became a respected agent with a distinguished list of authors. Most of the work was serious nonfiction—science, philosophy, and self-help. The authors appreciated Brockman's ability to secure unusually favorable contracts for these kinds of books. Gregory Bateson, for instance, referred to Brockman as "my scoundrel," explaining that every writer needs a scoundrel to deal with unscrupulous publishers. In the mid-'70s, Brockman himself authored a series of paperbacks based on new technology: two volumes of *The Pocket Calculator Game Book*, then *The Kids' Pocket Calculator Game Book*, *The CB Handbook*, and what he claims was the first computer book for general readers, *The Home Computer Handbook*.

Despite his successes, life seemed dull. "Katinka and I had been wondering for years where the action was. Life during the '60s had been very exciting. The '70s were very unexciting.

They found their answer in 1982 when efforts to computerize the agency led them to attend COMDEX, the biggest computer trade show, held every year in Las Vegas. There they saw an "incredible energy...a different kind of people." At

COMDEX Brockman heard "a buzz from these eighty-thousand people that was energizing and exciting."

Having written a home computer book in 1978 and having been an intellectual playmate of cyberneticians, Brockman was already aware of the ferment in the industry and its vast social and cultural implications. In 1982 he realized its implications for him. He often says that by the end of 1985 there will be 25 million personal computer users, all of whom will be not only software buyers but also potential software authors.

Surveying the scene in 1982, Brockman reasoned: the creation of software "is an act of writing [that] results in a copyrighted work. Our business for the last 10 years had been in dealing with copyrights for authors. But there was no such thing as a software agent."

This idea set fire to Brockman's imagination. He started wooing both publishers and authors—at first to little effect. But he was sure he had hold of something big. He set up dozens of lunches with publishers. When *Time* made the computer its "Man of the Year," he shot off copies of the article in all directions. Soon he landed his first client, a software company called Bruce and James, and made his first deal: distribution by Simon and Schuster of *Wordvision*, a simple word processor for the IBM PC. The product would be sold in book stores for $50, a large cut under the retail price of most word processing programs.

Then the dams broke. Amidst predictions that the Vision line of software would be selling at the rate of $25 million annually within two years, both software companies and publishers started pursuing Brockman. One call came from a man in Chicago with a foreign-sounding name.

When Brockman went to meet Sat Tara Khalsa, he found a cheery Montana-born American dressed all in white, with a bushy red beard and a turban. Khalsa is a convert to the Sikh religion and founder of Kriya Systems. By the time of their meeting, Khalsa had three successful educational programs on the market. For his *Typing Tutor III*, Brockman pulled off another high-priced deal with Simon and Schuster. Though exact amounts were not revealed, the rumor of an advance exceeding a million dollars escaped, and estimates of potential royalties were pitched extravagantly high (to the extent that one newsletter, after quoting them, assured its readers that they hadn't seen a misprint).

Further headlines were made in 1983 by Brockman's book deals. In his original estimate of the consumer revolution he was hooking into, Brockman took into account the fact that the average computer buyer invests in eight to 10 computer-related books. Noting that, while the book industry in general was faltering, computer-related books and magazines were the fastest growing category in publishing history, Brockman moved to sign up every computer how-to book writer he could get hold of. An *InfoWorld* columnist later observed that he had "cornered the book market like the Arabs with the oil market."

In addition, Brockman figured out a new strategy for producing and marketing the books. "Rather than dealing with separate authors, I went to *PC World, InfoWorld, Whole Earth Catalog, LIST* magazine. I convinced them to become packagers and sell a series of books."

The result was gargantuan advances for all of them: $800,000 for *PC World*'s series of ten books, $600,000 for *InfoWorld*'s series of six, and the highest nonfiction advance in history—$1.3 million—for Stewart Brand's *Whole Earth Software Catalog*.

John Brockman rode the wild tide of competition and speculation like a cowboy on a bronco, exhilarated and crowding the edge of recklessness. Repeatedly he referred to the scene as a Wild West show, a gold rush, where anything goes. Deals, he declared, have nothing to do with some Platonic Idea of a product's absolute value. "A book is worth what someone wants to pay for it. It was my job to create conditions where books seem so valuable that the publishers *had* to get in on it. In the heat of an auction, you get the situation where winning is as important as acquiring the property."

Some people raised questions. What if the books (or the disks) don't do well enough? What if they cancel each other out, fail to make back their advances? Brockman washed his hands of it. "I'm not interested in the welfare of the publisher," he sometimes says. "I represent authors." And more colorfully: "In a gold rush, the people who make money are the ones who sell eggs for ten dollars apiece."

Brockman paints the picture of a world in which software will be a mass commodity, and we will all be buying our floppies at bookstores. In this world, the small independent companies that have dominated the software industry will be pushed out by huge media conglomerates with "deep pockets" and many years of marketing experience. "Putting ads in *PC* and *Byte* and then dumping products in Softsel (the largest software distribution company), isn't marketing," he says. "Marketing is fielding a sales force in all available channels, being in Toys 'R Us and K-Mart."

Khalsa adds, with beaming approval, "A 10-million-dollar company can't compete with Gulf + Western and its three-point-nine *billion*." (Simon and Schuster is a division of Gulf + Western.)

Big publishers and media conglomerates seem to agree with this analysis. Those who have set up divisions for software and "bookware" include CBS, Warner Communications, Random House, E.P. Dutton, Simon and Schuster, Harper & Row, Macmillan, New American Library, Harcourt Brace Jovanovich, Prentice-Hall, and McGraw-Hill.

Dissenters point out that a floppy disk, despite the fact that it has an author and a copyright, is in many ways *not* like a book. For one thing, people who buy software often need technical advice. "Book publishers," observes a Microsoft manager to an *InfoWorld* reporter, "never get calls from irate users who tell them that this book doesn't work with my bookshelf." Again, unlike books, software needs to be constantly updated to stay abreast of new technical developments. Those who are skeptical about Brockman's vision doubt that conglomerates can fill these needs. They also point out that the first of his spectacular deals seems to have collapsed. Bruce and James took 18 months to get *Wordvision* to the market, by which time, having missed its chance to be the first low-cost word processor, it expired with a whimper.

Needless to say none of this slows down Brockman or his ability to make new deals. He goes to every major computer show in search of new contacts, and has developed a special style for cultivating them. Part of the strategy is a luxury hotel suite as close as possible to the fair. Another part of it was referred to in a *Popular Computing* story as "sartorial overkill." It doesn't take much to make the best-dressed list among the techies, but typically, Brockman plies his trade in a brand-new Giorgio Armani suit and Matson accompanies him down the endless aisles in something white, plain, and very elegant.

There have been a lot of changes at John Brockman Associates since it yielded itself up to the computer revolution. Brockman no longer relates much to individual authors. His clients are companies and his contact people the presidents of them.

As a literary agent Brockman used to read book proposals his authors submitted. As a software agent he has little or nothing to do with the products. "My clients are industry experts. They're totally uninterested in what I think of their software. They want to make deals."

Brockman now describes his agency as a computer company that also does books. If a young writer should come along with a book of radical epistemology, Brockman admits he wouldn't be able to help.

On the other hand, the agent's life hasn't changed that much. Brockman and Matson still live in the same rather small and dark rent-controlled apartment on Central Park West. They can afford a lot more help in the office and plenty of baby-sitting, but Brockman has remarked that the only time he feels rich (and gets away from the telephones) is when he's behind the wheel of his new Mercedes. Most weekends he drives the family, and often a client or two, out to the house they rent in the Hamptons. In a small room in that country house, Brockman keeps a Compaq computer. Early in the weekend, he uses it to add up the financial results of the previous week's deals. But later, a visitor may be privy to an unexpected event: the sight of a John Brockman who by his own account belongs in the past, returning to the keyboard to peck at a work-in-progress, a serious book about science entitled *Einstein, Gertrude Stein, Wittgenstein, and Frankenstein*. It's several years behind schedule but, Brockman promises (sounding much like an author), very close to completion.

Doug Carlston

"I've never been interested in business"

▶ **BEST-KNOWN VENTURE:** Broderbund Software

BORN: 1947

RAISED: Iowa City, Dubuque, and Beaver Dam, Iowa

FATHER'S OCCUPATION: Presbyterian minister and professor of New Testament studies

FIRST DOLLAR EARNED: Cutting brush and mowing lawns

SCHOOLING: B.A., social psychology, Harvard University; J.D., Harvard Law School

ORIGINAL FINANCING: $12,000 saved from his private law practice

PERSONAL NET WORTH: 27 percent of Broderbund Software

HOME: Sausalito, California

FAMILY: Married

PERSONAL TRANSPORTATION: Toyota Celica

♛ Brøderbund Software

BRODERBUND SOFTWARE INC.: A leading game company that has successfully expanded into other types of software for home use.

► BEST-KNOWN PRODUCTS: *Choplifter!*, *Lode Runner* (arcade-style games); *Bank Street Writer*, *Bank Street Speller* (for word processing)

YEAR FOUNDED: 1980

EMPLOYEES: 75

HEADQUARTERS: San Rafael, California

SALES: $12 million (1983); $20 million (1984 projection)

OWNERSHIP: Privately held by founders and employees (55 percent) and outside investors (45 percent)

In the winter of 1979 Doug Carlston and his dog, a mastiff named Judge, were doing their best to cross the Great Divide. A heavy snowstorm caught up with them in Snake River, Wyoming, and Carlston's '68 Impala began to give up. Smoke billowed up from the floor; the highway disappeared. Driver and dog stuck their noses out opposite windows: one struggling to see, the other calmly eating snowflakes. They plowed ahead, not daring to shut the engine off, even for gas stops. At last they rolled triumphantly down the slope into western Oregon, leaving the snow behind, and clanked to a halt within a local phone call of where Doug's younger brother Gary was living. The car never moved under its own power again. But Doug and Gary Carlston were about to embark on a new venture they named after the Swedish word for brotherhood: Broderbund Software.

Doug Carlston talks about a "quixotic element" in his soul that made him leave the East and a promising legal career. In the 15 years before he landed in Oregon, his life alternated between spells in big urban-academic centers and flights to the Northeast woods, where he'd live, work, and ski until he'd go "stir-crazy" and run for cosmopolitan society again.

Meeting Carlston now, one feels he has found something he can stay with. In the midst of the pressures that have come with Broderbund's spectacular success, he seems relaxed and brushes off suggestions that he's done anything special. He dresses in blue jeans and sweaters and likes to describe himself by saying that his hair has been within an inch of the same length since high school. Asked if it ever occurred to him that his software business would make him rich, he replied, "No, I think it was more, 'Oh boy, now we're going to be able to trade software with everybody and we'll have the world's largest software collection.'"

The Carlston kids—three boys and two girls—grew up in Iowa, where their father was first a Presbyterian minister, then a seminary professor. Doug recalls his childhood happily: lots of football, basketball, and library books. "I've only broken four bones in my life—my arm once, Don's collarbone once, and Gary's collarbone twice. Dad got me six books every day. I read every piece of fiction and nonfiction in the children's section. We all grew up believing we could do absolutely anything."

He describes the family's economic status as "honorable poor," though they were able, when he was 12, to go to Germany for his father's sabbatical year. There Carlston attended a Waldorf school—part of the worldwide movement in education founded by the philosopher/mystic Rudolph Steiner. The German school strongly emphasized artistic creativity and Carlston loved it, but when he got back to Iowa he nearly flunked out of the eighth grade. He hadn't learned prepositions and other basics taught to seventh graders in the Dubuque public schools, so the system judged him unfit for college preparation and sentenced him to shop and mechanical drawing. He beat a retreat to a private school in Wisconsin (on a scholarship) and four years later was a National Merit scholar at Harvard.

Carlston's first taste of computers came in 1964, at a summer institute run by the National Science Foundation. When he started college a year later, he got a job cleaning toilets but soon concluded that he'd rather be programming. A little persistence landed him a job at the computer center. He majored in social psychology, went to Africa in his junior year, and came back in 1968 when college students all over the country were demonstrating against the Vietnam War. Carlston was against the war but had little taste for mass rallies, especially the kind where heads were crunched. He describes himself as "one of the most nonviolent people in the world" and in the late '60s limited his political action mainly to signing petitions.

Carlston abhorred another major preoccupation of students of that era, psychedelic drugs. He explains, "partly because I'm a real controlled personality and that kind of escapism bothers me a lot. Opium is the opiate of the masses."

While at Harvard, Carlston began his life of swinging back and forth between city and country. He apprenticed with a contractor in Maine one summer and later took to building and selling houses on his own. On one construction project he hired his brother Gary, sister Cathy, and a few friends. "One of my major oversights, which shows my personality, was that I just assumed everybody would work seven days a week. No weekends planned at all. Five weeks into the summer there was a rebellion. People just sat down and said, 'Sorry, Doug, it's a nice day.' I said, 'Yeah, you get rainy days off.' They said, 'We're going to take a nice day off.' And they went."

After graduation, when he wasn't doing construction, Carlston tried a variety of academic and professional pursuits, but none of them seemed to last. A fellowship lost its funding. Writing textbooks alone during the Maine winter left him so lonely that he applied to Harvard Law School "to improve my social life." Asked how that went, Carlston replies, "My basketball got a lot better." He managed to stay two years at a big Chicago law firm he joined after passing the bar; but then, with the prospect of 50 years of "one hundred man law firm goes out and saves Westinghouse from General Atomic," he quit to move back to Maine. His colleagues gave him a chainsaw as a going away gift.

Back in the woods, Carlston opened a private law practice, built a few more houses, and bought a Radio Shack TRS-

80 Model I personal computer. It was 1978, and this was the first time he had touched a computer in 10 years.

Carlston set out to program the TRS-80 to help him with his legal practice, but nine months after buying it he closed down the law office to program full time. By that time he'd written 150 programs. Many were designed for legal work, but Carlston's whimsical streak led him to also write a couple of games.

What eventually turned into *Galactic Empire* began as a program to simulate life choices: Should I go to college, should I get married, etc. He then turned to science fiction: A universe of 20 worlds is set before you. You have certain places already under control, certain resources like maps and instruments, certain knowledge about how to build things, where and when you can travel, and how long a journey takes. Your goal is to conquer the universe.

Carlston sent *Galactic Empire* to several software publishers. The quickest response came from Adventure International in Florida. He mailed the program on a Thursday, and on Monday he got a call from Alexis Adams, wife of Adventure's founder, Scott Adams. "Not only do we want to publish it," she said, "but we'll be shipping tonight. I've already sold fifty copies." Carlston imagined himself as just one of a stable of hundreds of free-lance software writers being handled by the company. Later he found out he was their first outside author.

Carlston wrote several variations of *Galactic Empire*. The series (called *Galactic Saga*) brought Carlston a steady income, averaging a thousand dollars a month for the next few years. At that time (late 1979) there was no such thing as exclusive rights, so Carlston sold his game to all interested publishers on the same terms. Royalties were around 20 percent of the $14.95 purchase price. Naively assuming that a "publishing house" would provide "editing," he sent out his games loaded with bugs, meaning they had unintended programming errors that could cause the game not to work properly. *Galactic Empire* went through 23 versions before it was finally bug-free. "I'd be sitting there and all of a sudden I'd think, 'Oh my God!' I'd realize some other problem. Sometimes there'd be three or four packages in the mail at once, and with the last one I'd say,

'Ignore the previous three versions.'" Carlston praises Adventure International for keeping up with him and continuing to revise the versions they sent out (unlike some of the others, whose businesses have since folded).

This was the juncture at which Doug and the mastiff crossed the prairies and mountains, stopping to visit all their friends along the way. Doug's vague intention was "to go on programming and visit Gary." He had $12,000 saved up. In Eugene, he found his brother, "as usual, completely out of money and starving to death."

From Doug's description, Gary (six years Doug's junior) comes off as a happy-go-lucky sort. Gary had majored in Scandinavian studies at Harvard and went to Sweden five times in eight or nine years. "He typically went over with about five dollars in his pocket and an optimistic sense that the world would provide. He spent most of his free hours there doing what he loved best—playing basketball." Gary's joy in that game led to his being hired as a women's basketball coach; he shepherded his team to the Swedish national championship.

But in 1979, Gary was back in Oregon trying to sell silver animal-shaped bicycle reflectors imported from Scandinavia. They were cute, but few people wanted to pay the $6 apiece he charged for them.

Doug gave Gary some of his programs to try to sell to local computer stores. He naturally went to Radio Shack outlets, since Doug's programs were written for TRS-80 computers, but found them to be "hopeless, absolutely hopeless." They had no more luck calling stores from lists they collected out of catalogs and the yellow pages. Writing to Radio Shack's headquarters was worse: "It took six months even to get a rejection, and it was a form letter. I'm not sure they even looked at the games." A successful sale was a rare enough occurrence to warrant a celebration: the brothers would "go out and have a hamburger."

The Carlstons began to wonder whether they were cut out for the vocation they'd picked. Doug remembers "going to the early [computer] shows when Scott [Adams] was cutting deals left and right. We sort of watched him in awe—we weren't cutting any deals with anybody. We figured that we had a lot to learn."

Inspired by Adams's example, the Carlstons manned a booth at the fifth West Coast Computer Faire in San Francisco. Sure enough, a group of Japanese traders appeared trying to sell some excellent games for the Apple computer. The Carlstons pursued the Japanese, determined to do some deal cutting of their own, but it was to no avail. The Japanese disappeared back to their homeland and all attempts to find them failed. In desperation the brothers published a letter in a Japanese magazine, urging the programmers to contact them.

Meanwhile, in May of 1980, the Carlstons decided to start writing games that would work on Apple computers as well as on the Radio Shack machines. There were many more distribution outlets for Apple software, and besides, they could do graphics in color. They had to invest a big chunk of their fast-dwindling assets to buy an Apple for Doug so he could convert his games. By June "we'd run out of money and were on the last of the Visa and MasterCard extensions," Doug recalls. Gary went to San Francisco to visit a friend (who supplied a one-way ticket), and while there tried peddling programs to stores that sold Apples. That was Broderbund's breakthrough. He sold $3,000 worth in three days.

Promptly, and without warning, the prodigal Japanese appeared on the Carlstons' doorstep. After they cemented a partnership, Broderbund had seven products—three games from Japan, three by Doug, and one by the third Carlston brother, Don.

In 1980 the video arcades were becoming a craze, heating up the interest in home computer games. With hardly any competition, Broderbund closed the year with $100,000 in sales— $55,000 of it in December. For most of that year Gary and Doug did all the work. "Sitting there duplicating disks took forever. Duplicating cassettes took ten times forever," Doug says. Eventually they hired three part-time employees and moved to a larger house in Eugene with a big garage.

In the fall Doug Carlston heard about Robert Leff, who was just launching Softsel, a software distributing company. Leff responded enthusiastically when Doug telephoned him, suggested they send out 400 attractively packaged sample disks, and offered to underwrite the costs. Within two months Broderbund's sales quintupled. When an order came in for 2,000 copies of *Alien Rain,* one of the Japanese games, the Carlstons couldn't afford to buy the blank disks on which to duplicate the program. Softsel came to the rescue with a $5,000 advance.

Three thousand miles away, Cathy Carlston was celebrating her promotion to the position of buyer at Lord & Taylor's department store in New York City. Her pleasant mood was interrupted when a tremendous racket drew her to the window. Bank robbers and police were engaged in a gun battle on the street below. It didn't take her long to phone her brothers in Eugene. Did they have work for her? Cathy joined Broderbund as office manager in March 1981, and later took on responsibility for advertising and marketing.

Soon afterwards, in August, Doug decided to move the company closer to the action. Broderbund's new home in San Rafael, California, was just north of San Francisco, fifty miles from Silicon Valley, and near several of their suppliers. It was also a much more convenient place to meet with their Japanese partners.

The move also brought Broderbund closer to another group of people. "I'd never heard of venture capital, frankly," says Doug. "All of a sudden we had people knocking on our door trying to give us millions of dollars, telling us that we needed this, that, and the other to run the company." He resisted their advances at first. But a year later, despite the rapid growth of the business, Carlston watched Broderbund's checking account balance dip close to the red enough times to appreciate the value of a nice cushion of cash. He decided to accept an investment of $1 million from the firm of Burr, Egan, Deleage & Co. in return for one-fourth of the company's stock.

In mid-1984 Broderbund was selling a million dollars worth of software every month. Though great leaps in revenues are common in the computer industry, Broderbund's increases since 1980 are more astronomical than most: 1,200 percent a year. Carlston attributes this growth rate to the quality of their products. "There's a kind of a company culture about quality," Doug says, and tells tales about "strange fights" they have over whether one type of label will be more tacky than another. He admits that writers claim they can be published elsewhere six months earlier than at Broderbund because of the Carlstons' perfectionism. "We're convinced that the last 5 percent of the [programming] code that takes so long to do represents 50 to 60 percent of our sales, or more."

Broderbund games have remained best-sellers and award winners since 1982. Their biggest success is *Choplifter!*, with over 200,000 sold. The object of that game is to rescue 64 peace delegates who are being held hostage by The Bungling Empire. Other hits are *Alien Rain, David's Midnight Magic, Serpentine, Lode Runner,* and *The Arcade Machine.* The last of these enables players to program their own games, and more than one *Machine* creation is being sold by a rival software publisher.

Broderbund's relationship with the Japanese programmers has been consistently rewarding. The Japanese tend to outdo even the Carlstons in perfectionism, which may be why they get along so well. One game by the author of *A.E.* (a bestseller in which a genetic engineering experiment goes awry, terrifying the universe) almost went to an untimely demise in a Japanese garbage can. Gary Carlston fished it out and convinced the dubious authors that it was good enough to sell.

As president of Broderbund and administrator of 75 people, Doug Carlston is no longer a software author, but he still says the biggest thrill in running Broderbund comes from creating new products. Writing is hardly ever a one-man show these days. Gary Carlston is in charge of product development, which is organized into editorial, animation, and storywriting staffs. It works like this (as described by Doug): "A programmer will come in and say, 'I've got a neat routine. It kind of gives an effect of sliding over ice. What can I do with it?' So everybody gets together and the animator works on little characters, the story guy works on story line, and the editors come in and try to contribute towards character development and the theme. Together they come up with a complete game."

If Doug Carlston had any remaining doubts about his ability to wheel and deal, they should have been dispelled by the results of his arrangements with outside software suppliers. In 1982 he outbid Apple and Atari for the publication rights to

Bank Street Writer, a word processor from a group of Boston programmers. The $70 program was reviewed in *Time* and became the number two seller nationally for six months in 1983, averaging 10,000 copies sold every month.

Bank Street products have grown into a "home productivity" series, one of three main lines of products. The second consists of "edutainment," the word Doug Carlston coined to express the educational intent of Broderbund's games, and the third, scheduled for a late '84 release, is computer literacy products with Jim Henson's Muppets as guides.

In August 1984, at age 37, Doug Carlston embarked on another adventure—his first marriage. Mary Crowley, his wife, is also an entrepreneur. She founded Ocean Voyages, a yacht brokerage, which offers charters in exotic locations all over the world. The honeymoon they planned was in character: "by boat, going up the coast of China from Hong Kong to Shanghai, and then over to Seoul, and then to Japan."

Bill Gates

"Software is a great combination between artistry and engineering. When you finally get done and get to appreciate what you have, it is like a part of yourself that you've put together"

► **BEST-KNOWN VENTURE:** Microsoft

OTHER VENTURE: Traf-O-Data

BORN: 1955

RAISED: Seattle, Washington

FATHER'S OCCUPATION: Lawyer

FIRST DOLLAR EARNED: Programmed class schedules on a computer while in the seventh grade

SCHOOLING: Two years at Harvard University (no degree)

ORIGINAL FINANCING: Personal savings

PERSONAL NET WORTH: $100 million

HOME: Bellevue, Washington

FAMILY: Single

PERSONAL TRANSPORTATION: Mercedes

MICR☉SOFT™

MICROSOFT CORPORATION: Largest developer of software for personal computers in the United States.

▶ **BEST-KNOWN PRODUCTS:** MS-DOS, M-BASIC; *Innovative Windows, Microsoft Word, Multiplan; Adventure, Flight Simulator,* and *Olympic Decathalon* games

YEAR FOUNDED: 1975

EMPLOYEES: 620

HEADQUARTERS: Bellevue, Washington

SALES: $100 million

PROFITS: $15 million (estimate)

OWNERSHIP: Private

This is not a rags-to-riches story. Although William H. Gates III may sometimes look as if he's dressed in rags, it's not because he can't afford to buy the very best clothes, nor does it reflect any humble origins. Bill Gates grew up in a well-to-do family. His father was—and still is—a prominent Seattle attorney. His mother, Mary Gates, is very active in Seattle society. They sent their only son to private schools, and they were delighted when he was accepted by Harvard, figuring that he would outgrow his childish mania for computers and follow in his father's footsteps to become a lawyer.

Gates never did finish Harvard. He left in 1975 at the end of his sophomore year (he's still listed as being "on leave") to get in on the early start of the personal computer business. He did get in on the ground floor, and now he's pretty close to the top. The company he co-founded, Microsoft, had sales of more than $100 million in 1984 and ranks as the largest software supplier in the industry. Bill Gates is believed to own nearly half of all the Microsoft shares—the company has never sold stock to the public—and his personal fortune on paper, has been estimated at more than $100 million.

Descriptions of Bill Gates are remarkably consistent. *People* magazine, profiling him in 1984, said he "still might be mistaken for a stockroom clerk. Like everyone at Microsoft, he dresses in Eddie Bauer casuals—a sweater, corduroys, and running shoes." *People* also said that with his "unruly" cowlick and boyish grin, there was a touch of Andy Hardy about him. Three months later, in its April 16th issue, *People*'s sister magazine, *Time*, put the 28-year-old Bill Gates on its cover, describing him as looking "like an undernourished grad student... His gray sweater has patches on the elbows; his shoes are scuffed; his ginger hair flops over a pair of steel-framed glasses." *Business Week*, in 1983, reported that Gates "is frequently described as immature." *Fortune*, in 1984, had this to say about Gates: "He is childishly awkward at times, throws things when he is angry, and fidgets uncontrollably when he speaks."

Why all this attention to young Bill Gates? Because today a lot of companies can make a computer (there are well over 100 brands) but what makes it work, what turns it into a useful tool for writers or business planners or investors or game players, are programming languages, operating systems, and application programs—software—and Gates's company has emerged as the leading software designer in the industry. More than two million computers are now driven by Microsoft software, ranging from the operating system that powers the IBM personal computer to the *Flight Simulator* program that enables you to sit in front of your computer and experience the same problems a pilot has in flying a Cessna Skylane from Chicago to Seattle. Trying to explain to its readers the significance of this work, *People* put it this way: "Gates is to software what Edison was to the light bulb—part innovator, part entrepreneur, part salesman, and full-time genius."

Bill Gates has always displayed this combination of traits. He was a whiz kid in school. He was a very early entrepreneur. His first experience with computers came when he was in the seventh grade at a private school in Seattle. The school's Mothers' Club had donated money to give their progeny a chance to buy time on some big mainframes. Gates became an instant convert, as did a ninth grader, Paul Allen. By his own description, Gates was "a hard-core technoid." His first big programming job was doing the class schedules for the school. He remembers living in the computer room the summer these schedules were devised. For that summer's work he earned $4,200.

In high school Gates and Allen became accomplished "hackers," like the Seattle teenager in the movie, *War Games:* they were so expert they could penetrate other systems and cause them to crash. In their book, *Fire in the Valley,* Paul Freiberger and Michael Swaine said that later on, when Gates wanted to establish his computer credentials, "he didn't display some clever programs he had written. He just said, 'I crashed the Burroughs; I crashed the CDC [Control Data Corp.].' Then they knew he was good."

Gates swore off computers for about a year after Control Data found that he had subverted their system, but Paul Allen lured him back when Intel fielded the 8008 microprocessor, "the computer on a chip." Together they started a little company called Traf-O-Data, which used the 8008 chip to track traffic patterns in the Seattle metropolitan area. Gates was then 15 years old; the company grossed $20,000.

The summer he was 16, Gates worked as a congressional page. That was the year Senator George McGovern was running for President against Richard Nixon. After McGovern dumped Senator Thomas Eagleton as his running mate, Gates and a friend bought up 5,000 McGovern-Eagleton campaign buttons for five cents apiece, which they later sold for as much as $25 each. (It was handy experience since the early software industry had a similar profit margin.)

Gates even took a leave of absence from high school for a year to work with Allen for TRW, which had heard about their computer prowess and hired them to develop software programs. Each was reportedly paid $30,000 a year. Bill Gates was 17 years old. He bought a speedboat and went waterskiing with Allen.

Gates and Allen stayed in touch, even after Gates went off to Harvard, ostensibly to take pre-law classes. What brought them back together as computer programmers was a 1975 cover story in *Popular Electronics* that described a $350 computer kit called Altair that was being assembled by an Albuquerque, New Mexico, company, MITS. It was a story that galvanized a number of early computer entrepreneurs. By that time Allen was working for Honeywell in Massachusetts, and he persuaded Gates that they should not pass up the opportunity to adapt the computer language BASIC (Beginners' All-Purpose Symbolic Instruction Code) for use in microcomputers. During February and March of 1975, the two worked steadily, often 18 hours a day, mostly in Daniels 312, a small dormitory room at Harvard. They were working with the second generation microprocessor, the Intel 8080 chip. MITS had told them that others were also working to adapt BASIC to microcomputers, so they knew they had to work fast.

"Our primary emphasis," Gates later explained, "was on a fail-safe BASIC that would always indicate a user error instead of crashing or producing the wrong result. Because we knew our software was going to be put in ROM [read-only memory] where it couldn't be updated, we needed to be extremely careful about subtle bugs. Our other major worry was that our simulator [in essence, the 8080 software, which they wrote for DEC's PDP-10 computer] might be incorrect.

"We agreed to take a paper tape of our BASIC to MITS to demonstrate it, knowing that if the simulator had made a mistake or we had misread the instruction manual [for the Intel 8080 chip], the demonstration would end our chances. The night before Paul left to go to Albuquerque, I stayed up reviewing everything to make sure it would run on the real machine. Paul wrote the bootstrap loader on the plane. Everyone, including ourselves, was amazed when this BASIC worked the first time. Many MITS employees who couldn't comprehend what to do with an Altair saw the value of the computer for the first time. Paul and I were ecstatic that all our work had paid off."

Allen quit his job at Honeywell, Gates left Harvard, and together they went to Albuquerque to start Microsoft. Allen actually went on the payroll of MITS as director of software development. Gates never did. He worked in a hotel across the street from MITS, refining and improving the BASIC programs for use with other computers. After a year with MITS, Allen left to work full time for Microsoft. MITS, the company that had the honor of introducing the first personal computer kit, didn't survive. The company was sold in 1977 and disappeared completely two years later. Also in 1977 Allen and Gates moved their company, Microsoft, to their home town, Seattle—more precisely, to Bellevue, a little town just across Lake Washington from Seattle. Already a veteran of this young industry, Bill Gates was then 21 years old.

Over the next seven years, as the personal computer industry moved from uncertain beginnings to explosive growth, Microsoft emerged from the pack as the pacesetter in the development of standardized software that makes the hardware (computers) more accessible to users. "The signal event in Microsoft's history was its selection by IBM to provide the operating system for its new personal computer. It started with a phone call from IBM in July 1980, at which point Microsoft had 32 employees. The IBM people wanted to come and see Gates. He said yes, and canceled a previous appointment with Ray Kassar, the president of Atari. For IBM, he and his associate, Steve Ballmer, even put on suits. The eventual agreement brought Microsoft into a very close working relationship with the IBM task force in Boca Raton. It was probably the closest linkup IBM has ever had with an outside supplier. And they seemed to hit it off very well. There was an electronic mail linkup between Bellevue and Boca Raton, and there were a lot of red-eye flights between Seattle and Miami. The timetable was intense. IBM and Microsoft first met in July 1980; IBM was able to announce its personal computer, with the Microsoft operating system, in August 1981. "I don't know how many people have read Tracy Kidder's new book, *The Soul of A New Machine*," Gates remarked to David Bunnell of *PC World*, "but it was like that—and everybody really did get their just desserts of being recognized and knowing what part they put into it. People worked incredibly hard. I guess there was a kind of an anticlimax when I got a form letter from IBM a week after we'd finished the thing, which said, 'Dear Vendor: You've done a fine job.' But they've apologized an appropriate number of times for that."

With so many computer makers wanting to be compatible with IBM, the Microsoft operating system was licensed to 100 other companies. As a result, MS-DOS (Microsoft Disk Operating System) was established as the dominant operating system for the personal computer industry in the United States. Far from resting on its laurels, Microsoft, under the prodding of Bill Gates, set out to use this victory as a springboard for entry into all phases of the software business. Microsoft stands ready to work with every computer maker in the world. It was a Microsoft design that made possible Radio Shack's Model 100, a lap-held computer. When Apple Computer brought out its Macintosh in 1984, Microsoft was on board with a bunch of software, and Bill Gates, no loyalist to IBM, pronounced "the Mac far easier to use than anything we have seen before." In Japan, Microsoft introduced its MSX design as a way to standardize the manufacture of low-powered home computers. Microsoft will get a royalty on each machine sold. Microsoft has developed the most comprehensive line of software applications in the industry, including programs that go head-to-head with such popular sellers as *WordStar* and *VisiCalc*. Jean Yates, one of the industry's leading market researchers, depicted the Microsoft strategy as one of trying to "preempt everybody else's products." She seems to be right on target. Toward the end of 1983, when Microsoft introduced its new *Windows* program, enabling computer users to juggle different jobs, the product was endorsed by 23 computer makers, and Bill Gates threw down this gauntlet: "This isn't just another software product—it's a change in the foundation that people built software on top of." No one ever accused Gates of setting his sights too low.

Read anything that Bill Gates has said or written—in interviews or articles—and you quickly get the picture not so much of an abstracted scientist as of an ambitious, analytical man who is completely at home in this new technology. In the far-ranging interview with Bunnell, Gates expounded as follows: "In five years the cost of computation will really be effectively decreased. We'll be able to put on somebody's desk, for an incredibly low cost, a processor with far more capability than you could ever take advantage of. Hardware, in effect, will become a lot less interesting. The total job will be in the software, and we'll be able to write big, fat programs. We can let them run somewhat inefficiently because there will be so much horsepower that just sits there.

"I expect over the next five years, between us and others, a heck of a job will get done. You'll be able to sit at your desk and do whatever it is you want to do with information or presenting data or interchanging data incredibly effectively. In other words, we will have changed the way people work."

Gates made that statement in 1982. A year later he was still singing the same tune: "No longer do we need to go out and build better, more powerful hardware to achieve productivity improvements: we can simply develop a new software package, and people can put it to use immediately in their existing machines. The revolution is here—and it is soft."

One of Gates's concepts is "softer software," by which he means programs that are intelligent enough (because they have been designed that way) to change their own behavior over time, having learned from experience. As an example, he cites the possibility of a program that "remembers" the user always wanting right-hand justification and a particular heading on a page whenever double-spacing is requested. Having "learned" that by observing the habits of the user, the program will tell the computer to do it automatically. Charles Simonyi, a research manager at Microsoft, once expanded on this subject, predicting to *InfoWorld* that the future computer "will be a working partner in the sense of anticipating your behavior and suggesting things to you. It will mold itself based on events that have taken place over a period of time."

Prior to joining Microsoft, Simonyi put in seven years at Xerox's Palo Alto Research Center, alma mater of many top-flight computer scientists (John Ellenby, Bob Metcalfe, Ben Wegbreit, Alan Kay, and Larry Tesler). Simonyi was 35 years old in early 1984, which made him one of the oldest people at Microsoft, where the average age was 28. Two other key people at Microsoft are Kazuhiko (Kay) Nishi and Steve Ballmer. Nishi hooked up with Gates in 1977 when he, like Gates, was 21 years old and a college dropout (from Tokyo's Waseda

University). Nishi serves as Microsoft's Japanese connection. He publishes several computer magazines in Japan and functions simultaneously as a part-time vice president of Microsoft. Thanks to Nishi's evangelizing, some 50 Japanese manufacturers have incorporated Microsoft software into their machines. And it was Nishi who found, at Hitachi, the element—an eight-line liquid crystal display—that made the Radio Shack 100 model possible. Ballmer, vice president of corporate staff at Microsoft, also goes back a long way with Bill Gates. He lived down the hall from Gates at the same Harvard dormitory where the BASIC microcomputer program was written. Gates used to visit with Ballmer after losing money at late night poker games. Following graduation from Harvard, Ballmer spent two years at Procter & Gamble and then a year at the Stanford Business School before dropping out to join Microsoft. He and Gates are reported to have an extraordinary rapport. "It's important to make money," Ballmer once told an *InfoWorld* reporter, "but if that's all that people think about, it bugs me and it bugs Bill. We like to be hard-core dedicated to the stuff we are doing."

Paul Allen, co-founder of Microsoft, serves as executive vice president of the company. He never graduated from college. He had to lighten his load at Microsoft in 1983 after he was found to be suffering from cancer. With the disease in remission, he returned to full-time duties in early 1984. With expected sales of $100 million in 1984 and a staff that now exceeds 600, Microsoft is no longer a cottage industry—and Gates has encountered some problems in management.

In 1982 he reached down to Oregon to hire James C. Towne away from Tektronix. Towne was installed as president and chief operating officer, a move Gates said would free him "to spend more time designing products." Towne was known around Microsoft as "the suit" because of his coat-and-tie dress. He lasted less than a year. "He was sort of random," Gates told *Fortune*. To replace him, Gates reached to Fort Worth and hired Jon Shirley, former computer merchandising vice president for Radio Shack, a major Microsoft customer. Shirley, who was 46 years old in 1984, had spent 25 years with Radio Shack.

There's speculation about what will happen to Microsoft next. Here are three scenarios: (1) The company will continue the way it is, re-investing profits back into development; (2) IBM will buy it out; and (3) Microsoft will continue to grow and sell stock to the public in 1986. Going public or selling out to IBM would enable Gates and other shareholders to make a ton of money. Gates himself still works very long hours and rarely takes vacations. He has a $750,000 home overlooking Lake Washington, with a 30-foot indoor swimming pool, and it takes him only 14 minutes to drive his Mercedes to Microsoft headquarters. He is still single.

Bill Gates came away from the IBM experience with a healthy respect for IBM and the way it works. As he told David Bunnell, "There's some supersmart people there. I was very, very impressed with the team they put together. They used most of the people who had their own personal computers. Employees within IBM who have the oomph to go out and get their own personal computer and be kidded by their fellow workers are, in general, a pretty good class of individuals." Gates also believes his mother helped get him the IBM assignment. When Don Estridge, the head of the IBM personal computer project, told IBM chairman John Opel that Microsoft might be involved, Opel said, "Oh, is that Mary Gates's boy's company?" When he was stationed in Seattle for IBM, Opel had served on the board of United Way with Mary Gates.

Fred Gibbons

"If I were to summarize the people I know in this industry, the vast majority of them come from modest, middle-class backgrounds"

▶ **BEST-KNOWN VENTURE:** Software Publishing

OTHER VENTURES: A ski bag company, sold catamarans on Cape Cod

BORN: 1949

RAISED: Boston, Massachusetts

FATHER'S OCCUPATION: Captain of a commercial ship

FIRST DOLLAR EARNED: Selling canvas ski bags

SCHOOLING: B.S. and M.S., computer engineering, University of Michigan; M.B.A., Harvard University

ORIGINAL FINANCING: $50,000 savings

PERSONAL NET WORTH: Between 15 and 20 percent of Software Publishing

FAMILY: Single

PERSONAL TRANSPORTATION: 1968 Mustang, Cessna Turbo 210

pfs:

Software Publishing Corporation

SOFTWARE PUBLISHING CORPORATION: Makers of moderately priced business software without bells or whistles.

▶ **BEST-KNOWN PRODUCTS:** *pfs:file, pfs:report, pfs:graph, pfs:write*

YEAR FOUNDED: 1981

EMPLOYEES: 107

HEADQUARTERS: Mountain View, California

SALES: $10 million (1983); $20 million (1984 projection)

PROFITS: $1.4 million (1983, after taxes)

OWNERSHIP: Private; over 50 percent held (in equal shares) by founders Fred Gibbons, Janelle Bedke, and John Page

Fred Gibbons is a natural entrepreneur. Everyone says so—his partners at Software Publishing Corporation (SPC), his associates, and Gibbons himself. Janelle Bedke, who has known him for years and is now vice president of marketing at SPC, describes Gibbons as "an entrepreneur from day one."

Gibbons likes to generalize about computer entrepreneurs and neatly fits himself into his own generalization. "The vast majority of them come from modest, middle-class backgrounds. They come from the Midwest. They have the gumption to pick up stakes and build their own companies. First generation wealth is being created out here [in California's Silicon Valley]. I like to think of my own case. I moved out to California and didn't know anyone. Now, eight years later, here I am president of my own soon-to-be $20 million company." That company, Software Publishing, has consistently hit the bestseller charts with its *pfs:* line of software packages.

Gibbons always assumed that some day he would start his own company. Most of the people he admired and worked for as a kid ran their own businesses, like his father, a sea captain in Boston. Gibbons started running his own businesses while he was still in school. At the age of 17 he designed a canvas bag for skis; a seasonally unemployed sailmaker ran them up for him in the winter. The profits kept Gibbons in college—and on skis—for a couple of years. At 19 he had a Hobie Cat franchise on Cape Cod.

At the University of Michigan, Gibbons earned first a B.S. and then an M.S. in computer science. He liked the subject because "it is an ordered world, very structured. Programming is easy, it's rote, it's either right or wrong," and Gibbons, by his own admission, "never thought about things in the abstract."

Gibbons describes his life in terms of the disciplines that he's picked up one after the other as needed; first he learned how to run a small business, then he acquired a technical education. After college, he received some practical business experience at a small computer company, Stewart Systems in Massachusetts. When he and his friends/advisors at the Cape Cod Lounge—where he bartended for one summer—decided he needed more business skills, he entered Harvard Business School. No missed chances or sowing of wild oats for him. By age 24, Gibbons was educated, experienced, and eager to "find out how to be number one."

Gibbons lacked, as he tells it, one more "piece of plank": the experience of a large corporation. He joined Hewlett-Packard in California and rapidly shot up the ranks. He claims he became the youngest marketing manager H-P ever had. "I proved to myself that I could be successful in a large corporation. It was like a post-graduate degree in the real world of running a company." Gibbons put that degree to work when he left H-P to set up his own company, Software Publishing.

The idea for the company came to him in 1979 while he was at H-P. Gibbons had been watching the still-infant personal computer industry from the sidelines. He noticed that there was no data base system available for personal computers. Neither Ashton-Tate's *dBase II* nor Lotus's *1-2-3* were out yet. Gibbons took the idea to his bosses at H-P, but they turned him down. He did find two allies, though, among his peers at H-P— Janelle Bedke and John Page.

Bedke, an Air Force brat as a child, always liked math.

But, she bristles, "I wasn't a nerd. I was a normal child." She earned a B.A. degree in math and computer science at the University of Utah. When she joined H-P in 1969, she was their only woman programmer. Later she spent three years in management there.

Bedke describes Englishman John Page as "the philosopher. He's the one with the ideas. He makes order out of chaos." During the eight years Page worked as a research designer at H-P, he wrote the data base system for the H-P 3000 minicomputer. Now vice president of software development at SPC, Page designed the company's original products. He told *InfoWorld,* "I aimed the software at the guy sitting next to me on the plane who says, 'Oh, you're in computers, I don't know anything about them.'"

Gibbons, Bedke, and Page stuck to their original concept of simple, uncomplicated, and inexpensively priced software, "without a lot of bells and whistles." Bedke told us, "We apply the 80/20 rule: 20 percent of the features are used 80 percent of the time." SPC would cut out the 80 percent of the features that are rarely used and would charge about $150 per package—one-half to one-third of the price of many competitive programs.

During that first year, Bedke set up the SPC "office" in her Atherton garage. "One of the first things I did that first year as chief cook and bottle washer was act as technical liaison between Apple Computer and John Page," Janelle says. She wrote the manual for *pfs:file* while Page worked nights and weekends perfecting the data base system for the Apple II. He and Gibbons continued to work days at H-P. Gibbons would come by the garage nights, and he gave Bedke half of his H-P paychecks. That, plus his life savings (about $50,000), kept her and the company going.

By September 1980, *pfs:file* was ready. Bedke sent announcements to Apple dealers around the country. She remembers, "the phone started to ring, packages started to go out. UPS would stop at my door and we'd load it up with packages." Within six months Page and Gibbons felt secure enough to quit their jobs at H-P. The three decided that "we didn't want to be a mom-and-pop shop—a garage operation." So they met with well-known venture capitalist Jack Melchor, who rounded up a quarter of a million dollars from Les Hogan of Fairchild, Bob Noyce of Intel, Bob Maxfield and Ken Oshman of Rolm, and attorney John Friedrich. In 1982, they raised another $1 million in venture capital.

Bedke, Gibbons and Page retain over 50 percent of the company, each holding an equal share. Why? "How do you decide which of the three [talents] is more important?" Bedke asks. "We decided they were all equally important."

SPC has introduced a best-selling software program every year since its founding in 1980. The four programs, *pfs:report, pfs:graph, pfs:write,* and *pfs:plan,* all give their user less than ten options to choose from. The SPC strategy is to quell user panic by using the "principle of least astonishment." Avoiding the kind of high-priced, big menu, and integrated software of Lotus *(Symphony)* and Ashton-Tate *(Framework),* SPC has stayed with its original market plan of easy-to-use, low-priced software.

Four of SPC's *pfs:* packages have made the various "top-ten" lists of best-selling software. During 1983 and 1984 *pfs:file* sold over 130,000 copies, second only to *dBase II* among data base programs. Radio Shack carries *pfs:file* and *pfs:report* in Software Publishing's own packaging rather than Radio Shack repackaging; SPC's products are the only software so honored. IBM recently struck a deal with SPC in the summer of 1984 to market *pfs:* software under the IBM label.

When we talked to Fred Gibbons at SPC's leased offices, we met with him in a cubicle that was identical to every other employee's work space. He was busy at his IBM PC when we entered. "There's no status in the company," he claimed. "I don't have a secretary. Everybody has vocational [mundane work that has to be done] work, even me." He stresses the years of management experience he and his partners accumulated at H-P, and the H-P influence is clearly evident in the egalitarian working conditions and close-knit feelings that prevail at SPC.

The unforeseen risks that Gibbons eschews as a businessman turn up in his recreation. Gibbons, a tanned, fit man with preppy good looks, is every inch the outdoorsman he appears to be. He devotes three weekends a month to the "physical stress of individual sports like windsurfing, skiing, and flying. If I had another career, I'd have been a DC-3 pilot in East Africa." Aside from sports, Gibbons's personal life is not flashy. He lives in the same house in Palo Alto that he moved into when he came out from the East Coast in 1975. He drives the same car he received as a high school graduation gift, a '68 Mustang that now has 200,000 miles on it.

David Gordon

"He who dies with the most toys, wins"

▶ **BEST-KNOWN VENTURE:** Datamost

OTHER VENTURES: Programma International

BORN: 1943

RAISED: Brooklyn, New York

FATHER'S OCCUPATION: A mechanic in the garment industry and personnel officer

FIRST DOLLAR EARNED: As a Hollywood bean-counter

SCHOOLING: M.A., accounting, California State University at Los Angeles

ORIGINAL FINANCING: Family loans and savings

FAMILY: Married; two sons

PERSONAL TRANSPORTATION: Corvette

DATAMOST INC.: Publishers of best-selling computer games and books.

▶ **BEST-KNOWN PRODUCTS:** *Snack Attack, Cosmic Tunnels, Super Bunny, Market Mogul,* and *Ankh* computer games; *Using 6502 Assembly Language* and *Kids and the Apple* books

YEAR FOUNDED: 1981

EMPLOYEES: 60

HEADQUARTERS: Chatsworth, California

SALES: $1 million a month

OWNERSHIP: Private

D atamost's founder, David Gordon, hardly fits the image of the slick, cool, corporate type. He weighs in at 300 pounds (one of his first software hits was called *Snack Attack*) and reports cheerfully, "I've been fat all my life." He has a passion for expensive jewelry and sports a pinkie ring, gold bracelet, and a $15,000 gold Piaget wristwatch (definitely *not* digital).

As we followed him through the crowd at the West Coast Computer Faire, he stopped every few feet to greet yet another friend in the loud tones of his native Brooklyn. Either Gordon is the most inspired glad-hander in the computer business or he's an incredible extrovert with a phenomenal memory for names and faces. Whichever one he is (and we'd vote for the latter), he's no mousey accountant—despite the 16 years he worked as one.

What would lead a man who's firmly entrenched in one of the most cautious of professions—accounting—into the make-it-or-break-it world of computer entrepreneurs? In David Gordon's case, it was his unbridled passion for his latest hobby—his hobby in 1977 was his Apple II computer.

When this man becomes obsessed, he goes hog-wild. As a bowling fanatic, he bowled in three leagues. Four weeks after meeting and falling in love with Arlene at a B'nai B'rith youth party, he married her. He's still married to her 17 years later. He calls himself a "pack rat" who loves to collect things. He owns between 5,000 and 7,000 record albums of all kinds of music.

Gordon is a self-proclaimed "gizmo freak." His old Corvette is laden with every imaginable doo-hickey. Computers are made to order for a man who believes, "He who dies with the most toys wins." He encourages that attitude in his two teen-aged sons who, while we spoke with Gordon, were busily exchanging Datamost games to get other computer games.

Gordon was a teenager himself when his father, a garment industry mechanic turned personnel officer, moved his family from Brooklyn to Los Angeles. At Cal State Los Angeles, Gordon earned an M.A. in accounting—it was the one major that had no language requirement. In 1964, Big Eight accounting firms would not hire Jews (according to Gordon) so he worked for entertainment companies like Warner, Gulf + Western, and Paramount. "I think I had seventeen jobs in thirteen years," Gordon laughs.

One of Gordon's biggest thrills came when he met Fess Parker, the actor who played Daniel Boone on TV. "That, to me, was the dream of all dreams," Gordon enthuses. You believe him because he seems so sincerely moved.

It was perhaps predictable what would happen when Gordon got his hands on his first personal computer in 1977. Gordon reacted much like many other early buyers of the machine—only more so. David Hunter of *Softalk* explained, "His enormous appetite for software drove him to user-group meetings, software stores, and the homes of fellow Apple owners. A hustler, a trader, a Brooklyn-turned-L.A.-bum, Gordon copied and traded software as if they were bubble-gum cards."

Before long Gordon was spending all his spare time tracking down Apple software. Continuing to work as an accountant didn't make any sense. Gordon kept looking around to find a way to make money pursuing his hobby. In 1978, Gordon quit his job as an accountant and founded Programma International, along with a man named Mel Norell. Programma sold hundreds of different programs, mostly on cassette tape. And it was very successful partly because Gordon was so well-known in the relatively small personal computer industry of the late '60s.

David Gordon repeatedly insists that he's in the computer business "to make money and have fun. We always have fun. When it stops being fun, I'm gone." After two years of running Programma, it stopped making money and it stopped being fun, but Gordon didn't get out, he was thrown out.

He explains, "We grew too fast and we were bickering too much, which forced us to sell the business to Hayden." He doesn't mention that many of the games they offered were of poor quality and prompted many returns. As *Softalk* reported: "Gordon's enthusiasm got the better of him and many of the programs he picked up for Programma were often embarrassingly inadequate—riddled with bugs or just plain crude." Hayden ousted Gordon soon after they bought Programma. Hayden eventually dumped Programma completely.

Gordon swallowed the bitter pill of Programma's failure and tried again—this time on a more modest scale. In the fall of 1981, Gordon, his wife Arlene, brother Allan (who now runs his own company, Overbyte), and sister-in-law Ina started Datamost in Gordon's living room with $10,000. In its first year of operation Datamost scored big hits with two computer games, *Snack Attack* and *Aztec*, and a technical book, *Using 6502 Assembly Language*. That first year they released dozens more games and titles, including the best-selling *Kids and the Apple* (and other computers) series by Ed Carlson. Sales grew to $1 million a month. Gordon replaced his family ("You shouldn't work with your relatives. It's bad.") and some of his "hobbyist" employees with a crack management team. In keeping with its founder's flamboyant style, the company's booth at the Softcon trade show in New Orleans in early 1984 featured several leggy young women in Judy Garland-style top hats and tails handing out advertising brochures.

There were rumors of trouble in Gordon's paradise when we met with him in March 1984. He admitted they had to lay off 20 people in a cutback on software. He remembered the painful lesson learned at Programma. "I can build the company into failure, just overexpanding," Gordon conceded. Even though he had to cut Datamost's staff back to 60 people, he included the survivors in a stock plan.

Datamost's catalogs trumpet: "We're the guys with the rubber wallpaper in our conference room. The street legal loonies." Gordon keeps talking fun, but this time around he's proceeding with caution. In late June 1984, Datamost asked its creditors for a 45-day grace period in paying off its debts.

In its new 43,000-square-foot facility in Southern California, Datamost handles all aspects of production, including artwork and typesetting. They can deliver a book from manuscript to retail shelf in a staggering six to eight weeks.

David Gordon had three goals in life: (1) to hire a tax accountant to do his taxes (accomplished); (2) to buy a fancy wristwatch (also accomplished); and (3) to make a round-the-world trip without touching his principal (not yet accomplished). He says when questioned about the changes in his material success, "At least I can buy fancier jewelry now."

Gordon, who sees himself at 40 as the "typical consumer," leaves us with his observations about himself as the typical entrepreneur: "Working seven-day weeks and twelve-hour days, always pushing myself, always spending more than I earned no matter what I earned. I think you'll find that a trait of most entrepreneurs. Doing things emotionally. Oh, another thing. Entrepreneurs like to open their own mail."

THE GOLD RUSH ALMANAC

Ownership Preferences

37 lead privately held companies.

17 have taken their companies public.

7 lead merged subsidiaries of larger firms.

Age at Founding

20	Under 30
30	30 to 39
14	40 to 49
1	Over 50

Year Founded

7	Before 1970
14	1970 to 1975
30	1976 to 1980
10	Since 1981

Trip Hawkins

"My view of learning has always been that play is an important way to learn"

▶ **BEST-KNOWN VENTURE:** Electronic Arts

OTHER VENTURES: The Accu-Stat Game Company, Strategic Simulations Inc.

BORN: 1953

PARENTS' OCCUPATIONS: Father—works in the electronics industry; mother—has a Ph.D. in American history

FIRST DOLLAR EARNED: Designing and marketing a football simulation board game

SCHOOLING: B.A., strategy and applied game theory, Harvard University; M.B.A., Stanford University

ORIGINAL FINANCING: Several hundred thousand dollars from the sale of Apple Computer stock

PERSONAL NET WORTH: $7.5 million in Apple stock (1980)

FAMILY: Married; "Big Brother" to an 11-year-old Korean boy

PERSONAL TRANSPORTATION: Mercedes coupe convertible

ELECTRONIC ARTS: Markets unique, award-winning games while promoting "software artists" with Hollywood flash.

▶ **BEST-KNOWN PRODUCTS:** *Archon, Pinball Construction Set, M.U.L.E., Hard Hat Mack, Music Construction Set, Dr. J and Larry Bird Go One-On-One*

YEAR FOUNDED: 1982

EMPLOYEES: 65

HEADQUARTERS: San Mateo, California

OWNERSHIP: Private

Trip Hawkins believes that to start a company, you must have a big idea. He thinks Electronic Arts has such an idea. While most computer companies treat software programmers much like engineers or other technical personnel, Hawkins puts them on a pedestal and calls them "artists." He sees Electronic Arts as being similar to a record company or book publisher, and woos his "electronic artists" with large advances and promises of stardom. Electronic Arts games feature the software artist's name and picture prominently displayed on glossy, full-color record album-like covers. Tours and publicity for the artist aim for the sort of promotion usually reserved for rock groups.

Hawkins came up with his big idea while working at Apple Computer. Frustrated by a two-year delay in introducing a new computer, Hawkins began to realize what was causing the problem: The software programmers could not invent on a schedule. "They had a hard time coming to work and living in the same little cubicle as everybody else and getting the same paychecks and not getting treated like the special people they are," he remembers. A brainstorm hit him: "These software artists need a vehicle for getting their products commercially successful." And Hawkins could be their vehicle.

Hawkins talks about his artists and Electronic Arts in an odd mixture of business jargon, pop psychology, show-biz lingo, and the philosophy of John Dewey. He describes Electronic Arts' products with such words as "simple, hot, deep, emotional, rich, social, and artistic." Hawkins sees Electronic Arts' games as educational because of John Dewey's dictum that we learn best by doing. Hawkins interprets that as also meaning "playing is an important way to learn."

At no point does Hawkins falter when talking about these varied subjects. Combined with his boyish good looks, Hawkins's easy fluency and understated self-assurance make him seem like a perfect candidate for a TV reporter. We talked with him before he was to address several hundred people at a computer conference gathering. Just prior to his scheduled talk, he was told he was expected to speak for 45 minutes. He laughed, saying he had understood he was only to speak for 15 minutes. "No problem," he said. He pulled a piece of paper out of his jacket, jotted down a few more notes, and returned to our interview without evidence of further concern. His subsequent 45-minute speech sounded as if it were written out well in advance.

As a boy in Southern California, Hawkins always liked games. Sports, board games, dice, cards, fantasy games—any game with competition. A game became the product of his first business, Accu-Stat, which he started at age 19 while a freshman at Harvard. He marketed his football strategy game with $5,000 that he borrowed from his father, a sales and marketing executive in electronics. He sold a few hundred games through the mail—enough to realize that he loved being an entrepreneur.

Although neither of his parents were entrepreneurs, both were well-educated (his father at Dartmouth, his mother at Wheaton), and believed in self-reliance. Hawkins remembers that in high school he had to pay his father 10 cents a mile when he used the family car.

At Harvard, Hawkins discovered computers and talked the administration into creating a special field of study for him—Strategy and Applied Game Theory. For his senior thesis Hawkins built a computer simulation of World War III to illustrate how easily we could blunder into another war. He graduated *magna cum laude* and won two prestigious grants from Harvard and the Kennedy School of Government for his work.

Always a highly organized fellow, Hawkins sat down during the summer after his junior year in college to map out his future. He was determined to be running his own company by 1982—before he turned 30. He even said it would be a software company. His summer job that year was with a big computer software company called Systems Development Corporation.

The first step was to learn more about business. So, after graduation in 1976, Hawkins moved back to California to go to Stanford Business School. He got his first job while at Stanford by volunteering to do market research for Fairchild (for which he arranged to get college credit at Stanford). His next intern job was with Creative Strategies International, which hired him to write and publish forecasts on the then brand-new personal computer industry.

Hawkins could not have had a more fortuitous assignment. His conclusion, based on his extensive research, was that Radio Shack would be the sales leader in the field in 1978. When the report was published, he got two irate phone calls— one from Steve Jobs, the other from Mike Markkula, the founder and president, respectively, of Apple Computer. They insisted that Hawkins was wrong. But the cool, unflappable Hawkins stuck to his guns and impressed Apple's honchos enough that they offered him a job. Hawkins's prediction later proved correct.

Hawkins was the first M.B.A. hired by Apple. When he started work there, the company had only 50 employees and about $4 million in business. Hawkins set up the market research department and co-wrote the original proposal for Lisa with Steve Jobs. The one-half of one percent Apple stock Hawkins had turned out to be worth $7.5 million. "By the time I left Apple, working was not a financial issue. It was a personal love," Hawkins says.

After two years at Apple, Hawkins grew frustrated with the burgeoning size of the company—and besides, the 1982 deadline for starting his own company was drawing nearer. He had been on the board of an "esoteric computer game company," Strategic Simulations Inc., for two years, but that wasn't the big idea for a company that he was looking for.

In 1982, with a couple of hundred thousand dollars of his own money, Hawkins started Electronic Arts in San Mateo, California. In just the first year, Hawkins paid out $350,000 in advances to his artists. He's since raised $5 million more in venture capital. Of the 65 employees, 50 work in such areas as the talent department, where six producers do everything from funding new software artists to holding hands of touchy, established artists, to producing the packaging and promotion.

Apparently, the rock-star treatment and flashy packaging is working. Electronic Arts' games for Atari and Apple, such as *Music Construction Set* (written by 16-year-old Will Harvey), *Hard Hat Mack*, *M.U.L.E.*, and *Archon* receive good reviews and are consistently in the *Software Merchandising* top 20 best-sellers. Many of those $40 games are bought by teenage boys, the same group that buys record albums.

One of Hawkins's best-selling artists is Bill Budge, a 30-year-old programmer who worked with Hawkins on the Lisa computer at Apple. Budge wrote the *Pinball Construction Set* game for Electronic Arts. He lives in a quarter-million-dollar house in Piedmont, California, that is strewn with software, a childhood erector set, and science-fiction books. Budge watches reruns of "Leave it to Beaver" before he leaves for work in the morning. Electronic Arts captured him with a $250,000 package of stock, advances, and royalties. Budge is number one in a stable of prima donnas—"the really talented software people should be put on a pedestal because they are extremely unusual," according to Hawkins.

Hawkins no longer sees himself as a "worker bee." Though he puts in 60- to 65-hour weeks, there is no working on weekends. He uses that time to replenish the "psychic energy that's drained," and to be with his new wife at their new house in well-to-do Hillsborough, California. Hawkins drives a Mercedes coupe convertible equipped with a phone, but he says he's not a materialist. "I still don't even own a video tape recorder," he points out. The most important use of money, he finds, is to "buy back my time."

Hawkins spends some of his time—a day once every week or two—with an 11-year-old Korean boy named David. Hawkins has done this as a member of Big Brothers of America since 1980.

James Johnson

"This field is boring. Where else do people get excited about integrated spreadsheets? My main goal is not to be bored"

▶ **BEST-KNOWN VENTURE:** Human Edge Software

OTHER VENTURE: Psych Systems (automated psychological testing systems)

BORN: 1940

RAISED: Perry, Iowa

FATHER'S OCCUPATION: Personnel manager for the Milwaukee Road

SCHOOLING: B.A., philosophy, University of Washington; Ph.D., clinical psychology, University of Minnesota

ORIGINAL FINANCING: $600,000 from his partner

PERSONAL NET WORTH: Became a millionaire from the sale of Psych Systems

HOME: Atherton, California

FAMILY: Divorced; remarried; three children

PERSONAL TRANSPORTATION: Jaguar XJ12C, Audi 5000S

⊞ HUMAN EDGE

HUMAN EDGE SOFTWARE CORPORATION: First in the field of "psych-out software."

▶ **BEST-KNOWN PRODUCTS:** *The Sales Edge, The Negotiation Edge, The Management Edge*

YEAR FOUNDED: 1983

EMPLOYEES: 25

HEADQUARTERS: Palo Alto, California

SALES: $900,000 (December 1983 through August 1984)

OWNERSHIP: Private; James Johnson and Ronald Dozoretz, his silent partner, each own 50 percent

James Johnson not only identifies and analyzes life's little games, he masters them. He played student until he received a Ph.D. His turn at salesman landed him a $10-million order his first sale. As a professor, Johnson wrote over 100 papers in clinical psychology. He co-founded, and later sold, a successful business in his budding entrepreneur phase. Now that Johnson is the founder and president of Human Edge, he seems to be playing for keeps.

Johnson, at age 44 in 1984, reflected a little of each phase he'd gone through. He sported the three-piece suit, white shirt, and tie of his IBM days. Human Edge employees remark on his professorial air. The academician is still evident. When we interviewed Johnson, he charted out his theories on the entrepreneurial character on a blackboard.

The entrepreneur part of Johnson goes back a long way, to his hometown of Perry, Iowa. Because Johnson's father worked for the Milwaukee Road, the family received free train passes. Johnson started to travel alone by train in the third or fourth grade. During the summers he'd ride to South Dakota to buy firecrackers, then resell them in Iowa where they were illegal. Johnson also sold candy, seeds, and comic books door-to-door as a boy. His first major business in the seventh grade—a mimeographed newspaper that sold in the local grocery store—was eventually banned at school for its satirical comments on teachers and students.

His early taste for travel by land led to a desire for travel by sea. After a short stint at the Merchant Marine Academy in New York, Johnson sailed the U.S. Lines in the Far East for six months. He later wound up at the University of Washington at Seattle, because it was the only school he could find that would accept his academy credits for courses like knot-tying and sail-making.

Johnson pointed out to us that "what you do in life is determined by chance," an idea only partly borne out by his own history. It was boredom that pushed him out of his chosen major, psychology ("they were just into rats"), and into philosophy ("you get to do debates in class"). After graduation, he received a fellowship for graduate study at the University of California at Berkeley.

Johnson recalled, "At that point [1964] we had the Kennedy thing, the beginning of the Vietnam War, the Free Speech Movement [leader Mario Savio was also in the philosophy department]. I was never arrested at demonstrations. I just became involved in the whole thing, became a drop out."

The man who is now a multimillionaire and resides in the superposh Bay Area suburb of Atherton spent his Berkeley years "starving a lot" in the black section of Albany, a working-class town. He had a baby daughter and a wife who worked in a department store. Johnson himself could no longer find the retail jobs he had previously worked because he looked like a hippie. "So I cleaned up and got a job selling Jell-O for General Foods. I got a free car and food I could trade."

A new offer jelled on a family visit to the Midwest. His sister in Des Moines suggested he apply for a job selling computers for IBM. He got the job and moved to Des Moines, where he learned to program and later became a data processing salesman. Even though Johnson brought in a $10-million order as his first sale, he didn't like the corporate life. "The fact that I would occasionally go march in a peace parade on weekends got me into trouble periodically. They say they like 'wild ducks,' but they don't necessarily promote 'wild ducks.' I wanted to go back to school. I believed in a Walt Disney approach to academics—that you get a Ph.D., become a professor, get tweed jackets with arm patches, smoke a pipe, and life would be wonderful."

After two years at IBM, Johnson amassed $200,000 from sales commissions and stock trading. He quit his job and entered the clinical psychology department at the University of Minnesota in 1968. His large income from his stock portfolio supported two new cars and a cabin cruiser on the Mississippi River while he went to school. "I was the radical at IBM, but on the university campus, a capitalist."

Not for long. Johnson lost his money in the stock market crash that year, but stuck it out at school. And he found a way to integrate his previous careers: "I got interested in the whole area of computerized interpretation of psychological tests. You have a computer background. You know how to program. You have a logic background from your old philosophy days. It makes perfect sense to computerize it."

As a professor—first at the University of Utah, then at Eastern Virginia Medical School, and finally at the Illinois Institute of Technology—Johnson went beyond the Walt Disney image of a professor. He mastered grant writing and learned that "if you want to do something in the academic world, you hit the road giving papers, presenting papers, getting papers accepted in the *New York Times*. It was 1974, but Johnson still came up against the "touchy-feely '60s" while he tried to push "dehumanizing" computers for psychological testing.

"Being an innovator, an entrepreneur, is not popular, period." Johnson did research by day and 40 hours of private practice in psychotherapy by night. Johnson wanted out of small-time academia and he wanted to market his idea of testing. "I found out the rules," he recalls, and he played by them to start a new graduate school in professional psychology at Eastern Virginia Medical School and a new company, Psych Systems. He stopped doing psychotherapy, but he admits, "my house was in hock as well as everything I owned. I couldn't see out of the cellar except that I couldn't quit either because if you quit you're really in trouble. In the process of my working all the time, in 1979 I had my entrepreneurial ritual divorce. All entrepreneurs have divorces."

Johnson believes that most psychologists end up in therapy because of the pressure. "There is no other thing that can give you such brain-out," he says. As the professor in Johnson waned, the entrepreneur took over. The idea of Psych Systems—selling computerized diagnostic systems to the medical community—took off slowly, but in 1982 his firm made an initial public offering for $6 million.

Johnson had a new idea, though. And he acts on ideas. "When you think of the good ideas you have, you're lucky if you have one in a lifetime." The idea was to gather information about another person, feed that into a computer with information about yourself, and come out with an interpretation of how the two of you will interact. Johnson decided to gamble on his idea and devote himself solely to making it work. "I had spent my whole life doing two or three different things at the same time and I was really tired of it. I didn't need to set it up halfway and be pissed off at the fact that I am only a small part." (He owned only 10 percent of Psych Systems.)

With $600,000 from Virginia professor Ronald Dozoretz, Johnson founded Human Edge Software in 1983. Although he and Dozoretz each own half the company, Johnson has only seen him four times since the two "cut the deal in five minutes" at a meeting in Miami in 1982.

Armed with research into operations research, artificial intelligence, decision theory, and computer technology, Human Edge came out with three "expert systems," which means a condensation of an expert's knowledge into easily understood terms. *The Sales Edge* helps a salesman "sell dirty," as Human Edge's ads proclaim, by telling him how to adjust his personality and style to each customer. *The Negotiation Edge* and *The Management Edge* both detail strategies and plans of attack for the user.

Last year the *Financial Times* of London conducted a simulated test using *The Sales Edge*. It answered the 20 minutes of personality questions the computer asked using the characters of Ronald Reagan and Margaret Thatcher. If Thatcher wanted to sell Reagan her plan on NATO spending, she should know that, according to *The Sales Edge* program, "R.R. is inclined to seek the limelight, to perform for others. Appeal to R.R. with flattery and by acknowledging his accomplishments." The *Times* concluded that if Reagan has an "edge—perhaps Thatcher should too."

Other observers are not so sure. Detractors call the $250 programs "manipulative software," "Orwellian," and no substitute for personal perception. Perhaps his own experience with the "entrepreneurial ritual divorce" provided the spark behind an upcoming Human Edge program, *The Life Strategy,* that is supposed to do everything from renewing a marriage to encouraging slow-learning children. However the programs are finally received, Human Edge has the field of "psych-out software" all to itself.

Johnson likes it that way. He sees his expert systems as truly unique. "The computer industry is the disseminator of clichés," he insists. "This field is boring. Where else do people get so excited about integrated spreadsheets? My main goal is not to be bored. I'm not interested in clone products, I'd feel like a crook." Johnson observes that Henry Ford didn't copy anyone, and that the history of entrepreneurs is not a history of "me-toos."

Although Johnson is a millionaire, he claims, "I honestly care so little about money that I pay my taxes." Still, he drives a Jaguar to and from his Atherton home and his Palo Alto office.

Mitch Kapor

"It's a balancing act between people and profits"

▶ **BEST-KNOWN VENTURE:** Lotus Development

BORN: 1950

RAISED: Freeport Long Island, New York

FATHER'S OCCUPATION: Owner of a cardboard-box factory

FIRST DOLLAR EARNED: Rock 'n' roll disc jockey

SCHOOLING: B.A., psychology, Yale University; "three-quarters of a master's degree," Massachusetts Institute of Technology's Sloan School of Management

ORIGINAL FINANCING: Venture capitalists Ben Rosen and L.J. Sevin

PERSONAL NET WORTH: Over $5 million in cash and more than $50 million in stock at Lotus's initial public offering

HOME: Outside of Harvard Square, Cambridge, Massachusetts

FAMILY: Divorced; remarried to a psychiatrist

PERSONAL TRANSPORTATION: Audi 5000

▛▞ Lotus

LOTUS DEVELOPMENT CORPORATION: Phenomenal rise, in one year, from nowhere to manufacturer of the best-selling business software.

▶ **BEST-KNOWN PRODUCTS:** *Lotus 1-2-3, Symphony*

YEAR FOUNDED: 1982

EMPLOYEES: 600

HEADQUARTERS: Cambridge, Massachusetts

SALES: $53 million (1983)

PROFITS: $14 million (1983)

OWNERSHIP: Public (October 1983); Kapor owns 18 percent

Mitch Kapor's best-selling software program— *Lotus 1-2-3*—put the words "integrated package" on everybody's lips in 1983. Kapor himself has had to work hard to integrate the package of his own personality. It's no wonder. In just a decade, Mitch Kapor has gone from unemployed Transcendental Meditation teacher and sometime rock radio disc jockey to multimillionaire head of the hottest software company in the personal computer business. Or, as *Business Week* put it in a feature article on the baby boom generation: "The thirty-three-year-old Kapor is an extreme example of baby boomers who have turned from protest to profits."

One wouldn't expect the career path of such a person to be like an arrow speeding to its target. Mitch Kapor wandered widely. At Freeport High School on Long Island, he was sharp in math but shied away from it. At Yale he studied psychology and moonlighted as a disc jockey. It was the turbulent period of the late '60s and early '70s. He played the Byrds and the Dead, the Fugs and the Mothers. He supported radical political groups and started doing Transcendental Meditation. When he finished his B.A., instead of making a beeline for graduate school, he became a full-time disc jockey for a radio station in Hartford, Connecticut.

By 1973 Kapor was in Boston, a TM teacher and unemployed. Serendipitously he wandered into a job as an applications programmer for a consulting company. His task was to turn the data from market research questionnaires into reports for big companies like Levi Strauss and Polaroid. What did he learn from that first exposure? "I really learned that I hated IBM mainframes, but I was still attracted to the mystique of systems programming. Also, I learned to program in BASIC."

The job was boring, and Mitch taught piano in his spare time. He was unhappy. His marriage broke up. He flew to Maharishi International University in Iowa and meditated a lot. Then he went to the world capital of TM, in Switzerland, for an "enlightenment-or-bust" course. After six months, he was through with organized meditation. He'd noticed that as he became more and more committed to matters transcendent, his earthly life became more and more miserable. He withdrew from the Maharishi scene, which he now describes tersely, "There's less there than meets the eye."

Continuing on his errant pathway, Kapor went for a master's degree in counseling psychology, had a brief stint as a hospital counselor, and withdrew after concluding that he "could make a tremendous contribution to the field of human services by getting out of it."

His next idea was to become an academic. Around 1978, while waiting to get into a doctoral program in psychology, Mitch started to fool around with microcomputers. He bought a Radio Shack TRS-80 Model I, then an Apple II, and soon he was reading all the magazines and "hanging out in the one computer store on the East Coast." Short on funds, he started helping people set up computer programs for their personal needs. His first client was an ophthamologist who wanted to track the progress of cataract patients. Mitch never went for his Ph.D.

An interviewer for *Softalk* notes that Mitch Kapor seems like a good guy, the sort of guy you'd like to be friends with. It was this friendly quality, no doubt, that prompted him to do some free work for a grad student at MIT. Mitch was interested in the student's problem, wrote a program that worked, then mused, "I bet people would pay money for this." With some help from Dr. Eric Rosenfeld of MIT, Mitch wrote *Tiny Troll*, which did line charts, statistics, multiple regressions, and editing. Yes, an integrated software package.

Kapor's speed was picking up. At an early meeting of the first Apple user group on the East Coast, he met Bob Frankston, one of the two creators of *VisiCalc*. Frankston connected him with the people at VisiCorp (then called Personal Software), with whom Kapor signed a contract to develop two new programs based on *Tiny Troll*. Introduced in 1981, *VisiPlot* and *VisiTrend* brought him royalties of half a million dollars in six months. Because Kapor's 1979 contract gave him 33 percent of sales (today the norm is 10 to 15 percent), VisiCorp bought him out in 1982 for $1.5 million.

Now Kapor was moving more like an arrow. Not pausing to notice if he was rich, eager to create more products, and unwilling to leave the publishing and marketing to others, he started Lotus Development. At that point he had already teamed up with Jonathan Sachs, who was a *real* programmer (unlike himself, a "BASIC hacker"). Kapor designed, Sachs wrote; they dreamed and brainstormed together about creating a powerful electronic spreadsheet with data processing and graphics functions.

When IBM announced its PC in August of 1981, Kapor and Sachs knew what to do. They correctly presumed that the PC, with its 16-bit processor, was the wave of the near future. All the software on the market was geared to eight-bit processors. By modeling their product to the more powerful PC, Kapor and Sachs figured they could grab an incalculable lead over potential competition.

But wait, there's another chapter to the story. It's called "money." Kapor needed lots of it to launch his product. It so happened that Ben Rosen, the high-tech venture capitalist, had purchased *Tiny Troll* for his own use. Kapor had spoken with him on the phone when Rosen needed help with the program. Now it was Kapor's hour of need and he approached

Rosen with a brief summary of his business plan. Six weeks later Rosen and his partner, L.J. Sevin, took Kapor to dinner and over salad offered him a million dollars. Mitch dropped his fork. He soon picked it up again and was able to stand the shock some months later when a second round of investors (including Sevin and Rosen) gave him $3.7 million more.

That shining triple lotus was placed before the public at the Fall COMDEX 1982, a major industry convention. Lotus spent most of the venture capital on an unprecedented advertising blitz for a single software product. Full-page ads appeared in major newspapers and magazines across the country. *Lotus 1-2-3* reached the top of the best-selling software charts by April and 60,000 copies were delivered by July. In October, a mere 18 months after founding, Lotus sold its stock to the public for the first time. Mitch Kapor walked away from the stock sale $5.4 million richer. That's in cash. The shares he held on to were worth over $50 million. The investors didn't do badly either. The venture capitalists saw their investments of about $5 million mushroom to more than $100 million in Lotus stock at the time of the public stock offering.

Kapor is getting into his wealth slowly. "For many years I made nothing, so it's taken some years to feel comfortable about spending my salary. I've never wanted a Mercedes. And how much can you spend on a stereo? Or on a vacation, even if you fly first class?" He let himself pay $100,000 extra for a house just to get a good location, near Harvard Square. He is remarried to a psychiatrist, Dr. Ellen Poss. There's a housekeeper three days a week, "because my wife and I both hate housework." And there's some art collecting—not investment in old masters, but support of young artists to help them get a break.

There's also glory. While we were interviewing Kapor for this book, the phone rang. It was the young founder of Apple, one of the emperors of the computer world. After talking to him, Kapor remarked, "It's nice that Steve Jobs, who is one of my heroes, who is like God, wants to see *me*. It's great."

Just as Mitch Kapor's mathematical talent didn't get lost in the years devoted to psychology and meditation, his interest in consciousness continues to pervade his life as a software star.

He attributes part of Lotus's success to his gut-level insight into the user's state of mind. Comparing himself to Bill Gates, "a technical guru of the first order," Kapor says he's more like a typical user, "smart but lazy," not wanting to get into a battle of personalities with the machine. Lotus programs are designed to be powerful but lazy. At the same time, Kapor likes to be out front in terms of technology. He explained to *Industry Week* that as a toddler his mother couldn't keep him in the crib: "I was always trying to get out and wander around and see what was going on. I like being just inside the cutting edge."

Kapor and his co-workers chose musical names for their second product—*Symphony* for the program, Composer for the command language—because metaphors "let you make emotional connections with people rather than technical, analytical, rational ones; if you want to communicate, it's good to have emotional connections." He describes his process of working with Jonathan Sachs in terms of music and lyrics, concepts and architecture.

The Lotus organization also reflects Kapor's interest in emotions and relationships. He doesn't like bureaucracy or hypocrisy, and has had "lots of trouble with organizations, feeling that they were bad for people." And he has seriously tried to adhere to many of the ideals of the '60s and early '70s. He told us that he is trying to make Lotus relatively "soft," open, and responsive, a place where there are many channels of communication, both formal and informal, and where consensus and collaboration are valued. He holds weekly meetings attended by all the company's 500-plus employees, and he has gone out of his way to hire women and minorities. And he told *Business Week*: "It's possible to make money and at the same time to have a company where people are proud to work and can be happy. On the other hand," he emphasizes (again recalling his familiarity with early '60s subcultures), "Lotus is not a food co-op." People have real responsibilities and are accountable for making things happen.

When Mitch talks about competitors, he sometimes reveals a more primitive consciousness: "We're killing them in sales! We're blowing them and everybody else out of the water!"

Lotus has taken some flack for being a one-product company. Wall Street pundits grumbled a little about the instability of the enterprise, and they compared the exhilaration of the first investors and stockbrokers to the intoxication of the lotus-eating sailors in *Odyssey* (who were eventually smeared over the dream landscape by boulder-throwing monsters). But Mitch Kapor got his lotus metaphor from the Hindus, not the Greeks. In India, the lotus is a symbol of perfect enlightenment. In the summer of 1984, Lotus introduced *Symphony* amidst a second round of critical applause—and another multimillion-dollar TV advertising campaign launched during prime-time Olympic Games coverage. *Symphony* combines graphics and financial management with word processing and the capacity to receive and transmit data by telephone. Mitch Kapor, looking like a cross between Brahma and an orchestra conductor, is still sitting pretty, wielding his magic baton.

SPIRITUAL PURSUITS

At some time or other, with more or less seriousness, the entrepreneurs involved themselves in these nonmaterial interests:

Epistemology	John Brockman (John Brockman Associates)
John Dewey's philosophy	Trip Hawkins (Electronic Arts)
Eastern mysticism	Steve Jobs (Apple Computer)
Transcendental Meditation	Mitch Kapor (Lotus)
Sikh religion	Sat Tara Singh Khalsa (Kriya System)
Gary Hart's new ideas	Regis McKenna (Regis McKenna P.R.)
est	William Millard (ComputerLand)
Scientology	George Tate (Ashton-Tate)
Intentional community	Jim Warren (West Coast Computer Faire)
Arica Institute (human potential movement)	Camilo Wilson (Lifetree Software)
Tibetan Buddhism/ hypnotism	Ihor Wolosenko (Synapse Software)

Sat Tara Singh Khalsa

"I think my goal is to be an information mogul"

▶ **BEST-KNOWN VENTURE:** Kriya Systems

OTHER VENTURES: Foot Sweaters

BORN: 1953

RAISED: Hamilton, Montana

PARENTS' OCCUPATIONS: Father—owned a hardware store and was a city clerk; mother—managed a hospital office

FIRST DOLLAR EARNED: Radio announcer

SCHOOLING: B.A. and M.A., psychology, University of Chicago

ORIGINAL FINANCING: Profits from Foot Sweaters

PERSONAL NET WORTH: 33⅓ percent of Kriya Systems

FAMILY: Married; lives with his wife and seven other ashram members

PERSONAL TRANSPORTATION: Rolls-Royce, Cessna Skyline airplane

KRIYA

KRIYA SYSTEMS: Developers of educational home software products for the mass market.

▶ **BEST-KNOWN PRODUCTS:** *Typing Tutor II* and *III, Learning Lab*

YEAR FOUNDED: 1982

EMPLOYEES: 9

HEADQUARTERS: Chicago, Illinois

SALES: $1.5 million (1983)

OWNERSHIP: Private; equal partnership of the three founders

H e smiles winningly from the cover of *InfoWorld:* sparkling eyes, even teeth, immaculate white turban and shirt, a big, frizzy red beard, an expression that radiates intelligent good humor. His head tilted lightly on a supporting hand, he looks relaxed in the spotlight.

Sat Tara Singh Khalsa, a convert to the Sikh religion, gets up most mornings at 4:30 for two hours of yoga and meditation. He is something of a religious teacher to the eight people who live in his ashram (spiritual retreat), as well as to a score of others in the Chicago area. But none of this religious discipline gets in the way of his driving a Rolls-Royce, flying his own airplane, or embarking on a national tour in which he is billed as a "software star."

"The Sikh religion encourages success in the world," Khalsa says. His own teacher, an Indian named Yogi Bhajan, is quite pleased with his accomplishments.

Khalsa's company, Kriya Systems (*kriya* is Sanskrit for "completed action"), is proprietor of a few educational programs that teach people to type and read faster. Its most successful product so far, *Typing Tutor II,* sold 250,000 copies in its first year and a half.

But that is not what makes Kriya and Khalsa so news-worthy. The news is that they are at the forefront of a large experiment in the software industry, one that is being conducted not by technological wizards, but by media masters. The experiment is to see whether computer programs can be mass marketed like paperback novels, and whether their authors can be promoted like best-selling book writers, through radio, TV, print media, and personal appearances. This idea, which burst on the software scene in 1983, was, in 1982, a gleam in the eye of literary agent John Brockman.

Sat Tara Singh Khalsa heard about it and gave Brockman a call. Khalsa had read Brockman's books on radical epistemology in the '60s and had a feeling they would get along. They did, but what impressed Brockman most of all was the lack of clutter in Khalsa's office on the 55th floor of posh Lake Point Tower in Chicago. Khalsa's desk had absolutely nothing on it—no computer, no telephone, no pencil, not even a scrap of paper.

Off to Publisher's Row they went with a package of four programs—*Typing Tutor, Learning Lab* (introductory computer literacy), *Letter Invaders* (a *Space Invaders*-type game to improve typing skills), and *Speed Reading Tutor.* The first two had already sold well to Apple and TRS-80 users; the other two were new. All four would be made available for several other micros as well. Brockman and Khalsa modestly proposed that the package should be worth $15 to $20 million in royalties. One big publisher reportedly reacted to the offer "with incredulous laughter." But another one didn't. Simon & Schuster, a division of Gulf + Western, was fully committed to electronic publishing and fishing for the ideal software for their first offering. They wanted something that had wide appeal, a proven track record, and exciting promotional possibilities. Brockman convinced them that *Typing Tutor III*—an updated version with color graphics, interactive features, and a highly photogenic proprietor—was it. In late 1983 they signed a contract for an undisclosed amount. (One newspaper said the advance was over $1 million.) They were willing to disclose, however, their intention to launch an unprecedented promotional campaign featuring Khalsa. The *Wall Street Journal* said he would appear on talk shows "touting the mind-expanding possibilities of combining yoga with learning to type on a computer." Al Reuben, the S&S software division's vice president for sales and distribution, had more details. With *Typing Tutor III* scheduled to reach the market in April 1984, Khalsa would start on an 11-city tour in March: "He should hit most of the major television talk shows and radio programs. He'll also give press interviews, speak with user groups, and autograph packages in retail outlets."

At the time this itinerary was being planned, the nascent celebrity was 30 years old. Up to the age of 20 he had been known as Jim Hefty. He grew up in a small town in Montana, where his father owned a hardware store for a while, then worked till retirement as the city clerk.

As a boy, Jim liked science and public speaking. In junior high school he and his friends fabricated gunpowder, using it to propel homemade rockets. In high school he debated and ran for student body president as a sophomore. This was so unorthodox that the school principal actively campaigned against him. Hefty lost, but recalls with satisfaction that the principal ended up looking like a jerk. At graduation, his classmates voted him most likely to succeed.

Hefty went on to the University of Chicago, where he majored in psychology. Fascinated by a course taught by Erica Fromm on altered states of consciousness, he formed a "mind exploration group" with a couple of friends. They took up hypnosis, various types of radical therapy, Buddhist meditation, and yoga. In 1973, Hefty started going to yoga classes at the home of a university medical doctor who had become a Sikh. The exercises left him feeling higher than he remembered feeling during his earlier experiments with LSD. Soon he was going for daily predawn yoga and meditation sessions at the doctor's house. In January 1974 he met Yogi Bhajan, changed his name, and put on a turban.

After graduation, Khalsa worked at a research institute, studying criminal psychology, and then at a private psychiatric hospital, where he helped treat patients and train therapists. In retrospect, what seems most important is that there, in 1977, he got his first chance to work with a computer—a toggle-switched Altair. He had learned to program in college, but the math department's approach to computers didn't inspire him. The hospital director, knowing he liked the machines, turned him loose to investigate ways of programming a computer to recognize speech. Funds ran out just as Khalsa was arriving at a practical approach to the problem, but he had a great time and learned a lot. Then he went back to school where he used a computer to do research for his master's degree in psychology.

It was then that he got his first taste of entrepreneurship. He was casting about for an enterprise that might support him in graduate school, when a friend returned from a stay in Afghanistan. It was the dead of winter in Chicago, and the friend was wearing some terrific, thick Afghan socks. Soon Khalsa was in the sock business. Calling the product Foot Sweaters, he and his associates sold about 150,000 pairs in the next three years.

"I walked into Bloomingdale's and the men's accessories buyer totally flipped out. He thought they were the greatest things he'd ever seen. They were the most popular item in Bloomingdale's men's accessories department for two years."

Two friends ran the business at home, while a third acted as agent in Afghanistan. Just as Lord & Taylor was about to take on the line, the agent disappeared from the face of the earth. "We never figured out if it was the Russians or bandits." That was the end of Foot Sweaters.

In 1979, Khalsa met Dick Ainsworth, whom he describes as "a wild, crazy guy, one of those brilliant idea people." Ainsworth was working for Image Producers, an ad agency in the process of converting itself to a software company. Soon Khalsa signed on as a programmer. He felt there were organizational problems in the company, and started doing "guerilla management." As time went on he spent less and less time programming, and more and more time managing. His bosses were not enchanted. In 1982 they fired him, then laid off nearly everyone else. Ainsworth, Khalsa, and a woman at Image named Ram Dass (a fellow Sikh) together formed Kriya Systems.

Kriya managed to escape with *Typing Tutor* and a few other

programs designed by Ainsworth. This was possible for two reasons: (1) Image owed Ainsworth a lot of back royalties; and (2) no one but Khalsa, by his own report, recognized what "hot commodities" these programs were. Khalsa hired a specialist law firm—for stiff fees—to deal with Image. He didn't draw any salary from Kriya for six months. He kept busy, though, working with Ainsworth on an enhanced version of *Typing Tutor* and talking to manufacturers about deals to sell the program with their machines. A contract with Epson for rights to *Typing Tutor* and *Learning Lab* provided Kriya's first significant influx of cash ("reliable sources" say Epson paid half a million). Microsoft continued to handle *Typing Tutor*'s retail marketing, as it had done since 1980.

Then came Brockman, whose vision Khalsa shared. Between May 1983, when they started stalking publishers, and November, when the Simon and Schuster deal was sealed, Khalsa passed up new offers from manufacturers in the conviction that the mass market, via media conglomerates, would provide a fabulous new flood of wealth to software makers.

Whether this vision will materialize remains an open question. But surely there will be more differentiation among types of software makers. Kriya is one of a type John Brockman likes to call "software boutiques"—relatively small and engaged only in producing programs. Somebody else publishes their work and (according to the Brockman/Khalsa/S&S strategy) promotes it as a creative achievement for which both the artist and the company should get at least recognition, possibly fame. Sometimes Khalsa says his aim is to make Kriya a household word. But it's clearly Khalsa himself who cuts a figure in the media. He grants it, commenting, "Chrysler is a difficult concept to hold on to, so Lee Iacocca becomes a celebrity."

In the same vein Brockman comments, "You don't go into a store and ask for a Random House novel or a CBS record."

One flaw in this reasoning seems to be that popular novels and record albums cost under $10; Kriya's software is closer to $50. Books and music also provide their readers and listeners with emotional experiences. They excite passions and ignite fantasies. Educational computer programs don't, as a rule, stir the blood.

There were some delays in getting *Typing Tutor III* ready for the market and in launching Sat Tara on his full-scale tour, but, in August 1984, Kriya's offering appeared in stores across the country and on the Softsel *Hot List*.

Khalsa expresses the ambition to be an "information mogul" in the coming age of information-driven culture. At the same time he professes detachment from his worldly achievements. When asked about the relative importance of Kriya's success and his religious practice, he says the business is "miniscule by comparison," little more than "nice gravy." If it it should all disappear, he claims, he wouldn't be terribly upset. Khalsa continues to live in the ashram he heads, some of whose residents also work at his company.

He is also president of the Illinois Chapter of 3HO (Yogi Bhajan's Healthy, Happy, Holy Organization) and is helping to computerize the Sikh group's operations nationwide.

Half expecting another answer about the rewards of yoga and meditation, we asked if there was anything missing from his life.

"Skiing," he replied. "I didn't get out skiing this year."

BIRDS OF A FEATHER

Where They Were Hatched

State	Number
New York	11
California	10
Overseas	9
Pennsylvania	4
Illinois	3
Iowa	3
Massachusetts	3
Michigan	3

Where They Came To Roost

State	Number
California	40
Massachusetts	6
Illinois	2
New York	2
Ohio	2

Gary Kildall

"The biggest change due to the success of the business is that you always have to fight for your time in terms of being a technologist"

▶ **BEST-KNOWN VENTURE:** Digital Research

BORN: 1942

RAISED: Seattle, Washington

FATHER'S OCCUPATION: Merchant marine barge captain and teacher at Kildall's Nautical School (founded by Gary's grandfather)

FIRST DOLLAR EARNED: Taught navigation after high school at his grandfather's school

SCHOOLING: B.S., M.S., and Ph.D., computer science, University of Washington

FAMILY: Separated; one daughter, one son

PERSONAL TRANSPORTATION: PITS biplane, Sea Ray boat, horses, Porsche 914, 1984 Corvette, Rolls-Royce, Star Crown, four-wheel-drive pickup truck, all-terrain three-wheel cycle, motorcycle, two mopeds, jet skis

█◐ DIGITAL RESEARCH™

DIGITAL RESEARCH INC.: Developed and marketed the standard operating system software for eight-bit personal computers.

▶ **BEST-KNOWN PRODUCTS:** CP/M, DR Logo, Pascal/MT, C-BASIC

YEAR FOUNDED: 1976

EMPLOYEES: 665

HEADQUARTERS: Monterey, California

SALES: $44.6 million (1983)

OWNERSHIP: Privately held by Gary Kildall and venture capital groups

At the 1984 West Coast Computer Faire, the good-old-boy network of computer pioneers waxed sentimental about the good-old days of computers. Speaker after speaker got up to congratulate himself and his colleagues for their entrepreneurial spirit and smarts. One computer wizard, however, was not content to rest on his laurels. Gary Kildall, founder and resident genius of Digital Research, blasted his peers out of their nostalgic reverie for the '60s and into the future of the '90s, with a startling presentation about his new pet technology: linking personal computers with videodisk players.

When Kildall, the inventor of the landmark CP/M operating system, comes up with something new, the computer industry listens—and in this case, looks. *Vidlink* connects personal computers, videodisk players, and color TV and adds a huge storage capacity. A single disk can hold the equivalent of 54,000 still-video images, 180 rolls of microfilm, or 10,000 floppy disks of information. *Popular Computing* called *Vidlink* a "daring move" that could, if successful, put Kildall "once more on the threshold of a major industry."

That's just where Kildall likes to be: on the cutting edge of a new technology. If it hadn't been for his thirst for a challenge, he'd still be in his native Seattle, Washington—the third generation to teach navigation at Kildall's Nautical School, which his grandfather founded in 1927. Gary taught at the school after high school, from 1960 to '62.

He soon recognized that navigation was "the old technology." He told us during an interview in his new office complex in Monterey, California, that he thought navigation skills were going to be obsolete because of the new electronics and computers. Gary wanted to go to college "to get a technical education for the future."

Gary had not been a good high school student, preferring to work on cars and gadgets rather than studies. He built an automobile burglar alarm, a machine to practice Morse code via tape recorder, and a flip-flop binary switch. In school he only liked the "mechanical stuff" associated with practical mathematics and engineering. So he studied to be a high school math teacher at the University of Washington while he worked part-time at the navigation school. But in his junior year, two courses in computer programming redirected his future. He even got a job working on the Burroughs 5500 at the computer center. So much for navigation.

Like many another computer whiz, Kildall often saw "the sun rise over the computer center" as he played with the Burroughs at night. Another college computer friend, Dick Hamlet, later started a time-sharing computer company in Seattle where Bill Gates and Paul Allen hung out. These two Seattle teenagers later set up Microsoft, arch rival to Kildall's Digital Research.

Facing the draft during the Vietnam War, Kildall joined the Navy—mainly because it allowed him to get his master's degree in computer science before being sent to Monterey, California, to teach at the U.S. Naval Postgraduate School. While he taught, he worked on his Ph.D. dissertation (in compiler code optimization) from the University of Washington.

It was in 1972, just after he received his doctorate, that

Kildall saw the notice on the Naval school's bulletin board that would change his life. "Computer on a chip—$25" was what the ad read. The ad intrigued Kildall. "I thought, 'God, that's a pretty good deal considering the [IBM] 360 [mainframe] we had in the school cost 3 million dollars.'" The ad was placed by Intel, then a small semiconductor manufacturer in nearby Silicon Valley. Intel was advertising its 4004, the first microprocessor on a chip. Kildall knew that a $25 chip was not going to replace a big IBM mainframe, but he sensed that the idea of a computer on a chip "was going somewhere, there wasn't any question about that." Wanting to keep abreast of the latest technology, Kildall immediately responded to the ad.

At the time, Kildall was still teaching computer science at the Naval school in Monterey. But he was clearly not wedded to teaching. "Teaching is one of the best scams there is in the whole world because of the vacations and the free time," Kildall told us. "You can work on your own projects and you are rewarded for it." With his doctorate out of the way, he was looking for other projects to pursue. Programming the Intel 4004 looked good.

A hotshot programmer like Kildall didn't need to see the actual chip. He had Intel send him the manual for the 4004. The microprocessor chip wasn't any good without about $2,000 worth of surrounding circuitry. But Kildall's specialty wasn't engineering the physical chips and electronic circuitry. His forte was writing programs to make the bundle of electronics useful. Always a very practical-minded fellow, Kildall instantly understood uses for a tiny computer using the Intel 4004 chip. For one thing, ships could use it for navigation. "My father had always talked about doing a little calculator that would do navigation problems," Kildall recalls. "His idea was to turn this crank"—and out would come the answer. So Kildall started programming away, using the Intel 4004 chip manual. He also started visiting Intel's offices to see if he could interest the company in his work. He became acquainted with company founder Bob Noyce and several Intel engineers, including Bob Garo.

Intel wasn't particularly interested in Kildall's navigation applications, but it was interested in some math programs he had written. In exchange for Kildall's math routines, Garo gave him a prototype microcomputer machine, the Sim-04, which contained the 4004 chip plus other electronic circuitry—one of the world's first microcomputers. (Kildall still has this prototype microcomputer in his home in Skyline.) The year was 1972. Gary Kildall was a forerunner of an entire industry that would not come into being for several more years. It would be three years, for instance, before Altair kits (usually called the first microcomputers) became available to computer hobbyists.

Intel's Garo also asked Kildall to do some software consulting work on a more advanced microprocessor chip, the 8008. He developed a Programming Language for Microcomputers (called PL/M) for the 8008. At this point, the amazing little microprocessor chips, with accompanying circuitry and sophisticated programs written by people like Kildall, could perform arithmetic calculations or sort information, much like a mainframe. But big computers could be connected to magnetic tapes to store data, while microprocessor development systems were connected to more clumsy punched paper tape devices. Fortunately for Kildall and his colleagues, some others in Silicon Valley were hard at work at creating storage devices for microprocessors.

Kildall visited Shugart & Associates, founded by Al Shugart, which was busy developing floppy disk drives that could be used with microprocessor systems. Kildall talked one of his friends there into giving him a test disk drive. Kildall tried but failed to get the disk drive to work with a microprocessor chip board. But again, Kildall wasn't interested in fooling around with hardware. Kildall just assumed that at some point an engineer at Shugart or elsewhere would get the floppy disk drive to work right. Instead, he concentrated on writing the programs (called, together, an operating system) that would coordinate the disk drive with the microprocessor. He named it Control Program for Microcomputers (CP/M), and it took him two months of focused effort. At the same time he was teaching at the Naval school, working from six in the morning to six in the evening every day, plus a few hours at night. By the end of the project, he often worked nonstop for a couple of days in a row.

The CP/M operating system was to make Kildall's fortune. But apparently no one, not even Kildall himself, considered it a "major product" at this point. He offered it to Intel, but the chipmaker turned it down. Although people there recognized that microprocessor chips would be used in other electronic devices, they were dubious about the future of small computer systems based on their "computer on a chip."

Kildall wasn't particularly discouraged. He just went ahead and worked on other computer projects that interested him. He even helped a friend build an astrology machine with a microprocessor in it. It was installed in several places in San Francisco. A passerby could walk up to it, turn the dials to his or her birthday, drop in a quarter, and the machine would print out an appropriate astrology chart. The invention was a flop, though, because the dials were too complicated to operate.

Almost two years after he had written it, Kildall's CP/M operating system came into demand. The technology caught up with Kildall when others developed microcomputers, also known as personal computers. Kildall began selling CP/M for $75 to hobbyists through mail orders from an ad in *Dr. Dobb's Journal*, and in 1976, he and Dorothy McEwen, his wife at the time, formed their own company, Intergalactic Digital Research (the Intergalactic was dropped when another company with the name Digital Research went out of business) and housed it in a yellow, two-story Victorian—complete with company cat—by the sea in Pacific Grove.

CP/M soon became the standard operating system for most personal computers. Kildall quit his teaching job at the Naval school in 1977. He hadn't been spending much time on teaching anyway. Many days, he admits, he'd "think up my lecture driving to school. It is definitely the second-best business to be in. This [his current occupation] is the best 'cause you get paid better."

He is philosophical about his sudden success: "There are so many things you do that don't go anyplace. You do them and you find out they aren't any good. If you just do enough things, eventually some of them are going to be successful."

There's a story going around about Gary Kildall that illustrates his disregard for corporate maneuvering in favor of his pursuit of his own interests. Computer industry wags—and *Barron's*—joke that when two IBM executives came to Kildall's office in 1978 looking to buy the DRI CP/M operating system for their new personal computers, Kildall was too busy flying his private plane to come down to earth to cut the deal.

In fact, Kildall did talk to the IBM executives. He flew with them from California to Florida before he caught a flight to the Caribbean for his vacation. But it is typical of Kildall that he didn't cancel his two-week vacation to clinch the deal. As Kildall explained, "In the meantime, Microsoft had gotten in there and made a deal with them. When we got back, they [IBM] were pretty cold." Because of the popularity of IBM's PC, Microsoft's MS-DOS operating system now outsells Digital Research's CP/M by a wide margin, and Microsoft is the bigger company. Yet, when talking with Kildall, you get no sense that he thinks he botched the deal. Given the same choice as he faced in 1981, Kildall talks as if he would not delay a planned Caribbean holiday for one business deal. Gary Kildall gives the impression that he invariably does precisely what he wants to do.

Maybe it really doesn't matter. After all, from those very modest mom-and-pop beginnings, Digital Research has grown into a company of 665 employees with 1983 revenues of $44.6 million. And Digital Research has succeeded in getting contracts from IBM, AT&T, and other giants. By all outward appearances, it seemed to be doing well in mid-1984.

Kildall told us, "I'm not particularly interested in spending lots of time on the business aspects. [Digital Research president] John Rowley is my right-hand man. He does most of that," Kildall says. Right now he figures he spends 60 percent of his time "being a technologist," and 40 percent on business.

Despite criticism of their original CP/M "crappy documentation," as Kildall says, Digital Research's products are considered high quality, especially their language and software development tools. The last language Kildall worked on was DR Logo, educational software advertised by Dennis the Menace (whose creator, Hank Ketchum, is a fellow Monterey Peninsula resident).

Digital Research's expansion has created its own casualties along the way. The new big-company-style management of salary guidelines and a distinct hierarchy John Rowley instituted after joining Digital Research in 1981 alienated some of the early employees. One who quit was an engineer with 22 years of programming experience and a Ph.D. in mathematics. He told *InfoWorld* in 1984: "Outsiders started coming in and they were making more money than we were. Our efforts weren't appreciated. Gary had the attitude that he was the only one that worked there, that no one else sweated or worried or put their soul into the place." He bitterly compared the 200 shares he earned after three years with Digital Research to the 1.5 million shares the Kildalls owned. Kildall insisted that "not that many" had left and that: "It's never pleasant when anyone leaves the organization, but there are certainly a lot of changes, and of course people tend to move on in the face of all that."

Another change affected Kildall's personal life. Kildall and McEwen, high school sweethearts who were married for more than 20 years, separated recently due to "pressures of business, I guess," Kildall admits. McEwen still works as vice president of operations at Digital Research. A former business associate and friend calls Kildall and McEwen "nice folks who have been done in by money."

In addition to his research and development duties, Kildall also enjoys the "toys" his money can buy. He flies a company-owned Aerostar and his own biplane. He tries to get his projects finished in the spring, so he can take up to a month off in the summer to water ski behind his 20-foot Sea Ray. For land use, Kildall owns two mopeds (for his teenage daughter and son), as well as a restored Porsche 914, an '84 Corvette (his third), a Rolls-Royce previously owned by 007 actor Roger Moore, a Star Crown (used to haul his boat around), a four-wheel-drive pickup truck, a motorcycle (which he often drives to work), and an all-terrain three-wheeler. He also keeps horses in Pebble Beach, near his home in Skyline.

Today, Kildall is no longer interested in writing the kinds

of software that created his company and made him a fortune: operating systems and compilers (which translate a programming language into machine code). "It's not a lot of fun for me to write operating systems or even compilers at this point. I've gone through more compilers than I'll ever want to go through." Besides, "enough people know how to do it. It's not interesting." Instead, Kildall has turned to video: "I think the reason I'm interested in it is that it is a lot of fun—real interesting and a lot of fun. With video, you can see the potential for that." Kildall compares the video situation today with the work he and others were doing that led to the first practical personal computers a decade ago. And others have pointed out that wherever the cutting edge of the industry is, Gary Kildall seems to be there.

Kildall speaks rapidly and with intensity. He conveys the kind of self-assurance you would expect of the son and grandson of sea captains. He seems to think others will naturally follow in his wake.

Although Kildall insists that he has no intention of retiring early (he's in his early forties), he no longer works as hard as he did ten years ago. "I usually come into work maybe eight-thirty or nine a.m. and work until evening. I don't spend all-night sessions working on this," he says. After all, he needs some time to play with his toys.

WHEELS OF FORTUNE

Number owned

Mercedes-Benz	27
Porsche	9
Rolls-Royce	8
Cadillac	6
Toyota	6
Corvette	5
Jaguar	5
Audi	4
Ferrari	4
BMW	3
Honda	3
Ford	2

Seymour Rubinstein

"It's really not how I originally envisioned it, being rich. Unless you're a dissipated type, your life really doesn't change"

▶ **BEST-KNOWN VENTURE:** MicroPro International

OTHER VENTURES: Seymour Rubinstein Associates; ProData International Corp.

BORN: 1934

RAISED: Brooklyn, New York

PARENTS' OCCUPATIONS: Father—distributor of arcade machines; mother—billing clerk for food importer

FIRST DOLLAR EARNED: Helper on a food truck

SCHOOLING: B.S., psychology, Brooklyn College

ORIGINAL FINANCING: Mortgaged his home

PERSONAL NET WORTH: Received $7.5 million at initial public offering; retains 29 percent of MicroPro stock

HOME: Belvedere, California

FAMILY: Separated; one son

PERSONAL TRANSPORTATION: Gold Corvette

MicroPro

MICROPRO INTERNATIONAL CORPORATION: Develops and markets the best-selling word processing program for personal computers.

▶ **BEST-KNOWN PRODUCTS:** *WordStar, MailMerge, InfoStar, SpellStar*

YEAR FOUNDED: 1978

EMPLOYEES: 425

HEADQUARTERS: San Rafael, California

SALES: $45 million (1983)

PROFITS: $4.8 million (1983)

OWNERSHIP: Public (1984)

Seymour Rubinstein fought his way up from the streets of Brooklyn to become the developer and seller of the most popular program in the early history of personal computers: *WordStar*. It's *WordStar* (among other software packages) that turns a computer into a word processor. We used *WordStar* to write this book. Rubinstein is not an engineer nor is he a mathematician. He's a hyper salesman who drives a hard bargain—and who drives himself very hard, too. In early 1984, when he was 49 years old, he suffered a mild heart attack. It occurred just as he was taking his company, MicroPro, public. The sale made Rubinstein a millionaire and he was soon back in the saddle, although he lightened his duties somewhat. In the prospectus that took the company public, Rubinstein was listed as chairman of the board, president, chief executive officer, secretary, and director. MicroPro now has a new president.

Rubinstein was born during the Depression and knew adversity early on. His father, a distributor of pinball machines, died when Seymour was seven years old, forcing his mother to go to work as a billing clerk for a food importer. "I wore hand-me-downs," Rubinstein recalls. He went to Brooklyn's Tilden High School, where he was an indifferent student. His working career began when he was 12, helping out on a fruit truck; later he worked in his uncle's jewelry store. About 1950, he learned how to repair television sets, which were then novelty items. He also became a ham radio operator.

It took Rubinstein 13 years to get a college degree. He was admitted first as an engineering student at City College of New York but was ill-prepared for that kind of academic regimen—and dropped out after flunking most of his courses. A direction-less Rubinstein married, but he quickly had it annulled; he worked for a while as a TV repairman. He might have continued wandering had he not become involved with a New York organization called the Institute of Applied Psychology. That group made him realize, as he put it, "I was letting the world pass me by, that the world was prepared to give me anything I wanted if I worked for it."

Rubinstein was living in Manhattan then, near the Queens Midtown Tunnel on Second Avenue, and working during the day and going to school at night, majoring in psychology at Brooklyn College. And he was getting good grades. A minor disaster that turned out to be fortuitous struck in the summer of 1964.

He had completed all the requirements for a degree except for a second year of German, and he got permission to take a 12-week crash course that summer at Long Island University. As he was speeding across the Brooklyn Bridge, on his way to take a final examination for the first half of the course, he was stopped for speeding. He was late for the test, no makeup was allowed, and he couldn't get credit for the course. The 30-year-old Rubinstein, goal-oriented now, had to return to Brooklyn College in the fall to finish with German. But the thought of taking only German appalled him. So he looked for another course to take—and he found Computer I. It constituted the entire computer science curriculum at Brooklyn College at that time. There were 38 students enrolled, and only 12 finished. Seymour was one of the 12. He loved it. In his own words, "I went bananas over it."

Rubinstein, who acquired his B.S. in psychology from

Brooklyn College, put his new computer skills to work at Sanders Associates, a Nashua, New Hampshire-based supplier of sophisticated electronic equipment to the military. He got hands-on experience there in programming, working on IBM mainframes. He learned how to take them apart and put them back together. He worked at Sanders for five years, was remarried, fathered a son, and met, on a trip to San Francisco, a man who was to have a big influence on him. That was Bill Millard, who, at that time (1967-68), was in charge of data processing for the city of San Francisco. After working for several small companies and doing some independent consulting, Rubinstein called up Millard, who had left his municipal job to start his own software company in Oakland, California. Millard invited him to come west to join his company, System Dynamics. And Rubinstein did, moving his family from New Hampshire to Oakland. It was 1971; Rubinstein was 37 years old. System Dynamics closed its doors nine months later.

Rubinstein turned to independent consulting again, specializing in setting up data processing systems for law offices. He also moved his family across the bay to San Rafael in Marin County, which was then becoming celebrated nationally as the playground for the self-indulgent, "we-want-it-all-now" crowd. But Rubinstein wasn't having much of that. He was working too hard, still true to his New York roots. He merged his consulting business into a new company, ProData International, of which he was a 20 percent owner, and he landed at Varian Associates, a company located south of San Francisco, where he developed various data management systems. Varian sent him to Switzerland where he set up a branch banking system using the software he had developed. Univac bought Varian data machines, placing the Rubinstein-developed software called *Pronto* into 1,500 installations. So Seymour Rubinstein had seemingly arrived as a big-time developer of special applications. It was only 10 years from Computer I at Brooklyn College.

When he returned from the Swiss project in early 1977, Rubinstein passed a new store called the Byte Shop near his San Rafael home. It was selling computer kits. He spent $700 and in a few weeks put together a microcomputer. It turned out that the kit was being manufactured by a new company, IMSAI, which had been started by his old friend, Bill Millard. Before long Rubinstein was again working for Millard, as director of marketing. Millard was essentially a salesman, and he may have recognized a kindred spirit in Rubinstein, although Millard was never able to get the Brooklynite to share his enthusiasm for est, the self-help movement that was all the rage then in the Bay Area. Rubinstein was a tough negotiator, a trait he's still proud of today. At least he related to us, with obvious relish, how he bought the CP/M disk operating system for IMSAI from Gary Kildall, who was then a professor at the Naval Postgraduate School in Monterey, California. IMSAI was the first manufacturer to buy CP/M to run the disk drives in its computer. Kildall had been selling CP/M for $25 a copy. Rubinstein negotiated a deal for a flat fee of $25,000 for all the CP/M programs it needed.

We asked: "Was it a good deal?"

"It was a steal!" Rubinstein exclaims, "It wasn't a good deal. It was a steal! You know, I said, 'Gary, how come you wanted to sell this to us for so cheap?' And he said, 'Well, that way a lot more people will use it.' I said, 'That's true!'"

In their book, *Fire in the Valley*, Paul Freiberger and Michael Swaine tell another story to illustrate Rubinstein's "remorseless" negotiating ability. On behalf of IMSAI, he bought software programs from Microsoft, the company founded by Bill Gates. According to Freiberger and Swaine, "Gates left their meeting thinking that he had done well for Microsoft, but a few days later he began to have doubts. Rubinstein, on the other hand, knew at once what kind of deal he had made. 'Everything but the kitchen sink,' he chuckled, 'including the stopper and the faucets.'"

Rubinstein was with IMSAI a year and a half, during which time, he says, sales went from $300,000 to $1.2 million a month. He left in 1978 to start his own software company, MicroPro. Having outwitted software sellers as a buyer, he reasoned he could do well on the other side of the fence. He wouldn't sell to manufacturers directly, nor to end-users via the mail. He would distribute through dealers. It was once again a move across San Francisco Bay. IMSAI was based in San

Leandro in the East Bay, and Rubinstein set up shop first in Rohnert Park, a small town in Sonoma County, just over the Marin County line. He later moved his headquarters closer to his home in San Rafael. "It was just a matter of choosing the right time and place to leave and start my own company," Rubinstein told us. "When I left, I was forty-four years old. I had less than 8,500 dollars in the bank, a mortgage, a wife, and a kid." IMSAI went down the drain a year later, just as Micro-Pro was beginning to take off.

Rubinstein's first move after leaving Millard's company was to hire one of the industry's top programmers, Rob Barnaby, who had left IMSAI two weeks before Rubinstein. Barnaby created MicroPro's first two products, *WordMaster*, a video text editor, and *SuperSort*, a data management program. Working together, Rubinstein and Barnaby improved on *WordMaster* to come up with *WordStar*, which was introduced in mid-1979. It was an instantaneous success, having decided advantages over other word processors.

How did they pull it off? "I spoke to the dealers almost daily," Rubinstein said. "And they told me what they wanted. They wanted an integrated system that had a combination of editing and printing. And so I worked with Rob, specifying what the end product should look like and criticizing and looking at this and that and making marketing plans and so on." It was made possible also, added Rubinstein, because "I was willing to starve. I basically did not take five cents out of the company for the first nine months. I mean, nothing! I went into debt because I had no personal credit, nothing." Barnaby, by the way, "sort of retired" after writing *WordStar* and *Mail-Merge*, according to Rubinstein. But Rubinstein was unwilling to state the terms of Barnaby's contract or whether *WordStar's* author receives a royalty on sales of the program.

WordStar was one of the shooting stars of the early growth of the personal computer market, fueling MicroPro's growth. Although it's priced at $495, it is widely discounted; and even though it's widely copied, over 800,000 copies have been sold. It has been a perennial best-seller on the software charts. MicroPro's sales hit $45 million in the fiscal year ending August 3, 1983, and they went over the $100-million mark in fiscal 1984. But it wasn't all great for Seymour Rubinstein. He was separated from his wife. He had to give up managerial control of the company to venture capitalist Fred Adler. He is no longer chief executive officer. He had a heart attack. Still, there are compensations. When the company went public in March 1984, Rubinstein sold one-quarter of his shares, thereby coming away with $7.5 million. Interviewed by Denise Caruso of *InfoWorld* shortly after the public offering, Rubinstein said:

"It's really not how I originally envisioned it, being rich. Unless you're a dissipated type, your life really doesn't change. You might increment some things. I mean, I've got a nice house, I've got a very nice car, that gold Corvette downstairs— but I got that actually last April, a year ago. And the house I bought in August. And okay, so I'll decorate the house. I'll buy some furniture. So maybe I'll spend another couple hundred thousand but most of the money will be used for investment, not to go on some wild spending spree."

Rubinstein's house is in Belvedere, one of the lushest enclaves of Marin County, overlooking San Francisco Bay. It boasts one of—if not *the*—highest per capita incomes of any town in the United States. His wife and son live in the San Rafael house they bought together three years ago.

When MicroPro went public, would-be buyers of the stock were warned: "The microcomputer applications software industry is highly competitive and subject to rapid change. The rate of obsolescence of software products cannot be predicted with any certainty." Those who did buy were burned badly. The offering price was $10.50 a share. Four months later MicroPro stock was selling for less than $5 a share.

THE MOUTHS OF BABES

IBM is known as a responsive corporation: it listens to its customers. In November 1983 it introduced the PCjr computer, the company's first attempt to reach the home user. The PCjr was criticized for its "chicklet" keyboard and its relatively low memory capacity. Eight months later, in the middle of 1984, IBM introduced an upgraded PCjr with a full typewriter keyboard and expandable memory. Those who had already bought a PCjr were offered a new keyboard free of charge.

To show off its improved PCjr, IBM staged a press conference in New York to which it brought a group of school children from North Carolina, Texas, and Washington, D.C. They had been using the PCjr during the past year in a "Writing to Read" educational program. One of the students paraded on stage was Melinda Garner, a six-year-old first grader from the Grove Park School in Burlington, North Carolina. She said her parents had promised her a computer for Christmas. When asked what make, she announced to the large group of attending reporters: "I want an Apple."

Sherwin Steffin

"When I was an entrepreneur, I had my freedom but not the economical resources. Now I've got the economical resources, but not my freedom"

▶ **BEST-KNOWN VENTURE:** Edu-Ware Services

BORN: 1935

RAISED: Detroit, Michigan

FATHER'S OCCUPATION: Retail lamp and shade store owner

FIRST DOLLAR EARNED: Street-gang social worker

SCHOOLING: B.S., experimental psychology, Ed.M., instructional technology, Wayne State University

ORIGINAL FINANCING: His father

PERSONAL NET WORTH: Sold Edu-Ware Services for $1.5 million in stock and a percentage of future profits

HOME: Thousand Oaks, California

FAMILY: Single

PERSONAL TRANSPORTATION: Porsche 944

EDUWARE

EDU-WARE SERVICES INC.: No-nonsense educational software for home and school.

▶ **BEST-KNOWN PRODUCT:** *Prisoner 2*, an interactive fantasy

YEAR FOUNDED: 1979

EMPLOYEES: 30

HEADQUARTERS: Agoura Hills, California

SALES: $1.6 million (1983); $4.5 million (1984 projection)

OWNERSHIP: Subsidiary of MSA

We received an unusual photograph from Edu-Ware's public relations office. It shows a middle-aged man at home removing a newspaper from the mouth of, not a dog, but a little R2D2-style robot. The man is Sherwin A. Steffin, founder of Edu-Ware, a leading supplier of educational microcomputer software. The machine is a "pretty bright little robot" that Steffin programmed himself.

There's nothing unusual in computer types fiddling with high-tech gadgets and gizmos, of course. But Steffin came later than most to computer entrepreneurship. He founded Edu-Ware in 1979 at the age of 44 after a 20-year career in education. His partner, Edu-Ware co-founder and president Steve Pederson, was a 20-year-old economics undergraduate when they met in the late '60s at UCLA's campus radio station.

The unlikely business duo set up a company in Steffin's apartment supported by unemployment insurance, hamburger stand earnings, and a few thousand dollars from Steffin's father. Four years later, Management Science America (MSA), the largest independent software manufacturer in the country, bought Edu-Ware for a million-and-a-half dollars. Sherwin Steffin bought himself a new townhouse in Thousand Oaks, California, and took possession of a new Porsche, which was part of his contract. Steffin had come a long way from his first job as a $5,000-a-year social worker who nearly got killed by the street gang he worked with in Detroit.

Steffin grew up in Detroit. His father had a lamp and shade store for 30 years, but Steffin had no desire to run a business. "If you had asked me a year before [founding Edu-Ware] if I ever wanted to go into business, I would have said no," Steffin claims. He graduated from Wayne State University in Detroit with a degree in psychology and began working with street gangs in the city. The job helped turn Steffin into "a very cynical individual." In 1959, "I was making the magnificent sum of about $5,000 a year working 14-hour days out on the streets. I lost a lot of my altruism. Most of the kids I worked with in those days were very resistant to change, like good viruses." During a rumble, he got hit in the back of the neck with a "zip gun" made out of a car antenna. "Another quarter of an inch and no Edu-Ware," Steffin remarks.

He decided teaching was safer, as well as "an honorable and secure position." Steffin taught junior high and high school in Michigan and Illinois. But again he was disillusioned. "What I hadn't reckoned with was the youth movement of the '60s. My first year was very quiet and nice. But it got worse every year because of the generation gap, the flower kids, and all that stuff."

Like many people fleeing from bad memories, Steffin came to Southern California, where he landed a job in UCLA's instructional television department. In 1978, he made a very important purchase—his first Apple computer. "I didn't know anything about personal computers," he remembers. "But I had all these wonderful dreams of what you could do with a computer if you had one. I found you could do most of them."

Steffin taught himself programming and wrote a couple of educational programs. He saw the potential for instructional computing right away. In the wake of his previous classroom experiences, Steffin appreciated the fact that he didn't have to work directly with students. Through his job in instructional television at UCLA, Steffin met Steve Pederson, who had more highly developed programming skills. When Steffin was laid off, the two friends decided to enter a business in which "fools walk in where angels fear to tread," recalls Steffin.

At the beginning, it looked as if the two men were indeed fools. The first program they attempted to sell was *Compu-Read*, designed to help increase reading speed and recall memory. Pederson worked part-time at a McDonald's and then worked with Steffin at the latter's apartment until four in the morning. Steffin's father bought stock for $7,500, which allowed Edu-Ware to hold on through the tough opening months when they tried to sell *Compu-Read* directly to computer retail stores. They would type the labels and the serial numbers on the disks, Xerox the single-page documentation, and stuff it into a plastic baggie. Times, Steffin admits, were pretty lean.

But the two unlikely entrepreneurs held on. Their programs were highly sophisticated and won rave reviews from educators. Finally, Steffin says, "We really started to hit the numbers: In August of '81 we did 9,000 dollars worth of business and in October we did 30,000 dollars worth." What put them over the top was *Prisoner*, a highly regarded and very popular game—or "interactive simulation" as Edu-Ware calls it. David Mullich, a young programmer Steffin had met at a computer store, based *Prisoner* on the TV cult classic of the '60s. That game, as well as the educational fractions and decimals programs, established Edu-Ware—and moved the business out of Steffin's apartment. "If I had a family, they would have divorced me." Edu-Ware now operates out of a 7,500-square-foot building in Agoura Hills, California.

Unlike other educational software companies, Edu-Ware stresses education over entertainment. Steffin remains the vigilant academic and frowns on juicing up education to seduce kids. He has written dozens of articles on the debilitating effects of video game arcades on youngsters, and he firmly believes that "people enjoy learning." Although Edu-Ware offered a few games in the beginning, including a "dope-smoker game," Steffin dropped them because they were "trivial."

Edu-Ware's four software lines stress learning to read, spell, do math, and write poetry (*Science of Learning*); educational play (*DragonWare*); real world situation games like *Prisoner*; and imagination stretching exercises.

But the Edu-Ware story does not have a happy ending—at least not for Sherwin Steffin. One year after the MSA buy-out in July 1983, Steffin left Edu-Ware because of a dispute with MSA. Steffin claimed that MSA did not honor certain financial obligations to him, and he planned to sue MSA.

But Steffin is not brooding about the fate of Edu-Ware. He's busy thinking up new educational programs for the Apple Macintosh to introduce at the Consumer Electronics Show in January 1985.

FAITHFUL FOUNDERS' CLUB

Years of Continuous Service

Andrew Kay (Kaypro)	31
Jack Tramiel* (Commodore)	30
Arthur Rock (Arthur Rock & Company)	23
Pat McGovern (International Data Group)	20
William Hambrecht (Hambrecht & Quist)	16
Reid Anderson (Verbatim)	15
Jerry Sanders (Advanced Micro Devices)	15
Jeffrey Wilkins (CompuServe)	15
Regis McKenna (Regis McKenna Public Relations)	14
Takayoshi Shiina (Sord Computer)	14
Thomas Perkins (Kleiner Perkins Caufield & Byers)	12

* Resigned in January 1984

George Tate

"I have always worked in my hobby, whatever that was at the time"

▶ **BEST-KNOWN VENTURE:** Ashton-Tate

OTHER VENTURES: Softwaire Centre International, Softeam

BORN: 1943

RAISED: Greenville, South Carolina

FATHER'S OCCUPATION: Furniture store owner

FIRST DOLLAR EARNED: Worked in a TV repair shop

SCHOOLING: Dropped out of twelfth grade

ORIGINAL FINANCING: $7,500 combined personal savings with partner, Hal Lashlee

PERSONAL NET WORTH: $50 million

DIED: August 10, 1984

SURVIVED BY: Jill Weissman-Tate and their daughter, Michelle Nicole

ASHTON·TATE

ASHTON-TATE: The fifth-largest independent supplier of software programs for computers.

▶ **BEST-KNOWN PRODUCTS:** *dBase II, dBase III, Friday!, Framework*

YEAR FOUNDED: 1980

EMPLOYEES: 350

HEADQUARTERS: Culver City, California

SALES: $40 million

PROFITS: $6 million

OWNERSHIP: Public; Tate's estate and Hal Lashlee each own about 34 percent

George Tate was a bearded, down-home Southerner who managed to do what many of us never get to do: live pretty much the kind of life he wanted to live. When we interviewed him in April 1984, he told us: "I've never been willing to do anything that I didn't enjoy doing. I won't do anything that I don't enjoy doing. Nothing." Four months later, at age 40, he collapsed and died of a heart attack in the Los Angeles offices of Ashton-Tate, the company he and Hal Lashlee, an accountant, started in 1980 to distribute software programs to computer users.

The business was first run out of Tate's garage in Silverlake, a shabby Victorian enclave in the heart of Los Angeles. In 1981 they moved to industrial quarters in Culver City, a mile from the MGM studios. By that time they were well underway with marketing one of the hottest products in computer software: *dBase II*, a data management system that worked so well in so many different applications that Ashton-Tate sold more than 200,000 copies by the end of 1983. By 1984 Ashton-Tate was sailing along at an annual sales clip of $40 million. The company sold stock to the public in November 1983, raising $15 million. Tate himself sold 220,000 shares at that time, collecting $3.1 million—and he still owned 34 percent of the company, worth about $60 million.

Becoming a millionaire did not seem to have turned George Tate's head. Easygoing and low-keyed, he was the opposite of pretentious. You could hear the grits in his Southern drawl. He dressed casually. He still spent his time doing what he wanted to do—and it wasn't all work. His hobby was flying planes and he owned two, including a one-third interest in a Citation jet. He drove a Toyota Supra, a new one every year. And he lived in Manhattan Beach, certainly not one of Los Angeles's most fashionable addresses, with Jill Weissman, whom he had met at Ashton-Tate. She is the company's sales manager, and had been the seventeenth employee hired. Their daughter, Michelle Nicole, was born in early 1984.

Tate was a stubborn cuss as a youngster, the despair of his father. He was born in Tennessee and raised in Greenville, South Carolina, where his father and uncle had a furniture business. His father, a Phi Beta Kappa in college, was sorely disappointed in his firstborn son's progress as a student. "I was never happy with school," George told us. "I was always bored. School never addressed what it was I wanted addressed. As far back as I can remember, I had an interest in mechanical and electronic things. That's what I wanted to be involved in. So while I might take shop in school, the books they had were way out-of-date. They had nothing to do with what was really going on. And my interest was to really get in and learn by hands-on."

That was still his interest two decades later. When we saw him, Tate had been tinkering all day with his IBM personal computer, experimenting with his company's new program, *Framework*. He explained that he didn't like to follow manuals. "I have a hard time learning just from reading," he said. "The way I tend to learn is to have the machine and spend some time with it. Once I have become 90 percent familiar with it, then I'm likely to read the manual."

Tate saw his first computer, a big IBM mainframe, when he was 13 years old. An IBM engineer who rented a house from his parents took him down to see it at the Liberty Life Insurance offices in Greenville. When he was 15, he began working after school in a TV repair shop—not to make money but because he enjoyed it. "At one point," his mother Irene told us, "I was told he was the only one in all of South Carolina who could repair little Sony TV sets." His school marks were, as he put it, "zero in essence," and he decided to drop out in the twelfth grade.

"Daddy was very upset about this," he said. "He felt like there were two things I could do: go to military school or join the service. So I did. I joined the Air Force."

Tate was in the Air Force for two-and-one-half years—during which he learned how to repair teletype machines. When his uncle died, his father arranged for George to get a hardship discharge so that he could join the family business, Tate Industries. So George went back to Greenville to work in the furniture store. That lasted only six months. George was bored. He went off to Atlanta, where he became a convert to L. Ron Hubbard's philosophy, Scientology, which taught that, as George put it, "all people are basically good and the only reason someone does less than the ideal in any situation is based on his own past pain. So if you can go in and clean up all those things that happened in the past, then you end up with someone who can now function perfectly in the present."

His interest in Scientology brought him to Los Angeles, the motherland of sects. He was working in the Santa Monica outpost of Pacific Stereo, repairing stereo sets, when the historic January 1975 issue of *Popular Electronics* appeared with its cover story on the Altair computer kit made by MITS of Albuquerque, New Mexico. He described his reaction to us:

"There was a place where you could order one, so I did. That computer had no memory—I think it had 256 bytes. It had switches on the front panel. So I got it built, and I knew where the on switch was, obviously. I could trace that. But I didn't have a clue about what to do after that point. I could turn it on. But as far as the switches and registers, I knew nothing. So I started at that point learning and understanding computers."

Later on, with memory boards ordered from Processor Technology, a used CRT terminal, an old paper tape reader, and help from a "godlike" person who understood Bill Gates's adaptation of the BASIC language for the Altair, George Tate got his computer up and running—and he was, he recalled, "stunned. After that point there was nothing in my life but computers. That's what I lived and breathed." He became a free-lance computer repairman, calling himself "The Computer Doctor."

Tate was a founding member of the Southern California Computer Society, where he met Hal Lashlee. By 1980 Lashlee was working as a controller for a Los Angeles mortgage banking firm, and Tate was western sales manager for a computer terminal maker, Atlanta-based Intelligent Systems. They pooled $7,500 to start a company to compete against Lifeboat Associates, the industry's first major software program house. They called their company Software Plus, and it offered discounts, fast delivery, strong customer support, and a toll-free telephone number.

Their business did well, but the galvanizing factor was *dBase II,* which was invented and developed by Wayne Ratliff, an engineer who worked at NASA's Jet Propulsion Laboratory in Pasadena on unmanned planetary space shots. In his spare time, he embarked on creating software for a robot. He began by adapting the Lab's mainframe data base program (JPLDIS) to his homebuilt IMSAI 8080 computer. But he got so interested in programming the data base that he soon forgot about the robot. A year later, after countless hours of patient work, he was satisfied with his data base program. He christened it *Vulcan* in honor of the birthplace of "Star Trek"'s Mr. Spock.

Ratliff's efforts to sell the program he'd labored over so long amounted to a couple of ads in the back pages of *Byte* magazine. The response was predictably poor. Only 50 copies sold in a year. Since his job with NASA was paying the rent, the *Vulcan* project remained on the backburner. That is, until an unknown caller telephoned Tate's Software Plus and, upon discovering they didn't carry *Vulcan,* began to extoll its wonders. Intrigued, Tate and Lashlee made contact with Ratliff.

Tate says he couldn't believe what he had. "It could do everything it was supposed to do"—a rarity among software programs. Tate signed an exclusive contract with Ratliff, giving him a royalty on sales that was to make Ratliff a multimillionaire. But it was to make Tate and his partner, Lashlee, even wealthier.

Ratliff's program—renamed as *dBase II*—put Ashton-Tate on the map.

dBase II succeeded because of its incredible versatility—it could perform a multitude of data management tasks—and because it was the right product at the right time: personal computer sales were beginning to take off and here was a product that made useful a computer in the home or on the top of an office desk. *PC Magazine,* in February 1984, cited a few of the more common tasks to which *dBase II* is put. Used in restaurant management, *dBase II* keeps track of sales, analyzes each item on the menu, counts customers by meal, and prints out a regular summary of payroll, including tips. Schools use it to give them an instant picture of students who are frequently absent or late—and why they are. Used in a political campaign, *dBase II* can keep tabs on contributions, volunteers and schedules. And—wouldn't you know?—an ex-jockey has created "Harness Race Horse Handicap," a *dBase II* application that feeds gamblers all the information they need to know about a race before betting.

George Tate and a Los Angeles advertising man, Hal Pawluk, are also to be credited with the merchandising flair that helped popularize *dBase II. Vulcan* had to be dropped because it was already the name of an operating system used by Harris, a manufacturer of mainframes. Pawluk came up with *dBase II* out of the blue. It's a catchy term that has a technical ring to it and implies an advancement over "dBase I." Of course there never was a "dBase I." It was just an adman's trick.

Pawluk also coined the name, Ashton-Tate. Ashton doesn't stand for anyone or anything; Pawluk simply liked its stuffiness, and he didn't like the feel of Tate & Lashlee or Lashlee-Tate.

Tate and Pawluk shared what Stan Brin, a writer for *Popular Computing,* called "a boisterous, Barnumesque instinct for promotion." They introduced *dBase II* in January 1981 with an ad and picture carrying the headline, "*dBase II* vs. the Bilge

Pumps." (The manufacturer of the depicted Bilge pump screamed.) And at one dealer show Tate had a blimp emblazoned *dBase II* "circling" above the floor of the Las Vegas Convention Center. It didn't actually circle because the show organizers wouldn't let it. Tate had it tethered to the Ashton-Tate booth.

George Tate was having a lot of fun, and he also seemed to know what he could do and what he wanted to do. In the summer of 1983, as sales were soaring, he gave up the chief executive's title to 31-year-old David Cole. "One day I realized this was getting out of hand," he said to *PC Magazine.* "I knew we were no longer a seat-of-the-pants kind of company. We'd gotten big [over 250 employees]. It was time for me to move on."

In May 1984 Ashton-Tate introduced a successor to its top-selling product: *dBase III.* It was a calculated risk since *dBase II* was then accounting for 80 percent of Ashton-Tate's sales. But Cole said: "I think it's better for us to eat our own flesh than to have others eat it." Later in 1984 Ashton-Tate introduced *Framework,* a $695 integrated software package designed to compete against *Symphony,* Lotus's successor to its top-selling spreadsheat, *1-2-3.* They both combine word processing, data base, and spreadsheet functions, as well as graphics and communications software, in a single-program package. Ashton-Tate bought $4 million worth of television time during the summer 1984 Democratic Convention and Olympic Games to introduce *Framework.*

George Tate remained a country boy. He had interests in two other companies, Softwaire Centre International, a chain of software-only retail stores, and Softeam, another software distributor. But he told us that he was mostly concerned, on a day-to-day basis, with "doing all I can to create a good atmosphere for the people who work here."

Tate was proud that people at Ashton-Tate "loved what they were doing." His father, though, was thunderstruck by his son's success. "I would call him up," George related to us, "and say, 'Dad, we started this business in a garage.' And he would say, 'Well, how are you doing?' I would say, 'We're doing great, we did $5,000 this month.' It got a little embarrassing after a while because his business had never done more than a million dollars a year, and all of a sudden we were one million, two million a month. He just couldn't understand."

Tate is survived by his father and mother, a brother, four sisters—and Jill Weissman and Michelle, who now share Tate's 34-percent stake in Ashton-Tate. The couple had been planning to marry. They were searching, according to Jill, for a place big enough to hold all the people George wanted to invite: everyone who worked at—or with—Ashton-Tate. Jill, who was 28 in 1984, legally adopted the Tate name after George's death. She continues to work in the company, as she told us, to keep it the kind of company George envisioned: a place where people like to come to work.

Ken and Roberta Williams

▶ **BEST-KNOWN VENTURE:** Sierra On-Line

OTHER VENTURES: Financial Decision Systems, Softsel, *Softline*, Calsoft

BORN: Ken—1954; Roberta—1953

FATHERS' OCCUPATIONS: Ken—Sears TV repairman; Roberta—agricultural inspector

SCHOOLING: Ken—California State Polytechnic University at Pomona, Control Data Institute, Glendale Community College, San Fernando Valley College (no degrees); Roberta— high school graduate

PERSONAL NET WORTH: Jointly own over 50 percent of Sierra On-Line

FAMILY: Married; two sons

PERSONAL TRANSPORTATION: Porsche 928, four-wheel drive Bronco, boat, three motorcycles, three windsurfers

SIERRA ON-LINE INC.: Popular, independent publishers of home computer software.

▶ **BEST-KNOWN PRODUCTS:** *Wizard and The Princess, Frogger, Dark Crystal, Homeword*

YEAR FOUNDED: 1980

EMPLOYEES: 93

HEADQUARTERS: Coarsegold, California

SALES: $10 million (1983)

OWNERSHIP: Privately held by Ken and Roberta Williams

You wouldn't describe their mansion in the woods as tasteful. It's a huge pile of stone shaped like a castle with 10,000 square feet of living space. Besides the vast game room and gym, the house features three hot tubs and a racquetball court with a floor design in the shape of the Apple Computer logo—the computer on which Ken and Roberta Williams designed their first adventure game. The bathrooms, family room, and front door sport stained glass windows of scenes from Roberta's best-selling computer games.

They like to collect "toys," as Ken says. Three motorcycles, three windsurfers, a Porsche, a Bronco, lots of computers, and a boat clutter up their 10 acres of land in the Sierra foothills near Yosemite. But Ken and Roberta Williams are not exactly *nouveau riche*—they're not pretentious enough for that.

Ken jovially refers to the mansion as "outrageous, ridiculous, and fun." Even Roberta, who designed the estate, admits she "overdid" it a little. Ken freely identifies his motivation in building one of the most successful personal computer companies as "greed. I'd sweep floors for the money. I just wanted it. I could always spend it faster than I got it."

Besides their success and candor, the Williams are notable

in the computer world for their enduring marriage. Ken met Roberta when he was 15 years old. In 1984, at 30, he and Roberta had been a married team for over 10 years, and a business team for half that time. Quite a record for a couple who describe themselves as once having been "losers."

When Roberta and Ken met back in their teens, she was a timid, "lazy, loner" with no ambition to go to college, or do much of anything. Ken, on the other hand, had just graduated from high school at the age of 15 as a math whiz.

Always an ambitious child, Ken wanted to get out of the lower middle-class life his parents led. He lived with his father (a TV repairman for Sears), his mother, and three siblings in a two-bedroom house in the Los Angeles suburb of Pomona. Unlike the dashing, rich heroes Ken so admired in his favorite Harold Robbins' novels, Ken sold newspapers and delivered pizza while he learned how to repair radios, TVs—anything electronic. He had his ham radio certificate at the remarkably young age of nine.

Maybe he had pushed too hard for too long, or maybe Roberta was a bad influence, but when the A student entered California State Polytechnic University, Ken only had time for drinking with his frat buddies. He flunked out with a D average. He married Roberta and, when she got pregnant, he took a nine-month computer programming course that was advertised on late-night TV. Eventually, it led to a series of programming jobs.

Meanwhile, Roberta wasn't playing the stereotypical role of suburban Los Angeles housewife. Between diaper changes, she got involved in real estate speculation. "At this time, real estate was a real lucrative business," Roberta says. "House prices were going up like crazy, and you could sell a house overnight. So we would buy a house one place, and I would spend most of my time fixing it up—painting or wallpapering and fixing up the yard—until it looked really nice, and we would put it up for sale and start looking for something else. I was usually the one who decided when to sell and how much and where to buy the next one." The way Ken tells the story, they'd move in and put up the "For Sale" sign the next day. They bought and sold 11 houses in five years.

Ken was earning a good salary at Informatics General, a software company, but the job was more important for whom he met rather than what he did. He became a close friend of Bob Leff, another workaholic who, like Ken, had a passion for backgammon and money. While playing 300 to 400 backgammon games a week, Leff and Williams thought about money. They gambled $8 to $10 a point while they schemed how "to get rich and famous. It was our goal in life," Ken says. Leff remembers that Ken was "real, real bright, with more energy than anyone I've ever seen. I'd seen him work forty-eight hours without sleeping and still function."

Ken moonlighted up to 60 hours a week in various computer industry ventures in addition to his job at Informatics. After leaving Informatics, he worked as a consultant. One of his ventures was the distribution of software for the still-infant personal computer industry. He entered that business after meeting Scott Adams at a computer fair. Adams gave Ken the Southern California distributorship for his Adventure International microcomputer games.

Meanwhile, Ken wasn't the only Williams excited by computer games. Ken had brought home a computer terminal that tapped into the mainframe at his consulting job. He and Roberta played *Colossal Cave*, the original text adventure game.

Roberta loved *Colossal Cave* and played it compulsively. According to Steven Levy in his book, *Hackers*, Roberta remembered her obsession, "I had a baby at the time; I totally ignored him. I didn't want to be bothered." The game appealed to her because "it's like reading a book, only you are the main character." The appeal, she says, is to "actually feel like you're there and have control over your story." Remembering her childhood ambition to be a writer, Roberta decided to write the first visual adventure game for a personal computer.

As a child living in the foothills of Southern California's San Gabriel mountains, Roberta considered herself a storyteller. A dreamy-eyed bookworm, she haunted the public library of La Verne, California, for fairy tales, and wrote and illustrated stories for her younger brother and friends. Her father, an agricultural inspector, thought Roberta was overdoing the reading; she needed glasses in third grade—proof, he said, that she was ruining her eyes.

But her bookishness finally paid off. Roberta wrote *Mystery House*, a whodunit reminiscent of Agatha Christie's mystery *Ten Little Indians*, and drew the graphics. Ken made a technological breakthrough programming *Mystery House* on his Apple II by turning his wife's drawings into a series of computer-generated images, or scenes, with text at the bottom of the screen. The hi-res (high-resolution) adventure game was born.

But how could the Williamses—with their spendthrift ways that always left them financially strapped—afford to market their new game? They decided to sell the software distribution company that Ken operated "out of the back of his car" to Bob Leff for $1,300. The money allowed Ken and Roberta to start Sierra On-Line. To save money on typesetting for their first ad for the game, Roberta cut and pasted letters out of a magazine. The $200 ad yielded 40 orders right off. Things picked up—sales were $167,000 the first year, enough to finance their dream of moving from Los Angeles to the foothills of the Sierra Nevada mountains.

Leff made out even better. Two weeks after the sale he sold a half-interest in the company to Dave Wagman for $10,000. Today their company, Softsel, is the largest personal computer software distributor in the country.

Sierra On-Line's success was not quite so dramatic. For the first six months, the new company consisted of Ken and Roberta, working together in their den. Roberta works fast—she can crank out an adventure game in about a month. Working on paper—sometimes giant sheets of wrapping paper—she scribbles notes and pictures that go off every which way; she does not use a computer.

Roberta didn't know much about programming, but maybe that's why she thought her games would work. Her next game, *Wizard and The Princess*, was in color. It didn't bother Roberta that adventure games didn't come in colors. She knew Ken would figure out how to program the color in. She was right. *Wizard and the Princess*, the first adventure game in color, hit the top of Softsel's *Hot List* and stayed there for a record-breaking year. It sold more than 60,000 copies.

The Williamses were in the big money now. Sierra On-

Line sold $10 million worth of games and software in 1983. When they started the company in 1980, all they were sure of was that they wanted to get out of the city and move to the country. The dream came true, just like a fairy tale. They moved to their castle in the woods and lived happily ever after—the wizard and the princess, just like Roberta's game. But there was no magic involved and no fairy godmother. Ken and Roberta worked long hours for a decade to make their wish come true.

Ken claims he still works 16-hour days, but Roberta says he "exaggerates." In 1983 Ken experimented with leaving the business end of Sierra to businessmen. He hired Dick Sunderland—a man who was once Ken's boss at Informatics—to be his main man. Ken wasn't satisfied with Sunderland, so he again took over as co-president with Roberta.

Steven Levy, in his book *Hackers,* described Ken as "characteristically sloppy—a burly, big-gutted man with swollen features, a hole in his red T-shirt, and a hole in his jeans. His shoulder-length, dark blond hair covered his head in an uncombed matting." He and Roberta, with her Farrah Fawcett hair and denim skirts, look anything but the chief executives of a multimillion-dollar outfit. Ken seems happiest programming new products, like the $50 word processor *Homeword* that Sierra On-Line introduced in 1983. Half of the company's revenues now come from home educational and productivity software.

Will Ken and Roberta continue to dispense fantasy and adventure from their never-never-land high in the mountains? Or will the forces of competition and dwindling game sales make their dreams vanish in a puff of smoke? Tune in next year.

Camilo Wilson

"That was my whole challenge: how do I make this bag of transistors useful to somebody?"

▶ **BEST-KNOWN VENTURE:** Lifetree Software

BORN: 1947

RAISED: Santiago, Chile, and Oakland, California

MOTHER'S OCCUPATION: Personal secretary to the executive vice president of Bethlehem Steel in Santiago

FIRST DOLLAR EARNED: National Science Foundation grant recipient

SCHOOLING: B.A., mathematics, University of California at Berkeley

ORIGINAL FINANCING: $15,000 from a friend

PERSONAL NET WORTH: 60 percent of Lifetree

HOME: Monterey, California

FAMILY: Single: "available"

PERSONAL TRANSPORTATION: Honda Accord

LIFETREE
SOFTWARE INC.

LIFETREE SOFTWARE INC.: Producers of the first working word processing program for the IBM PC.

▶ **BEST-KNOWN PRODUCT:** *Volkswriter*

YEAR FOUNDED: 1982

EMPLOYEES: 35

HEADQUARTERS: Monterey, California

SALES: $5 million (1984 projection)

OWNERSHIP: Private, Camilo Wilson holds 60 percent

Camilo Wilson's mother was crazy about the United States. Her home was littered with American magazines like *Reader's Digest*. There would be nothing unusual in that if she had been living in, say, Kansas. But she was a Chilean living in Santiago, Chile. She was determined to give her only child, Camilo, the best of everything. To her, that meant going to the United States.

She saved money from her years of secretarial work at American companies in Chile. She married a man who worked for RCA (although he never lived with Camilo) and introduced her son to her boss at a subsidiary of Bethlehem Steel. Camilo remembers the boss as a "fairly major influence in my life. He taught me how to drink, among other things."

Camilo's mother taught her son English at the age of seven and enrolled him in private schools in anticipation of the day when he would attend an American university. When Camilo turned 15, his mother left her job and the two finally headed off to live in the United States.

All through the long boat trip via the Panama Canal, and the three-week car ride through the United States, Camilo and his mother had a plan: get Camilo into the University of California at Berkeley to study physics. Camilo knew exactly what he wanted even though he was only 15.

He received a "terribly valuable education in 'Black English' at Oakland Technical High," he says. "I was fairly bored to death with studies." So Wilson filled in the time with the math club, where he got his first chance to play with the school computer. "It looked like a green refrigerator and was called a Bendix G-15. I became the resident computer genius—a hacker."

He was awarded a National Science Foundation grant the summer before he entered Berkeley in 1964 as a physics major. The grants allowed a dozen kids from across the country to learn computer basics at the Survey Research Center at Berkeley. He loved the idea of making the computer useful for the social scientists who needed computer studies for their research. Wilson worked at the center all through college and for seven years afterward.

That's not all he did. He switched from physics ("too bloody hard") to mathematics and political philosophy. He put the minor, philosophy, to work in his involvement in the Free Speech Movement at Berkeley. Joining political demonstrations was probably not what his mother had in mind when she brought her son to the Golden State, but Camilo had learned the American penchant for independence from parents. "Between working and studying and partying and politicalizing, that pretty much took up all of my time," Wilson says.

But he had time for one more important outlet—Arica. Like many other human potential organizations, Arica grew out of the social reforms and ideas of the '60s. Like its cousins—encounter groups, Rolfing, the Esalen Institute, and est—Arica appeared in the early '60s and attracted Wilson because it had a particular emphasis on physical health and fitness. Perhaps the fact that it was founded by Oscar Ichazo, a Bolivian, and named for a town in northern Chile, also exerted a pull on Wilson. The Arica style of "confrontational honesty" encounters appealed to Wilson: "I did always like the emphasis on being out front and being plain honest."

Wilson went to New York in 1972 to work as Arica's director of publishing, giving up computers in favor of a "very unique community of a couple hundred thousand people." Over the next four years, he published 25 self-help and meditation books, including such titles as *Psycho Calisthenics*. By 1978, Wilson was bored with his job and no longer found Arica intellectually stimulating. Still, he credits his publishing job with teaching him "that having a good product is essential, but you also have to know how to market it." It was also during his years at Arica that Camilo became a U.S. citizen. He changed his last name from Femenias to Wilson at that time.

For the next three years, Wilson had a ball. He took a lot of vacations to the Caribbean and made a lot of money as a consultant in his beloved field of mainframes. He advised clients—among them Merrill Lynch, Chemical Bank, Blue Cross, and American Express—on computerization. He liked the challenge and he loved New York. But, like the Duke of Windsor, he gave it all up for the woman he loved.

He lived in romantic bliss with her in Monterey, California. Not surprisingly, his career suffered. He commuted six hours, four days a week, to San Francisco where he taught computer science. His attempt to attract clients to his computer seminars flopped. To make matters worse, he was convinced that the personal computer world had passed him by. "I said, 'Oh my God! I am too late for this—the market is too big for me.'"

But then the rumors started to fly about the release of the IBM personal computer. "If I know anything about this business," Wilson thought, "IBM is entering into the world to change this business from a hobby business to a real business." He saw his chance: he would write the first book about the IBM PC. Wilson signed a contract with And/Or Press of Berkeley. He then immediately plunked down all his savings in advance for an IBM PC and began to call ComputerLand in San Francisco every other day to check on his order. He received one of the first 10 IBM PCs to hit California and sat down to write. That is, at least he tried to start writing.

The original infamous IBM word processor, *Easywriter*, squelched that plan. "You could not do anything, much less write a book with it. This is crazy. What I should be doing is writing a word processor." Within a week, Wilson decided to go into the software business by writing a decent word processing program. Wilson realized that he had both the publishing and software know-how to start a successful software business: "It was obvious. The cost of publishing is basically zero compared to its potential revenue."

Three months later, in March 1982, Wilson introduced the fruit of his labor at the West Coast Computer Faire. The name Wilson chose for his new word processor, *Volkswriter*, reflected his old attraction to simplicity and down-to-earth reliability, the qualities the Volkswagen Beetle represented. Everybody was promising a word processor to replace the despised *Easywriter*, but only the tiny company, Lifetree (a company that consisted solely of the man in the booth at the fair— Wilson), could deliver immediately. The booth was mobbed.

The Lifetree literature modestly states that "the company is a classic example of the importance of being in the right place at the right time with the right product." He knew he had to work quickly before *WordStar* (popular on other machines) was rewritten for the IBM PC. He worked 14-to 20-hour days to increase his initial lead.

Luck may have contributed to the initial success of *Volkswriter*, but performance and price ($195 for the original and $295 for the deluxe model) explain the continued popularity of the software. *Volkswriter* sold 40,000 copies by early 1984.

Wilson no longer takes his vacations in the Caribbean. Since founding Lifetree (the name is a combination of software companies Peachtree and Lifeboat) in 1982, he's been running hard to "turn the company into a company, which is a whole different ball game" from anything he'd done before. For a company that zoomed from zero to $2 million in sales in just two years, Lifetree operates with an extremely lean staff, only 35 employees. Wilson observes, "It's very easy to get bloated in this business. I'm trying very hard not to do that."

One of the members of Lifetree's lean staff is Peter Pirner, who worked for years at Mattel. Wilson calls him "every entrepreneur's dream"—someone who can run his company and who also knows marketing.

Wilson is not the kind of man to run himself ragged forever. That's not what he wants. He says that if Lifetree doesn't sell $5 million worth of *Volkswriter* in 1984, he'll get out.

Alas, *Volkswriter* cost Wilson the woman he'd followed across the country. The strain of founding Lifetree was just too much. Wilson says he "suffered horribly" because of the breakup. But, he says philosophically: "It's the price you pay. I've learned that maintaining a relationship and starting a business don't mix. It's a hard way to learn a lesson."

Ihor Wolosenko and Ken Grant

▶ **BEST-KNOWN VENTURE:** Synapse Software

OTHER VENTURE: Wolosenko—Ihor Photography

BORN: Wolosenko—1948; Grant—1947

RAISED: Wolosenko—Queens, New York; Grant—Pasadena, California

SCHOOLING: Wolosenko—B.A., drama and psychology, City University of New York; Grant—B.A., computer science, University of California at Berkeley

ORIGINAL FINANCING: $1,500 cash each

PERSONAL NET WORTH: Each owns 45 percent of Synapse

HOME: Wolosenko—Lucas Valley, California; Grant—Kensington, California

FAMILY: Both are single

PERSONAL TRANSPORTATION: Wolosenko—Mazda RX-7; Grant—Mercedes 240, Piper Seneca, Cessna

synapse

SYNAPSE SOFTWARE: Self-made computer gaming company that rode to prominence on *Slime, Chicken,* and *Picnic Paranoia.*

▶ **BEST-KNOWN PRODUCTS:** *Blue Max, Shamus, Zaxxon,* and *Necromancer* games; *Relax,* stress-reduction system

YEAR FOUNDED: 1980

EMPLOYEES: 100

HEADQUARTERS: Richmond, California

SALES: $6 million (1983)

OWNERSHIP: Privately held by Ihor Wolosenko and Ken Grant, 10 percent reserved for employee stock options

When Ihor Wolosenko gets bored, something interesting is sure to happen. He got bored being a photographer for a Boston, Massachusetts, TV station in the '60s. Four-day weeks, great pay, benefits, security—you know, boring. He decided his time was too important to sell 40 hours of it every week to somebody else. So he set up his own studio and became very successful shooting photos for newspaper and magazine advertisements for classy department stores, such as Filene's. He and his staff of seven worked out of a renovated carriage house, and for a while it was pretty interesting. But the work eventually began to seem no more than a series of petty exchanges with his various art directors, who insisted on adjusting a model's teacup 27 ways during a shooting session. Extremely boring.

In 1979, Wolosenko disposed of his business and moved to Berkeley, California. He had been reading a lot about Zen and Tibetan Buddhism, and wanted to talk to Tarthang Tulku, a Tibetan monk who lived there. At the same time, he developed an interest in the relationship between culture, language, and experience: how language shapes experience, how experience shapes language, and how culture shapes both. After studying for nine months with Tarthang Tulku, Wolosenko took up neurolinguistic programming, a kind of training and therapy developed by two psychologists at the University of California at Santa Cruz.

His favorite authors in those days were Gregory Bateson, the psychologist-anthropologist-philosopher who had also written about the role of language in reality-making; Milton Erickson, the psychiatrist famed for his uses of hypnosis; and Noam Chomsky, the linguist. His hero was Jacques Cousteau—a man who did exactly what he wanted to do. Because what Cousteau wanted to do was so imaginative and compelling, and he did it so well, people eventually supported him to do it. The search for security certainly didn't come first.

Security had never played a large part in Wolosenko's life. Born in Austria of Ukrainian parents, he came to New York in 1949, at age one. He can still speak Ukrainian. At an early age he had his own darkroom and a very sophisticated basement chemistry lab. ("I would be down there and something would explode, and my mother would think I was dead.") He also liked theater—he acted in high school plays, majored in drama and psychology at City University of New York, and did lighting design at a New York playhouse for a while after graduation. His interest in hypnosis started at about 11, when he read a Melvin Powers book, then took to hypnotizing his friends. He was good at it.

His skill at hypnosis came in handy. In 1980, having depleted his savings, Wolosenko was running workshops and seeing private clients in neurolinguistic programming and Ericksonian hypnosis in the Berkeley area. This enabled him to afford rent, food, and video games. Lots of video games— *Space Invaders, Missile Command, Star Raiders*—a torrent of quarters went down the slot. At the same time, he was studying computer languages, pursuing—through their more systematic and simplified medium—his old interest in the structure of language.

That he would buy a computer was inevitable, but which one? Here's how he made the crucial decision: "I played *Star*

Raiders on the Atari and it was just great. I asked them to show me the equivalent on the Apple and it was terrible. I don't care how much software is out there for the Apple. If the Atari can do *Star Raiders*, that's the machine I want." Wolosenko admits that he vacillated between trying to be rational and yielding to his desire for a toy. When the moment of truth came, he went for the toy.

As fate would have it, Ken Grant had gone to the same dealer a month before and bought *his* Atari. It was the fall of 1980, and fellow users were sparse. "If anyone else buys one," Ken told the manager, "please let me know." The manager did; Ken called Ihor and suggested they might get together.

Ken Grant is Ihor Wolosenko's opposite. A technological kid practically from the cradle, he grew up in Pasadena, California, and considered the California Institute of Technology at Pasadena's computer center his childhood playground. As an undergraduate at UC Berkeley he was so well-versed in the use of the IBM 360 that the Federal Reserve Bank hired him in his junior year to help convert their systems to it. Fifteen years later he was still at the Fed, a senior vice president in charge of 300 employees and a $30-million budget.

"Sure, let's get together," said Wolosenko. Naturally, they talked about computers, and Grant brought out some office management programs he'd written for the Atari. Wolosenko played with them and found them promising. Spurred by the fact that there was no business software at all for the Atari, he suggested that they get Ken's data base in shape and try to sell it.

It took a year to get it in shape—much longer than either of them had expected—but they kept at it. Grant did the architecture; Wolosenko, the graphics and interface. Meanwhile, they met another Atari user who'd written a game called *Dodge Racer*. With two products, they felt ready to go to market. In those days there was so much demand that you could advertise a little, tie your product up in a plastic bag, and get more orders than you could handle. Wolosenko ran the business, now called Synapse, from his one-bedroom apartment (the company occupied half of the bedroom). Both men were still working at their old occupations. Wolosenko would generally spend daylight hours on his workshops and clients, move to the computer work around nine o'clock, and continue until something like four in the morning. They picked up a second game, *Protector*, and Ihor began designing new games with the help of other programmers. Out came *Slime*, *Chicken*, and *Picnic Paranoia*.

In August 1981, Wolosenko moved to a two-bedroom apartment, and the company had a whole bedroom to itself. One way to chart Synapse's growth in the next year-and-a-half is to trace its frenetic scramble for space. Within six months, the partners got a five-bedroom house where they stayed six more months, until *it* was bursting. Then they moved to a 6,500-square-foot space, which lasted about eight months. Their 33,000-square-foot facility in Richmond, north of Berkeley, has seemed adequate since March 1983; but they're dreaming of building a grand headquarters in a nearby industrial park. Between the beginning and end of 1983, the number of Synapse employees jumped from 25 to about 100. Sales were $6 million in 1983. There has been no outside investment: Everything has grown from the original $3,000 put in by Grant and Wolosenko.

Synapse has seven business programs, the beginning of a new line called "personal healthware products," and a few dozen games. The games—a fair number of which have been award-winners and best-sellers—include flying-and-shooting sagas (where you pilot space skimmers, vintage biplanes, and subterranean blimps), mysteries, and fantasies. Reviewers praise the graphics: one called *Rainbow Walker* "an artistic masterpiece"; another quoted Fellini's response to Kubrick's *2001* in lauding the dreamlike intensity of *Zeppelin*. The games are also appreciated for their complexity and originality.

Blue Max, a sophisticated World War I airborne fighting game, was introduced with a thrilling promotional event. At a dirt-strip airport north of San Francisco, assembled reporters were treated to wild rides in a World War I-type stunt plane. Leaning out of the open cockpit, the ladies and gentlemen of the press were supposed to aim flour-sack bombs at a 25-foot circle on the ground while dealing with the variables of wind and altitude change. When they weren't flying, the journalists were playing *Blue Max* in a tent, facing even more complicated challenges than the flour-sack bombers above them.

Synapse's business philosophy consists of two rules that obviously rise from the bedrock of a more fundamental law: Keep Ihor unbored. The rules are: (1) You are only as good as your last product; and (2) What sells today won't sell tomorrow. Many a game company, the partners insist, has written its own epitaph by sticking to what was once successful. And, they further insist, what's needed is not just new games, but new concepts, whole new types of products. Wolosenko likes dreaming of possible futures and of products that will slide into the contours of those futures.

For instance, an item introduced grandly in the spring of 1984 is called *Relax* (unfortunately we can't reproduce the lazy, melting scrawl of the word as it appears, under a stretch of white clouds and blue sky, on the promotional materials). *Relax* is a "stress reduction system" that includes features not usually associated with software: a biofeedback device in the form of a headband that measures muscle tension and transmits the measurements to the computer; an audiotape that guides you to "deep relaxation" states; and a 150-page workbook by a psychologist who specializes in the causes and cures of stress. The program includes several options for representing your tension on the screen. You can choose a standard line graph; a kaleidoscopic pattern that flows with colors coded to tension levels; a face that appears scrunched up when you're tense, then gradually opens up and smiles as you relax; or a balloon ride that sends you flying over different kinds of terrain that change according to your tension levels.

Although such a product is unprecedented in the software industry, it's no surprise that Wolosenko came up with it. It integrates his studies of hypnosis, Tibetan physical-spiritual exercises, and "programming" the nervous system through language. He brushed off the suggestion that there might be anything sinister in these do-it-yourself conditioned-learning kits, but the question bears thought.

Wolosenko thinks the next major innovative thrust at Synapse will be something called Electronic Novels, a new genre already being published by other companies.

Characters will have their own knowledge, abilities, and "emotional valences." They react differently depending on whether you talk to them politely or rudely. ("If you kick a guy, maybe he won't tell you anything for a long time.")

The novels are being composed by collaborative teams of literary authors and programmers, with the primary impetus from the literary side. (Author says, "I want to do this;" the programmer figures out how to do it.) Synapse has created a new language for its fictions and is commissioning real novelists to write them. The group of tales being worked on in 1984 included *Brimstone* ("a combination of Dante's *Inferno* and Gawain's quest," narrated in third person) and *Enigma*, in which you find yourself lying face-down in sand at the beginning and have to figure out who you are.

The two founders of Synapse feel their lifestyles and personalities have been little affected by sudden wealth. Wolosenko did buy a Mazda sports car, and Grant has an old Mercedes and two airplanes. But Ken was a pilot and plane owner long before Synapse existed. Ihor thought about Porsches and decided he didn't like them. On the other hand, he decided he *would* like a house in fashionable Marin County, just north of San Francisco, to fulfill his need for more solitude and contact with nature.

"I don't do it for the money," he said of his current career, "or because I want to run a big company. I do it because it's fun to do. When it stops being fun I won't do it anymore." We naturally asked what he might do in such an eventuality. "I want to write children's books," came the reply, "and I want to produce more movies." (He's already produced some commercials.) "Oh yeah, and I'd also like to live in the South Pacific. There's just an endless, endless number of things that are interesting."

Women Among Men In Silicon Valley

Women engineers and managers in Silicon Valley computer firms are about as rare as manual typewriters. "This is a very male-dominated culture, very macho," one woman engineer told the *San Francisco Examiner*. "To survive one needs to be very self-confident and aggressive, and those are typically traits that women do not have."

Two women who are surviving quite nicely in the man's world of computers are Carolyn J. Morris and Sandra Kurtzig. Morris learned that "aggressive is not a bad word," when she started her own software company, Savantek. She recalls that when she graduated from the University of Texas in 1966, the women there were not even allowed to major in engineering.

Sandra Kurtzig, founder and president of Ask Computer Systems in Los Altos, California, thought all she wanted was a part-time job and two children. She started Ask in a spare bedroom in her apartment in 1972. Twelve years later she had 23 sales offices around the country, 350 employees, and $64 million in annual sales.

Morris and Kurtzig are still the exceptions, not the rule. According to a 1982 study by the Commission on Civil Rights, women accounted for 14 percent of the managers, 17 percent of the professionals, and 25 percent of the technicians in the Silicon Valley.

Many educators believe the underrepresentation of women in the computer industry reflects the lack of girls in computer classes in schools. *Discover* magazine concluded that, although girls score just as high as boys in programming courses when the girls take those courses, girls shy away from computer electives and the male-dominated video arcades where many boys first learn to love computers. Elizabeth Sage, an educational psychologist at the Lawrence Hall of Science in Berkeley, California explains, "The arcade mentality of bombing and killing is really not that attractive to girls."

CHAPTER 3

INNARD ENGINEERS
& PERIPHERAL
PROVIDERS

Marty Alpert

"I'm very fond of Cleveland. On the West Coast you're just another kid on the block"

▶ **BEST-KNOWN VENTURE:** Tecmar

BORN: 1949

RAISED: Cleveland, Ohio

PARENTS' OCCUPATIONS: Father—worked in a factory; mother—worked in a bakery

FIRST DOLLAR EARNED: Built a device to catch fish automatically

SCHOOLING: M.S., systems engineering, and M.D., Case Western Reserve University

ORIGINAL FINANCING: Personal savings

HOME: Beachwood, Ohio

FAMILY: Married

PERSONAL TRANSPORTATION: Company-owned Porsche

TEC*MAR*

TECMAR INC: A leading producer of IBM-compatible peripheral add-on products.

► **BEST-KNOWN PRODUCTS:** *PC-Talker* (speech synthesizer), *Video Van Gogh* (video digitizer)

YEAR FOUNDED: 1974

EMPLOYEES: 425

HEADQUARTERS: Cleveland, Ohio

SALES: $100 million (1984 projection)

OWNERSHIP: Privately held by Marty and Carolyn Alpert and some of the engineering staff

J ust six weeks after the IBM Personal Computer was introduced to the world in the fall of 1981, Tecmar amazed the industry by introducing 20 gadgets that could be added onto the PC to make it more versatile. Many thought this previously unknown company must have had a spy within IBM. The computer giant had cloaked details of its PC in a shroud of secrecy that would have done the CIA credit. The truth of the matter was that Tecmar had its own secret—a whiz of an engineer/entrepreneur who has lived his entire life in Cleveland, Ohio.

Tecmar stands for "Marty's Technology." Marty is Dr. Martin Alpert, a former physician who is a technological genius. He is the president of the company, and his wife Carolyn, co-founder and executive vice president, manages the financial end of the business.

Alpert was born in 1949 in Cleveland, exactly one month after his refugee parents arrived in that city. They were survivors of several Nazi concentration camps and had met in one of them. Although they'd never heard of Cleveland, they decided to settle there; it was in Cleveland that their only child was to achieve the American dream.

While his father worked in a storm-door factory and his mother worked in a bakery, Marty began to show signs of precociousness by building an electronic fish-catching device at the age of nine. Although Yiddish was the language spoken at home, he learned English quickly and became an excellent student.

School may, in fact, have been too easy for him. At Case Western Reserve University, he was coasting toward a 4.0 grade point average when he suddenly decided to play pinochle for a semester instead of going to class. A typical act. To this day, Marty can't stay interested in anything that isn't a challenge.

He still graduated in the top 5 percent of his class and was awarded a scholarship to Case's graduate school, where he studied biomedical engineering. That lasted a year; then he switched to the university's School of Medicine, went back again to get a master's in engineering, and finally returned to complete his medical education. He practiced medicine at the university hospital.

"My primary interest was always in technology," he told us over coffee during a break in one of the many computer trade shows he attends every year. "I was interested in medical school only to have the credentials as a doctor and because I didn't want to have to work for a physician when I was building medical products. I ended up enjoying medicine a great deal, but then all the throats started looking alike, so I got bored with it." Still, despite his increasing success in the field of engineering, he didn't totally divest himself of his patient load until June 1983.

One area of interest that he hasn't become bored with is his wife Carolyn, whom he met on a blind date in 1971. Both were undergraduates at the time, he in engineering and she in biology. A highly motivated achiever like Marty, she continued her studies and worked two jobs while he was in medical school.

Marty's medical and engineering research led to the design of the Pulmonary Diagnostic Instrument (PDI), a computer-based machine for diagnosing lung problems. Building this apparatus took him five years, nearly $50,000 (accumulated through scrimping and saving), and the help of Carolyn and a Case graduate student named Ken Stern, who later became Tecmar's engineering vice president. Tecmar was incorporated in 1974, and the PDI was put together in the Alperts' Beachwood living room. Carolyn switched career plans to go after an M.B.A.

All this time, both Marty and Carolyn worked more than full time at their jobs. It was just as well, since Marty had trouble getting anyone to believe in the PDI at first. In the course of building the PDI, Tecmar designed microcomputer systems that could be used for other scientific research. Sure enough, demand for his systems grew, mostly through advertising in computer magazines, until the Alperts had a full-time business and their living room was impossibly cluttered.

Now it was decision time: continue with the PDI or market computer products? Marty chose the latter. In April 1981, Tecmar moved from the Alperts' house to a 10,000-square-foot office in Beachwood, and by the end of the summer there were 15 employees making 20 products with annual sales of about $1 million. These included digital-to-analog and analog-to-digital converters, as well as a broad range of laboratory hardware and software.

Tecmar created its own window of opportunity through a bold, swift move, characteristic of Marty Alpert. When IBM announced in August 1981 that it would start marketing a personal computer that fall, Tecmar decided to concentrate on enhancements for this new machine. In effect, Alpert hitched his wagon to IBM's star.

Since the PC wasn't out, the Tecmar team was operating on guesswork at first, and later with the aid of a mysteriously obtained copy of the PC's technical reference manual. The moment the PC was unveiled on October 7, 1981, Tecmar's vice president of marketing, Dave Wertman, flew to Chicago and bought the first two PCs ever sold.

Then the real crunch began. Working night and day, with food sent in, the Tecmar team tore apart ("de-engineered") the PCs to find out how other products could be attached, then raced to finish building these products. Subcontractors were hired to keep up the pace.

Why the rush? Because Marty and his crew realized that to be first and to get noticed were the keys to capturing the PC peripherals market, and because COMDEX, the most important computer trade show, was coming up in just six weeks.

For Tecmar's corporate gamble, the COMDEX site—Las Vegas—couldn't have been more appropriate. The gamble paid off. Crowds gathered, with mouths agape, around Tecmar's tiny booth, which proudly displayed 20 fully operational (not prototype) add-ons for the IBM PC.

Tecmar has never given up its lead. The company continues to develop an average of one new product a week for Apple and other machines besides the IBM PC. The line ranges from dust covers to memory extenders to disk drives. There's a cabinet that enables the IBM PC to be rolled from one desk to another, a device that lets business users save money by sharing one printer among several PCs, an encryption code designed to protect the security of bank information, a speech synthesizer that makes the computer talk, and a network that can connect PCs around the world.

Marty was anticipating 1984 sales of $100 million. In early 1984, Tecmar had 425 employees and was "hiring at an incredible rate again," according to him. Only a "very, very small percentage" of venture capital has been needed.

Has success spoiled him—much as he says his parents did? It is not obvious. Intense and driven, he still works "more than I did in my internship, which was one hundred and fifteen hours a week." There's little evidence of ego—often he modestly says "we" when he means "I," he insists on being called "Marty" rather than "Dr. Alpert," and he's quick to point out that he has an exceptional group of people working for him. "It's the most incredible engineering staff in the industry— many of them are at genius level," he says.

How does he attract and keep such a crew? One incentive is freedom: "They can do whatever they want, and we support it with equipment or whatever they need," says Marty. Some of the engineers also have a piece of the company. Then there are the perks, including a fleet of company Porsches, a wine cellar for employees, and a music room. But a major draw is probably Marty himself. "We needed to get a project done quickly, so we took all the engineers to our house. Now they enjoy it so much that we realized we're not getting our house back. So we're looking for another house," he says with a twinkle of amusement.

He and Carolyn are enthusiastic Cleveland boosters, pointing to the excellent art museums, orchestra, theater, and low-cost housing. (The two are culture lovers, although they rarely have time to indulge.) Marty thinks the Cleveland area could be Silicon Valley Central. "We couldn't have done what we've done in terms of product turnaround if we'd been in another state," he asserts. "In Cleveland, we can get things done for us. On the West Coast, you're just another kid on the block."

In 1982 Tecmar received some unsought publicity. Three IBM executives, who were planning to leave the corporation, offered to sell Marty some PC design secrets. With this inside information, they pointed out, Tecmar could surge even further ahead of its competitors. Marty smelled something unethical in the proposal, and after a night of worrying about what to do and discussing it with his wife, he told IBM. IBM then persuaded him to take on a most uncomfortable role: undercover agent. Nervously wearing a hidden tape recorder, he engaged the renegades in a series of incriminating conversations that resulted in their dismissal.

Marty claims no hero's medal for this. He says he didn't know what the three men really wanted, and that the company they were planning to start would have been a Tecmar competitor. Surprisingly, he was criticized and even insulted by some high-tech colleagues who sympathized with the "little guys" over IBM. "It was probably one of the worst things I've gone through," Marty says of his espionage experience. But generally the publicity was favorable, and IBM (a Tecmar competitor itself) was openly grateful.

At present, Tecmar is owned by Marty, Carolyn, and a number of the engineers. There were no plans to go public in 1984, although Marty concedes that they may do so in the future. As for Marty himself, his restless nature may well take him into something new. "I see myself changing direction every five to seven years—radical switches," he says.

Reid Anderson

"The most important thing is to be a survivor, to stick it out through thick and thin. This is something the venture capitalists often overlook "

▶ **BEST-KNOWN VENTURE:** Verbatim

OTHER VENTURES: Tempo Tuner (musical instrument tuner), Anderson-Jacobson (acoustic couplers for data transmission by telephone)

BORN: 1917

RAISED: Wheeling, West Virginia

FIRST DOLLAR EARNED: Teaching music at a summer camp

SCHOOLING: B.S., engineering, Denison University; M.S., physics and electrical engineering, University of Michigan

ORIGINAL FINANCING: Proceeds from a sale of Anderson-Jacobson stock, personal savings, bank loan, money from friends and relatives

PERSONAL NET WORTH: $50 million

FAMILY: Married (42 years); two sons, one daughter

PERSONAL TRANSPORTATION: Cadillac Cimmaron

◤ Verbatim

VERBATIM CORPORATION: The largest maker of floppy disks for the storage of computerized information.

▶ **BEST-KNOWN PRODUCTS:** Datalife, Verex, and Optima floppy diskettes

YEAR FOUNDED: 1969

EMPLOYEES: 2,800

HEADQUARTERS: Sunnyvale, California

SALES: $120 million

PROFITS: $14 million

OWNERSHIP: Public (1979)

For 23 years, J. Reid Anderson worked for others. When he finally decided to go out on his own at age 46, he picked a product with a very small market: a transistorized metronome/tuner for musicians. Despite dropping the ball occasionally since then, the quiet and unassuming Anderson has been able to go into semiretirement as a multimillionaire.

It's a far cry from Anderson's experience growing up in Wheeling, West Virginia, during the Depression. His father was a stockbroker. Anderson remembers the Big Crash of '29 as the time when his father didn't come home for four nights. The Anderson family struggled through the lean years, and Reid was able to go to Denison University in Ohio, where he majored in engineering science. Since there still weren't any jobs when he graduated, he went on to get two master's degrees—in physics and in electrical engineering—at the University of Michigan.

All this time, he pursued an unrelated interest: music. He began playing clarinet in his high school, and when he landed a job at Bell Laboratories in Murray Hill, New Jersey, he played in the New Jersey Little Symphony and in Bell Labs' own Murray Hill Orchestra.

Bell Labs was his employer for 17 years—interrupted by a four-year stint in the Navy during World War II. "Bell was like going to another graduate school," he says. "It was a great training ground, with tremendous people and a very nice, open atmosphere."

The trouble was, he decided, Bell had so many good people that the chances for advancement were limited. So, in 1956, when National Cash Register in Dayton, Ohio, offered him a job as director of physical research, he took it. But after Bell, NCR (which was just getting into electronics) seemed backward, and 18 months later he moved on to Stanford Research Institute in Palo Alto, California.

That's where he was bitten by the entrepreneurial bug. SRI did the early development of products and then turned them over to clients for manufacturing. The focus on innovation was exciting. One of the projects Anderson worked on was the first electronic desk calculator. "Every year, I felt like I was starting a new business," recalls Anderson. "That got me to thinking about going into my *own* business."

After five years at SRI, that is precisely what he did. For a product idea, he turned to the field that was his other love— music. With help from his youngest son, a college student, he built the prototype for the Tempo Tuner in his garage in Los Altos Hills. There wasn't much start-up cost involved. Anderson sold the first 100 metronomes to music stores and then went on to make the next batch. His wife Polly did the packing and shipping.

The Tempo Tuner wasn't exactly the road to riches. The profit per item was small, and so was the market. In fact, after three years he had sold the device to virtually all the potential buyers. Anderson was desperately looking for a new product to make when a mutual friend introduced him to business consultant Ray Jacobson. At the time, it seemed like a fortuitous meeting. Jacobson had a marketing and finance background; Anderson had expertise in acoustics. They set out to make display terminals but in 1967 the two were shown an acoustic modem (a device for transferring computer data over telephone lines) on a visit to SRI. Someone said, "This is what's really needed. This one doesn't work very well." Anderson asked how much it cost. "Several hundred dollars" was the reply. Looking inside the device, Anderson was shocked to discover that it contained fewer components (and of inferior quality) than those he had used in the Tempo Tuner he had sold for $26. The two left the building in animated conversation, and it wasn't long before Anderson-Jacobson had a license from SRI for modems called acoustic data couplers.

Although the partnership was successful financially, it was a disaster interpersonally. "We didn't get along, Ray and I," says Anderson. "He got me out of the company in 1968, against my will." One source of friction was Anderson's conviction, which Jacobson didn't share, that magnetized tape in cassettes would replace paper tapes for computer storage and that the company should start producing cassettes.

As if to prove himself right, Anderson started his own company the following year, Information Terminals Corporation (later renamed Verbatim), and hired an engineer from Memorex to make the best data cassette possible. He raised $300,000 from friends, relatives, and one venture capitalist. Then came the kind of windfall most entrepreneurs dream about. Anderson-Jacobson, which was doing well, offered stock to the public; as part of the offering, Anderson sold some of his stock, becoming an instant millionaire.

Verbatim's sales in the first two years were slow. It turned out that Jacobson was mostly correct: cassettes were not destined to become the prime storage vehicle for computerized information. In 1973 IBM introduced the floppy disk, a magnetic disk for the storage of data. Anderson asked for a license to make the product. IBM said yes—and Verbatim had the product that was to be its mainstay. In 1977 Verbatim secured a similar license from Shugart Associates to make a smaller disk—the 5-1/4-inch mini. So Verbatim has proven to be adept at picking up on the technology pioneered by others. Anderson put it to us this way: "We knew that this [the floppy disk] was one of the products you have to make or not be in business next year." Verbatim still makes data cassettes.

Anderson's company captured a sizeable chunk of the floppy disk market, and when Verbatim sold stock to the public for the first time in 1979, it raised more than $5 million. Anderson, then 62, was worth $14.7 million on paper.

However, it wasn't all clear sailing. Verbatim's success was marred by two problems: (1) It made some batches of disks that were faulty; and (2) It was not blessed with an over-abundance of sharp managers at the top. The two may have been related.

Without adequate testing, Verbatim changed the liner on its disk jackets. That caused the disks to fail quickly because they absorbed too much lubricant. Then Verbatim changed the chemical coating on the disks themselves—and that caused them to wear out rapidly, too. This double-whammy forced Verbatim into a massive recall of its floppies in 1980 and 1981. Profits were halved, and customer confidence in Verbatim was not exactly shored up.

One result: Peter McCuen, who was promoted to president in 1978, walked the plank—and Anderson, who had moved up to chairman, resumed the presidency of his company. In 1981, he found a new chief executive: Malcolm Northrup, who was recruited from Rockwell International. Northrup is credited with getting the company back on track. A key move was the introduction of a new Verbatim disk, the Datalife, which was sold with a five-year warranty, a first for the industry.

However, in 1984 product deficiencies cropped up again. IBM returned $2 million worth of Verbatim disks because the protective sleeves had once again been changed. The giant computer maker later removed Verbatim from its list of authorized suppliers, saying that the company's floppies resulted in too many computer errors.

As for Anderson, although he retired in January 1983, he hasn't given up entrepreneurship. He's investing time, advice, and money in four small companies—Datacopy (electronic cameras), Abacus II (electronic terminals for fast-food restaurants), Autobotics (industrial robots), and Speech Plus. And as chairman, he's still very much involved in Verbatim. His wife Polly, to whom he's been married for 42 years ("we're considered strange in California"), was an active board member until 1982.

Now there's more time to play the clarinet and to reflect on what it takes to succeed as an entrepreneur. "Knowing when to delegate and when to get help is important," he says. "And the most important is to be a survivor, to be able to stick it out through thick and thin and not let things get you down. This is something the venture capitalists often overlook."

Dennis Hayes

"At one time there was a question of whether I would go to art school or engineering school. I chose engineering. As it turns out, I'm successful and don't have much time to do art"

▶ **BEST-KNOWN VENTURE:** Hayes Microcomputer Products

BORN: 1950

RAISED: Spartanburg, South Carolina

PARENTS' OCCUPATIONS: Father—lineman, Southern Bell; mother—operator, Southern Bell

FIRST DOLLAR EARNED: Bag boy in a grocery store

SCHOOLING: Georgia Institute of Technology (no degree)

ORIGINAL FINANCING: Personal savings

PERSONAL NET WORTH: Large percentage of Hayes (won't disclose how much)

HOME: Norcross, Georgia

FAMILY: Married; one daughter

PERSONAL TRANSPORTATION: Buick Park Avenue

HAYES MICROCOMPUTER PRODUCTS INC.: Manufacturers of personal computer telecommunications equipment.

▶ **BEST-KNOWN PRODUCTS:** Smartmodems 300 and 1200; *Please* (data base program), *Smartcom II* (telecommunications program)

YEAR FOUNDED: 1978

EMPLOYEES: 310 (1983)

HEADQUARTERS: Norcross, Georgia

SALES: $50 million (1983)

PROFITS: Won't say

OWNERSHIP: Privately held by Dennis Hayes, Dale Heatherington, and employees

To hear Dennis Hayes tell it, he started Hayes Microcomputer Products because he wanted to work for a company like Hewlett-Packard, but no such firm existed in the Atlanta, Georgia, of the mid-'70s. Hayes admired the Silicon Valley firm because it was on the cutting edge of high-technology and provided its employees a great place to work.

Dennis Hayes has certainly achieved his goal. Not only has he provided himself a full-time job (and made himself a millionaire several times over), but bright, young electrical engineers from Georgia Tech send their applications to Dennis Hayes's burgeoning operation.

In the process, Hayes has also made his name synonymous with modems—small boxes that connect computers with telephones and allow computers to "talk" with each other over ordinary phone lines. Hayes's company makes about 65 percent of all modems purchased by personal computer owners.

Of course, there's more to the story. At the time Hayes founded his company in 1977, he was working as an engineer for a big Atlanta-based company that provides computerized data services for banks, airlines, and credit card companies. His specialty was telecommunications. If National Data's nationwide data network went on the fritz in the middle of the night, Hayes was hauled out of bed to figure out how to patch it up. The position at National Data was the last in a series of engineering jobs Hayes had held since entering Georgia Tech in Atlanta in 1968. All were related to computers, and all concerned telecommunications—linking computers by telephone.

Hayes grew up in a telephone family. His father was a lineman and his mother a phone operator for Southern Bell in Spartanburg, South Carolina. As a youngster, Hayes liked to make things, such as model airplanes and cars from kits. He was also enamored with creating Indian headdresses and costumes when he was an Eagle Scout. His love of arts and crafts from that period was such that he seriously considered going to art school. But he decided on an engineering career because, as he told us, "It was harder, and it probably had more career prospects. As well, I figured that if I was successful as an engineer, I could do art." But, he lamented, "As it turns out, I'm successful and I don't have much time to do art."

The Eagle Scout in Hayes is still apparent in the earnest manner in which he relates his life story. A large man, Hayes speaks with a quiet Southern drawl. He was an honors high school student but only a "mediocre" student at Georgia Tech. As he recalls it, "I just began to get interested in reading a lot. I'd spend time in the library when I should have been studying. Maybe I was working on something related to my studies and I'd let myself get off on a track and burrow into a shelf in the library. I'd learn a lot from that but it wasn't the stuff I was supposed to learn for my course."

Hayes had to work his way through college. He enrolled in Georgia Tech's co-op work program alternately working and studying every three months. His first co-op job was with AT&T Long Lines figuring out how to transmit radio signals over the Everglades with its shifting water level. Subsequent jobs were also related to telecommunications or computer programming. For financial reasons, Hayes did not, however, graduate from Georgia Tech—a fact which he downplays because he feels it may discourage others from finishing college. Hayes is conscious that his success makes him somewhat of a role model. He's proud, for instance, that the Atlanta Chamber of Commerce named him one of five "Entrepreneurs of the Year" in 1983.

Before Hayes caught the entrepreneurial bug, he got caught up in the personal computer craze in its earliest days. He and a friend, Dale Heatherington, bought an IMSAI computer and were founding members of the Atlanta Area Microcomputer Hobbyist Club. (The club still exists as the Atlanta Computer Society.) It occurred to Hayes that these personal computer owners would soon want to communicate with each other. To do so, the microcomputers needed modems. Though modems were commonplace in the commercial world, where big mainframes and minicomputers could exchange information with each other, no such device existed for small personal computers. Hayes and Heatherington set out to remedy the situation.

The two set up shop at Hayes's house in Atlanta atop a dining room table borrowed from a next-door neighbor. They assembled their first modem from a schematic designed by Heatherington. After they got a few built, they showed the modems to the computer club. "We got about 10 people who said, 'Yes, we'll take one.' That got things kind of started," Hayes recalls.

Hayes began a killer routine to get the modems built, tested, packaged, and shipped while he was still working full-time for National Data. "Between April and October of 1977 it was really crazy," Hayes says. "I'd take what little bit of money we had and go over and pick up the parts I needed to build a batch of modems. I'd take those parts home and work all weekend building them. On Sunday night I'd take them over to Dale's house where he had the [IMSAI] computer. All that next week every night he would test a few of them and give them to me the next day. I'd take them back home and box them. I'd go by the post office on the way to work to see if any orders had come in, and then I'd go by UPS and ship 'em.

"Pretty soon the thing had taken over the whole house. I had four or five people coming to the house every morning to help. I had to get an accountant to keep books. Then we moved out into a building."

But Hayes wasn't on easy street yet. He had quit his job a few months before they incorporated the new company in January 1978. He says he spent about two years "in poverty," before the company became profitable. Luckily, he was still single at the time and had no commitments, other than his house payment. His future wife, Melita Easters, earned more take-home money as a newspaper reporter than Hayes. She would have to give him gas money to make the four-hour drive back to Atlanta from her home in Lenox, in south Georgia, after he'd visit her on weekends.

All that scrimping is just a memory now. Hayes Micro-computer racked up $50 million in sales in 1983. A large part of those sales come from his original product, the Smartmodem. Hayes also makes one of the three best-selling telecommunications software packages—*Smartcom II*—which enables the modem and phone line to transfer information between two computers.

Hayes has no intention of stopping at telecommunications systems. In the summer of 1984, Hayes spent $3 million on an ad campaign to introduce *Please*, a new data base management program.

Hayes is proud of the fact that his company is still privately owned by him, Heatherington, and his employees. They have accepted no venture capital despite many offers. "The long-range objectives of the founder of the company and the long-range objectives of the venture capitalist are not the same," he believes. Hayes's aim has always been to "make a good living in the kind of place where I wanted to work, and to be able to provide for people who were like myself when I was in a technically oriented job. They should have the kind of environment that's good for them."

Apparently, Hayes has succeeded in that goal. In 1984 the *Atlanta Business Chronicle* voted Hayes Microcomputer one of the best places to work in Atlanta. Hayes offers separate career tracks for management and technical areas. That means a senior research engineer can make as much money as a director of the company. Dale Heatherington still works at Hayes as a senior engineer, for example.

Hayes has each employee create his or her own educational plan—from night school and special seminars to buying video tapes on specific subjects—all paid for by the company. Dennis Hayes set up his own study system to learn management techniques. In addition to reading the *Harvard Business Review* and management books, Hayes flies to La Jolla, California, every six months for a week-long series of classes at the School of Management and Strategic Studies.

Nor is Dennis Hayes's interest in education confined to studying business. When a friend challenged him to learn Japanese in six months (like the character in James Clavell's *Shogun*), he eagerly took up the call. Several years later, he's still at it. His explanation? Most people in the United States don't do enough to learn about other people's cultures, and (quoting *Shogun*), "If you want to think Japanese, you have to speak Japanese." He also collects Japanese prints. When we asked why he decided to make continuing education a part of company policy, he replied, "Modern business needs people who can solve problems. Our best asset is our ability to think, and the best way to develop a disciplined thought process is through education."

Hayes's interest in self-improvement and examining his knowledge of other cultures is not the stuff of the stereotyped southern "good ol' boy," a term Hayes professes not to understand. Still, Hayes gives in to a few southern insecurities at times. When we talked with him he twice quoted something that his uncle, who worked in California, once told him, "All these guys out here in California are just a bunch of smart guys like y'all back there in Georgia." When he told us that he drives a Buick Park Avenue, he quickly added, "I'm about ready to get a Mercedes. What kind of answers do you get [to that question from other computer entrepreneurs]? I bet you get a lot of sports cars."

But Hayes doesn't mind being underestimated. "Sometimes we've gone around in negotiations where people obviously took us as a bunch of hicks from Georgia, and when that happens, I do pretty well," he chuckles.

K. Philip Hwang

"If you have confidence in your idea, then do it, no matter how harsh it is. Don't give up and you will make it. That's what I experienced"

▶ **BEST-KNOWN VENTURE:** TeleVideo Systems

OTHER VENTURE: 7-Eleven store in San Jose, California

BORN: 1936

RAISED: Hungnam, North Korea, and Seoul, South Korea

FIRST DOLLAR EARNED: Cleaning U.S. Army barracks

SCHOOLING: B.S., electrical engineering, and honorary doctorate, Utah State University; M.S., electrical engineering, Wayne State University

ORIGINAL FINANCING: $9,000 savings from a 7-Eleven franchise

PERSONAL NET WORTH: $610 million (value of his stock when TeleVideo Systems went public)

HOME: Los Altos, California

FAMILY: Married; two daughters

PERSONAL TRANSPORTATION: Mercedes 500 SEL

❧ TeleVideo Systems, Inc.

TELEVIDEO SYSTEMS INC.: Manufacturers of the dominant "smart" computer terminal.

▶ **BEST-KNOWN PRODUCTS:** Video display terminals, personal computers

YEAR FOUNDED: 1975

EMPLOYEES: 550

HEADQUARTERS: Sunnyvale, California

SALES: $161 million (1983)

PROFITS: $22 million (1983)

OWNERSHIP: Public (1983)

The morning of March 16, 1983, many hard-working denizens of Silicon Valley opened their *San Jose Mercury News* to discover that the ranks of the inconceivably rich had been joined by a quiet neighbor named Kyupin Philip Hwang. Even those whose admiration was tinged with envy had to agree that the day TeleVideo offered its shares to the public was a good day for the American Dream. The story of Philip Hwang ranks among the most remarkable rags-to-riches stories of all time.

It begins in Hungnam, North Korea, in 1950 during the thick of the Korean War. MacArthur's troops have swept through the country and the North Korean Army has retreated into China. In this industrial harbor town, cut off from farmlands and badly bombed by the Americans, there is hardly any food. Philip Hwang, age 14, is already providing for his family. He cleans rooms for the occupying U.S. Tenth Army in return for C rations. It is easy to imagine him. To the GIs he must have seemed just another Korean street kid, like the ones often portrayed in the series "M*A*S*H."

Seven million Communist Chinese troops are poised above

the border, ready to strike at the United Nations forces. Mac-Arthur threatens A-bombs on Shanghai and Peking; meanwhile, one million United Nations troops are being evacuated from the North. Rumors say that when the Chinese invade they will execute anyone who worked for the Americans, and when the Americans are evacuated they'll drop A-bombs on Hungnam.

The Hwangs decide that Philip, being in double jeopardy, should try to escape first. Hwang convinces a couple of GIs to hide him behind a pile of surgical masks in a GMC truck being sent south by ship. The MPs at the dock don't see the small boy hidden toward the front of the truck. A crane picks up the truck and drops it on the ship. Hours later—well out at sea—his GI buddies locate the truck and yell, "Hey, Al" (they call him Al). He's safe, on his way to Pusan in the far South.

Philip has said good-bye to his parents, sister, and three brothers, not knowing if he would ever see them again. A few weeks later some GIs show him a *Saturday Evening Post* with pictures of Hungnam Harbor, where a million Koreans are trying to escape to the South. At the front of the throng is his family. Without hesitation Hwang sets off for the remote island of Kuja, which is packed with refugees and POWs. He searches unsuccessfully for his family but recognizes a former neighbor to whom he gives his address—the U.S. Tenth Army headquarters. Two years pass before the neighbor meets the Hwangs, who were dropped on a different island, and Hwang is tracked down.

1953: The cease-fire comes. After four years living next to the demilitarized zone between the two Koreas, and working as an errand boy for the Tenth Army ($5 a month plus food), the boy quits his job to go to school in Seoul. Young Hwang has ambition, but his life in South Korea seems indistinguishable from that of thousands of other street waifs. He lives with two friends in a tiny room behind a stationery shop. He shines shoes and sells pencils and paper pads to earn a meager existence. He studies English in addition to taking other classes at night. Already Hwang is working or studying 18 to 20 hours a day, something that is to become a lifelong habit. One of his roommates is adopted by a military doctor and goes off to the States. His letters say, "Come to America. You work much, much less and still can go to school." Hwang had a goal in life beyond day-to-day survival.

1964: Logan, Utah. The 28-year-old Korean is now a freshman in engineering at Utah State. After Hwang finished high school, he spent a couple of years in the South Korean Army and took two years of college in Seoul, before he was eligible to take exams to qualify for overseas study. He took them once, twice, three times. "So disgusting," he reminisces, "nobody passed." The fourth time, after special bone-up classes, he made it. He got a scholarship to Utah State that included tuition and a room in a dormitory.

When he left Seoul in September, he had only $50 cash. He survived for two months in the Land of Opportunity, but now it was December and he was hungry. Every day he kept going to classes—but no breakfast, no lunch, no friends. One evening he found a box by his door, filled with unlabeled, dented cans. The note inside said the local Presbyterian minister had dropped them off. Opening one of the cans, the starving student found something that was brownish-orange. Pumpkin pie filling, heated with water, became a kind of soup. Hwang lived on Reverend Blum's damaged cans till Christmas vacation, when he had to drop out of school for a semester to earn enough money to eat.

1966: Romance. Gemma, a woman he met in Seoul while taking the overseas exams, comes to Utah State to pursue a master's in food services administration. Within days of seeing her again in Utah, Hwang suggested getting married to save on rent. She was outraged at first but he eventually persuaded her of his sincerity.

The Utah years were lean. The couple worked summers at a Lake Tahoe casino washing dishes, busing tables, wrapping coins, and saving every penny to support themselves during the school year. An oft-told family tale describes Philip finding a $20 bill on the casino floor and, to Gemma's horror, insisting that they share it with his co-workers.

1973: Hwang becomes a full-time storekeeper; he owns a 7-Eleven franchise on Winchester Avenue in San Jose. He had graduated in electrical engineering from Utah State and had several jobs in his field—with Ford and Burroughs in Detroit (where he picked up a master's at Wayne State University), and then NCR in Dayton. But he made the mistake of taking a job in Silicon Valley as a chip designer with a start-up video game company that folded after several months. Times were tough in the Valley for engineers. Hence, the 7-Eleven. The 16-hour days, seven-day weeks were miserable. He hated the graveyard shift with its interminable Muzak. But he learned how to run a business and how to contend with children filching candy and employees depleting the stock. Gemma helped out in the store after coming home from her job as a hospital dietitian. They had two daughters.

1975: Gemma becomes the sole provider for family and company as Philip tries to start his own video game business with $9,000 in savings from selling the 7-Eleven store. The obstacles he overcame would have thwarted a meeker man. His two original partners deserted him because they didn't think they could afford to buy video display monitors—a required part of a video game package in those days. Philip embarked on a frantic series of flights to his homeland in search of subcontractors to supply the monitors he desperately needed. The Korean monitor makers demanded larger orders than Hwang could offer; and when he did get a purchase order from Atari for 6,000 home game machines, he had to put up his house, car, and furniture to obtain the credit to satisfy the Koreans. Even when he was commuting across the Pacific twice a week, he would haul his luggage and often a video monitor two miles to catch a 10-cent bus instead of paying for the $2.50 taxi to Seoul.

Hwang realized that he was onto something much bigger than video games. All kinds of people needed a good, cheap monitor. Not only that, but by adding a $10 microchip, the "dumb" terminal—which then dominated the market—could be given information processing capabilities and memory.

Hwang unleashed 100 percent of his unstoppable energy on producing "smart" terminals. For several more months he commuted to Korea, training his suppliers' employees and setting up exacting quality control procedures. Then, ignoring the comments of manufacturers who thought he had lost his senses, he ordered enough parts to assemble 50,000 terminals with fancy molded plastic cases. Says Hwang: "After technology comes packaging. That's the way to make your product go bang, bang, bang!"

When Hwang's competitors, the makers of "dumb" terminals, saw the product he was offering and its price, they took him for a flash in the pan selling below cost to gain a foothold in the market—a familiar method of committing high-tech suicide. The next time they looked it was too late to catch up with him.

Everyone wanted Hwang's smart terminal. His supply never ran out, and the price didn't go up because Hwang knew how to keep costs down. TeleVideo has a factory in Korea and an assembly plant in Puerto Rico. Many employees in his California plants are young Korean immigrants. And much of the testing of equipment is computerized ("cost savings of 30 percent, quality control five times higher").

1983: Philip Hwang offers his stock to the public. At the close of trading of the first day on the market, Hwang's 69-percent share of the firm was worth $610 million—making him one of the 100-richest men in America. His company's sales that year were $169 million, up from $2 million just four years earlier.

By 1983 TeleVideo was into more than computer terminals. In fact, over half of the 1983 revenues came from a much more risky push into personal computer systems. Just how risky can be judged by watching the rise and fall of TeleVideo's stock price—and Hwang's net worth. At one point, with the stock at $40, Hwang was a billionaire (at least on paper). At the end of August 1984, the stock was closer to $5, and an article in *Fortune* magazine was referring to TeleVideo's losses stemming from "its ill-timed move into the personal computer business" and mentioning a strong, new competitor in the terminal business—an immigrant from Hong Kong (Bernard K. Wyse of Wyse Terminals.)

Hwang's schedule remains predictably intense. He travels nearly half the time. When he's in town and there's no business dinner, he usually gets home around nine o'clock. There's no time for frivolous reading. He devours electronics magazines, but with the *Wall Street Journal* he is very selective: he checks on how his stock is doing, then scans the headlines and the ads to see what his competitors are up to. Occasionally a movie is endured (for the sake, he avers, of wife and children). His one regular recreation is racquetball, which he enjoys three mornings a week at six o'clock: "Go hit the ball, take a quick shower, jacuzzi for 10 minutes. That's the best time of the day. Think about what I'm going to do."

A fervent Christian, Hwang feels that the fruits of spiritual life are here rather than in some distant heaven. "My faith helps me run my business. There are tensions, legal problems, marketing—I can laugh sooner than the others because of my faith. Of course I'm a human being, I get nervous. But as soon as I calm down, I pray: This matter is all up to You. Every day I pray, for my employees, their families, the vendors who supply parts, my customers, of course, my family and friends. And I pray for myself. But as soon as I start to pray for somebody else, I get—Pow!—more energy."

Actually Hwang seems to get—Pow!—more energy no matter what he does. Maybe that's because he doesn't stop to notice what has happened to him. Though his personal wealth puts him in a league with the Bechtels or William Hewlett of Hewlett-Packard, Gemma still works part-time at the hospital. (They have, however, acquired a $3 million Los Altos house built to look like a Welsh castle; its dining room is big enough to seat 400 for dinner.)

"I'm not successful yet," he says. And just to make sure that no one catches him succeeding, he adds, "I don't have a goal." By this he means an ultimate goal. He admits having case-by-case goals. But even these return to a strangely austere formula: "My first objective is to survive, not complicated. My next goal is the same. Survive." The emphasis Hwang gives the word conveys something of how much further than most of us he is willing to go to ensure that goal.

President, chief executive officer, and chairman of the board, Hwang is passionately involved in company activities at every level—research, design, production, marketing, and employee relations. Characteristically jocular and as energetic as a meteor, he can also flare into vivid anger. According to an often-told story, he once stormed out of his office and fired the first five people he ran into. While denying that the people were fired, Hwang told us laughingly, "Yeah, I agree, I have a bad temper. A lot of people quote that. But I'm not a bad guy. Am I?"

Porter Hurt

"When you hang sheetrock for ten years, you know what it is to work"

▶ **BEST-KNOWN VENTURE:** PH Components

OTHER VENTURES: Actrix Computers, Testology

BORN: 1940

RAISED: Baltimore, Maryland, and Anaheim, California

FATHER'S OCCUPATION: Engineer at Lockheed

FIRST DOLLAR EARNED: Busboy at Knott's Berry Farm

SCHOOLING: High school graduate

ORIGINAL FINANCING: Poker winnings; loan on his home

PERSONAL NET WORTH: 100 percent of PH Components

HOME: Palo Alto Hills, California

FAMILY: Married; two children

PERSONAL TRANSPORTATION: Ferrari GTS, Jaguar, helicopter, 40-foot Formula 402 speedboat

PH components, Inc.

PH COMPONENTS INC.: Electronic circuit board assemblers and component distributors.

▶ **BEST-KNOWN PRODUCT:** The lawsuit that began the scuttling of Osborne Computer

YEAR FOUNDED: 1975

EMPLOYEES: 170

HEADQUARTERS: Fremont, California

SALES: $50 million

PROFITS: $10 million (before taxes)

OWNERSHIP: Private; 100 percent held by Porter Hurt

Porter Hurt thinks most would-be entrepreneurs underestimate the role of gambling. He should know. His $50-million-a-year, highly successful behind-the-scenes parts supplier would not exist if Hurt had not been willing to bet all he had time and time again. In fact, Hurt would not even be involved in the computer business were it not for the poker games he used to play after spending his days as a construction worker, pounding nails into sheetrock for 10 long years.

Hurt's remarkable success story starts back in the late '60s, when California's Silicon Valley was just beginning to boom. Hurt worked as a laborer building homes and factories. Some nights he'd go out riding with a San Jose motorcycle gang. When asked whether his escapades could be compared with those of the Hell's Angels, Hurt once told a *Wall Street Journal* reporter: "[I] never did any of the really bad stuff." The reporter commented, "He doesn't count his bike rides through a YMCA and a crowded restaurant as bad stuff."

But it was how Hurt spent other evenings that made the difference. It's not that Hurt never made money playing poker.

He often did. He told the same *Journal* reporter of his willingness to bet everything he owned at the twice-weekly poker games: "That's why I look like I am sixty years old instead of forty-two." It was at these poker games that Hurt met several fellows who were beginning to make it big in the area's burgeoning electronics business. Hurt grew tired of seeing his poker-playing buddies wave to him from inside their expensive Porsches while he was hanging sheetrock. That's why he took his first big gamble.

Hurt quit his $1,500-a-month construction job to take a $450-a-month warehouse stock boy job with Kierluff Electronics, a distributor of electronics components located in Palo Alto. It was 1967, Hurt was 27 years old, and his wife was pregnant and jobless. He told us that he took the job "to learn the business." He elaborated, "I think a lot of people have opportunities and don't realize it. I think the gambling aspect is very, very prominent. I have risked everything I ever owned three different times to make things happen. I mean *everything*."

Hurt's first gamble paid off. It didn't take him long to reveal a natural sales talent and three years later he was making $60,000 a year as Kierluff's general sales manager.

Many former sheetrock hangers would have been pleased with such a quick progression. Not Porter Hurt. He had bigger things in mind. Sure, he could make a lot of money working for somebody else, but he could make even more working for himself. That meant he'd have to throw the dice again. For his second big gamble, Hurt hocked his house (for $20,000) and set up PH Components, an electronic parts distribution company, in 1975. He ran it out of his kitchen, taking orders by phone in the morning, tracking down the parts all afternoon, and delivering them in the family car in the evening.

PH Components was doing fine, and it could have been a thriving small electronics distributorship today. But Hurt wanted to make it big. So, two years after he launched the enterprise, he took his third big gamble. As he described it to us, "I felt a crunch coming in the market." A shortage of electronics parts would mean that anyone with a big supply could name his own price. He again hocked everything he owned to buy as many parts as he could. Soon components that had cost

Hurt 20 cents were fetching $4 each. "I made a couple of million dollars on that little episode," Hurt told us.

With the profits from the parts shortage "episode," Hurt started a new company, Testology, which became his biggest success. Hurt knew that his customers sent the components they purchased from PH Components to other companies for assembly onto the printed circuit boards used in most electronic devices. Testology offered one-stop service for parts and completed boards at a price 30 percent lower than other suppliers. Hurt also offered a one-year guarantee. The industry, which was accustomed to a 50 percent parts-failure rate, rushed to place its orders.

Testology's customers included Hewlett-Packard and several other well-known names, but one of them, Osborne Computer, became a thorn in Hurt's side by failing to pay its bills. The gamblers' code does not leave room for welching. So Hurt called Osborne's bluff, suing his errant customer for nonpayment of about $5 million worth of bills. The $100-million-a-year company later collapsed under the weight of all those who followed Hurt's example.

Hurt had another reason for resenting Osborne. The way he saw it, the portable computer maker was doing little more than putting a package around Testology's assembled boards. Why not make a portable computer himself? It just so happened that one of Testology's customers, Ted Pollard, owned a company that was about to make the portable computer now called Actrix. When Pollard asked Hurt to invest in his new enterprise, Hurt responded by offering to buy him out. Pollard promptly threw Hurt out of his office. But a few weeks later, in June 1982, Pollard reconsidered and accepted $2.1 million for 80 percent of Actrix.

A rather different picture of Hurt is drawn by Adam Osborne in his book, *Hypergrowth*, self-published in 1984. Getting even with all his enemies, Osborne describes Hurt as looking like "a pork barrel" and goes on to charge collusion between Hurt and Tom Davidson, who was production manager at Osborne Computer. According to Osborne's story, Porter Hurt drove a hard bargain with Davidson—hard for Osborne, easy for Hurt. It supposedly obligated Osborne Computer to pay for all components supplied by one of Hurt's companies, PH Components, even if they were not used in the ultimate boards supplied by the other Hurt company, Testology.

Hurt's Actrix gamble was not as successful as the gruff entrepreneur's other ventures. When Hurt first introduced Actrix's computer (then called the Access Matrix) *InfoWorld*'s John Dvorak commented that the machine had "everything but a wet bar." In addition to its two disk drives, it had a built-in printer and modem, and an exceptionally large bundle of software that came with it. Hoping to sell 65,000 computers at $2,190 each, Hurt stood by mystified when the public failed to pay attention to his new machine. He hired Joe ("Where's the Beef") Sedelmaier to create three elaborate television commercials, only to see them scrapped when a lawsuit by an Ohio company named Access Computer forced the name-change to Actrix. It shook Hurt to discover how high the ante had been raised in the marketing of computer hardware. "We didn't have fifty million dollars to compete with IBM and Apple," he laments.

While the demise of Actrix is a blow to Hurt's ego, it hasn't done as much damage to his pocketbook. His other two companies, which he is merging into one—PH/Testology—have reached combined sales of $50 million a year. Porter Hurt, the sole owner, says his gross profit margin is 20 percent. Despite the 80-hour week which Hurt puts in, he somehow finds time for two "vices": golf and a $250,000 speedboat he is preparing for offshore racing.

Every morning Porter Hurt emerges from his home in Palo Alto Hills and hauls his stocky frame aboard the chauffeur-piloted helicopter that whisks him off to work. Ten minutes after take-off, Hurt descends to his private landing pad behind the Fremont building that houses PH/Testology. As he flies to work, the gold chain-bedecked entrepreneur (he regularly wears $15,000 worth of gold jewelry) can gaze down on smoggy Silicon Valley. If he looks hard, he can see homes and factories where he used to hang sheetrock everyday. He might also be able to spot some of his more cautious former poker-playing friends who have to tool to work in their Porsches and Mercedes.

GONE FISHIN'

As far as most corporate executives are concerned, once you've been an entrepreneur, you're unemployable. Those same qualities that make an entrepreneur successful— nerve, independence, single-mindedness—frighten off companies looking for "team players." So what does an out-of-work entrepreneur do with himself? Alan Shugart decided to go fishing.

Shugart's company, Shugart Associates, was a pioneer maker of small, floppy disk drives, before he was pushed out of his own firm in 1974 by the venture capitalist investors when then sold it to Xerox. "I finally said, 'Screw it,' and quit. I probably would have gotten fired anyway," Shugart says.

Before starting his own company, he had put in over 18 years as a team player for IBM, and another four at Memorex. He knew he didn't want to go back to that. Shugart bought himself a fishing boat and set himself up as a commercial fisher of salmon.

For five years, he fished out of Santa Cruz and San Francisco, California. "I never made any money at it, but I used to catch fish and sell them. Oh, it was a fun time," he recalls. But once an entrepreneur, always an entrepreneur. Shugart sold the boat and founded a new company (to manufacture hard disk subsystems for personal computers) with Finis Conner in 1979. He claims he found the name in the dictionary when he looked for a seven-letter word that began with an "s," ended with a "t," and had a "g" in the middle, like Shugart. But the name he chose, Seagate, would look fine across the stern of a boat, should he ever change course again.

EAVESDROPPING BY THE RULES

Silicon Valley bars and restaurants overflow with local shop talk, just like hangouts anywhere. But when that shop talk runs to new computers not yet introduced by the likes of Apple and Hewlett-Packard, you're talking an earful—and pocketful—of very valuable information.

To protect themselves from little spies with big ears, Valley technocrats have evolved an unspoken—but clearly understood— code of behavior for acceptable eavesdropping:

—Never use a tape recorder.

—Do not join into overheard conversations.

—Refrain from tailing loose talkers to their offices.

—Watch whom you sit near—if he or she is a competitor, move.

Of course, a little technical knowledge wouldn't hurt the budding eavesdropper. And one should always know where the best listening is. The Lion & Compass Restaurant and Rodeo, both in Sunnyvale, and Eli McFly (especially for Apple people) in Cupertino are all good listening posts.

Above all, never feel queasy about eavesdropping. Aaron C. Goldberg, an analyst for International Data Corp., told the *Wall Street Journal*, "You can be passively sleazy. If you're out there drinking a beer, you shouldn't have to wear earplugs."

When The Bloom Is Off The Rose . . .

High-tech Layoffs in July 1984

Atari	Home computers	1,000
Qume	Printers	600
Victor Technologies	Business computers	400
Diablo Systems	Printers	300
Franklin Computer	Home computers	160
VisiCorp	*VisiCalc* marketers	110
MicroPro	Business software	100
Software Arts	*VisiCalc* authors	65

Reincarnations

Entrepreneur	Company Name	Former Company Name
George Morrow	Morrow Designs	Thinker Toys
Chuck Grant/ Mark Greenberg	North Star	Kentucky Fried Computers
William Millard	ComputerLand	Computer Shack
Lee Felsenstein	Community Memory	Loving Grace Cybernetics

Terry Johnson

"While I might not be a great leader, I'm not a very good follower. I just got thrown out of the nest"

▶ **BEST-KNOWN VENTURE:** MiniScribe

BORN: 1935

RAISED: Ogden, Utah

FATHER'S OCCUPATION: Rancher

FIRST DOLLAR EARNED: Cowboy

SCHOOLING: B.S., University of Utah; M.S., electrical engineering, University of California at Berkeley

ORIGINAL FINANCING: Savings and $1 million local venture capital

PERSONAL NET WORTH: $31 million (14 percent of MiniScribe at public offering)

HOME: Ranch near Longmont, Colorado

FAMILY: Married; three children

PERSONAL TRANSPORTATION: Mercedes 500 SCL; gray Arabian horse named King

 **MiniScribe**

MINISCRIBE CORPORATION: Second-largest producer of hard-disk drives for personal computers.

▶ **BEST-KNOWN PRODUCT:** Hard-disk drives for the IBM PC-XT

YEAR FOUNDED: 1980

EMPLOYEES: 1,650

HEADQUARTERS: Longmont, Colorado

SALES: $76 million (1983); $140 million (1984 projection)

PROFITS: $4.8 million (1983)

OWNERSHIP: Public (1983)

I n September 1980, Terry Johnson went on a hunting trip in the mountains above Steamboat Springs, Colorado. It was (or so he thought) one last fling before settling down to run MiniScribe, the company he'd founded that July. Before leaving, he had made several presentations to venture capitalists and assured his partner and five employees that the money would be forthcoming.

But when Johnson led his string of horses down the Rockies and back to civilization, he called his wife and learned that he no longer had a company. His partner had been "turned around" by another company, and of the other five employees, only one showed up for work the next day. As for money, who'd take a chance on such a bereft start-up?

This apparent disaster is typical of the setbacks that modern-day cowboys/entrepreneurs have to learn to take in their stride in the the new Wild West. Terry Johnson quickly dusted himself off and started another roundup, which in his case turned out to be quite lucrative.

Johnson was a reluctant entrepreneur, "thrown out of the

nest," as he describes it, when corporate management decisions went against him. "Although my father had always been self-employed, and I always had a feeling that I'd like to have my own company or something like that, I honestly never thought I'd have guts enough to do it," he says.

Certainly no one who knew him in his formative years would have said he was headed for self-made wealth. He grew up in Odgen, Utah, "the kind of person who pretty much melted into the woodwork," as he puts it. He followed his older brother into an engineering career. Four years as an electronics technician in the Navy convinced him he'd found something he was good at, so he went back to school to study electrical engineering, ending up with a master's degree from the University of California at Berkeley.

His first job after that was with IBM in San Jose, California. There he received what he calls "a postgraduate course in how to design machines for mass production and for tremendous reliability." At first, he was excited by all the responsibility he was given as a design engineer. But after seven years—all but one of which he spent working on disk drives— he still wasn't a manager, so he left.

It wasn't an easy decision for him. "Leaving IBM is like renouncing your U.S. citizenship," he says. "They do a fantastic job of convincing you that it's the greatest company in the world." In fact, he says he might have stayed if his boss hadn't concealed from him that another group at IBM was prepared to offer him a management post. Yet he admits that working for IBM was perhaps a little too predictable. "It was like being out on the Great Plains and seeing your future out there a thousand miles in front of you."

The next two companies he worked for—Memorex and Storage Technology—offered three primary inducements: management opportunity, challenge, and stock equity. He wanted to be in management not because he liked controlling people's lives, but because he didn't like having to live with decisions made by other people behind closed doors. The challenge came from being in on start-up ventures at both companies. He also appreciated having a piece of the action. "I've always managed to spend all the salary I get," he says, "but the [stock] equity I've been able to save."

All this time he was still making disk drives. At Storage Technology, after developing "one of the company's most successful disk drive products," he became director of engineering for the disk division. But after that, things began to go downhill. Johnson clashed with his superior and found himself demoted. That was enough to push the bird—feathers ruffled—out of the nest.

What now? He had some financial security thanks to the Memorex and Storage Technology stock, but no plans. Soon though, people who had worked with Johnson began to suggest, "Gee, why don't you put something together, we'd like to join you." So, off he went to the spring 1980 National Computer Conference in Anaheim, California, looking for a product to develop. Naturally, disk drives came to mind. At the conference he ran into Jugi Tandon, who expressed interest in having Johnson start up a new operation for Tandon's disk drive manufacturing firm. This sounded good to Johnson, so he went to work on a risk analysis.

As the analysis progressed, the idea began to look so hot that Johnson decided he didn't need Tandon—he'd do the whole thing himself. There was just one problem: "I'd been in the engineering monastery all this time. I knew engineering and a little about manufacturing, but I knew absolutely nothing about finance or marketing."

Fortunately, through a colleague he'd known since his Memorex days, he met Glen Klimek, a co-founder of Dysan who was now dabbling in venture capitalism. Once Klimek showed him how to prepare financial models, Johnson had fun doing the projections on his computer. He made some presentations to potential investors and pulled together a staff. And that's when things fell apart during the hunting trip.

From then on, life had more ups and downs than Johnson's beloved Colorado mountains. Up: Johnson was able to assemble another staff. Down: He was turned down "by every venture capital group in Northern California." Up: He finally raised $1 million through friends and other small investors, and the initial MiniScribe disk drive was developed in Johnson's very atypical basement, which overlooks a 65-acre lake on his ranch in Longmont, Colorado.

Down: Even after the company had a real office in Longmont, customers didn't exactly flock to MiniScribe. "'What's MiniScribe, where's Longmont, and who cares?' was their attitude," says Johnson. Larger firms, such as Seagate and Tandon, held on to most of the 5¼-inch disk drive business.

Up: On a sales visit to Tandy in Fort Worth, Texas, Johnson's chief engineer, John Squires, ran into a brutally candid buyer. After looking at MiniScribe's proposed product, the Tandy man said, "You guys are wasting your time and mine." He then tore their design to shreds and told Squires what he thought it would take to make their product competitive. Squires reported to his boss with the words, "Johnson, I think we've been riding the wrong horse."

MiniScribe completely redesigned the drive and was able to introduce a much-improved product by June 1982. Down: Despite some success at raising additional capital, MiniScribe still wasn't making a profit, and the company had to cut back its work force by 15 percent.

"It was October of 1982 when things finally started to fall into place for us," recalls Johnson. "We got contracts with North Star, Altos, Fortune—and then IBM. The fourth quarter of 1982 we did 3.5-million dollars in revenue, and in 1983 we did about 76-million dollars. We had just incredible growth. We went from 93 employees in June of 1982 to 1,500 by the end of 1983."

About 60 percent of that growth could be attributed to business from Johnson's old alma mater, IBM, especially a contract to supply hard disk drives for the IBM XT personal computer. In November 1983 MiniScribe went public, raising $24 million. Johnson owned (and still owns) 14 percent of the company's stock himself, worth $31 million at the time of the offering.

Given MiniScribe's history, it isn't surprising that this peak was followed by a sudden valley. In January 1984, IBM cut back its orders, and MiniScribe stock plummeted 42 percent in one day, from $12 to $7 a share.

Still, Johnson got back on the figurative horse. MiniScribe

found some new customers and pushed Tandon out of second place (Seagate remains first) in manufacturing hard disk drives. Despite previous setbacks, Johnson's enthusiasm hasn't flagged. He loves being out of the engineering cloister: "Working with the investment bankers, the lawyers, the customers, getting involved with the marketing aspects—all of that is tremendously interesting and varied. Just wonderful."

He's finally bought the first new car he's ever owned (a Mercedes) and is taking the flying lessons he used to think he couldn't afford. He still keeps up his ranch at the foot of the Rockies, and he and his family now vacation as far away from home as Australia. He's even been known to sneak off on hunting trips.

Jerry Sanders

"I work absolutely as little as possible and that turns out to be more than any human being should work"

▶ **BEST-KNOWN VENTURE:** Advanced Micro Devices

BORN: 1936

RAISED: Chicago, Illinois

FATHER'S OCCUPATION: Traffic light repairman

SCHOOLING: B.S., electrical engineering, University of Illinois

ORIGINAL FINANCING: Severance pay from Fairchild

PERSONAL NET WORTH: Over $28 million in AMD stock alone; 1984 salary and benefits amounted to almost $1 million

HOME: Cooperative apartment on Russian Hill, San Francisco; houses in Bel-Air and Malibu, California

FAMILY: Divorced; three daughters

PERSONAL TRANSPORTATION: Bentley convertible, Rolls-Royce Silver Spur, Cadillac limousine, Volkswagen Rabbit, Rolls-Royce Corniche convertible, two Blazer S-10s

ADVANCED MICRO DEVICES ⊐

ADVANCED MICRO DEVICES INC.: Fifth-largest maker of silicon chips in the United States.

▶ **BEST-KNOWN PRODUCTS:** 550 different types of chips for computers and other electronic devices

YEAR FOUNDED: 1969

EMPLOYEES: 13,000

HEADQUARTERS: Sunnyvale, California

SALES: $583 million (fiscal 1984)

PROFITS: $71 million (fiscal 1984)

OWNERSHIP: Public (1972); Siemens, a German electronics firm, owns 19 percent; Jerry Sanders owns 4 percent (or 778,121 shares)

Jerry Sanders believes in the traditional American ideals of honesty, loyalty, and hard work. And he's bought the American dream of material rewards for effort—with a vengeance. Sanders didn't stop at a house and two cars in the garage. The garages of his "magnificent" homes in Bel-Air, Malibu, and San Francisco, California, hold a total of seven cars, including two Rolls-Royces, a Bentley, and a Cadillac. He never misses the chance to tell anyone who asks that his enormous ambition is fueled by one thing: money. "My dreams were very simple," he says. "I just wanted to make a lot of money."

He has succeeded fabulously. Since founding Advanced Micro Devices (AMD) in 1969, Sanders has built it into the fifth largest maker of silicon chips in the United States. In 1984, his stock was worth over $28 million. His cash compensation for 1983 was $948,000, making him one of the best-paid executives in the semiconductor industry. By 1985 AMD was expected to approach Sanders' oft-stated goal of becoming a "gigabuck" ($1 billion in sales) company.

At 48 years of age in 1984, Sanders seems to have gotten everything he ever wanted and believed in. But behind the super salesman's slogans and the free enterprise evangelism lurks a new introspection. The man a colleague described as the "world's greatest fortune cookie writer" now wonders, "What, after a gigabuck, what do I do then? The answer to that really is not clear."

Somehow, this soul-searching Sanders is almost shocking. For 15 years, the flamboyant Sanders has delighted journalists looking for good copy in often dull Silicon Valley. Sanders, with his gold chains and snow-white hair setting off his tan, could always be counted on for a catchy phrase or an outrageous opinion.

Everything about Sanders is excessive and exaggerated. He throws Christmas parties for 8,000 employees and guests at places like the Moscone Center in San Francisco, site of the 1984 Democratic Convention. The 1983 party "outdazzled Hollywood's tribute to the Queen of England," according to the *San Francisco Examiner.* It featured 25 bars and rock bands on two stages. Sanders himself rode into the convention center in a sleigh.

In the photo of Sanders for AMD's 1984 annual report, he wore the typical blue business suit, but the foot that rested on a polished wood table was shod in an attention-grabbing red-white-and-blue cowboy boot stamped with the initials "W.J.S. III." But no matter how outlandish Sanders appears in print, he's extremely likable in person.

Jerry Sanders likes to thumb his nose at the staid business community. He exemplifies the modern maxim, "Living well is the best revenge." He's getting his revenge for growing up poor and unwanted on the south side of Chicago. "I saw people who had clean hands and haircuts and nice clothes and took baths every day," he says. He wanted that. It pleased him immensely that when he went back to Chicago for his 25th high school reunion in 1979 "there wasn't another guy there that had a net worth one-tenth of mine. Maybe not even one-hundredth of mine."

Sanders's parents never could get along. His father was a traffic light repairman for the city of Chicago; his mother had her hands full with Jerry and his brothers and sisters. They farmed out one son to the maternal grandparents, and Jerry's paternal grandparents took him in. "With a certain degree of reluctance. Somebody's got to raise the kid. You can't just throw him in an ashcan," Sanders remembers ruefully. "I was your basic love-starved kid."

To curry favor from his stern grandfather, Jerry became an overachiever. He was the valedictorian of his high school class and won a scholarship to the University of Illinois to study engineering ("because it paid the most"). After graduating in 1958, he wanted to put as many miles as possible between himself and the rigid class system of his childhood.

Young Jerry was painfully aware of his wrong-side-of-the-tracks background. "In Chicago, I would have always been identified with the University of Illinois and the south side of Chicago. I didn't go to Northwestern; my family wasn't from Winnetka. I was tired of it." To fulfill his American dream of upward mobility, Sanders chose that most mobile of dream states, California. He believed California to be "the transparent society where you will move as far and fast as your abilities will take you without that excess baggage that you didn't go to the right school."

Sanders worked for Douglas Aircraft when he first went to California in 1958. He stayed at Douglas a year during which time he designed the air conditioning system controls for the DC-8 jet. He then joined Motorola, first as an applications engineer and then as a semiconductor salesman.

Again his motivation was money. "I made the observation that people in sales didn't know anything and made more money than I did, had an expense account, and a company car. I was not in engineering because I had a great desire to create, or design, or invent. I was in engineering as a vehicle to improve my standard of living." Sanders has always assumed that everyone is mostly interested in making more money, and he made that a major employee motivator when he founded his own company years later.

His unique personal style evolved during that time: cocky, self-assured, and wild. He received so many speeding tickets in his yellow Corvette that he lost his driver's license for 90 days

—a fate worse than death for a salesman. Motorola understandably wanted to fire him, and he lost all feeling of loyalty to them when they failed to pay him the homage he thought he deserved as a top salesman.

He went over to the competition—Fairchild—where he demanded a Chevrolet Bel-Air convertible as part of his employment terms. They agreed. At Fairchild, he became, at the age of 31, one of the youngest marketing directors in the industry. His meteoric rise sputtered out in ignominy when a new management team pushed him out. Sanders claims he was too much a "hot-shot and smart-mouth" for the management, but he dismisses as "nonsense" reports that he wore pink pants and boots to an IBM meeting and owned a silver briefcase. The only unusual style he admits to affecting at that point was a black Cadillac convertible company car, when everybody else was driving Fords. "I thought that was only appropriate. I was a star!"

He was enough of a star (or troublemaker), to merit a full year's severance pay when the axe fell at Fairchild. It must gall Fairchild that Sanders used his severance pay as seed money to get AMD started, especially since today AMD is bigger than Fairchild.

Sanders didn't start AMD to get back at Fairchild. But, as everyone told him, what could a star do other than run his own vehicle? Because Sanders had neither the engineering expertise nor the money for research and development to make his own semiconductors, he decided to produce already-existing silicon chip designs that he would guarantee for quality and reliability—and make customers pay more for the service.

On the strength of his own personality and track record in the industry, and the fact that, he says, "I always got what I asked for," Sanders started AMD in 1969 with $1.5 million from venture capitalists. But it wasn't all that easy. Because Sanders needed technical expertise, he rounded up seven engineers and offered them a piece of the company for their knowledge. "That's what entrepreneurs do," Sanders says innocently. "You go and find someone that has the skill you need and you get them to do it for you."

At one fund-raising meeting, a venture capitalist told Sanders, "I've investigated all the people in your group and they're second-rate. You're the only star in the group." The comment still rankles Sanders. It seems to be against his credo to denigrate the contributions of others who've helped him build AMD. But he is quick to point out that his sense of fairmindedness when forming the company has hurt his pocketbook today. Looking back, Sanders says he made two mistakes with AMD: he founded the company with too many people; and he did not give himself a high enough percentage of the company. "I was too stupid and I was too fair. I got six percent; everybody else got four-and-one-half percent. And they were upset even with that! I thought, 'Jeez, you guys are really assholes.'" Of the eight original founders, only Sanders remains at AMD today.

At first Sanders took a textbook approach to running AMD—literally. He read Peter Drucker's *Managing for Results,* a book he calls the "*Mein Kampf* of AMD." But Sanders quickly institutionalized his hard-learned value system: loyalty, honesty, responsibility, and quality work will be rewarded with money. That and advertising "sloganeering" became the organizing principles of AMD. The Silicon Valley office walls are papered with glossy promotional posters, like the one that proclaims "The Age of Asparagus." Sanders often compares AMD's growth to that of the asparagus because they both need a few years to mature before paying off with a fine crop.

AMD's crop has come in, and it's because of Sanders. The *San Jose Mercury News* wrote, "Through all the twists and turns of the market over the past decade, AMD has made no fundamental mistakes," like concentrating on the game market, or on any single customer. No single customer represents more than 10 percent of sales, but such firms as AT&T, IBM, Nippon Electric, DEC, Burroughs, and Olivetti purchase one or another of AMD's 550 different types of chips. In many cases, AMD is sticking to its original strategy of being a "second source" for these chips; that is, it licenses the design for the chip from another company and manufactures it for sale. For instance, AMD has been a second source for some of the microprocessor chips created by Intel that power the IBM PC. But as AMD has become a bigger player in the industry, it has developed its own research-and-development arm. Now, almost 40 percent of AMD's sales come from chips developed in-house.

Sanders and AMD are almost interchangeable to most industry minds now. AMD co-founder Edwin J. Turney told the *Mercury News,* "Sanders is AMD. He had a number of people working for him. They were the band and he was the orchestra leader and he got them to excel."

Sanders is not above whipping his employees into production frenzies with his incentive contests. He's offered an extra week's wages and a drawing for a fire-red Corvette to boost employees' work levels to achieve greater sales. And he's not oblivious to the media attention such events command. In 1980 he personally handed the first of 20 years of monthly checks for $1,000 to an AMD assembly line worker when she won the drawing for a new home. He was accompanied by the local press, of course.

Pay raises and benefits are based on merit. "The better job you do, the more promotions you get, the more money you make, the more fun you have," Sanders tells his troops. He organizes his employees into teams with names like the "Super Rabbits." The teams are part of "directorates," which are headed by managing directors (Sanders, the Julius Caesar of Silicon Valley, calls them "my centurions"). "The entire company is structured entrepreneurially," one managing director asserts.

Now that Sanders's voracious appetite for money is becoming sated, he's looking deeper to his feelings of loyalty and responsibility for his employees to motivate him. "I think that what drives me now is I feel very responsible for my, let's use the word, 'flock.' It fits with the evangelist." He continues, "We got really good core values. We don't have beer busts; we don't have fancy gymnasiums. We just provide an environment where people can improve their economic condition and we don't compromise their principles."

Sanders is a self-proclaimed "world-class spender," but conspicuous consumption does have its limits. "I've got shoes I've never worn; ties I've never worn. That's weird. I've got televisions and video tape recorders that I don't even know how to use," he says. In the five years that he owned a Ferrari (before giving it to a girlfriend as a going-away present when they split up), he never bothered to figure out how to operate the radio. "That's not my personality type, to go reading manuals," he says.

From all outward appearances, Sanders seems to be the same outrageous and rich playboy he's been since his divorce a few years ago. He offers: "I've got a Volkswagen Rabbit—a white one—for my girlfriends to drive around and so I don't have to give them any of my better cars. And so when I don't want to drive them home, they drive the Rabbit. Or as my current girlfriend refers to it, 'the chicks' car.'" She is only 22 years old, a year older than the oldest of his three daughters. He claims that "next to sex, skiing is my favorite thing to do."

But he'll admit that he has nothing to talk about with a 22-year-old girlfriend. He dreams about surviving a heart attack so that he wouldn't feel guilty about taking some time off from his rigorous schedule of four days a week in Silicon Valley and weekends working out of his Beverly Hills office. "I worked every day for three years," he remembers. "I felt that the first 10 years of the company it was like being in prison. I know it cost me my marriage."

For all his brash demeanor, Sanders is willing to reflect on the price of his success. He wants people from the outside to "recognize the cost." What about Silicon Valley? What about the divorce and the alcoholism and the drugs and the pressure and the strain? "There's a lot of it going on."

Early in its history, AMD started an ad campaign featuring Sanders' smiling face over the caption, "Can this man run a million-dollar company?" A few years later they were running the same ad with the figure changed to $10 million; then it went to $100 million. Now that the company is approaching the $1 billion mark, Sanders says, "I'm going to tell [the ad department] don't run a 'Can this man build a $10 billion business?' I don't want to work that hard."

Go Sugiura

"I was young and impatient with a lot of hot blood. I like to be on my own. I like to be free"

▶ **BEST-KNOWN VENTURE:** Amdek

OTHER VENTURES: Steel import company in Venezuela and Sakata International (electronics) in the United States

BORN: 1936

RAISED: Osaka, Japan

FATHER'S OCCUPATION: Import/export entrepreneur and automotive parts manufacturer

FIRST DOLLAR EARNED: Importing Japanese goods to South America

SCHOOLING: University degree in economics

ORIGINAL FINANCING: Own pocket

PERSONAL NET WORTH: 50 percent of Amdek

HOME: Western suburbs of Chicago, Illinois

FAMILY: Married; three children

PERSONAL TRANSPORTATION: Toyota Cressida

AMDEK CORPORATION: First video company to market quality video displays especially designed for personal computers.

▶ **BEST-KNOWN PRODUCTS:** Green and amber monochrome monitors; composite and high-resolution color monitors

YEAR FOUNDED: 1977

EMPLOYEES: 65

HEADQUARTERS: Elk Grove Village, Illinois

SALES: $50 million (1983)

OWNERSHIP: Privately held by Go Sugiura (50 percent), close associates (20 percent), and venture capitalists (30 percent)

G o Sugiura is one manufacturer who wishes consumers would complain more often. "American consumers are very poorly treated," says the Japanese-born Sugiura. "American consumers are extremely understanding, patient, and forgiving, and American manufacturing companies are sort of spoiled and abuse that easy environment. That's what I really want to change."

Sugiura welcomes demanding consumers because he believes his company, Amdek, can stand the close scrutiny. Amdek's computer products, particularly the high-resolution video monitors that use a screen surface of very fine nylon mesh to cut glare and reflection, get high marks for quality. Amdek was the first company in its field to offer two-year warranties. And Sugiura claims to read every single letter of complaint Amdek receives.

It's no coincidence that the companies Sugiura mentions as ideals of quality-consciousness are Japanese. Go Sugiura considers himself to be a very traditional Japanese, right down to his arranged marriage with a woman from his hometown of Osaka.

Sugiura maintains his ties to his culture even though he left Japan over 23 years ago and has spent most of his adult life in South and North America. By American standards, Sugiura seems quite formal in his speech and manner—he bows Japanese-style to guests, for instance. By Japanese standards, though, he's almost an iconoclast. Even though he makes frequent trips to Japan (and Taiwan) to look for new electronic parts for Amdek to market in the United States, Sugiura admits that he's not "the typical Japanese of Japan. Whenever I go back to Japan, I always feel funny."

The life Sugiura leads—moving between America and Japan, but belonging to neither—is not unusual for a Japanese trader. What is unusual about Sugiura is his entrepreneurial spirit. An overseas trader for Mitsui, or C. Itoh, for example, might spend his entire career with the same firm. But Sugiura was, by his own account, "young and impatient with a lot of hot blood. I like to be on my own. I like to be free." Always in search of that freedom, Sugiura founded his own company three times.

Sugiura inherited his entrepreneurial spirit from his father, whom Sugiura calls "unconventional." The elder Sugiura, himself the son of a Christian minister, chose to go into the small (at that time) business of imports and exports. Go was about five years old at the start of World War II. His father put aside importing to manufacture automotive parts for the military. After the war ended, he returned to a successful career importing from the United States.

He would have liked Go, his only son, to continue on in his business, as is common in Japan, but Go had ideas of his own. He accepted his father's advice to go into world trade, but chose to go overseas with a small Osaka electronics importer.

Although he had studied English while he took his degree in economics, it turned out that what he needed was Spanish. At age 24, in 1960, Sugiura found himself in Caracas, Venezuela. For the first few years, Sugiura busied himself with learning Spanish and importing Japanese consumer electronics. Then, Sugiura recalls, he started his own company because "I wanted to seek my own opportunities." His new company moved into a new area of importing: steel. Sugiura didn't care so much what he traded, just as long as it was profitable.

Sugiura was now heading his own company, but still his "hot blood" drove him on. He wanted to be where the action was—the United States. So he sold his young company and moved to Chicago.

Sugiura signed on with a Japanese semiconductor exporter named Sakata as its U.S. sales representative. He was not an employee at first. He worked out an arrangement whereby he headed his own firm under the name Sakata International, almost like a franchise owner.

Sugiura always had the energy, but rarely the capital, needed for international trading. In effect, an importer must pay up front for everything he buys. Eventually, the demand for the products Sugiura imported exceeded his ability to pay for them in advance. His company merged with the mother company and Sugiura became, once again, not his own boss but an employee.

He tried to be a docile employee for Sakata, but youthful impatience can't be denied forever. Age 40 loomed threateningly on Sugiura's personal horizon. "If I wanted to do something on my own, I really wanted to start before I got to forty," he says. In 1977 Sugiura began importing car radio components. He randomly picked the name Leedex for his company, and later just as randomly picked the name Amdek to replace it, after an Ohio manufacturer named Leedex complained.

There was nothing random about Sugiura's trading sense, however. He realized that a whole new market devoted to personal computers was emerging, and he wanted in on it. But he was no engineer—how could he know what products were needed by the computer industry? That's when he remembered Ted McCracken.

McCracken was a professor of computer science at the University of Missouri, and the first Apple computer dealer in the state of Missouri. Sugiura had met McCracken at the foreclosure of an electronics company. McCracken was a consultant for the bank handling the proceedings, Sugiura was one of the creditors. The two hit it off and Sugiura occasionally called McCracken for technical advice. Within a few years, their association would make them both fortunes and put Amdek at the top of the pack of video monitor manufacturers.

Sugiura remembers how it happened. "That was just about the time—1977 or '78—Atari was making some games and Apple was starting to make some noise, but there was no monitor specifically made for personal computers." On one of his trips to Taiwan, Sugiura found a video terminal. At just about the same time, halfway around the world, McCracken was watching Mike Markkula, then president of Apple, demonstrate an Apple computer at a computer show in Dallas. McCracken was impressed. He advised Sugiura to adapt the Taiwan-made monitor to Apple.

"I don't know anything about the personal computer," Sugiura reminded us, but within months he found himself at a computer fair in Texas in the summer of 1978 with a sample video terminal. "I split the cost of a ten-by-ten booth with another guy, and I put my three-foot table on one side. My share of the cost was about 375 dollars. So I put the one and only sample [monitor] on a table and just did black-and-white spread sheets [on the screen]. I was really surprised that there were a lot of people who came to our booth and showed interest." Sugiura decided to order 500 monitors from Taiwan and sell them for $129—$50 less than the only other monitor available.

By 1981 Amdek was selling 2,000 to 3,000 black-and-white monitors a month. Sugiura then thought he'd try selling color monitors as well. He was off to Tokyo and made an agreement to buy one made by Hitachi.

McCracken built a board to adapt it to the Apple computer and they priced the color monitor at $1,000. Their first prototype was ready just in time for the 1982 West Coast Computer Faire in San Francisco. As had happened with the black-and-white version, the color monitor was a hit.

But Amdek's fortune was made by what Sugiura calls "a totally unexpected, uncalculated, happy coincidence." In 1982

IBM started shipping its personal computer. It was capable of displaying color, but IBM didn't offer a color monitor. It just so happened that IBM announced its PC almost the same day Amdek received their first shipment of 500 Hitachi-built color monitors. New IBM PC owners snapped up Amdek's color monitors, despite the $1,000 price tag. For over a year after the IBM PC was announced, Amdek had the field to itself. IBM and others now offer their own color monitors; still, by mid-1984 Amdek had sold over 600,000.

Today, Amdek makes interface boards and plotters, as well as green, amber, and color monitors. Amdek was one of the first companies to offer three-inch disk drives (also made by Hitachi).

So far, so good. Amdek did $50 million in sales in 1983. McCracken and other personal friends of Sugiura's put up $250,000 for about 20 percent of the firm's stock. Sugiura owns approximately 50 percent, with the rest owned by venture capitalists. McCracken, who took a leave of absence from teaching last year, travels with Sigiura to visit Japanese and Taiwanese manufacturers three times a year. The rest of the time, he remains in Rolla, Missouri, with 11 engineers; Amdek's other employees work in offices in Elk Grove; Dallas; and Costa Mesa, California.

Sugiura dislikes the bureaucratic set-up of Japanese companies. He's proud of the casual atmosphere at Amdek where "everybody calls me 'Go'." But a shade of the paternalism Japanese companies are famous for does creep into Amdek. An employee's mother was hired to cook for employees so "nobody goes out for lunch," Sugiura reports.

Sugiura is so busy running Amdek these days that he hasn't been able to indulge in his one hobby—golf—for almost two years. He has lived in the same house for 11 of the 17 years he has been in the United States. He still drives a Toyota. He remains in the marriage arranged over 20 years ago by his family's minister. He and his wife and three children go to church every Sunday. Although Sugiura will probably remain in the United States for the rest of his life, he says, "I'm not an American. I see great value in this country, which I respect and admire, but I value Japan's cultural background."

Jugi Tandon

"I have always been very effective when I overload myself. If I have a lot of free time, it sort of runs into my busy time and nothing gets accomplished"

▶ **BEST-KNOWN VENTURE:** Tandon Corp.

OTHER VENTURE: Infomag

BORN: 1942

RAISED: Barnala, India

FATHER'S OCCUPATION: Criminal attorney

FIRST DOLLAR EARNED: Waiter at the Flagship Restaurant in Washington, D.C.

SCHOOLING: B.S., Howard University; M.S., mechanical engineering, Kansas State University; M.B.A., University of Santa Clara

PERSONAL NET WORTH: $100 million

FAMILY: Married; three children

PERSONAL TRANSPORTATION: 14 or 15 cars, including a Lamborghini, a couple of Rolls-Royces, three Mercedes, Ferrari, BMW, truck, jeep

Tandon

TANDON CORPORATION: World's-largest producer of microcomputer floppy disk drives.

▶ **BEST-KNOWN PRODUCTS:** Disk drives, read/write recording heads for disks

YEAR FOUNDED: 1975

EMPLOYEES: 1,550 domestic; 2,000 overseas

HEADQUARTERS: Chatsworth, California

SALES: $303 million (1983); $400 million (1984 projection)

PROFITS: $23 million (1983)

OWNERSHIP: Public (1981); Jugi Tandon holds 10 percent (3 million shares)

I lead a very simple, ordinary millionaire's life," says Sirjang Lal "Jugi" Tandon. What that means to Tandon is owning an armada of 14 or 15 cars, including a couple of Rolls-Royces, a Lamborghini, three Mercedes, a Ferrari, and a jeep, and thinking, "this is funny, I don't like to drive." Tandon goes on to say, "Cars are definitely toys. They don't serve any useful purpose, especially when I live only two-and-one-half miles from my work. It's ridiculous. You got a company worth half-a-billion dollars, you better spend it."

While Jugi Tandon works hard to spend some of the $100 million he's worth, he pays workers at a factory owned by his relatives in his native India $38 per month to manufacture Tandon Corporation's disk drives. Skilled laborers who had been left jobless when their former employer, IBM, pulled out of India in 1977, receive $63 per month. Tandon dismisses charges of exploitation by pointing out that he buses them to and from work and subsidizes their lunches.

Cheap labor is one factor that helped make Tandon the world's-largest independent maker of small computer disk drives. A highly automated plant in Singapore competes with the Tandon factory in Chatsworth, California, because Tandon feels "that's healthy." The Southern California plant apparently lost the competition. In the summer of 1984, at least 1,000 employees in the Chatsworth plant were laid off. Tandon defends how his firm handled the layoffs: "We went through a great deal of expense getting people other jobs. Anybody who wanted to get a job, we have gotten them a job. Tandon is a very good name, so when we train them their market value is significantly higher."

Jugi Tandon can be very generous. He threw a $400,000 Christmas dinner party for 2,400 employees at the Los Angeles Convention Center in 1982 because he thought it would be nice to have a "family get-together." But is Tandon much of a family? Unlike the happy faces of staffers sprinkled liberally through most company annual reports, Tandon's 1983 report features one face only: Jugi's. The other photos are of anonymous hands building electronic components.

Jugi Tandon began his fantastically successful career inauspiciously enough as an immigrant student and part-time waiter in Washington, D.C. He had been born into a wealthy professional family (his father is a prominent criminal attorney) in Barnala, India. He could have let his parents take care of him until he was settled down and married, as is the custom, Jugi says, but he chose to accompany his older brother to the United States in 1960 to get an education in engineering.

The Indian government wouldn't allow him to take more than a couple of thousand dollars out of the country, "so it made me a very responsible person," Jugi says. "I had to make my own living." The inexperienced 18-year-old supported himself as a waiter while he completed a B.A. degree at Howard University (the most inexpensive school he could find) in two-and-one-half years. "I overloaded myself because I wanted to graduate as soon as possible," Tandon recalls. "I have always been very effective when I overload myself. As a matter of fact, I got my M.B.A. [at the University of Santa Clara in California] in one year while I was working full-time [designing office building heating systems]."

Not content with an M.B.A., he applied for (and received)

scholarship aid at Kansas State University so he could get a master's in mechanical engineering. After that he returned to California, where he worked as an engineer for Beckman Instruments in Fullerton, and then for IBM as a project engineer in 1967.

He was perfectly happy at IBM, but he'd always planned to move back to India, so he did. Although he got a job with IBM in India, it wasn't the same. The plant wasn't very advanced and he felt unchallenged. "But I did accomplish something in India—I got married," he says.

It was an arranged marriage, in which the parents made the decision and the couple met in formal, chaperoned settings to decide whether to confirm it. All of Jugi's seven brothers and sisters had arranged marriages and all are successful, according to Jugi. "You get to know each other after the marriage anyway," he laughs. There was no reason not to confirm the marriage, in Jugi's mind. He and his wife Kamla made up their minds in three days and married in 10. "It's been going okay so far. My biggest hobby is my family."

Ten weeks after the marriage, in 1968, Jugi and Kamla returned to California—again without much money. He wanted to go back to work for IBM, but he was told he'd have to wait two or three weeks to clear it with IBM corporate headquarters. "I can't wait," Tandon replied. "I have a wife and no money, and I'm staying in a friend's apartment. I have to go to work tomorrow." So he joined Memorex instead.

"That was probably a good break for me," he says now. "If I had gone back to IBM, knowing what a good place it is to work, I would never have left it to start my own company."

For five years he worked at Memorex, mostly on magnetic heads (devices that read memory disks) for floppy disk drives. It was a time when new companies were sprouting up all over, and Tandon began to get the entrepreneurial itch himself. "I made several attempts to leave and start my own company," he says. "I was one of the guys who initiated Infomag, called CCTC today. But I didn't stay very long because I was offered 30,000 dollars worth of stock back at Memorex."

But Tandon had the entrepreneurial bug. He left Memorex in 1973. It was the same year Al Shugart left the same company to start his own floppy disk drive firm, Shugart

Associates. Although the two knew each other and had even played golf together (Tandon has a 14 handicap), Shugart didn't ask Tandon to join him in his enterprise. "That was the biggest mistake he ever made," says Tandon. His company was to become one of Shugart's hottest competitors.

The competition started out a bit uneven. "Alan Shugart was a big name in the industry—he was an executive vice president at Memorex—and I was a project engineer with no business or management experience. I was not able to raise any money at that time," recalls Tandon.

So he took another tack. In return for a $25,000-a-year salary and a $70,000 bonus, he started up a floppy disk drive business for Pertec Computer Corporation in Chatsworth. It wasn't an ideal match; Tandon was wildly enthusiastic about the floppy disk market while Pertec was only lukewarm. But Tandon was only biding his time until he had enough money to start his own company.

In 1975, with $7,000 in savings from the Pertec bonus and from some real estate ventures, Tandon launched the firm that bears his name. "I knew I wasn't going to put together a team because not too many people would join me, and I wasn't going to go to a bunch of people and raise money because no one would give me any. I was able to do it myself—in a very frugal way." He was willing to take the risk because, he says: "If you are a good engineer, you can always get a job. That gave me the courage."

With his wife soldering the wires and cutting cables, he labored in a little building in Los Angeles, developing a magnetic head for floppy disk drives. His strategy was, and still is, to make a product that was as good as the competition's but less expensive.

"Everybody was selling 50-dollar heads [to companies like IBM, Radio Shack, and Commodore]. I sold them for 18 dollars, and I was making them for 10 to 12 dollars. From the first month, we were profitable," says Tandon. Another key strategy for being a low-cost, high-volume producer is vertical integration, which at Tandon means making 80 percent of the products internally rather than contracting them out. This ensures a steady stream of components and eliminates suppliers' markups.

For the first three years he didn't hire anyone with experience in technology. "I just wanted honest people who worked hard because I had my own very definite way of building." He was also reluctant to hire anybody unless he felt it was okay for them to take the risk of joining the fledgling company.

For most of those early employees, the risk has paid off. The company's growth has been both steady and dramatic, and when Tandon went public in 1981, employee shareholders profited handsomely. Among them was Joyce Arnold, Tandon's first employee, who was able to pay $400,000 cash for a house.

Another early employee, vice president Gerald Lembas, saw his $17,000 investment mushroom to stock worth $20 million. Of course, the biggest winner of all was Jugi, whose stock was worth more than $100 million.

Now Tandon makes all kinds of drives—hard and floppy—and claims to be the world's largest producer of floppy drives. Tandon sells disk drives to 480 customers, the largest being IBM. One computer account Tandon doesn't have is Apple. Chairman Steve Jobs explained to the *New York Times*, "We expect our vendors to jump through hoops for us. Jugi never really exhibited enough interest in selling to us." Even without Apple, however, Tandon made enough sales to earn *Forbes* magazine's designation as the "Up and Comer of the Year" in November 1983. That year sales were $303 million; projected sales for 1984 were $400 million.

Although a multimillionaire, Jugi Tandon works as hard as ever—10 hours a day. Even when he's on vacation he keeps in constant touch with the office. His "free" time is spent with his wife and three children, and occasionally he gets in a round of golf. He is a devout Hindu who retains close ties to his old town in India, where he built a $3-million hospital. As though the entrepreneur's life weren't enough of a gamble, he sometimes goes with his wife to Las Vegas, Nevada, to play cards.

He figures he's won the gamble of entrepreneurship just by playing the game. "When you go and try something that you really want to do, whether you succeed or not you are really a winner. Fortunately, I succeeded to the wildest dream of anybody."

James Toreson

"There are probably a thousand things that could cause an entrepreneur to fail. A loser will pick up on one or more of these things and start to fall in love with it. For a real entrepreneur, losing is just absolutely not possible"

▶ **BEST-KNOWN VENTURE:** Xebec Corp.

OTHER VENTURES: Toreson Construction, Microcomputer Systems

BORN: 1942

RAISED: 20 miles west of Detroit, Michigan

FATHER'S OCCUPATION: Builder/contractor

FIRST DOLLAR EARNED: Helping his father pound nails

SCHOOLING: B.S. and M.S., electrical engineering, University of Michigan

PERSONAL NET WORTH: $43 million

HOME: Houses in Mountain View and Lake Tahoe, California, and Minden, Nevada

FAMILY: None (went through three wives)

PERSONAL TRANSPORTATION: Cadillac Fleetwood, Lear jet, underwater research vessel in the Caribbean

XEBEC CORPORATION: Makers of disk drive controllers and subsystems for computers.

▶ BEST-KNOWN PRODUCT: S140 Intelligent Disk Drive Controller

YEAR FOUNDED: 1974

EMPLOYEES: 500

HEADQUARTERS: San Jose, California

SALES: $57 million (1983)

PROFITS: $6.1 million (1983)

OWNERSHIP: Public (1983); James Toreson retains 37.3 percent of stock

A xebec is a three-masted vessel favored by pirates who used to roam the Mediterranean. A model of a xebec stands behind the huge desk in James Toreson's corporate office in California's Silicon Valley.

Mustached, brusque, and with a ramrod-straight military bearing, Toreson cuts a macho image. He's an energetic doer who has little patience for passive dreamers or people who settle for less than what they really want. He was determined to be a millionaire by the age of 40, but he made it well ahead of schedule. "I've been through three wives," he admits. "I'm dedicated to career and achievement and women come second."

He'll even tell you how he lost wife number two. It happened a decade ago, not long after Toreson took a job with Spectra-Physics, a high-tech engineering firm in California's Silicon Valley. Spectra was under the gun to deliver a reader for those little bar codes (like the ones you find on your groceries) to NCR in six weeks. They offered a job to Toreson, then an engineer at Hewlett-Packard. Being a man who "likes to be challenged to the point where there is absolutely nothing left," Toreson accepted the job. Toreson threw himself into the project, "I was crazy enough to grab hold of that thing by the reins and try to make it happen." He made it. "I worked right through New Year's Eve and January first. That's what cost me my second wife," he says with little regret.

Toreson has now divorced wife number three and heads a major firm that makes a variety of memory storage devices for personal computers. He has never been content to hold down only one demanding, full-time job. For example, at the same time that he had a full-time job at Bell Labs—his first employer after college—Toreson got a master's and did the course work for a Ph.D. in electrical engineering. But he left Bell Labs because it was "a little slow for me."

He preferred the quicker pace he found working with some ex-Bell Labbers on a start-up venture, making microcomputer devices. That folded after a few months, so he got engineering jobs— first with Memorex and then Hewlett-Packard. To keep himself busy while working full time at H-P, he started Toreson Construction, which built residential housing, and took classes at the University of Santa Clara. And once his bar code assignment was completed at Spectra, Toreson agreed to do some outside work wih Metasystems while continuing to work full-time for Spectra.

The partnership with Metasystems paid off handsomely. Metasystems had asked Toreson to design an add-on that improved the floppy disk drive for minicomputers. Because the product sold well to various minicomputer manufacturers, Toreson received $25,000 in royalty payments. With that money, Toreson left Spectra, dissolved his partnership with Metasystems, and with $8,000 in savings incorporated his own company, Microcomputer Systems Corp., in October 1974.

In the family room of his house in west San Jose, Toreson produced MSC's first baby: a hard disk controller (a device that enables a computer to store data on, and retrieve it from, the disk drive). This particular controller connected a Control Data large disk drive to a Hewlett-Packard minicomputer, using microprocessor technologies. He sold the first one over the phone to the Naval Air Station in Alameda, California, and the company took off.

Toreson went to computer makers like H-P, IBM, and Memorex, who needed component development but didn't want to do it themselves. MSC contracted to develop the components and sold them to the manufacturers, but kept title to the technology. With this way of getting business, MSC became the country's largest independent supplier of disk drive controllers. When the personal computer explosion took place, MSC was in a perfect position to exploit that market as well, building controllers for disk drives used by a variety of personal comptuer makers. In 1982, the year before MSC went public, sales were $26 million.

Toreson's original strategy for MSC was an unusual one: he planned to start up new ventures, get them rolling on their own, have them attact their own venture capital, and go public while the parent company remained privately held. But in the dynamic world of high-tech, circumstances change, and he had to adopt the opposite strategy. Like any good corsair, Toreson was able to roll with the waves and steer a new and profitable course.

In 1980, MSC bought rather than spawned an offspring. This was Xebec Sytems, a competitor. "They were making basically a junk product," says Toreson. After buying Xebec, MSC spiffed up the Xebec product line and, when MSC went public in 1983, took over Xebec's logo and its name.

Why did MSC go public, when the original plan was to stay private? "What we tried to do is take Xebec Systems public, but that didn't go over too big with the investment bankers, so what we had to do is take Xebec Corporation [the parent] public. So now it's a publicly held company which has privately held companies reporting to it. But the concept is essentially the same."

This central concept is what Toreson refers to as "distributed entrepreneurship." The heads of subsidiaries are given a piece of the action and get to act like entrepreneurs— which in fact they are. Sometimes Xebec seeks out someone to start a new venture; sometimes an entrepreneur approaches Xebec for financing a good idea; and sometimes Xebec purchases an already-existing company. In any case, the parent corporation tries to let them function as independently as possible. In addition to salaries, MSC engineers get royalties based on gross sales.

But does a true entrepreneur want to have a parent company controlling the purse strings? Says Toreson, "Entrepreneurs have less of a hassle dealing with Xebec than with a venture capitalist. We empathize with the entrepreneurs because we're entrepreneurs. Venture capitalists are Harvard M.B.A.-types and portfolio managers who really don't have an understanding for the marketplace and the technology and how you beat one against the other," he adds in typically aggressive phraseology.

Entrepreneurs, he feels, don't really mind constraints—constraints are what make business fun and challenging. What they do mind is "constraints they can't deal with logically."

Toreson knows what to look for in an entrepreneur—someone like himself. "He has to have the three Ds—desire, dedication, and determination. It's determination that separates the men from the boys. An entrepreneur is also a high risk-taker, but they're calculated risks; the key is being able to control your risks.

"There are probably a thousand things that could cause an entrepreneur to fail. A good achiever will somehow or another cut through all of those and he'll win. A loser will pick up one or more of these things and start to fall in love with it as a reason for failing. He will feel comfortable with accepting a loss. For a real entrepreneur, losing is just absolutely not acceptable. He may have all sorts of intermediate setbacks, but ultimately he'll get to where he wants to be."

A perfectionist, Toreson adds, does not make a good entrepreneur. "They try to play the game, but everything they do they try to justify as being right. That's not good either." Toreson himself is a perfectionist in the sense that he considers zero defects a reasonable goal, and is contemptuous of manufacturers who don't. The Japanese, he told *Computer Systems News*, are the only disk drive vendors who pay real attention to quality, "but our company would rather buy from American companies than from the Japanese, and we're sure a lot of other companies feel the same way."

Toreson says he has a good nose for choosing the kind of company and entrepreneur he wants for Xebec. Subsidiaries now include Datamac (marketing), Datapoint Corp. (disk/tape drive manufacturing), Microscan Systems (optical scanners for reading bar codes), and Information Memories Corp. (thin-film media, used for storing large amounts of information in hard disk drives). The products are mainly designed for microcomputers and 5¼-inch Winchester disk drives. Toreson estimates Xebec has 50 percent or more of the market.

Xebec's own principal manufacturing operations are in a 40,000-square-foot plant in Gardnerville, Nevada, south of Reno. This plant, which opened in 1983, employs robots purchased from IBM. Toreson shrugs off criticism of robots displacing people. "Jobs can't be eliminated by robotics as fast as they can be eliminated by CEOs making a decision to move them to the Far East. These CEOs can make value judgments in three narrow seconds that will blow away thousands of people."

However, Xebec itself has a large plant near Rome, Italy, which supplies Xebec products to the European Economic Community.

In addition to his home in Mountain View, Toreson owns a house in Lake Tahoe, California, and one in Minden, Nevada, "but most of the time I'm on the road doing business." As obsessed as he is with business achievement, Toreson has used his wealth to purchase "a few thrills": a Cadillac Fleetwood (in keeping with his buy-American philosophy), a Lear jet, and an underwater ocean research vessel—like a smaller version of Jacques Cousteau's *Calypso*, not a pirate ship—in the Caribbean.

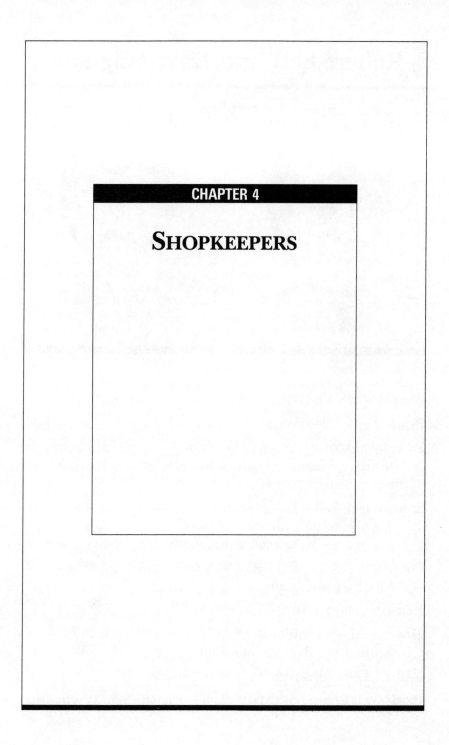

CHAPTER 4

SHOPKEEPERS

Robert Leff and Dave Wagman

▶ **BEST-KNOWN VENTURE:** Softsel Computer Products

BORN: Leff—1947; Wagman—1951

PARENTS' OCCUPATIONS: Leff—father owns a chain of movie theaters; Wagman—father and mother ran a western wear store and a feed-and-seed store

SCHOOLING: Leff—B.A., business, and M.S., computer science, State University of New York at Albany; Wagman—B.A., economics, Armstrong State College

ORIGINAL FINANCING: Leff—$1,300 from savings; Wagman—$10,000 from savings

PERSONAL NET WORTH: Each owns 35 percent of Softsel

HOME: Leff—Hermosa Beach, California; Wagman—Manhattan Beach, California

FAMILY: Leff—divorced; Wagman—single

PERSONAL TRANSPORTATION: Leff—Porsche 928; Wagman—Porsche 930

SOFTSEL COMPUTER PRODUCTS INC.: Leading wholesale distributor of software for personal computers.

▶ **BEST-KNOWN PRODUCT:** *Hot List*

YEAR FOUNDED: 1980

EMPLOYEES: 340

HEADQUARTERS: Inglewood, California

SALES: $85 million (1983)

OWNERSHIP: Privately held by Robert Leff and Dave Wagman, 30 percent held by venture investors

R obert Leff and Dave Wagman have a business marriage made in computer heaven. By supporting each other in a single-minded quest for money, the Softsel twins have amassed a multimillion-dollar fortune since founding, in 1980, the largest software distribution firm in the country.

It would be hard to find two more similar buddies and partners than Leff and Wagman. Both men could easily make any eligible bachelor list. Young, rich, and good-looking, Leff and Wagman affect the well-tanned casual look of upwardly mobile Los Angelenos: designer jeans, blow-dried hair, and sports cars. But neither has the time to cultivate the playboy life. Leff, whose wife divorced him because he was a workaholic, describes his and Wagman's schedule in the first year of Softsel:

"We worked 90 hours every week. During the typical week we'd go in at 10 o'clock or so, and work until two or three in the morning. Saturdays we would meet for brunch and work all day, and since we didn't have much time for women, they didn't have much time for us, so we might go out to dinner Saturday night together. You know, women don't like to go out on a date and then have somebody call them eight weeks later and say, 'Hi, do you want to go out on another date?' You have to pay more attention [to women] than that."

Even though Leff and Wagman no longer work quite as much as they used to, it takes more than 40 hours a week to run a company that did $85 million in sales in 1983 and expected to do over $150 million in 1984. Softsel markets more than 4,000 products from 300 manufacturers to over 5,500 dealers around the world. They have warehouses on both coasts, as well as in the Midwest and England.

It all started with a trunkful of software, a selling technique they called, "Dialing for Dollars," and another close friendship, this one between Robert Leff and Ken Williams, founder of Sierra On-Line.

Leff met Williams at Informatics, a mainframe software company, in the mid-1970s. Leff remembers that Ken "had an insatiable appetite for money and toys—boats and motor homes and things like that." Williams, in turn, claims that Leff also liked money.

The two men played hundreds of games of backgammon at work, as well as at gambling parlors where they bet eight to 10 dollars a point, and dreamed of money-making ventures. Both men grew bored with Informatics. Leff says, "The idea of sitting in a back room for a year or so working with four or five other people, arguing about where a comma should be in de- signing [a programming] language wasn't my idea of a good time." He moved on to Transaction Technology Inc., a subsidiary of Citibank located in Santa Monica, California. Leff became the person responsible for changes made in the automated teller machines. He also moonlighted as a consul- tant with Ken Williams.

Williams relates an odd story about Leff and his wife from this period. "I remember his wife calling me one night and say- ing she was divorcing Bob because I had him working too many hours. Either I was going to tell her that I would fire him, and he'd never know why, or she was dumping him. I told her that if Bob wasn't working for me, he'd work for somebody else. He was just a workaholic and always would be."

Eloise Leff dumped Robert, and now he had extra time on his hands, as well as the need for extra money for a divorce settlement. The ever-enterprising Williams happened to have a little personal computer software distribution business that he had been operating out of the trunk of his car. It wasn't much of a business, because at the time there were few good programs. Many were still being offered on cassettes rather than on the technologically superior floppy disks, and the packaging was amateurish for the most part. But Williams needed some quick money to finance an adventure game for computers that he and his wife Roberta had designed, so he offered to sell his little business to Leff. Leff, by his own admission, "knew nothing about selling," but decided to buy it. They haggled briefly over the price and settled on a figure of about $1,300. Neither remembers the precise figure.

Leff also knew nothing about personal computers or the software he was now peddling from *his* car trunk to computer stores. But within a month he grossed between $6,000 and $7,000. After the divorce, Leff's house in Mar Vista was almost empty, so he set up his blossoming business in the den and got himself an Apple II computer. What he next needed was a partner with some capital to invest. He settled on a friend and fellow worker at Transaction Technology, Dave Wagman.

Leff speaks about Wagman in affectionate computerese: "We interfaced a lot. He was matrixed to me." And the ultimate compliment, "He's much more of a techie than me. He can make his PC dance." But the affection didn't stop Leff from doing a little bit of a snow job on Wagman. Leff took Wagman down to some computer stores in Orange County—the first time Leff himself had ever tried to sell his software there. "I sold 6 or 7,000-dollars worth of orders, which was equal to my previous month. David is very impressed and I'm saying, 'Oh, just another normal Saturday down in Orange County. You know, it happens every day.' So we decided to become partners as of that moment."

Two months after Leff had bought the business for $1,300 from Ken Williams, he charged Dave Wagman $10,000 to buy in as a partner. Williams was incensed when he heard the news. "I refused to talk to Leff for a month, I was so mad at him. Because this little kid Wagman, who was not very impressive in those days, had just borrowed the money from his grandmother, and I figured Leff had just suckered him out of it. I was really pissed. I couldn't believe he had taken advantage of this poor guy Wagman, but as it turned out, Wagman made a good investment for his money."

No kidding. Wagman himself finds the whole story amusing—he's laughing all the way to the bank. "It's funny," he smiles. "Every time Bob tells that story, the amount of sales that we made in Orange County gets bigger. But it was incredible! Bob had talked about going out and doing a couple of hundred dollars on a weekend and making 50 dollars to put in his pocket. It sounded interesting enough to me. We went out and we probably did, I don't know, 1 or 2,000 dollars that day. It was dynamite!"

In the early months, Leff and Wagman went around to the 15 or 20 computer stores in the area and showed their samples of software in Ziploc bags with a bit of mimeographed documentation and a cassette or floppy disk inside. Wagman describes their sales method. "We played a game that we used to call 'Dialing for Dollars.' We had a list of Apple dealers and we would get on the phone on a Saturday, or in the afternoon, after work, and just figure if we could get a 200-dollar order, it would sure as hell pay for the phone call. So we'd just pick up the phone and dial and call these dealers. Neither Bob nor I are sales people by inclination, but we were selling on like 50 percent of the phone calls that were cold calls."

Leff realized that if orders could be taken over the phone, and if UPS ships everywhere, then Softsel could sell everywhere. They did not have to operate out of the back of their car. Their potential territory was the entire country. It seems obvious to everyone now, but Softsel claims they were the first to come up with the idea. As Wagman says, "We didn't know any better."

In August, Leff and Wagman sold $12,000 worth of goods and in September they did twice that. Wagman quit working for TTI in October, when they again more than doubled their sales, to $56,000. Leff quit TTI the next month, when they were up to $85,000, and in December they sold products worth $150,000. They hired their first employee in January 1981, while they were still working and practically living at Leff's house in Mar Vista. By the end of the year they had 40 employees and 12,000 square feet of warehouse. By December 1981, they had built sales to $1.5 million.

Leff and Wagman stumbled upon a real gap in the computer industry. Software publishers couldn't really establish a network of retail dealers for their products. Retail dealers couldn't really evaluate the software they received. Leff and Wagman tested and compared software. They stepped in first, solved the problem, and made themselves rich.

Not surprisingly, both Leff and Wagman are sons of entrepreneurs—although their parents certainly never made a fraction of their sons' wealth. Leff's father owned a dozen or so theaters in the Albany, New York, area. Wagman's folks operated two stores in Savannah, Georgia: a western clothing shop with his mother in charge, and a feed-and-seed store handled by his father.

Leff's assessment of himself as a "pretty dull kid," is echoed by Wagman's claim, "there is almost nothing remarkable about my childhood." Both men received undergraduate degrees in business, with additional training in computer science. Leff received an M.A. in computer science at the State University of New York at Albany in 1971. Wagman studied computers for a couple of years at Georgia Tech.

After graduate school, Leff kicked around the mainframe world for a few years, working for RCA, coming back to Rochester to play with a Univac, and finally putting in a stint in Germany with the giant chemical company, BASF. Leff describes his life in terms of the jobs he held, but his personal relationships precipitated the major shifts in his career. His marriage to a California woman was the reason he left Germany—to please her. He found work in Southern California at Informatics. Later, at Transaction Technology, it was his divorce expenses that motivated him into buying the business that would become Softsel.

Even though Leff was the one with the degree in computer science, Wagman was the techie. "I just instinctively sensed that computers were for me. It [a college course in computers] was the start of a 16-year love affair," Wagman gushes.

Wagman worked as a programmer for a commercial credit

company, and later, for Nixdorf Computer. Unlike Leff, with his steady progression, Wagman "burned out and blew a fuse!" He planned to move West and relax for three months, but after one month, work withdrawal set in and Wagman looked for his next fix: a job at Transaction Technology.

That's where Wagman learned that Leff was the "one guy that I knew I could always go to and only have to explain something once." Leff felt the same way about Wagman: "He understood what I was talking about and I understood what he was talking about." Wagman feels that Leff is the more aggressive, so they complement each other, just like partners in a good marriage.

This particular business marriage keeps coming up with money-making ideas, such as a 24-hour turnaround on orders, a dealer advertising co-op program, and disk formatting and duplication service. Softsel's *Hot List* runs each week's top-selling products and is widely respected. Softsel employs eight people who do nothing but test the 300-odd programs submitted each month, selecting usually only four or five.

What are the Softsel twins doing with the 70 percent of the private company they control? They've moved into beach houses in neighboring towns in the Los Angeles area, and they keep tan and fit: Wagman skis and flies airplanes; Leff plays racquetball.

But more free time? "That's not my inclination," Wagman says. "This is a great business and it fascinates me. I like being at a focal point in the industry—both as an opinion maker and as a decision maker. I like having the press and researchers call me up and ask what I think. It's a nice perk that comes with the job."

LEAST FORMAL EDUCATION

Jack Tramiel (Commodore)	Completed fifth grade
George Tate (Ashton-Tate)	High school dropout
Porter Hurt (PH Components)	High school graduate
Roberta Williams (Sierra On-Line)	High school graduate
Sheldon Adelson (Interface Group)	College dropout
William Gates (Microsoft)	College dropout
William Godbout* (CompuPro)	College dropout
Dennis Hayes (Hayes Microcomputer)	College dropout
Regis McKenna (Regis McKenna P.R.)	College dropout
William Millard (ComputerLand)	College dropout
William von Meister (The Source)	College dropout
Ken Williams (Sierra On-Line)	College dropout

* *Later received an honorary doctoral degree*

Lorraine Mecca

"Don't try to fit into a man's world. Just be yourself"

▶ **BEST-KNOWN VENTURE:** Micro D

BORN: 1949

RAISED: Haddonfield, New Jersey

FATHER'S OCCUPATION: Engineer, RCA; currently personnel director, Sammons Communications

FIRST DOLLAR EARNED: Junior high school teacher

SCHOOLING: B.A., Arizona State University

ORIGINAL FINANCING: $25,000 from the sale of her house

PERSONAL NET WORTH: $59.1 million (1983)

HOME: Huntington Beach, California

FAMILY: Divorced; remarried; one daughter, one son

PERSONAL TRANSPORTATION: Chevrolet Caprice

MICRO D

MICRO D: One of three largest personal computer equipment distributors.

▶ **BEST-KNOWN PRODUCTS:** "Middlemen" between manufacturers and 7,000 retail computer stores

YEAR FOUNDED: 1979

EMPLOYEES: 200

HEADQUARTERS: Fountain Valley, California

SALES: $71 million (1983)

OWNERSHIP: Public (July 1983); Mecca holds 51 percent

Teaching English to eighth graders is a lot harder than running a multimillion-dollar corporation, according to Lorraine Mecca. "To be locked in a room with forty kids is definitely the most physically and mentally taxing job I've ever had." There are other reasons she has no regrets about leaving the classroom. When Micro D went public in 1983, Mecca (who is referred to by her last name by her employees) was worth nearly $60 million. She is one of the few women to head a major firm in an industry often thought of as a male preserve. A stunningly beautiful woman, Mecca is a favorite on the microcomputer convention circuit. Those who watch her lecture to large groups of software publishers and retailers can still discern a bit of the schoolmarm in her authoritative manner.

Mecca's road to multimillions was quick but not easy. She arrived in Los Angeles in 1975, after teaching for two-and-a-half years in Litchfield Park, Arizona, near Phoenix. The first job she landed was with Connector Distribution Corp., a wholesale distributor of electronic components. Like many liberal arts graduates with no business experience, Mecca started at the bottom. She answered phones, relayed telexes, entered orders into a computer, and handled cash receipts. But she was happy to no longer be in front of a classroom of young teenagers. She figured that even at $4 an hour, she was making more money than she did teaching. Her employers were happy with Mecca, too, and she rapidly rose to operations coordinator, where she learned the nuts and bolts of the electronics distribution business. She also shared an office with a man who changed her life.

Geza Csige came to the United States in 1956, an 11-year-old refugee from the Hungarian revolution. Fascinated by electronics as a child (he built a laser in high school), Csige had encountered the world of computers when he worked as a lab technician at the University of Southern California and took some college classes in advanced electronics and math. While working at Connector Distribution, Csige and a partner opened one of the first microcomputer stores in Southern California in 1977. Called Computer Playground, the store at first resembled a video arcade. Ten micros were installed along the walls, and people could come in and rent time to play games or program on their own. But customers were more interested in buying machines than renting time on them, so Csige soon started to sell them.

Csige and Mecca married and both quit their jobs— Csige to devote full time to his computer stores, Mecca to go to El Camino College to study business. One of her work-study projects involved producing a weekly fashion show at the Marriott Inn in Marina Del Rey. She detested typing out the script of the show every week. Her new husband had the solution: "Why don't you use my word processor?"

Mecca, who had not previously paid attention to Csige's electronics hobby, immediately fell in love with his Radio Shack TRS-80 Model I microcomputer and its *Electric Pencil* word processing program. "It made writing creative," Mecca recalls. "My shows got much better." Much more important, Mecca saw the business potential of personal computers. "I realized that if I, who was an extremely nontechnical person, could enjoy computers that much and find them so useful, then anyone in the world who wrote, or anybody working in any office would be using home computers or personal computers in the future."

Mecca launched her business from bed during her first pregnancy when sickness forced her into unaccustomed inactivity. "At the end of three months, I was going crazy," Mecca said. "I wanted to do something." She knew that microcomputer store owners like Csige had no difficulty getting the computers themselves, but getting the peripherals—monitors, printers, modems, and other items needed to make the system work— was another matter. She decided to apply her experience in electronics distribution.

In July 1979, Mecca, who was nearly six months pregnant, incorporated Micro D using $25,000 from the sale of a house from her former marriage as capital. She set up shop in a rented building in Orange County. Her first employee was her cousin who made deliveries with his van: "I remember telling him, 'Don't worry, you only have to work a few days a week. Stores don't open till ten o'clock; you can sleep late every day; the stores are closed on Mondays, so you don't have to work on Mondays.' That was true for about a month." In the first six weeks, Micro D sold $60,000 worth of computer peripherals and software. The company was profitable from the beginning, partly because Mecca was able to negotiate credit terms with vendors she knew from her previous work at Connector Distribution, while her customers paid COD.

Mecca's energy gave Micro D its flying start. When her daughter was born on November 8, 1979, she had worked the previous day, had the child at midnight, and was home again the next morning: "When I got home they had moved the computer to my bedroom and forwarded the office phones there. We were up and running the next day. There was no alternative. There was nobody else to do it."

Mecca, however, soon convinced her husband to give up his computer stores and work for her full time. She retained full ownership of the firm in her own name. When asked whether Csige became a partner when he joined the company, Mecca replied, "No, he doesn't own anything. But he trusts me. He knows I need him."

Micro D had a stroke of good fortune in early 1980 when

Apple Computer decided to discontinue selling its machines through outside distributors. Micro D's main competitor in Southern California decided to become an exclusive Apple representative, leaving distribution of Apple peripherals to Micro D. During its first full year of operation, Micro D did $3.6 million in sales.

In late 1981, Micro D opened a warehouse in the Dallas area, and a year later opened a branch in Maryland. In typical fashion, Mecca moved to Maryland and helped set up that operation herself.

In early 1983, Mecca decided to take her company public. That spring, firms like TeleVideo and Altos were raising spectacular amounts of money by selling stock to the public, but an uncanny premonition made Csige insist that the party would be over by the end of July. Mecca rushed to line up New York venture capitalist Fred Adler and together they prepared their public offering in half the time it usually takes. Micro D sold its first stock to the public on July 12, 1983, at the last possible moment before Wall Street went sour on new high-tech company offerings. "We got absolutely maximum value for the company," says Mecca. "We raised twenty-five million dollars. It's given us an incredible edge over our competition." The timing also made Mecca, then 34, a wealthy woman. At the initial stock offering price of $16 per share, Mecca's 3.4 million shares (51 percent) of Micro D stock were worth over $59 million.

The company still specializes in microcomputer peripherals, selling 900 different hardware items (modems, printers, monitors, and disk drives) manufactured by 90 different firms, as well as 3,000 software packages produced by 150 software houses. Micro D sells these goods to 7,000 retail outlets, mostly small, independent dealers who buy less than $2,000 a month. Mecca prefers the smaller customers, "They don't haggle over price since they're often only buying one of an item."

Mecca and Csige are proud that Micro D is so computerized. "We were on computer from the day we opened the doors," Mecca says. "We're the only distributor in the microcomputer industry with an on-line order entry system across the country."

In mid-1984, *Nation's Business* did a cover story on Mecca in which she was asked what she found most difficult about being an entrepreneur. She said it was realizing that she couldn't be nice to everyone: "There were times when I had to make a choice between who was going to make a profit on the sale—me or somebody else. And it was hard to decide that it had to be me. I was used to sharing!"

She has also learned that running your own business requires a very different kind of commitment from working for someone else: "You do not have time to exert any mental effort in any direction other than your business. You have to be happy with either fidelity or celibacy."

Mecca offers some advice for women who want to emulate her business success. She told us that they should "get a wife, someone who can take care of things a wife would take care of if she was staying at home and not working—a housekeeper, a babysitter—that sort of thing." She also suggested, "Wear high heels so you can see. A woman in a male industry goes into a social situation and she can't see." Finally, Mecca said, "Don't try to be too masculine. Don't try to fit into a man's world. Just be yourself."

Has Micro D's success changed Mecca's life much? She admitted that when she had her second child she took six weeks off work, though she quickly added, "But I was on the phone every day." Mecca actually took a week's vacation in October 1983—to go scuba diving. She still works from eight in the morning till eight at night, while Csige puts in an even longer day. A live-in housekeeper babysits their two children in a house overlooking a harbor in the wealthy suburb of Huntington Beach. (Mecca had yet to take a dip in the ocean when we talked with her six months after she had moved in.) Her one hobby is karate, but nowadays the instructor comes to her office.

William Millard

"I am the biggest winner of all in the microcomputer industry"

▶ **BEST-KNOWN VENTURE:** ComputerLand

OTHER VENTURES: IMSAI, System Dynamics, IMS Associates

BORN: 1932

RAISED: Oakland, California

PARENTS' OCCUPATIONS: Father—railroad clerk for Southern Pacific; mother—secretary for Montgomery Ward

FIRST DOLLAR EARNED: Delivering magazines door-to-door

SCHOOLING: University of San Francisco (three semesters, no degree)

ORIGINAL FINANCING: Savings, bank loan

PERSONAL NET WORTH: $1 billion (estimate)

HOME: Piedmont, California

FAMILY: Married; three daughers

PERSONAL TRANSPORTATION: Mercedes

ComputerLand ®

COMPUTERLAND CORPORATION: An international chain of franchised computer stores—545 in the United States and 137 abroad (as of summer 1984).

▶ **BEST-KNOWN PRODUCTS:** Computers and computer accessories

YEAR FOUNDED: 1976

EMPLOYEES: 1,100 corporate (10,000 including stores)

HEADQUARTERS: Oakland, California

SALES: Stores—$1.8 billion (1984 estimate); ComputerLand Corporation—$144 million (1984 estimate)

PROFITS: $30 million (estimate) for ComputerLand Corporation

OWNERSHIP: Privately held by William Millard

ComputerLand is Bill Millard's company, although for a lot of years hardly anyone knew that. He had Ed Faber, an ex-Marine captain and ex-IBMer, fronting for him. Many outsiders, especially writers who covered the business scene, thought ComputerLand was Faber's company. It was not only not Faber's company, but, despite the fact that he was president throughout its formative years, Faber hardly owned any stock. One of Bill Millard's trademarks is that when he's involved in an enterprise, he *is* the owner. He doesn't like to give stock to anyone. In fact, according to *Forbes*, Faber was given 5 percent of ComputerLand's stock only with the condition that he sell some back to Millard every year. In 1983, Faber's holdings were down to 3 percent. In 1984, he left ComputerLand to do what he liked best: shoot ducks and hook fish. If he had stayed any longer, his stock position would have been wiped out.

It was then that Bill Millard took center stage and began

granting interviews to the press. He claimed that his Computer-Land franchisees had demanded that he assume this role. "As the game became larger," he told Mary A.C. Fallon of the *San Jose Mercury News*, "the franchisees got concerned. The more reclusive I was, they just went crazy to know who's behind this."

The man behind the ComputerLand chain of 682 stores (as of mid-1984) is a disciple—and good friend—of Werner Erhard, founder of est, the self-help movement that teaches people to be assertive. It has always been a good idea, if you wanted to advance in a Millard enterprise, to go through est. At est you learn a trait Millard admires, not to accept failure. He has a salesman's propensity to look on the bright side. And he is also full of homilies. He told us, for example, that "ComputerLand is probably the number one place to work on the planet earth." Why? "My purpose is to be viable so that we have the opportunity to have a place where we can live out our lives together. In a way that really and truly is nurturing to myself and everyone else who is here, and to other people who we interact with and deal with from the outside. And that is the truth." Another time a reporter asked him why Computer-Land didn't sell stock to the public. "Why should I do that?" he asked. "I am fully engaged in this organization and in achieving objectives that happen to transcend pure business."

ComputerLand doesn't own a single store. They are all franchised to local owners. The chain has expanded by using other people's capital (a franchise costs $75,000), not Millard's. He provides the idea, training, support services, and central buying. And then Millard collects eight cents of every dollar taken in by each and every ComputerLand store.

Forbes got a look at some financial statements that indicate what a money machine ComputerLand is for Bill Millard. In 1982 ComputerLand took in $25.5 million in franchising fees, netting $10.8 million on that gross before taxes, which may be negligible because Millard is known to be a fancier of tax shelters. (Among his side ventures have been a fish farm and a 300-acre vineyard.) In 1985 ComputerLand will be generating close to $200 million annually in revenues for Millard. He has already made the *Forbes* 400 roster of the richest people in

America. His net worth was estimated in 1983 as "at least 500 million dollars"—and given the sensational growth of ComputerLand, he may now have reached the billionaire level. "I am the biggest winner of all in the microcomputer industry," he told *Forbes*.

This big winner of the computer jackpot is a short, thin man who looked, in 1984, 10 years younger than his age: 52. He's rather humorless but has an incredible intensity. Not once during an hour-and-a-half interview did he break eye contact. His desk is remarkable for its lack of clutter. As Fallon noted, he deals with "one piece of paper at a time."

Bill Millard did not have an easy time of it as a boy or as a young man trying to make his mark in the business world. He is mostly self-educated. As far as the computer industry goes, he happens to have been in the right place at the right time—and he made the most of his opportunity. But he didn't enter the industry as an idealistic enthusiast of the technology. More than others around him, he looked upon the end uses of a computer, and he grasped early that the way to get ahead and make money was to serve the end users. He also had such a strong drive to succeed that he became a charismatic leader. And finally, Millard was willing to gamble on his hunches and to persist. He struck out in his first two ventures but he hit a home run with his third.

Being willing to gamble is an attitude Bill Millard may have adopted in reaction to his father: "I'm not going to be like him," he told us. But it's also not that simple. In talking to us about his childhood, Millard displayed what seemed to be a hurt pride: there was resentment, but he was not about to put his family down. He was born in Denver, Colorado, but when he was three his family moved to Oakland, California, where he grew up. It was in the midst of the Depression, and times were not easy. Through a relative, his father landed a job at the Southern Pacific Railroad in 1936; he worked there, as a clerk and cashier, until his retirement. His mother also worked, as a secretary at Montgomery Ward & Co. Young Bill went to St. Elizabeth's parochial school and worked, too, from the time he was nine, delivering magazines door-to-door. Later on he had an *Oakland Tribune* route. During those early years he was an only child. His parents started having children again when he was 10 and the Depression was over.

"One of the truly great gifts from my father is the work ethic," Millard said. "They came out of the Depression and they were really hurt by that. It was life-threatening. You got a job, and it was like, boy, security. He surrendered opportunity for security. He created a home that was full of love and he took care of the family and all of that. But I have never seen anyone so loyal to the company. You couldn't say a bad thing about that railroad. I thought it was terrible, of course. I had my own pictures about my father—like the greatest—but I just felt he was locked into this union situation, that structure where seniority is everything. There was no ability in that structure to really be acknowledged on your performance." (It must have been with no little satisfaction that 40 years later this railroad clerk's son paid $2.5 million to Southern Pacific for one of its properties.)

Young Bill Millard was determined to be different: "I came out of this saying, 'Listen, I don't know what I am going to do, but give me opportunity—to hell with security.' Actually, that's very easy for me to say because of the security that he always provided me with, and the self-esteem. I was always tremendously validated by my parents. They were very strict, and I always thought their restrictions were vastly more than was appropriate, but I never had a doubt about the purpose behind them. They thought that was the right thing to do."

Millard has a similar ambivalence about having to work as a kid. He was never given an allowance. On the contrary, he contributed to the family's earnings. Looking back today, he recalls: "The paper route was incredibly demanding. It was an afternoon route. If you were more than a half an hour late leaving school, you would start getting complaints from your customers. And it was every day, three-hundred-and-sixty-five days a year, Christmas included, New Year's, Thanksgiving. And I remember there were times when it really got to me. I mean, this is a kid who is twelve years old, thirteen, fourteen, fifteen, sixteen—and it's not something where once a week you could get somebody to cover your route. It meant that playing basketball or football or whatever—that wasn't really available to me.

"I didn't turn bitter about it, but it just bothered me. That is what I had to do, and that was it. It was obviously a trade-off, you know. I felt like I missed a lot. The truth is, I didn't miss a lot. I had acknowledgment. I did a good job, I was proud of my route and proud of how few complaints I got versus anybody else. In all of those things I had self-esteem. I have always had a job, since I was around eight or nine, and the truth is, I have always loved it."

There was also no question what Millard would do when he got out of high school: work. He dug ditches. He went to Nevada to work in a copper mine. He worked on Southern Pacific's commuter trains into San Francisco. Then he enrolled at a Jesuit school, the University of San Francisco, for three semesters, meanwhile holding down two part-time jobs. He never finished college, because (1) It was too expensive; (2) He didn't know what he wanted to study; and (3) He was not a scholar in the traditional sense. "I didn't enjoy home-work," he explained. "If you could get me with a teacher and I could sit down and be in some dialogue, interact with questions, that was great. But the educational system is not set up that way."

At 21, when he looked like a 14-year-old altar boy and still lived at home, Millard took a job in Oakland with a small loan company, Pacific Finance. His job: going door-to-door in West Oakland, a tough, low-income neighborhood, to collect bills. "I had to produce results," he recalls. "I deliberately went with this company because I was told that if I got the job done, I would be promoted. So I knew that I had to do it better. I worked seventy hours a week, and I didn't get paid for it, by the way. There was none of this overtime crap. And I had to persuade people. Do you understand? Can you imagine some kid demanding that you [pay up]? I could appeal to their integrity—I had to do it with relationships. And not only with customers but with the people in the office. This company had people of all ages. It was expanding very rapidly. And I aspired to the top."

Young Millard seemed to be on his way to the top. He advanced, in rapid order, to credit interviewer, collection manager, manager of credit, assistant branch manager, and then branch manager, in two years. At 23, he was the youngest branch manager the company had ever had. He also met his bride, Patricia Nolder, at Pacific Finance. They were married in 1956 when he was 24 years old.

It turned out that Pacific Finance was owned by Lockheed, which, since the finance company was doing so well (better than the aircraft company), pushed for its expansion into computerization. Pacific Finance took possession of a Univac computer in Los Angeles, the twenty-sixth Univac off Sperry Rand's line. Bill Millard was offered a chance to get in on the ground floor of this new data processing unit; he took it, thinking this would be a quicker path to the top. He and his wife went off to Los Angeles in 1958. It was his introduction to computers.

He did well, advancing from trainee to programmer to systems manager. But then he hit what he calls "a lid." Bill Millard had grown up in an environment where a college degree was rare. "I had never met an attorney in my life," he told us. "Never met one. The only doctor I had ever seen was when I was in the hospital. I mean, professional people were just not in the circle of friends we had." It had therefore meant a lot to him when he joined Pacific Finance to be told that a college degree didn't matter: he could go as far as his ability carried him. In Los Angeles, he learned that this was not true. He was in a line of progression that led to controller of the company. One day he had a conversation with his boss's boss. "I'll never forget it," he said. "I was making 14,400 dollars, and he said, 'Bill, I have got to tell you that there is no way I can take you any farther in this company without a college degree.'" Looking back at it now, with a viewpoint cultivated by est, Millard sees it as "one of the greatest contributions I could ever have." He may have felt differently at the time.

Bill Millard's next opportunity surfaced when he was waiting in a coffee line in Pacific Finance's Los Angeles office and heard someone behind him say, "Did you see this ad?" It turned out to be a help wanted notice for a director of data processing for Alameda County, which includes Oakland and other communities across the Bay from San Francisco. Data processing was a relatively new field then, and Millard already had three years' experience in it. He got the job and returned to Northern California.

"It was an incredible time in my life," Millard recalled for us. "I loved it. It was a perfect job. Why? They really supported the hell out of me. First of all, I was supportable. I didn't lie, cheat, steal, and I really wanted to get the job done. And I had the capability of motivating people, acquiring people, organizing them, and getting the job done. The thing I loved about it, though, here's this kid—and I had free license to go anywhere in the county. I was a department head. I was able to meet with the chief of police, the sheriff, the heads of hospitals, the tax assessor, the whole thing. I got to play, 'How could computers help the hospitals? How can computers help the police, the tax assessors, the county controller?' I mean, hey, I was in my glory.

"And we did some breakthrough things there. The use of computers in state and local governments was just being thought about, and we did a lot of firsts. I was the one who developed the world-wide system known as PIN, Police Information Network. It was the world's first on-line information system to serve local law enforcement. I began to build a na-tional—and what became an international—reputation in this area of applying computer technology to the problems local and state governments had. I remember in one year, as a result of what we were doing, I had thirty-five hundred visitors."

The Alameda County data processing used IBM systems, and after working there for four years, from 1961 to '65, Millard (still sans college degree) joined IBM, where he had the title, Industry Specialist, State and Local Government. He traveled around the world "talking to people about what was possible and how to do it and how to make it happen." After only a year with IBM he made what he now considers to be—"the one time in my life"—a side step: he took the same job he had held with Alameda County in San Francisco County, across the Bay.

Compared to Alameda, San Francisco data processing systems were "in the dark ages," and Millard said he was "terrified" by the job "because it sounded like the railroad." So why did he take it? "See," he explained, "I didn't have anything else. I didn't have the money. I didn't have the education. I didn't have the so-on. I still needed to build a base. I went there to prove that it was me, that I could do it again. And that took some knock out of me, it was a step down in my self-esteem. But"—and here's the old est hindsight—"the truth is, it was incredibly valuable. Because San Francisco is a jungle. It is not Alameda County, from a political standpoint. I mean, there are marauding beasts over there. They act like it. It was a whole new ball game. And I went in there, bright-eyed and bushy-tailed, and there would be a glitch every forty-three-and-one-half seconds. The press just loved it. There were some fun clippings. Nonetheless, I had enormous support, and in thirty-six months we brought them up to certainly what I believe surpassed what Alameda County had."

In 1969, at age 37, Bill Millard quit his job and for the first time went into business for himself. He started a software company, which he called System Dynamics, to create computer programs that he thought would be better than IBM's. It was a novel concept because at that time software was provided by the manufacturer. A big problem, Millard now admits, "was that we chose to sell system software right down the throat of IBM. Not smart. Really not smart. But I had seen the need for data communications controls, which could multiply the volume on your computer as opposed to buying another machine. And I thought, 'Hey, people will pay for this.' So we mortgaged our home, found some investment bankers, bet everything we had, and started this company. In May of 1972 we had to close it down."

Millard reflected on why his first venture failed: "I learned there was a giant missing piece. I knew computers. I knew software. I knew the communications protocol and the stuff needed to make the terminals work. And I had directed many, many people—managed projects always—to completion and success. So I thought I had everything needed to go out and start a company and be its president and be a businessman. And the truth is I didn't. I was a manager, and I confused businessman with manager. I had giant gaps as a business person. I had never actually wrestled with a balance sheet. Never with a P&L [profit-and-loss] statement. Before I had been supported, whether it was by Pacific Finance or the various county governments or IBM. The whole premise of a businessman as opposed to a manager was a giant gap in my education. Some of the most valuable lessons are the most painful."

So in 1972 Bill Millard retreated to his home in San Leandro. "I didn't have any money. We were hopelessly in debt. We had mortgaged our home for more than it was ever worth. The truth is, we were really bankrupt but we didn't file for bankruptcy. I went to the bank and said something like, 'I don't have anything now. I don't know what I am going to do. I will pay you somehow, somewhere, some day.' The biggest thing that I remember was the feeling of being president of a company that is defunct, the loneliness: where shall I go, what shall I do?" Millard said he thought of going back to work for government or IBM, but guess what he found? "No one is looking for a president of a company that just closed its doors. You're an entrepreneur now. People are afraid of entrepreneurs. They're afraid to hire them." Millard was then 40 years old.

His previous work for county governments turned up the next lead. He heard that Los Angeles County was going to issue a contract for the design of an on-line information retrieval system, one that embraced fingerprinting and identification systems, so that the sheriff's department could rapidly search through its files. It was right up Bill Millard's alley, and he decided to bid for it, creating a new company for the purpose called IMS Associates, standing for Information Management Sciences. He thought that two people who had worked with him at System Dynamics—Seymour Rubinstein and Dick Gentry—might join him in the new venture, but they elected not to, leaving Millard as the sole "Associate." In the end, Millard got the Los Angeles contract jointly with the big aerospace company, TRW, which was becoming a data processing power by providing the on-line base to check for credit card deadbeats.

Bill Millard was back in business again, and he told us that this time he was more businesslike. "When I had my first company, it was inconceivable to me to lay people off. I had never laid people off in my life. So when business was bad, I kept on meeting the payroll. I felt responsible: I hired those people. It was like I was unwilling to do what you need to do. Do not accept the right to hire unless you also accept the responsibility to terminate when they need to be terminated." This time Millard hired people on a contract basis. "As soon as the job was over, the expenses stopped."

The problem now was the nature of the consulting business itself. It's the kind of business where you do one job and then the next time you have to do it all over again. You don't build up anything. It's boom-and-bust, and you have to worry whether the profit (if any) that you made on your previous job will last until a new one comes in. Any consulting contractor knows the feeling. But the advantage, Millard found, was that it kept him on the leading edge: if a product was already available, customers wouldn't be asking him for it.

The turning point for Millard—and IMS Associates— came in 1975 when he was desperately trying to fulfill a contract for a General Motors dealer who needed a computer to handle his accounting. Millard underbid the contract because it represented the window he had long been looking for. He knew that if he could deliver this special application computer system to this one customer, he would then have the right to sell it to other businesses—to drugstores, other car dealers, you name it. In retelling the circumstances nine years later, he was still excited: "Do you see what I'm saying? If we got it done, we had a product we could sell everywhere." It was a dream come true for a consulting contractor in this field. It was the kind of general purpose system that had built Ross Perot's Electronic Data Systems into a powerful, money-making machine.

But it wasn't an easy problem to solve. And to help solve it, Millard told us, his engineer began looking at the new Intel 8080 chip, the microprocessor. He remembers sitting with his engineer and saying, "Listen, that looks like a goddamn computer to me." Millard and his engineer weren't the only ones who had noticed the potential of Intel's 8080 chip. A company called MITS in Albuquerque, New Mexico, had actually built a small computer, called the Altair, using the 8080 chip. The Altair was announced in the January 1975 issue of *Popular Electronics*. Thinking the Altair could solve their problem with the General Motors dealer, Millard got hold of two Altairs, tore them apart, and rebuilt them for his own purposes. Once he had put so much work into rebuilding the Altair, though, Millard thought he might just as well try to sell his version of the small computer. He called his adaptation the IMSAI 8080, and placed a one-inch ad announcing its availability in *Popular Electronics*.

What happened next? "You ought to picture this," Millard told us. "I mean, here are five people—two of whom are myself and my wife—in this little place in San Leandro. And we're just trying to survive, okay? The mailman came in with the mailsack. We got 3,500 responses to our ad—our little one-inch ad. And he spilled it out on the counter, and we began opening these envelopes. And this would be on tablet paper, 'Here's my order for the IMSAI 80 kit.' And there's a check—699 dollars. Jesus Christ! We didn't even have an order form. And we began opening these goddamn envelopes and there was money! I mean, there were checks, prepaid orders! It was the first time we felt like we had a business! We had the opportunity to perform."

Bill Millard had become a manufacturer and marketer of microcomputers almost accidentally. He certainly hadn't set out to make computers. Putting the ad in *Popular Electronics* was, at most, an effort to make a few extra bucks. But now it was a new ball game. He got out of the consulting business. Millard saw that the Altair was intended for the hobbyist market, the computer enthusiasts. He didn't care about them. He had his sights set on the commercial market, computers sitting on desktops, not workbenches. He wanted to produce "industrial-grade" personal computers. The IMSAI 8080 was technically almost identical to the Altair, though it had a better power supply and eliminated the need for customers to hand-solder wires. IMSAI sales soon surpassed the Altair. Between 1975 and 1978 Imsai sold 13,000 microcomputers.

Paul Freiberger and Michael Swaine in their book, *Fire in the Valley,* had this assessment of IMSAI: "Technologically, the

IMSAI computer was no breakthrough. IMSAI's most important contribution was not a technological feat but a marketing one. Millard took an uninspired design and a dubious market and built a company that became a power to be reckoned with in the nascent industry."

It was a company, however, that failed to survive. Hindsight makes everyone a seer. As a new product, the IMSAI computer had a lot of bugs. Customer support was poor. And the financial underpinnings were very fragile, partly because Bill Millard refused to sell any of his stock to venture capitalists or to investors through a public offering. One would-be investor turned away by Millard was Charles Tandy, founder of Radio Shack. The IMSAI factory in San Leandro was padlocked on September 4, 1979. It was the second company that Bill Millard had to close.

But he was far from being down for the count. While IMSAI was busy turning out its computers, Millard had gotten another idea. The stores selling the IMSAI 8080s were mainly operated by hobbyists who had little business experience. Millard saw a window here and he saw it before anybody else did. He would start a franchise store system, patterned after McDonald's. ComputerLand Corporation was established on September 21, 1976, with Ed Faber (who had been IMSAI's sales manager) installed as president. A pilot store was opened in November in nearby Hayward. The first franchised store opened in February 1977 in Morristown, New Jersey; the second appeared in West Los Angeles.

Bill Millard's neatest trick was sheltering ComputerLand from IMSAI. The organization he formed in 1972, IMS Associates, became the holding company for IMSAI Manufacturing, ComputerLand, and other Millard ventures. IMSAI eventually filed for reorganization under the Chapter 11 bankruptcy act. It never emerged from that reorganization, but creditors were unable to transfer any of their claims to ComputerLand.

Millard does have one nagging problem, though, the Martin-Musumeci lawsuit. John Martin-Musumeci worked for ComputerLand as a franchising consultant in 1976. His service must have been valuable, because Millard gave him 1 percent of ComputerLand's stock, which he later sold for $250,000. In 1980 Martin-Musumeci, then running a software publishing company that folded in 1984, heard about a $250,000 note held by a Boston venture capital firm. It was an IOU from IMS Associates that had been amended to include as collateral ComputerLand and other Millard enterprises; and as a kicker it carried the right to convert the note into 20 percent of IMSAI's and ComputerLand's stock. It had been issued back in 1977, when IMSAI was tottering and ComputerLand was in its infancy. Martin-Musumeci bought that note for $400,000 in 1980 and has been trying ever since to convert it into 20 percent of ComputerLand. The case has gone through a number of California courts—and up to late 1984 Millard had lost nearly every skirmish. The worst case scenario is that he will lose 20 percent of ComputerLand, and have to deal with some nasty back-tax consequences as well.

Millard has placed ComputerLand's headquarters in a wooded, mostly residential area of East Oakland, not far from the neighborhood he grew up in. A plaque above the receptionist's desk says, "The respect and friendship of those we serve is the foundation of our progress. Make it happen." When we visited him in early 1984, he had just negotiated an agreement that will bring ComputerLand into China. He was excited, he told us, because China is the largest country on the planet and he "is with the biggest company in the biggest segment of the largest industry on planet earth. That is opportunity."

Millard's wife, Patricia, sits on ComputerLand's three-person board of directors—the only non-Millard is Ed Faber. The three Millard daughters, none of whom went to college, also work in the company.

The East Oakland boy who grew up delivering magazines and newspapers door-to-door, still works 70 hours a week, and claims to have taken only three weeks' vacation in the last 10 years, can now look back with some satisfaction. He helped bring government into the computer age. He founded one of the first companies to make microcomputers. He founded the most successful chain of computer stores. And he didn't start in a garage. He doesn't wear jeans. And he didn't hit it until he was past 40.

Ira Weise

"I like to start a new company. It entails not only getting a business plan, but calling the phone company, getting carpeting, getting space; I like little projects like that"

▶ **BEST-KNOWN VENTURE:** 800-Software

OTHER VENTURE: Associated Foreclosure Services

BORN: 1949

RAISED: Los Angeles, California

FATHER'S OCCUPATION: Accountant

FIRST DOLLAR EARNED: Paper route

SCHOOLING: B.A., psychology, University of California at Santa Cruz; law degree, University of San Francisco

ORIGINAL FINANCING: $600,000 from family and friends

PERSONAL NET WORTH: 30 percent of 800-Software and 100 percent of Associated Foreclosure Services

HOME: Oakland, California

FAMILY: Married; two children

PERSONAL TRANSPORTATION: Honda Accord

(800-SOFTWARE)

800-SOFTWARE: First mail-order firm in the industry to use a toll-free number and accept charge card payments.

▶ **BEST-KNOWN PRODUCT:** Mail-order software distribution

YEAR FOUNDED: 1982

EMPLOYEES: 35

HEADQUARTERS: Berkeley, California

SALES: $4.5 million (1983); $10 million (1984 projection)

OWNERSHIP: Privately held, 15 shareholders are family and friends of the founders

If you were a college radical in the sixties who got gassed at demonstrations in People's Park in Berkeley, California, and spent your free time tutoring minority children, you might be reluctant to identify yourself as a capitalist and entrepreneur today. Ira Weise is. The founder and president of 800-Software still feels ambivalent about his business success, although his ambivalence apparently doesn't interfere with racking up sales of almost $5 million in 1983.

We talked with Weise in his cluttered red brick warehouse in the industrial flatlands of Berkeley. The warehouse is definitely not a *chichi* conversion job. Young people, who look like very recent graduates of the University of California at Berkeley, pad silently in sneakers and jeans past scores of metal shelves full of software programs. Weise carries a tremendous amount of inventory because he refuses to take an order for software not in stock. In another part of the warehouse, telephone operators take orders over the company's 800 number, while six technicians are on duty 90 hours a week, answering phone queries about 800-Software's merchandise.

That's a lot of activity for a reluctant businessman to preside over. The company turned a profit in its second month of business in 1982 and today is one of the biggest mail-order software firms in the country. Faced with the facts, Weise admits, "Since I'm running two businesses and they're both profitable, I guess I'm an entrepreneur. I hustled, but it didn't cross my mind." Two minutes later he says enthusiastically, "I like new businesses. There's nothing I like more than getting a new subsidiary going."

In fact, Weise showed signs of the entrepreneurial spirit quite early. Because he "didn't like to pay rent," Weise built a house in the Berkeley hills while he was an undergraduate. He learned carpentry from a friend, and he and another friend paid for the land with their savings. He made enough money from his half of the sale of the house to put himself through law school. During his tenure as a real estate lawyer, Weise started his own foreclosure company (he still owns Associated Foreclosure Services). Three months later, when Weise was 32 years old, he and a law school friend, Steven Brown, started 800-Software.

Weise never thought of starting a business when he was a boy growing up in Los Angeles. His father was an accountant, but Ira wanted to be a doctor. Duncan Lindsey, a friend at the University of California at Santa Cruz, convinced Weise to become an elementary school teacher. "I wanted to save the world," he remembers. He taught school quite happily for five years, until he was laid off. That's when Duncan's older brother Buck took his turn in influencing Ira Weise. "I don't make any decisions on my own," Ira asserts. "Buck said, 'You should go to law school.' There was still a residue of the radical in me. There was the idea that a career in law could help someone." So Weise went to the University of San Francisco, where he later taught an evening class in real estate law while he pursued a practice in bankruptcy law. "That's very relevant to the software industry," he says now.

When Weise tired of law after a year and a half, the Lindseys again stepped in. They had founded Perfect Software, which published several well-known business software programs. Brother Buck advised Weise, "Why don't you try a mail-order software distribution company?"

Ira and Buck brainstormed for an angle to set his mail-order company apart from similar firms. Weise came up with several angles. He cites a long list of the "firsts" that his company introduced to mail-order, or as he calls it, TEMSSSCO (telephone, marketing, software, sales, and support company): "We were the first mail-order firm to use a toll-free number, charge cards, and text and telephone support. We'd back up a product when somebody bought it. We were the first to actually have the items in stock. Most mail-order companies collect 10 orders, then go out and buy 10 products and ship them. I have nearly a million dollars of inventory in our warehouse, so a customer orders and gets the product [at a 30 percent to 50 percent discount] in three or four days."

Once he had his plan, he needed help in implementing it. Weise must have picked up a little of the Lindsey persuasiveness—he used it successfully on his law school buddy, Steven Brown. "Ira talked me into it—he told me we could each work a couple of hours a week, plus my mom was looking for something to do a few hours a day," Brown told the *San Francisco Chronicle*. "My mother lasted about a month before she went bananas," because the business was growing so fast.

Weise had borrowed $60,000 from family and friends to get 800-Software going. He and Brown called manufacturers and suppliers of software from Ira's office. (Brown worked for the California Coastal Commission.) Within a month, Brown was the full-time vice president of marketing and his father, Arnold Brown, became the chairman and chief financial officer. As a retired chief finance officer at Kaiser Cement, the senior Brown had the financial acumen that the company founders lacked. With another $200,000 in capital for inventory rounded up from private investors, 800-Software took off. Sales increased from $1.5 million the first year to $4.5 million in 1983. Staff salespeople started to actively solicit orders from large corporations—the major part of 800-Software's business today. In mid-1984, the firm was selling at a rate of $1 million per month.

But the ambivalence about capitalism returns when Weise talks about executive style and employees. He believes that the low turnover rate among his 32 employees is explained partly by profit-sharing and lesser perks like the "French roast coffee and bottled water here; we recycle all the paper and aluminum and give stuff to the Sierra Club." Imagine any other CEO claiming the only limits he puts on employees are "we always have to wear shoes and there's no dope smoking during office hours."

The company style might also be influenced by its location—Berkeley. Weise tailors his lifestyle to the city. "No, in Berkeley you don't drive big cars. I got rid of an 11-year-old Volvo to get a Honda." Not exactly life in the fast lane for a man who could probably afford a racier lifestyle. Weise owns 30 percent of the privately held company.

"Steven and I both want people to like us," Weise says. Apparently people do. Half of his business comes from repeat customers buying the best-sellers on the Softsel chart. His employees also seem to like their employers. No security of any kind guards the million-dollar inventory and so far not one program has been stolen.

NOVEL FORMS OF FINANCING

Don Estridge (IBM Entry Systems Division)	International Business Machines
William Godbout (CompuPro)	Sold a counter-intelligence operation
Dustin Heuston (Wicat)	Foundation grants
Porter Hurt (PH Components)	Poker winnings
Steve Jobs (Apple Computer)	(Sold his Volkswagen bus and Steve Wozniak's calculators)
Lorraine Mecca (Micro D)	Sold home from a divorce settlement
Jerry Sanders (Advanced Micro Devices)	Severance pay from Fairchild Semiconductor
William von Meister (Source Telecomputing)	Inheritance

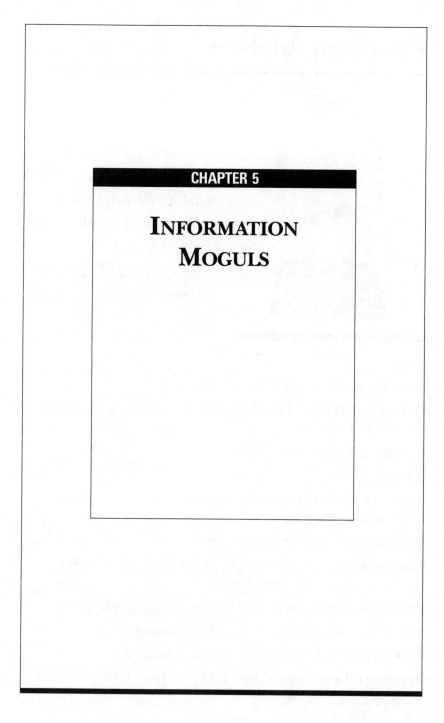

CHAPTER 5

INFORMATION
MOGULS

Sheldon Adelson

"A show is a magazine in the flesh. The advertisers become the exhibitors, and the readers become the attendees. I said, 'Hey, I got a magazine. I'd make a million dollars in three days'"

▶ **BEST-KNOWN VENTURE:** Interface Group

OTHER VENTURES: Dashel Associates, Adelson & Company, Vend-A-Bar

BORN: 1933

RAISED: Boston, Massachusetts

PARENTS' OCCUPATIONS: Father—drove a taxi; mother—owned a knitting store (retired)

FIRST DOLLAR EARNED: Soda jerk

SCHOOLING: Court reporting school; City College of New York night school (no degree)

PERSONAL NET WORTH: Majority of Interface Group

HOME: Boston and Cape Cod, Massachusetts

FAMILY: Married; three children; one grandchild

PERSONAL TRANSPORTATION: Jaguar, Mercedes

THE INTERFACE GROUP, Inc.

INTERFACE GROUP: Producers of COMDEX, the gigantic extravaganza of the personal computer show world.

▶ **BEST-KNOWN PRODUCTS:** COMDEX Shows, Byte Computer Shows, Interface Show, Federal DP Expo, Computer Showcase Expos

YEAR FOUNDED: 1973

EMPLOYEES: 300 permanent; 1,000 seasonal

HEADQUARTERS: Needham, Massachusetts

SALES: $175 million (1983)

OWNERSHIP: Privately held by Sheldon Adelson (51 percent) and five partners

The COMDEX computer fair is a gaudy carnival of excess, a sensory overload of glistening electronic gewgaws, gadgets, and gimmicks. The spring 1983 show featured Norman Vincent Peale conducting a prayer breakfast, while in another part of the hall, former President Jimmy Carter examined a software program his son had written.

The fall 1983 show in Las Vegas, Nevada, attracted 83,000 people to 11 miles of exhibit aisles jammed with booths of Marilyn Monroe look-alikes and Wild West get-ups complete with lasso contests. Most of the 1,400 exhibitors paid $2,150 each for the honor of being one of the "ten thousand people selling twenty products to each other," as one newspaper reported. For this five-day show, $100 million in equipment was shipped out to Las Vegas for display; $150 million found its way into the economy of Las Vegas; and $13 million enriched the coffers of the producer, Interface Group. And what enriches Interface enriches its majority shareholder and founder, impresario extraordinaire, Sheldon Adelson.

Adelson is not in the gargantuan show business for his

health or for his love of the computer industry. He's in it for the bucks. And he makes plenty. He shrugs off criticism by exhibitors and attendees that his shows are too unwieldy and trendy. "Let them go into a less volatile marketplace, like the gum eraser industry. The show merely reflects the industry itself," he told the *San Francisco Examiner*.

Some computer enthusiasts might find Adelson's attitude towards their industry a little cynical; but Adelson's philosophy comes from his own school of hard knocks, where he learned to earn millions and lose millions and then earn some more. He knows the value of his own myth-making. He refers to himself as "a little Jew boy from Carson Beach—you know, where the sewage came up on the beach." He says that he's "not really turned on by material things," but then he'll go on to remind you of the mansion he once owned that had 12,000 square feet, an elevator, and seven acres of land. He describes his year-round house on Cape Cod as "magnificent— sitting on top of a seventy-foot sand dune on the second highest point on Cape Cod Bay. And we have an indoor pool." He drives a Jaguar and his wife drives a Mercedes, "but I'm not going to buy a Rolls-Royce. I'm not turned on by cars," Adelson says with a straight face.

When it comes to employees, Adelson offers more conflicting statements. He admits that he has a reputation as a "tough son of a bitch," but he claims that he is not a "slave-driver. If they [employees] do perfection and they pay attention to detail, I can't ask any more of an employee."

Adelson asks a lot of others because he's always asked a lot of himself. He was born in the depths of the Depression in 1933 in Dorchester, a section of Boston Adelson calls a "Jewish ghetto." His father, an immigrant (possibly from Lithuania— Adelson says his father doesn't really know), drove a taxi; his mother, an immigrant from Wales, ran a knitting store. Sheldon and his three siblings lived behind the store in a one-bedroom apartment.

At nine, Sheldon sold newspapers. Later, he worked as a soda jerk and a delivery boy. He claims that with such jobs he managed to save a couple of hundred dollars by age 16 to buy his first business—Vend-A-Bar, a candy bar vending company.

Even more remarkable is the $3,000 or so loan he says he got from a credit union. The seller took a note and financed the $6,500 balance on the $10,000 company. He installed his own candy machines in factories and replenished the candy bars periodically. He repaired half of the 125 vending machines that were out of commission when he bought them. Adelson observed that candy bars melt in hot factories in the summer. Never one to miss an opportunity to make money, he bought a truck and ice chests and sold ice cream at the same factories during the summer months.

So far Adelson's life reads like that of a Jewish Horatio Alger. But then the Korean War interfered. He thought that if he went to night school to learn court reporting, it would keep him off the battlefields of Korea. So with the profits from selling his vending machine business, he marched off to school.

Court reporting may appear to be an odd twist in the career of a budding young entrepreneur. But young Sheldon had already proved himself adept at making the most out of any opportunity. He was young; he was poor; he was uneducated. He had one formal skill: court reporting. He used that single skill as the first link in an improbable chain of positions that led right up to his goal: multimillionaire.

When he could no longer stave off the draft, he enlisted in the Army, where his stenographic skills landed him a cushy desk job in New York City. After his discharge, Adelson, like many others, wanted "to start at the top" on Wall Street. But unlike other young men, particularly in the '50s, Adelson opted for a job as a private secretary to a top executive. Not only was he one of the male secretaries on Wall Street, he may well have been the only male secretary to a female executive.

Celia D. Wyckoff was herself a former secretary who had married her boss. She later divorced him and took over his financial magazine, *Magazine of Wall Street*. She was 70 years old when she hired Sheldon as her secretary. She soon promoted him to ad salesman and then advertising manager.

At first "everyone sounded like they were speaking Greek," Adelson remembers. He worked hard to learn the finance jargon. He even took night classes at City College of New York. He loved hobnobbing with the bigwigs on Wall

Street. It reminded him of his first brush with a celebrity when his court reporting school sent him to take down the memoirs of Emmett Kelly, the circus clown. He had considered that a "real turn-on," he said.

Adelson hustled ads for a variety of financial publications on Wall Street, but his real business was getting to know everyone who was anyone. He was preparing for the next step up the ladder—finder. Without education, or the proper credentials, Adelson had to rely on his shrewdness and persistence. As a finder, he'd use his extensive contacts to find small, privately owned companies who were looking to sell stock for the first time to outside investors. He'd match them up with Wall Street investment banking houses for a commission. He likens it to being a "traffic cop."

In 1963, he started Dashel Associates, an acronym for partner Dave Freedman and Sheldon. Freedman and Adelson wheeled and dealed together through the '60s, mostly refinancing mortgages during slow times in the securities market. By 1966, Adelson had started his own company, Adelson & Company, where he continued as a finder and mortgage financier. His deals were lucrative— Adelson says, "I think it's fair to say that I was a millionaire more than once."

He got cocky. Rather than finding venture capitalists to invest in companies, he put up his own money in everything from chains of carpet stores to valve companies. Then, in 1969, the market took a steep dive. "One day I woke up in 1970 and found myself a million-and-a-half in the hole," Adelson says. He was sitting in a big mansion that he could no longer afford, supporting a family and a domestic couple he had brought over from Korea.

Not one to dwell on failure, he refers to that incident as a "two-hour cry," as opposed to the "half-hour cry" he had a couple of years later when he lost $1 million in a condominium development that went bust.

Within a year, he had earned enough in consulting fees to buy out Douglas Communications, a small publishing company, which published a magazine called *Communications User*. He was no more interested in publishing than he was in quantum physics. It was just another company to invest in. At that time, 1972, the future computer show impresario saw condominiums, not computers, as the wave of the future. He was interested in financing condo conversions. It was condominiums that brought Adelson to a trade show in California. And that's where he got the idea that put him in the trade show business.

"I found out that the condominium show was owned by the people who published a magazine. A show is a magazine in the flesh. The advertisers become the exhibitors, the editorials become the conference, and the readers become the attendees. I said, 'Hey, I got a magazine. Why can't I do something like this? I'd make a million dollars in three days.'"

Back in Boston, Adelson informed his publishing staff, "We're going into show business. You're not getting anywhere with the magazine [*Communications User*] and I'm going to tell you guys what to do." So what if Adelson knew nothing about publishing? He knew about making money. He changed the name of the magazine to *Data Communications User*. The next year, 1973, Adelson put on his first Data Communications Interface show, sponsored by his magazine. Adelson's only personal experience with electronics prior to this had been "sitting in front of the TV watching the test patterns," back in 1946.

Adelson saw his new business as a great way to come back from the million-dollar fiasco with the condominiums. He put his energy into the shows and eventually got rid of the magazine entirely. The Interface shows offered a chance for manufacturers of computer and data communications equipment to show their wares to their customers—mostly data processing professionals who worked for large corporations.

The idea for COMDEX came to Adelson at 35,000 feet above sea level. Adelson was reading a copy of *Computer Systems News* while flying back to Boston from an Interface show in Chicago in 1979. He noticed from reading the articles and the ads that there had been a big change in the industry that nobody in the computer trade show business had yet noticed. Instead of selling directly to their customers, many manufacturers were working through middlemen—distributors and dealers. "This thing is all screwed up," he said to himself.

Adelson saw a chance to clean up. He decided to create a

trade show where manufacturers could show their wares directly to dealers and distributors. He couldn't even wait for Monday—he got on the phone that weekend. "If I see a need, I don't wait till next year," he explains. Even though he says putting a show together in eight months is "suicide," the first COMDEX (which stands for Computer Dealers' Exposition) show opened successfully in December 1979.

Adelson happened onto an idea that was also ideally suited to the still-infant personal computer industry. Shows like the West Coast Computer Faire enabled various manufacturers to show their goods to hobbyists and others who were buying personal computers. But there were no shows where the various manufacturers could appeal directly to dealers and distributors. COMDEX was the perfect vehicle.

COMDEX has become the largest trade show in the world. The three COMDEX shows—spring in Atlanta, fall in Las Vegas, and a new winter show in Los Angeles—have doubled in size every year since the start. Adelson's company, Interface, also produces McGraw-Hill's Interface '84, Byte Computer Shows, Computer Expos, and 30 other showcases here and abroad. Adelson is involved in a joint venture to build a 120,000-square-foot building at the Las Vegas Convention Center, and he owns one of the largest tour operators in the United States, GWV Travel. He is also in the process of setting up his own airline.

When Adelson puts on his Las Vegas show, the biggest annual industry show in the nation, he brings along 150 of his 300 employees, besides hiring an additional 500 locals. These shows require the kind of planning that would make anyone's blood pressure rise. In a tragic reflection of the pressures involved with setting up the fall 1983 show in Las Vegas, Interface partner Mitchell Halperin died of a heart attack on the convention floor the night before the show opened.

Adelson's next goal is to become big enough to be one of the Fortune 500. With revenues of $175 million, he guesses that puts him in the Fortune 1000 league; but it's that 500 club he wants to join.

FAMILY TREE

Roots

Number of Entrepreneurs Whose Parents Were Entrepreneurs: 30

Branches

Founders of Three or More Companies

Sheldon Adelson	Adam Osborne
David Bunnell	Chuck Peddle
Nolan Bushnell	Seymour Rubinstein
Gary Friedman	Go Sugiura
Fred Gibbons	George Tate
William Godbout	James Toreson
William Hambrecht	William von Meister
Trip Hawkins	Jim Warren
Porter Hurt	Ken Williams
William Millard	

David Bunnell

"I often thought of what if I had a personal computer when I was the president of the college SDS chapter. It meant that computer technology wasn't going to be strictly for big corporations and the guys in white coats"

▶ **BEST-KNOWN VENTURE:** *PC World* magazine

OTHER VENTURES: The first personal computer show; *Personal Computing* magazine; *PC* magazine

BORN: 1947

RAISED: Alliance, Nebraska

FATHER'S OCCUPATION: Managing editor of the Alliance *Daily Times Herald*

FIRST DOLLAR EARNED: Sports editor of the Alliance *Daily Times Herald*

SCHOOLING: B.A., University of Nebraska

PERSONAL NET WORTH: 32.8 percent of *PC* sale (still in litigation); undisclosed percentage of *PC World*

FAMILY: Married; two children from a previous marriage

PERSONAL TRANSPORTATION: Toyota Land Cruiser and Ford LTD

PC W●RLD

PC WORLD: The largest-circulation magazine devoted to the IBM PC.

▶ **BEST-KNOWN PRODUCTS:** *PC World* magazine, *Macworld* magazine

YEAR FOUNDED: 1982 (premier issue January 1983)

EMPLOYEES: 100

HEADQUARTERS: San Francisco, California

ADVERTISING REVENUES: $22 million

CIRCULATION: *PC World*—300,000; *Macworld*—200,000

OWNERSHIP: Subsidiary of CW Communications

An old computer industry associate calls David Bunnell "initially a knee-jerk liberal turned entrepreneur [who] likes money. A little bit dumb—obviously not very dumb because he's pulled off some great scams." The scams David Bunnell has pulled off are four computer magazines, including *Personal Computing, Macworld, PC,* and *PC World.* By a "little bit dumb," the associate certainly wasn't questioning Bunnell's intelligence; rather he was referring to Bunnell's gullible nature. He's been burned three times by publishers or investors who allegedly reneged on their promises to him.

And what about the "knee-jerk liberal?" Bunnell spent years teaching black ghetto kids, then American Indians on a reservation. Before that he served as president of the University of Nebraska chapter of Students for a Democratic Society (SDS). Bunnell, who sharpened his organizing skills in the antiwar movement, put them to good use in a recent magazine battle over *PC* magazine. He and his staff fought a lawsuit, set up an office, and turned out a brand new magazine within a month. That magazine, *PC World*, premiered with 310 pages—

it claims to be the largest first issue of any magazine ever. Another Bunnell talent is "being at the right place at the right time," as his associate says.

The small railroad crossing in the sand hills of Nebraska where Bunnell grew up hardly qualifies as anyone's idea of the right place. Bunnell, like almost all of his high school class of 140, "never had any thoughts of staying" in Alliance, the "Cattle Capital of Nebraska."

Bunnell wanted to be a writer, and he got some good training for that as a boy. While other budding journalists wrote for their high school papers, David was the sports editor of a real newspaper, the Alliance *Daily Times Herald*. He got the job because his father just happened to be the managing editor of the paper. David had to get up at five o'clock in the morning, pull out the wire copy, and write headlines before school.

His writing ambitions didn't end with sports reporting. Ernest Hemingway and Jack Kerouac were his heroes and "writing the great American novel was my goal in life," Bunnell remembers. But at the University of Nebraska in the late '60s, Bunnell spent most of his time with SDS protesting the Vietnam War. "The thing I'm most proud of," he says, "was I organized the single-largest demonstration in the history of Lincoln, Nebraska." Four thousand students marched on City Hall and took over the university administration building to get nondiscriminatory off-campus housing.

The idealistic Bunnell wanted to live his theories of equality in the big city. After graduation, he moved to Chicago where he taught poor black kids in the ghetto. He continued his involvement with SDS until he became disillusioned with "the radical elements—the Spartacus League and the Progressive Labor Party—that took over SDS" and turned it into what Bunnell calls "a sort of totalitarian, miniature communist soviet." Some of his last antiwar activities included attending the Chicago Eight Trial and later a march on Washington, D.C., in 1969 where he got tear-gassed.

Bunnell put in two years teaching in Chicago, then another two years on the Sioux reservation at Pine Ridge, South Dakota. That's where he was fired on again, this time with a regular bullet, which hit his windshield. It was during the time of the Wounded Knee occupation in 1973. Federal marshals traded shots with the Indians at the Wounded Knee village, about 50 miles from the village where Bunnell taught. "I identified with the American Indian Movement," Bunnell recalls. "I took food into Wounded Knee and I went to the funeral of the Indian—Frank Clearwater—who was killed there. I knew leaders Russell Means and Dennis Banks. I just didn't feel safe there anymore."

Bunnell decided to move as far away as possible from the violence of the rural reservation and big city life. With no reason other than the weather, Bunnell moved his wife, who was from his hometown, and two children to Albuquerque, New Mexico. For months he looked for a job. Albuquerque was turning out to be like Chicago and Pine Ridge: the wrong place at the wrong time. Finally, he got a job writing instruction manuals for an obscure electronics firm called MITS. He earned $125 a week.

Suddenly, Bunnell was at the right place at the right time—he was smack in the middle of the microcomputer revolution. Ed Roberts, a former Air Force engineer, inventor, and president of MITS, used the first eight-bit chip, the Intel 8080, to design the first personal computer, the Altair.

When the Altair appeared on the cover of *Popular Electronics* in January 1975, MITS took off. Bunnell rocketed through the company to become vice president in charge of advertising and marketing. He started a monthly tabloid for Altair owners called *Computer Notes*.

In 1976, Bunnell organized the first personal computer convention at an Albuquerque hotel, the World Altair Computer Convention. He was joined there by early computer innovators Roger Melen, Harry Garland, and publisher Wayne Green. He already knew Bill Gates and Paul Allen, who were living in Albuquerque doing programming for the Altair. Bunnell was now in the thick of the high-tech computer world, but he saw no jarring contradiction between computers and his old humanism. He believed that computer technology "could accomplish many of the political or social goals that weren't accomplished through the politics of the '60s—increasing the power of the individual, giving more access to information. I can see how the personal computer can be used for grass roots movements." The SDS activist had become a computer revolutionary.

All revolutions need a voice, and Bunnell thought he could be just that. He wanted to promote the "vision," as he calls it, to teach all people (not just hobbyists) what personal computers were all about through a magazine he named *Personal Computing*. He sent his idea to Benwell Publishing, which agreed to finance it. Bunnell was too naive in business to know that you should carefully check out prospective associates. All he knew about Benwell was that it advertised in his computer tabloid. That was apparently enough for him. Bunnell left MITS; and with editor Nelson Winkless and one secretary, wrote and laid out the first issue (January/February 1977) in Albuquerque and sent it off to Benwell's Boston, Massachusetts, headquarters.

The first burn: Benwell balked at giving Bunnell the 10 percent equity in the magazine that he wanted. According to Bunnell, Benwell told him that none of their other editors had such a deal. Still more committed to his ideals than to business, Bunnell decided he'd continue to do the magazine anyway. But, a year later, when Benwell wanted to move the magazine to Boston, Bunnell quit and moved (he separated from his wife) himself to San Francisco—the center of the computer business—where he began work on a book, *Personal Computing, A Beginner's Guide*, which was published by Hawthorne in 1978.

Although Bunnell took various computer jobs for money, he also "hung out and was kind of a bum," he says. In between writing the original documentation for *VisiCalc* and technical writing for GRT Corp., Bunnell read his poems in San Francisco coffeehouses and spent time writing short stories. He never wrote "the great American novel," although he had written an unpublished novel in college called *1, 2, 3*.

The second burn: A friend named Jim Edlin asked Bunnell to help him write a book, *Micro, the Next Watershed Invention*. They got a contract with Warner Books for $25,000. After the two finished 1,000 pages, Warner rejected the book and demanded the advance back. Bunnell says the publisher "reneged on the deal." At any rate, he "could barely afford to eat." Bunnell sold his car and borrowed money from his father.

Through his new fiancee, Jacqueline Poitier (now the associate publisher of *PC World*), Bunnell got a job as a word processing machine operator for the California State Bar Association. Bunnell didn't look at the job as a step down for a magazine publisher. He thought it was a "great experience" to learn to use a Xerox 860 and Wang system. Still, Bunnell had no intention of staring at a video screen for 20 years. When he saw a blind ad in the help wanted section of the newspaper for a managing editor of a small book publishing firm, he applied. The publisher turned out to be Adam Osborne. At that time, Osborne published computer books in Berkeley. He was as surprised and delighted to find a man with Bunnell's computer experience as Bunnell was to find a computer book publisher. Bunnell not only got the job, he also co-authored the second edition of *An Introduction to Microcomputers* with Osborne. Bunnell today credits Osborne with "rescuing" him from word processing.

The third burn: After ten months happily working for Osborne, Bunnell heard from his old friend and fellow vice president at MITS, Eddie Currie. Currie was now the vice president of Lifeboat Associates (a software publishing and distribution company) and its president, Tony Gold, wanted to start a computer magazine. Bunnell was ready to go back into the publishing fray because he still felt sad when he saw *Personal Computing* on the stands. "Number one, it was no longer my publication, and number two, it was so ugly now," he says.

It was the summer of 1981. IBM had just announced its personal computer. Gold's brainstorm was to publish the first magazine devoted solely to the IBM PC. Bunnell became so excited by the idea that he "was jumping up and down on my kitchen floor" while talking on the phone with Currie about it.

The excitement and the desire for his own magazine again dulled Bunnell's business sense. He knew only that Gold was "a Harvard M.B.A. and a banker who fell in love with computers and started the tremendously successful Lifeboat." Bunnell insists, "It's not that I made the same mistake twice. I was smarter this time. No handshake deal. We had a letter of agreement. I agreed to do it provided myself and key employees would get 45 percent of the magazine, which Tony agreed to."

Bunnell immediately resigned from Osborne with Cheryl Woodard (another Osborne employee) and set up production in his rented house in San Francisco. *PC* magazine was pasted-up in his living room (where spilled rubber cement spoiled his new Persian rug) by 14 employees, including his wife, Jacqueline. Gold put in $180,000 and Bunnell put in "sweat equity." Bunnell and his staff put in plenty of sweat in the seven issues they published. *PC* magazine grew from 100 pages to 400 in those seven issues; revenues increased from zero to $3.5 million per issue. The first issue came out in February 1982. By early November, Gold and the staff were locked in combat over the direction of *PC*. Selling the magazine was the only way out of the impasse. Several prestigious companies bid for the magazine, including CBS Publications, Prentice-Hall, Xerox Publishing, and International Thomson. Bunnell and the staff wanted Pat McGovern of CW Communications to buy *PC*, and Gold came to an agreement with McGovern on the Friday before Thanksgiving. Gold, Bunnell, and McGovern were scheduled to close the deal on Tuesday.

When Bunnell showed up at the *PC* office Monday morning, two representatives from Ziff-Davis were waiting for him. Gold had sold 100 percent of *PC* to Ziff-Davis. According to Bunnell, the lawyers for Ziff-Davis claimed Bunnell and company's 45 percent ownership was not valid because, among other things, the agreement had been written on personal stationery, rather than company stationery.

That night Pat McGovern arrived in San Francisco on a plane from Tokyo, ready to close the deal for *PC* the next day. When he heard Gold had sold to Ziff-Davis, he immediately offered Bunnell the support to start another magazine. By Friday, Bunnell had negotiated a contract with McGovern to launch *PC World* magazine. The agreement gives Bunnell, Poitier, Woodard, and other key staffers a piece of the ownership of *PC World*. On Monday, the staff of the new magazine spread their tale of woe and hustled 100 pages of ads on the sympathy vote at the COMDEX show in Las Vegas. Returning to San Franciso, *PC World* set up an office, hired 48 (out of 52) former *PC* employees, fought a lawsuit filed by Ziff-Davis over the name *PC World*, and put out the first issue of the magazine. Bunnell recalls that "it was just really very hectic and crazy. Ah, the adventures."

In 1984, the litigation continues with Tony Gold and the 45 percent "sweat equity" Bunnell and staff claim; but *PC World* has become the leading machine-specific magazine. Circulation is 300,000 (200,000 for *Macworld*).

With the power of the CW empire behind him, David Bunnell is flexing his muscles. He writes *Subroutines, the David Bunnell Newsletter for the PC Industry*, where he names names and gripes or praises. He premiered a new magazine, *Macworld*, for the Apple Macintosh. He pioneered disk advertising by offering the first demonstration floppy disk bound into a magazine. The 100,000 subscriber issues of the September 1983 issue of *PC World* contained a Microsoft disk that allowed the owner of an IBM PC or compatible computer to sample a new word processor, *Microsoft Word*. Unlike some publishers who prefer anonymity, Bunnell has his photo printed prominently along with his regular columns in all of his publications.

Will Bunnell be burned a fourth time? It's perhaps too early to tell. In his latest effort, he's involved with a man known as the "Mr. Nice Guy" of the computer publishing world. Whatever happens, Bunnell can't say he hasn't been warned about the dangers of playing with matches.

Adam Green

"If someone gets interested, they can buy me. Buy a book, buy a video tape, come to class. Software is less and less important. The important thing is selling Adam Green"

▶ **BEST-KNOWN VENTURE:** SoftwareBanc

BORN: 1956

RAISED: Brooklyn, New York

FATHER'S OCCUPATION: Computer consultant

FIRST DOLLAR EARNED: Lab technician

SCHOOLING: B.S., organic chemistry, State University of New York at Stony Brook

ORIGINAL FINANCING: $800 from savings

PERSONAL NET WORTH: 50 percent of SoftwareBanc

HOME: Arlington, Massachusetts

FAMILY: Married; one daughter

PERSONAL TRANSPORTATION: Toyota

SoftwareBanc, Inc.

SOFTWAREBANC INC.: Pioneers in software-training seminars.

▶ **BEST-KNOWN PRODUCTS:** Adam Green, self-promoter, super-salesman

YEAR FOUNDED: 1982

EMPLOYEES: 21

HEADQUARTERS: Arlington, Massachusetts

SALES: $5 million (1984 projection)

OWNERSHIP: Privately owned by Adam and Randy Green

Five years ago, when he was a chemistry major at State University of New York at Stony Brook on Long Island, Adam Green could not tell a byte from a bit. Today, the Brooklyn-born Green earns as much as $25,000 a weekend demystifying the intricacies of *dBase II*, a popular data management program, to computer professionals at seminars across the country. Green, who had nothing to do with writing or selling the program, is now known as the "Professor of *dBase II*" and has written the book—make that two best-selling books—on *dBase II*. His firm, SoftwareBanc, has one important and lucrative product: Adam Green.

Green became obsessed with computers after buying himself a TRS-80 Model I in March of 1980. By then he had spent a year and a half making synthetic drugs for a chemical company—long enough to realize that chemists need to put in 30 years to be considered knowledgeable. He realized that a highly motivated neophyte could, on the other hand, become an expert in the then-infant personal computer business. An impatient young man, Green quit his job, took a summer course in programming at Wesleyan University, and within months could claim that he was familiar with every major business software program for personal computers then in existence. In the fall of 1980, he took a programming job with CPU Computer Corp., a New England retail, wholesale, and mail-order company. By January 1981, Green had worked his way up to software and hardware product manager, meaning that he decided which items CPU would sell.

As product manager, Green had one rule of thumb: sell only products you like. Instead of 600 computer-related books, Green winnowed the list down to 30. Instead of an inventory of 3,000 products, Green featured 600. His strategy paid off. Sales doubled in six months.

Green's personal taste led him to buy early versions of *DB Master*, Ashton-Tate's *dBase II*, and *SuperCalc*. Despite Green's unerring track record, CPU's president refused to believe Green's prediction that *SuperCalc* would be "the biggest thing in the world." When he told Green that there was "no money in software," Green quit and started his own software mail-order house. With little more than his own sweat and good reputation, SoftwareBanc quickly became a significant player in a burgeoning industry. It was less than two years from the day he bought his first computer.

Green saw the need to expand beyond mail order. Instead of just selling computers, Green decided to sell himself. As one of the first *dBase II* users, he realized the inadequacy of the user's manual that came with the $700 program and quickly established himself as the commonsense expert. For those who want to buy Green's expertise, he offers Adam Green in print: his *dBase II User's Guide* at $29.95 has sold more than 90,000 copies. For those who want to be led by the hand, there's Adam Green in person for day-long seminars at $200 a pop. And for those who like their *dBase II* on TV, there's Adam Green on videocassette at $295. One of his ads for his various products features himself popping out of a box with a *dBase II User's Guide* in hand.

Why do people eagerly put down $29.95 to $295 for Adam Green? Leslie Miner, in a cover story on Green in *PC* magazine, explains: "Besides his enthusiasm for the subject, he has an actor's instinct, which combined with his considerable teaching ability, turns each of his classes into a command performance."

According to Miner, Green controls every aspect of his seminars with so much zeal that they remind people of Werner Erhard's est training sessions. He knows how warm the room should be, how many items of information to mention per minute, why coffee and cake are replaced with milk, yogurt, and cheese at the carefully timed breaks, and how to use audiovisual techniques. Green's principle of teaching is "KISS": Keep it simple, stupid.

Green sees applying his techniques to other subjects besides *dBase II*. Fully aware of the millions of dollars Jane Fonda has pulled in from her aerobics videocassette, Green says, "Somebody is going to do the Jane Fonda videocassette on microcomputing, and I want it to be Adam Green."

While Green is on the road, his wife, Randy, runs SoftwareBanc out of their office near Cambridge, Massachusetts. Green thinks she makes a good company president because "she likes to boss people around." In early 1984, SoftwareBanc was taking in $350,000 to $400,000 a month from the software mail order, books, videocassettes, seminars, and other enterprises. It has been quite profitable. Green figures that of the $25,000 in fees he gets from each weekend seminar, he has expenses of about $2,500.

Does Green see himself maintaining this dizzying pace indefinitely? Certainly not. In 10 years he hopes to have earned enough from the microcomputer business to retire permanently on a Caribbean island, before he turns 40.

Pat McGovern

*"My father told me,
'Son, there are only six
words that express what
you do in business:
find a need and fill it'"*

▶ **BEST-KNOWN VENTURE:** International Data Group

BORN: 1937

RAISED: Philadelphia, Pennsylvania

FATHER'S OCCUPATION: Managed a construction company

FIRST DOLLAR EARNED: Paper route

SCHOOLING: B.S., biophysics, Massachusetts Institute of Technology

ORIGINAL FINANCING: $135,000 in subscription advances

PERSONAL NET WORTH: $200 million

HOMES: Woodside, California, and Framingham, Massachusetts

FAMILY: Divorced; remarried to Lore Harp (co-founder of Vector Graphics); two children

PERSONAL TRANSPORTATION: An aging Mercedes on each coast

INTERNATIONAL DATA GROUP: Largest computer magazine
publisher.

▶ **BEST-KNOWN PRODUCTS:** *Computerworld, InfoWorld, PC World,
Macworld, Microcomputing, 80 Micro, inCider*

YEAR FOUNDED: 1964

EMPLOYEES: 1,400

HEADQUARTERS: Framingham, Massachusetts

SALES: $150 million (1983); $250 million (1984 projection)

OWNERSHIP: Privately held, Pat McGovern owns 85 percent
of stock

It's not every 15-year-old who builds a computer and programs it to be unbeatable in tic-tac-toe. Pat McGovern
did— and that was back in the early '50s when he was a
high school student in Bucks County, the northeastern suburb
of Philadelphia.

McGovern was always a whiz at science (he used to build
science projects for older students), and he was turned on to
computers by reading Ed Berkeley's book, *Giant Brains or
Machines That Think*. So for one month he saved the $4.60 he
earned each week from his newspaper delivery route and went
down to the local hardware store to buy 35 yards of bell wire,
300 carpet tacks, staples, and six 1.5-by-2-foot plywood pieces
that served as his circuit boards. He made his relay from little
strips of tin that he took off the edge of linoleum.

The result was a single-application computer that could calculate what the next optimum move would be in playing tic-
tac-toe. McGovern's computer would either win or tie—it
would never lose. However—and this tells you something
about Pat McGovern—he also programmed it so that every
fortieth move his computer would make an illogical move, one

that wasn't the optimum reply to an opponent's move. Why? To enable the player to win once in a while "and feel a little more secure in his human competence."

Delivering newspapers to the lawns of suburban homes was not the only connection to publishing that the teenaged McGovern had. He was also editor of his high school newspaper. And it was this combination—computer proficiency and journalistic curiosity—that enabled McGovern to become the James Boswell of the emerging computer industry. Most people enter the computer industry because they are intrigued with this new technology or they want to make a lot of money. With McGovern, there was always something more. He was fired up by computers and how the world was going to change because of them. And that thought made him wonder where he was going to fit in.

He was also influenced by his father, who worked as a manager for a construction company. McGovern explained that influence when he spoke in early 1984 at the West Coast Computer Faire: "I remember my father had told me, 'Son, the trouble with most things in life, people make it too complicated.' There are only six words that express what you do in business. You either have a left brain or a right brain concept. Your left brain concept says, 'find a need and fill it.' Your right brain concept says, 'do something useful for other people.'"

Those have been McGovern's two lodestars. Originally, he went for computers because he was excited about how useful this technology would be for "other people. It makes them intellectually charged, emotionally satisfied." And later on he went into the business of providing information to the computer world because he saw a gap there that could be filled.

The homemade tic-tac-toe computer iced McGovern's entry to the Massachusetts Institute of Technology—or as he has put it: "It attracted the attention of the MIT alumni association in Philadelphia. They decided to get me out of town and send me off to learn a trade in Cambridge." At MIT, which he entered in 1955 at age 18, he immersed himself in computer science. He developed a program that made possible interactive conversation with a computer. Although he had a scholarship, he had to work to put himself through school—and he landed a job as associate editor of a Boston-based magazine, *Computers and Automation*, which was published by none other than Ed Berkeley. After graduating he went to work full-time for the magazine—in effect, running it. When he took over, there were 5,000 subscribers; three years later, the circulation was 16,000.

McGovern says that 1964 was the turning point in his life. That's when he went down to New York to attend a press conference held by RCA, which was then trying to make it as a computer manufacturer. The RCA engineers were introducing a new device called Random Access Card Equipment. Here's McGovern's recollection of how it worked: "They take a punch card wrapped around with Mylar film, put it down, set it up about four feet away from a rapidly rotating cylinder, and then shoot these cards at random down the runway. They were supposed to wrap around the cylinder, be raised instantaneously, and shot back into the right slot. You can imagine, every hundredth card came out looking like a Polish accordian player by the time it got back to its original position."

McGovern approached the RCA people to determine why this product had been developed. Did it have something to do with accelerating the speed of access to files? No. Was it related to the increases in the size of a computer's memory? No. The engineers' answer went something like this: "We found out that we could do this. We have this new electromechanical technology and the sensor technique. So we produced this new product." Instead of finding a need and filling it, RCA made a product because it could make it, need or no need.

Amazed at this kind of behavior, the 27-year-old Pat McGovern walked across the street to check his impressions with Lou Raider and Lou Nofrey, the head and the planning director, respectively, of Sperry Rand's Univac division. They confirmed that companies were putting a lot of money into new, exotic technology without an apparent market—and one reason for this "flying blind" was IBM's market dominance. "We have about a 4 percent market share," they told him. "IBM has a 73 percent market share. We have very little information about what the customers are doing. IBM's large customer base tells them about market needs. And then they've got 23,000 field representatives gathering information about all the other prospects. Our salesmen are struggling so hard to catch up they hardly have time to do the paper work to keep us informed about the small base they're in touch with."

Well, the bells went off in McGovern's head: "find a need and fill it." The need was information about the computer market. Why not create a computer census? Send a questionnaire to every company with more than 500 employees, find out how many computers they have, what kind of computers they use, and what their needs are. It wasn't exactly a revolutionary idea. Market researchers in other fields had been performing this exercise for many years. But the computer industry was new—and no one was doing it, save IBM, which of course did not share its information with competitors. McGovern asked his friends at Univac whether they would be willing to pay $7,000 to $8,000 for such an information service. They told him that no one at Sperry Rand would believe the information was important if it was priced that low.

McGovern rushed home to Boston, started a company called International Data Corporation, put together a research proposal, priced it at $15,000 per annum, and sent it to 25 large companies. In two weeks he received acceptances—and checks—from 18 of them. He was in business. After registering the company, "I went to the most available source of labor, Newton High School, which was down the block. I gathered all the top science and math students and put them to work sending out questionnaires and doing telephone interviews. I would get the early students to work in the morning and get others to call the West Coast."

Pat McGovern's little census of the computer industry did not escape the attention of Big Blue. "I was going along," he said, "thinking I was making good progress when all of a sudden one day in front of my house, which I was working out of, came the big band—six Mercedes-Benzes and out of them came half a dozen representatives of the biggest law firm in Boston and six people from White Plains saying, 'We know what's going on here. Nobody can gather information about computer users without stealing our lists and you *must* be stealing our lists. We want you to stop what you're doing, close the door, wind up affairs, and go back to writing articles.' I explained that we were just doing this dumb thing, getting lists of companies, sending out questionnaires, calling people, and gathering information. Actually, we signed something that looked like the Hitachi settlement: you can come in anytime, day or night, look at our files, look at our records, and look under our bedsheets. Anything you find that looks like it belongs to you, you can have. They finally seemed mollified and agreed to let us stay in business without the burden of years of lawsuits. We just paid some small emolument to our one-man legal department. I think he aged five years in two weeks."

In three years McGovern was doing a market research volume of $500,000 a year—and, more important, he had laid the groundwork for the computer information empire that he now commands. In 1967, he launched *Computerworld*, a weekly newsmagazine of the computer field. If you've ever wondered why so many computer-related products and companies have squashed names (ComputerLand, Microsoft, *WordStar*), here's a likely explanation: McGovern put together his new magazine in a hurry, trying to get it out in time for an industry show three weeks from when he first got the idea. Of necessity, a great many decisions were made in the printer's office. When it came time to typeset the name he had chosen, *Computer World News*, the printer informed him that he could fit only the first two words and that there wasn't even enough room between them for a space or to capitalize "world." *Computerworld* was born and is now the largest trade magazine in the world, with a paid circulation of 120,000 and annual advertising revenues of $42 million.

Computerworld offices—and McGovern's headquarters—are in the Boston suburb of Framingham now, but in those early publishing years they were in Harvard Square. Like many founders, McGovern likes to recall the scruffy times. "We moved the office to the top of an Indian restaurant," he said. "We made a special deal that the chefs would start cooking the chutney and mangos at a very high boil about four o'clock. But we wouldn't let anyone leave the room until all the writing assignments had been done. As the afternoon wore on, the motivation of hunger would start to get stronger and stronger. Everyone was working more rapidly. Actually, we had a very beneficial environmental support. Back in 1967 in Harvard Square, if you remember what was going on in the student milieu at that time, if you had the right selection of students and put them in a big room, they would create a certain 'evaporous' atmosphere. People would sit there and say, 'I don't want to leave here, this is the nicest place I've ever worked at.' We had the most lovely crew. They never logged in overtime, they'd stay for 24 hours and have just a marvelous experience with all of us." (McGovern's obvious reference to the drug culture of the late 1960s brought the house down in laughter at the West Coast Computer Faire in 1984.)

It's a little different today. McGovern, who invariably dresses in pinstripe suits, presides over a multiproduct company with an international reach. His holding company is International Data Group. The research wing, which was the original business, logged sales of $25 million in 1983 and garners about 25 percent of the computer market research market. Large corporations pay up to $24,000 a year for the IDG's various market reports and services. The publishing arm, which has grown both by acquistion and internal expansion, had revenues of $85 million from more than 60 publications. These include 15 U.S. magazines—*InfoWorld*, *PC World*, and *80 Micro* are among them—and over 40 published in 17 other countries. The research operation is now called Interdata, the publishing unit CW Communications. The company has three main publishing centers: Framingham, Menlo Park, California, and Peterborough, New Hampshire. In 1982, when McGovern was interviewed in the *Boston Globe*, the headline called him: "The Lord of Computer Publishing."

McGovern owns 85 percent of International Data Group, and in 1983 *Forbes* included him on the roster of the 400-richest persons in the nation, estimating his net worth at $200 million. It would probably come to even more if he ever decided to take his company public. McGovern prefers to keep the company private, and he has started to sell his shares to his employees. When the company reaches $1 billion a year in sales, McGovern says he will own less than half the stock. He predicts IDG will top the billion-dollar mark by the end of the decade.

His life has changed. He was divorced from his first wife in 1975 and over the July 4th weekend in 1982 he flew with his two children to Zurich, Switzerland, where he married Lore Harp, a computer entrepreneur in her own right—she and her former husband founded Vector Graphics. They spent their honeymoon climbing to the base camp of Mt. Everest in Nepal, although McGovern's big frame hardly suggests much experience with fitness programs. However, since his remarriage, he has taken off almost 40 pounds. He maintains two residences. Harp lives with him in their luxurious Tudor-style home in the San Francisco suburb of Woodside, and McGovern commutes between there and Framingham. He logs more than 100,000 air miles a year.

It's difficult to find people in the computer industry who don't like Pat McGovern. His employees call him "Chairman Pat" and they like him so much that they created a second "Chairman Pat"—a life-size papier-mache dummy that sits in his office in Framingham, so that he's there even if he's not there. McGovern is known for working up to 18 hours a day; a former employee told the *Boston Globe:* "He is absolutely driven. It was never apparent when he slept." Another employee added: "He is very pleasant, charming and he remembers small details about people, like what you once said to him and when he saw you last. But he also doesn't give much about himself away. He doesn't let people know what he thinks."

The McGovern publications are known for their high pay and good benefits. Employees have a profit-sharing plan, a four-day work week in the summertime, and there's an annual all-expense paid trip to the Caribbean in the winter for an editorial meeting.

McGovern is proud of the fact that 13 of his original 18 staffers on *Computerworld* are still with him. However, there are small signs that this 'down home' environment may be changing. With 1,400 employees, it's hard to preserve a personal touch, and in Menlo Park in 1984, several staffers were fired— not by McGovern but by people he had appointed as managers—when they disagreed with new, more stringent workplace rules.

McGovern retains a childlike, almost missionary zeal for the computer industry and what it will do for people. It's a driving force in his life. Wendy Quinones, a Boston area writer, interviewed him in 1983, and he was not ashamed to tell her that his goal "is nothing less than working for the benefit of mankind." He really believes that. And Jim Warren, an industry pioneer who founded the West Coast Computer Faire and who knows McGovern better than most people, told us: "My personal impression is that he's one of the few big money people who has a hail-fellow, well-met, friendly, positive, congenial personality as opposed to, 'I'm gonna get you, I'm here to make money, and I'm going to screw your ass to the ground' approach."

MCGOVERN'S EMPIRE

CW Communications, Framingham, Massachusetts:
Computerworld, Computerworld Office Automation, Computerworld on Communications, Computerworld Buyers Guide, Micro MarketWorld (formerly *ISO World.*)

Wayne Green Publications, Peterborough, New Hampshire:
Microcomputing, 80 Micro, HOT CoCo, inCider, Run, jr, 73.

Popular Computing Inc., Menlo Park, California:
InfoWorld.

PC World Communications, San Francisco, California:
PC World, Macworld.

Argentina: *Computerworld Argentina.*

Asia: *Asian Computerworld.*

Australia: *Computerworld Australia, Australia Micro Computerworld, Australia PC World.*

Brazil: *DataNews, Micro Mundo.*

Denmark: *Computerworld Denmark, Micro Verden.*

France: *Le Monde Informatique, Golden, PC World France* (OPC).

Germany: *Commodore, CW Edition Seminar, Software Market, Computerwoche, Micro ComputerWelt, PC Welt, Computer Business.*

Italy: *Computerworld Italia.*

Japan: *Computerworld Japan, PersoCom World.*

Netherlands: *Computer Benelux, Micro/Info.*

Norway: *Computerworld Norway.*

Mexico: *Computerworld Mexico, CompuMondo.*

Peoples Republic of China: *China Computerworld* (50 percent joint venture).

Saudi Arabia: *Saudi Computerworld.*

Spain: *Computerworld Espana, Micro Systemas.*

Sweden: *ComputerSweden, MikroDatorn, Min Hemdator, Mikro.*

United Kingdom: *Computer Management, Computer Business Europe*

Merl Miller

"My best skill is being able to take something complicated and make it simple. One of the true signs of genius is being able to explain"

▶ **BEST-KNOWN VENTURE:** dilithium Press

OTHER VENTURES: Matrix Publishers (textbooks)

BORN: 1942

RAISED: Burns, Wyoming

FATHER'S OCCUPATION: Conductor for the Union Pacific Railroad

FIRST DOLLAR EARNED: U.S. Marine Corps

SCHOOLING: B.S., engineering, University of Wyoming

ORIGINAL FINANCING: $9 (left in checking account after a divorce), plus $1,000 loan from a friend

HOME: Lake Oswego, Oregon

FAMILY: Married and divorced twice; married to wife number three; two daughters, one son

PERSONAL TRANSPORTATION: Oldsmobile

 **dilithium Press**

dILITHIUM PRESS LIMITED: A leader in book publishing for novice computer users.

▶ **BEST-KNOWN PRODUCTS:** *32 BASIC Programs For...*(several computers), *Computers For Everybody, Nailing Jelly to a Tree, Instant BASIC, TeloFacts, From the PC to the Mac and Back*

YEAR FOUNDED: 1977

EMPLOYEES: 47

HEADQUARTERS: Beaverton, Oregon

SALES: $6 million (1983); $7.5 million (1984 projection)

OWNERSHIP: Private, 30 percent held by Merl and Patricia Miller

Merl Miller is a big bear of a man who is proud that no Wyoming high school student has yet broken his sprinting record for the 220-yard dash after a quarter of a century. He likes his life laid-back and his words plain and simple. The computer book publishing company he chairs, dilithium Press, embodies those same qualities.

Miller believes no subject, even computers, is too complex to be explained in clear, simple language that is easily understood by beginners. He aims his books at the eighth grade reading level—the standard for newspapers and magazines. As he told *InfoWorld*, "The *New York Times Book Review* said our books were too simple and were great for people in Iowa. We like publishing books for people in Iowa."

Miller, who claims he's not good at arithmetic, came to computers by a roundabout route that included football, Vietnam, selling used cars, and textbook editing. Miller was the first of seven children born to what he calls "poor shanty Irish from the wrong side of the tracks" in Burns, Wyoming. His father, a conductor for the Union Pacific Railroad, taught Miller that "Republican and son-of-a-bitch meant the same thing."

Five days after Miller graduated from a high school class of five in 1960, he entered the U.S. Marine Corp's boot camp. ("One less mouth to feed at home.") During his eight years in the Marine Corps he played football, received a degree in engineering from the University of Wyoming, and got shot down over South Vietnam in his F-4 fighter plane.

Miller characteristically downplays his war injuries. "Even though that was a terrible experience, it got me into this business. I'd probably be a colonel if I were still in the Marine Corps, but colonels just don't make what I do. My taxes support a whole bunch of colonels."

After his release from the Marines in 1968, Miller returned to Wyoming and took advantage of his crutches to make sympathy sales at a used car lot. He also sold roofing and Tupperware. Miller finally took a "real job" as a book salesman (and later technical book editor) in Chicago for Prentice-Hall, whose founder, R.P. Ettenger, is one of Miller's heroes. Ettenger wrote *Everything Happens to the Best*. But, even though he was working for his hero's company, Miller was induced to jump ship to West Publishing because they doubled his salary.

It was that second publishing job that gave Miller the motivation to start his own company. After two years at West, Miller realized that half of the sales in his division were due to him, so he proposed that he get half of the salaries. When West's president did not agree, Miller started his own engineering textbook company, Matrix, with a $1,000 loan from a friend, Richard Abel, and $9 of his own in the basement of his house in Champaign, Illinois. He met his current wife Patricia in Champaign and hired her to be Matrix's business manager. She now serves as dP's president.

About this time, 1975, Miller bought his first computer—one of the original Altair kits, which he tried to assemble on his kitchen table. The instruction manual was so poorly written that even Miller, an engineer, couldn't figure it out. He had to resort to phoning computer expert Rich Didday for advice. Miller's next idea was that those exchanges could be turned into a book. *Two to the Tenth Questions and Answers About Home*

Computers, by Rich Didday, sold in the neighborhood of 30,000 copies.

Miller saw how big the market for computer books could be and decided to set up a separate company to publish them. "We knew a lot of people in the computer industry were Trekkies," Miller says, so he named his new computer book company after the dilithium crystals that powered the "Star Trek" starship, *USS Enterprise.* The small "d" of the name is another Miller idea—the logo, dP, has no upside-down.

Despite the occasional flop, such as the robot books he published for five years (which may have been a little ahead of their time), dP maintains high interest in its books by staying one step ahead of the computer beginner. A glance through one of the 24 books Miller has written himself or with a co-author ("For someone who never wanted to be a writer, I've got a lot of books—almost three million—in print now"), reveals the dP style of easy-to-understand, light-hearted writing on computers. Some examples from *Computers for Everybody:* "Probably 5 to 80 percent of the programs and computers that claim to be user friendly are not. Many of them are user surly or user hostile. Some people even dislike being called a user." "All computers understand several computer languages. No, they don't converse fluently in French or Spanish, but most understand a language called BASIC." *Computers for Everybody,* written with Jerry Willis, sold over 500,000 copies—more than any other computer book. Other best-selling dP titles include the *32 BASIC Programs* series, *Computers for Everybody Buyers Guide,* and *Nailing Jelly to a Tree.* The spring 1984 catalogue listed over 150 titles. From sales of $38,000 in 1977, its first year, dP's revenues grew to $6 million in 1983.

The dP books are often written by two or three authors. Miller believes in the old adage that two heads are better than one. Miller's head is often better than any other, as far as computer books are concerned. The best-selling ideas for books are his. He estimates that he subscribes to 50 magazines for background and draws on a huge research staff. Many of these "managed" books are written by his frequent co-author, Jerry Willis, an education professor at Texas Tech University. According to Miller, Willis earned $250,000 in royalties from his dP books in 1983, and is the all-time best-selling computer book author. Six or seven other dP authors make over $100,000 a year in royalties (dP pays no advances).

Miller believes that the people at dP feel they belong there although they "probably wouldn't fit in any place else." The company is two-thirds women, from whom half of the executives and two-thirds of the managers are drawn. The company style is as relaxed as life in Oregon, to which dP moved shortly after its birth in 1977. All dP books and software contain a toll-free number to call for friendly advice and information.

In its usual style of demystifying computers, dP began putting disks into its books and selling computer books in general bookstores, where 95 percent of its books are now sold. The distinction between these books and dP's new ventures into software publishing is slim—one is a book with a disk in back, the other a disk with a book (the manual) in back. The only externally visible differences are the binding and price. Software prices are higher—and the package is shrink-wrapped so you can't peek inside.

Miller believes that a book is no different from a software package because "they're both ideas in a receptacle." dP's biggest program publishing effort to date is *TeloFacts*, a software tool for doing survey and poll analysis.

As head of a successful company that *Inc.* identified as one of the 500 fastest-growing private companies in the country, Miller no longer has time to write the science fiction stories he once wrote; but he is working on a science fiction adventure game. He believes his company should not think in terms of hobbyists or expert programmers, but "the ol' guy out there in the street." Miller and Jerry Willis dedicated *Computers for Everybody* to their mothers: "We wanted an intelligent adult with little or no technical background [as the typical reader]. We both chose our mothers."

THE SUPER HUMAN NAME

What's in a name? Much more than any mere mortal can comprehend, as far as Rodnay Zaks is concerned. When he cast about for a suitable moniker for his computer book and software publishing company, he entrusted the selection to a computer. After all, he though, his own name was a perfect example error-prone humans are.

Zaks's Polish-born parents wanted to give their Paris-born son an English name in memory of the years they had spent in England working for the Free French during World War II. Rodnay bears the result of his parents' apparent confusion over English spelling.

No such errors would happen when, in 1976, he founded his company simultaneously in Paris and Berkeley, California. He decided to program an IBM mainframe to spew out made-up names that existed neither in French, English, nor any other language. He knew some of the programmers at the University of California at Berkeley who had created the Exxon name.

Zaks, who holds a Ph.D in computer science from Berkeley, wrote a program in APL language that would combine two or three syllables using suffixes such as "ex" and "er," and prefixes such as "cy" (for cybernetics) and "sy" (for systems). He threw in a consonant or two ("B" for Berkeley and "P" for Paris), and turned the computer loose. Several hundred names poured out. "Once a computer gets going," Zaks says, "there's lots of output."

Surprise. Zaks's choice did not come from the computer. He liked the sound of "Cybex," but replaced the first letter with an "S." As Zaks points out, "ultimately the human element came into play."

To illustrate his satisfaction with the computer-picked name, Zaks relates a story. He asked a young job applicant if she was familiar with Sybex. She answered, "Oh yes, I've heard of Sybex before. My mother worked for the company 20 years ago."

William von Meister

"You can only eat so many steaks, or drive so many cars, or drink so many bottles of good California cabernet. As long as you can choose between soda water and champagne, then that's good enough"

► **BEST KNOWN VENTURE:** The Source

OTHER VENTURES: Control Video Corp., Telecommunications Industries (now Western Union Electronic mail), TDX Systems (now part of British Cable & Wireless), Digital Broadcasting Corp., Digital Music Company

BORN: 1942

FATHER'S OCCUPATION: Owner of Azoplate Corp., manufacturer of printing plates

FIRST DOLLAR EARNED: Racing cars professionally in college

ORIGINAL FINANCING: Inheritance

PERSONAL NET WORTH: He figures he lost two-thirds of the $20 million he's earned from his ventures

FAMILY: Divorced; one daughter, one son

PERSONAL TRANSPORTATION: Ferrari, Porsche, Mercedes, BMW, motorcycle

THE**SOURCE**

SOURCE TELECOMPUTING CORPORATION: Provides on-line
information services for home and business computers.

▶ **BEST-KNOWN SERVICES:** News and sports, electronic mail,
consumer information (airline schedules, stock quotes)

YEAR FOUNDED: 1979

EMPLOYEES: 135

HEADQUARTERS: McLean, Virginia

SALES: $25 million (estimate)

SUBSCRIBERS: 90,000

OWNERSHIP: A subsidiary of the Reader's Digest Association;
30 percent owned by Control Data

William von Meister grew up in a long shadow—the six-foot, seven-inch shadow of his stern and successful German father. In spite of this, or perhaps because of it, William's early life reads like the prototypical F. Scott Fitzgerald hero—bored, reckless, and filthy rich.

Unlike the dissipated Dick Diver in *Tender is the Night*, William turned his wild love of fun to the more constructive world of business. As an entrepreneur, von Meister continues to take risks. He is reported to have earned as much as $20 million from the five companies—including The Source—he started in 10 years, but he's lost about two-thirds of that on ideas that went bust.

Von Meister spent his early years in Glen Cove, Long Island, right next door to the "East Egg" of the Great Gatsby. He was the eldest son of a German who came to this country in 1925 to sell Maybach Diesel engines for yachts. In 1927, the elder von Meister challenged the New York Central Railway to a race down the Hudson against a yacht equipped with a Maybach engine. Unfortunately, the yacht ran aground, as did the entire yacht business with the crash of 1929. Von Meister's father eventually made a fortune as the owner of Azoplate, the largest manufacturer of printing plates in the country.

William remembers his childhood as "sheltered" by wealth. His family was living in a big, beautiful estate in Mendham, New Jersey, waited on by a large staff of servants. "I was eight or nine years old before I finally realized that not everybody had a chauffeur," he recalls.

When William graduated from prep school, his childhood ended and all hell broke loose. Rather than going straight on to Harvard, where he had been accepted, his parents sent him to a finishing school in Switzerland for a year to "mature." His maturation took a strange form: mining the ski trails with homemade bombs for fun and fooling around with the school maids. "I raised hell," von Meister admits. "I had such a 'wonderful' disciplinary record that Harvard wouldn't have me when I came back basically on a personal nonrecommendation from the Swiss headmaster, who said he never wanted to have anything to do with me again."

The elder von Meister was desperate about where to send his young hellion to college. Thanks to an old friend who was the dean at Georgetown University in Washington, D.C., William was admitted.

But he continued his wild ways. He was too busy driving race cars professionally to pay much attention to studies. He was sent to see the dean—the same family friend—constantly. It didn't improve his grades, but it improved his love life. He ended up marrying the dean's assistant, a Lebanese woman named Leila.

After William had been suspended from and readmitted to Georgetown four times, his family's friend retired, and the Jesuit who replaced him threw William out for good without giving him a diploma. William continued racing Ferraris, and later Ford Cobras on the grand-touring circuit such as at Daytona Beach, Florida. He only stopped when his father threatened to disinherit him and his wife threatened to leave him.

All of a sudden, William quit his wild ways. He entered American University's business school. "This time I was dedicated. I was ready to work at it," he says. He received his master's degree in 18 months, even though he had never received an undergraduate degree. But he was still not ready to work for someone else; he wasn't even sure that he wanted to work for a living at all. So he started scheming.

Scheme number one came to him through his childhood hobby— ham radio. One of his ham radio cronies was working for Western Union, installing new switching centers for the Air Force. He told von Meister he needed someone to remove the obsolete equipment. Von Meister bought it all for $750. He hired sergeants and their men on the Air Force bases to cart the stuff away. He sold the copper wire and teletype equipment for over $250,000 in less than a year. One year later, he sold many of the motors back to Western Union for $70,000. Von Meister says it was "lots of fun."

Scheme number two. He passed out 600 or so business cards he had made up, advertising himself as a consultant. Someone finally believed him. Bionetics Research Laboratories hired him to get their colony of 3,000 monkeys organized. They had to keep track of which monkey was injected for leukemia for the National Cancer Institute. It was 1962 and computers were just coming into vogue, so von Meister suggested computerization, even though he knew even less about computers than he did about monkeys.

He brazened it out and made a deal with some IBM salesmen. "I'll give you guys the job, if you promise that you won't tell Bionetics Labs that I don't know a thing about computers," he told them. "We put in a nice, old punch-card computer system and soon we had the monkeys under control."

Von Meister has made a career out of first getting the job, and then learning how to make it work. His combination of brash opportunism, quick wits, and unique ideas pays off more than half the time. When his friend at Western Union called him again to update their billing system, von Meister plowed right in. Seven years later, after completing "the biggest undertaking of my life," his computerized billing system for Western Union has been adopted worldwide.

Not only did that job teach von Meister all his communications theories, but it also stimulated his next entrepreneurial idea. In 1971 von Meister conceived of an electronic mail system. It provided a way a firm with a large mailing list could have Western Union send out an individually addessed form letter to hundreds or even thousands of people.

Although Western Union didn't believe it could work, they did agree to buy the idea if von Meister could get it going. Armed with their commitment, von Meister raised $1 million from a small Florida firm called Xonics to develop the idea. Two years later, Western Union agreed to buy the firm that had evolved—Telecommunications Industries—and von Meister made his first million. He made 20 percent of the $6.5 million sale.

Von Meister knew nary a thing about electronics, but he claims, "I didn't have to. All you've got to understand is the principles. I could never design the chips. I couldn't even design the circuitry. I was the inventor; there were other guys involved in the implementation."

Von Meister's next idea was to make a cheaper version of the Watts Box, the minicomputer-controlled switching set-up that would route telephone calls through the cheapest lines. Rather than buying a half-a-million-dollar Watts Box for your company, von Meister proposed hooking into a central location at a tenth of the cost. He called his new company TDX Systems, and it sold switches to Fortune 500 companies. Today it is worth $125 million. Von Meister sold his share to one of the original investors, British Cable & Wireless, a governmental company, in 1977.

Von Meister had made quite a few bundles of money by this time, but, as he points out, "I had a very expensive second wife and eleven thousand square feet of house in Virginia because she had six kids." Von Meister also had a daughter and a son of his own from his first marriage to Leila.

Von Meister's modus operandi consisted of his idea, rounding up the capital to implement the idea, and then selling his interest to the investor or investors. He continued along the same track for his next conception, Digital Broadcasting Corp. (DBC): using the subcarrier channel that every FM station has but doesn't use (subcarrier channels are what Muzak is broadcast over) to pass information to clients. He proposed to rent the subcarrier and transmit bad check, price change, or security information to such companies as Safeway.

Von Meister followed his usual M.O. to set up DBC. He was later to regret, however, his choice of a major investor. Jack Taub, a Bronx-born venture capitalist with a sixth-grade education, contrasted sharply with von Meister, the wealthy, privileged scion of an educated family. But before Taub and von Meister started fighting with each other, von Meister had another idea for DBC. The Source, as he called it, would offer information services to the computer hobbyist. Von Meister made a deal with Dialcom to provide computer service at night for 75 cents an hour, and he made the same deal with Telenet network. He hooked them up with news from United Press International, the *New York Times,* a wine buyer's guide, airline schedules and a stock service. He announced The Source information service in June 1979 at the National Computer Conference in New York. The favorable reaction at the show made it look like von Meister had a winner.

Before The Source got off the ground, however, Taub and von Meister became embroiled in a struggle for control of DBC. The struggle was a nasty one. During the suits and countersuits, Taub sold 51 percent of the company to *Reader's Digest* for $3 million. Since the initial investment had been $6 million, the sale represented quite a loss. The *Washington Post* reported at the time that: "they [Taub and von Meister] went through money like beer at a frat party." Von Meister eventually won his suit against Taub. His settlement amounted to about $1 million.

Von Meister was out of DBC (which Taub took into Chapter 11 bankruptcy proceedings) and out of The Source (another jinxed company, which continued to lose money under *Reader's Digest* and caused the resignations of a number of *Digest* executives). Von Meister was down, but not out. After all, there was always another idea to follow. But he was still on a losing streak. He lost $2 million when record companies yielded to pressure from the record retailers over his deal to offer digital transmissions of records into the home for legitimate taping. Digital Music Company would publish a list of new releases to its members, who could then tape a master quality record for $5 dollars rather than the $10 an album in the store would cost. DMC went down the tubes in 1982.

No crying into his beer for this entrepreneur. He cried into his "very good steak and very good wine at one of the nicer restaurants in Washington," where he came up with yet another idea. This made number seven. Using the back of a napkin at the restaurant, von Meister, his chief engineer, and chief software man sketched a system to enable someone with a personal computer at home to obtain video games over the telephone. This time, von Meister planned to set up the system so that the video games transmitted over the phone could not be recorded. After building a prototype with a little venture capital, and negotiating software licenses with video game companies, von Meister raised $9 million to start Control Video Corp. in 1983.

Again, von Meister's luck ran out. As soon as CVC began to ship its product out, orders dried up. The video game market had been oversold. They thought they could sell a quarter of a million; they sold less than 5,000. CVC laid off 18 of the 56 employees at its Vienna, Virginia, headquarters.

Von Meister, the president and CEO of CVC, gave up on the game market, moved toward supplying software for personal computers, and found a big, fat investor—Bell South. For an initial fee and a monthly service charge, a CVC user gets a modem bundled with software. Each month, CVC offers 10 new titles, as well as 30 other older titles that change every month. Bell South will begin marketing the system in the fall of 1984.

Von Meister's recent string of flops hasn't interfered with his lavish lifestyle. While he no longer supports the huge house needed by his second wife (and her six children), he still has a big place with tennis courts and a swimming pool in Great Falls, Virginia, where he lives with his "POSSLQ—person of the opposite sex sharing living quarters," he explains.

Although he no longer drives racing cars professionally,

he owns a Ferrari, a Porsche, a Mercedes, a BMW, and a motorcycle. The tennis, squash, shooting, and hunting he enjoys are holdovers from his upper-crust childhood.

Von Meister is emphatic about his financial success—he's made much more money than he ever inherited from his father. He competed against that long shadow and he beat it.

Von Meister admits that he's not a very good manager, but he doesn't seem to care much. "I'm very competitive and love it. I love making deals." He points out that people like working for him, a sign of how easygoing he is. He thinks his low blood pressure and ability to sleep very well are proof of his geniality.

He expresses his philosophy by quoting his father: "My dad told me that the most important thing in life is the freedom to choose." Von Meister interprets this in a way that his father probably did not mean. "As long as you can choose between soda water and champagne, then that's good enough."

▓ Jim Warren

*"All of us were just
drenched with sweat
and absolutely ecstatic
with information
exchange"*

▶ **BEST-KNOWN VENTURE:** West Coast Computer Faire

OTHER VENTURES: Founding editor of the first personal
computer software magazine, *Dr. Dobb's Journal of
Computer Calisthenics and Orthodontia;* founder of *Intelligent
Machines Journal* (later became *InfoWorld*)

BORN: 1936

SCHOOLING: B.A., Southwest Texas State University; M.A.,
mathematics, University of Texas at Austin; M.A.,
mathematics, University of California Medical Center;
M.A., mathematics, Stanford University

ORIGINAL FINANCING: $1,200 from partner Bob Albrecht

PERSONAL NET WORTH: $2 to $3 million from sale of West
Coast Computer Faire (estimate)

FAMILY: Single

PERSONAL TRANSPORTATION: Three Mercedes, Corvette,
dump truck

West Coast Computer Faire

WEST COAST COMPUTER FAIRE: The preeminent show for personal computer users and hobbyists.

YEAR FOUNDED: 1976

EMPLOYEES: 8 to 20

HEADQUARTERS: Englewood Cliffs, New Jersey

SALES: $1.5 million (1983 figures based on 800 exhibitors paying an average $1,300 per booth and 40,000 attendees paying an average $13 entrance fee)

OWNERSHIP: Prentice-Hall

For eight years, startled visitors watched Jim Warren career through the aisles and booths crowded with people and computers at the West Coast Computer Faire. It was a terrifying sight: a huge, bearded man—over six feet tall, weighing 265 pounds—hurtling through the masses on roller skates, with a walkie-talkie glued to his ear. This self-described "madman" on wheels was none other than the Faire's founder, and one of the seminal characters of the computer industry.

Jim Warren's computer lineage is impeccable. He was one of the early attendees of the Homebrew Computer Club, the first personal computer club in the country. He was the founding editor of *Dr. Dobb's Journal of Computer Calisthenics and Orthodontia.* He founded *Intelligent Machines Journal,* later renamed *InfoWorld.* He was the original host of the first weekly television show on computers, PBS's "Computer Chronicles." And he founded and directed the West Coast Computer Faire. When Warren won the first Sybex Computer Pioneer Award, his brass trophy was in the shape of a roller skate.

Today Jim Warren sits and broods about the M.B.A.s and "money-grubbers" (venture capitalists) who came into the personal computer industry around 1979 and turned it sour and nasty. He recalls the old days wistfully: "As soon as you found a solution to a problem, you ran down to the Homebrew Computer Club and told everybody. Nowadays you find a solution, you run off to the goddamned patent office, and lock it up for two years, or you keep it off the market because it might affect your bottom line by 3 percent if you introduce this enhancement now instead of in two years."

Warren is an unusual mix of hippie and techie, entrepreneur and anarchist. His disdain for the "money-grubbers" by no means interferes with the enjoyment he gets from the more than $2 million he received from the sale of the West Coast Computer Faire to Prentice-Hall in 1983. And the profits he received from the first Faire in 1976 allowed him to make the down payment on his 40-acre retreat on Kings Mountain, high above Silicon Valley.

His mountain estate reminds you of another founder of magazines, William Randolph Hearst and his San Simeon. Like Hearst's castle, Warren's mansion overlooks a hundred miles of the Pacific Coast. The house is crammed with a blend of high-tech and down-home elements: computers, printing presses, video equipment, and wood stoves. We spoke to Warren on the upper floor of his den—a 32-foot-diameter, 12-sided polygonal room with heavy beams cut from the surrounding redwoods.

As a boy growing up in San Antonio, Texas, Warren lived quite another kind of life. His parents divorced during World War II, and at first Jim lived with his mother. "Mom was a really good entrepreneur and pretty much a failure as a human being—very personable when she was wanting something from someone. She was a manipulative, conniving kind. I had a lot of problems with her and eventually moved out." At his father's place, Jim slept in the same double bed with his Dad and cooked his dinner on a two-burner hot plate on top of a half-size refrigerator. His father worked as a door-to-door salesman, a gas pump jockey, and later was the office manager of a small welding-supply company. "Dad was an exact opposite to Mom. As a business person, he was an absolute flop, but as a human being, just a delightful man. A sincere, concerned, gentle man."

Jim was "an insufferable wizard nerd" in mathematics at

San Antonio College and Southwest Texas State University, but he dropped out of school in his senior year in 1957. Even without a degree, he was able to teach high school math because San Antonio was desperate for teachers. Warren felt that a person's duty to society was to "put more in than you take out," and on a salary of $2,987 a year, he certainly wasn't taking much out. Fortunately, he had "hamburger taste" and loved his work. After five years of teaching, during which time he finished his degree at night, Jim's salary rose to $4,550 a year. By 1964, Jim had an M.A. in math from the University of Texas at Austin, and a bellyful of Texas society. He "hitched up a house trailer and drug it out here to California."

Warren discovered that California public school districts were just as bad as San Antonio's, so he eventually became the chairman of the math department at a private women's school, the College of Notre Dame, in Belmont, California. Finally, he discovered the California life he was hoping to find.

It was 1965. The Free Speech Movement was making waves in Berkeley and the Free Beach Movement was making its own waves at San Gregorio Beach, 10 miles from Warren's home in La Honda. After walking through the nasty litterers and radio-blasters on the clothed beach, Warren entered the golden, loving nude beach. It was a utopian vision to Warren. He invited several people to stop by his house on the way home, and about "twenty or thirty" took him up on it. Nobody knew anybody else and Warren had never thrown a party in his life, but it was a smashing success. They played rock 'n' roll, barbecued hamburgers, and took their clothes off. It wasn't an orgy, just a nice, friendly, no-clothes get-together.

Warren was ecstatic. This was what he left Texas for. He started throwing parties every two or three weeks for up to 150 people. "Greatest thing since sliced bread," he remembers. *Playboy* shot a spread on one of Warren's parties. BBC Television came to tape a party (in back-lit silhouette) for a special on California life. But the publicity did not go over big with Warren's employer, the Catholic women's college. In 1967 Warren resigned at their request, and devoted himself solely to his newfound communitarian/utopian vision.

Ironically, Warren still espouses his communitarian beliefs

even though he admits that he can't work for anyone else and doesn't like having partners. "I never had a wife. I've never had a family. I never got along with the family I did have. Maybe that's the reason I have these community and communal feelings and desires—because I've never had one, or never been able to get along with one," he speculates.

Warren threw all his energy into the Mid-Peninsula Free University in Palo Alto, the largest alternative school in the country. He picked up two more master's degrees at the University of California Medical Center and Stanford University (where he also had a programming job). He began doing more and more consulting in the computer field and eventually, at the People's Computer Center, met Dennis Allison and Bob Albrecht. They were the "D" and "ob" of *Dr. Dobb's Journal of Computer Calisthenics* (from BASIC exercises) *and Orthodontia* (referring to bytes), a newsletter of information exchange for the just-introduced Altair computer. Warren began to edit the newsletter for $350 a month. The heady days of "information exchange" on computers were on.

Even though the Bay Area was emerging as the home of the infant personal computer industry, Warren was the only computer magazine editor in the area. He revelled in his position at the center of the techno-gossip network. He never failed to attend meetings of the Homebrew Computer Club, which he saw as a continuation of '60s communitarian activities: informal, anarchist, and communicative. "My guess is that the industry is half-a-year to two years ahead of where it would have been if the Homebrew Computer Club had not existed," Warren says.

Warren started to hear about informal computer swap meets and conferences in the Midwest and East. He went to one such show in Atlantic City: "the crotch of the nation," he calls it. Even though it was held in a second-class hotel where the air conditioning broke down in 99-degree heat and high humidity, 3,500 people attended. Warren was exuberant: "All of us were drenched with sweat and absolutely ecstatic with information exchange."

He was determined to put on his own show in the Bay Area. Bob Albrecht put up the $1,200 deposit for the Civic

Auditorium in San Francisco, and Warren got on the phone to all his friends in the area: " 'Hey, we're going to do a Computer Faire! Do you want to be part of it?' They'd say, 'Sure, Jim.' 'Okay, send me money and we'll reserve a space for you.' I think it took us three or four days to go into the black."

Exhibitors at that first Faire in 1976 paid about $300 to $500 per booth, and 13,000 attendees paid $4 to $8 admission. Warren had expected 8,000 to 10,000 people. "It just burned our asses to the ground! We didn't know what we were doing. No one knew what they were doing. But everybody just had an exciting and challenging and informative time. We made all the mistakes without getting our balls cut off the first time around. And it's certainly been profitable, so we decided to do a second show." Warren started a tabloid to get information out at the Faire— *Silicon Gulch Gazette*. He brought in a third partner, "a very spacey dude" named Eric Bakalinsky, and the West Coast Computer Faire incorporated; each partner held a third of the business.

After the fourth Faire in 1979, Warren began to get bored. "I'd gone into it with no thought of it being a business," he says. "I wasn't a businessman. I didn't pay any attention to books." He decided that the personal computer industry needed a fast-turnaround news medium and started *Intelligent Machines Journal* (*IMJ*—after his first name in pig-latin). But he found himself reluctant to hustle his friends in the industry to take out ads in his new paper. Obviously, the paper's revenues suffered. Late that year, he sold *IMJ* to Pat McGovern of *ComputerWorld* for an amount "that was far more than my fondest expectations." It was well worth the price for McGovern. *IMJ* became *InfoWorld,* one of the largest news magazines in the business. But Warren was still bored and no longer had even his *IMJ*. He bought out his partners for "a couple of hundred thousand dollars" after the fifth Faire, but that didn't solve his boredom, either.

He continued to practice his communitarian ideas with his loyal Faire staff of 8 to 20 people, whom he affectionately calls "weird." They were folks "out of the bars in La Honda, ex-hippies, mountain folk—not your standard eight-to-five office employees. They sat out on the sun deck, went swimming, and soaked in the hot tub. But when things were heavy, they worked nights, weekends, the whole thing. I managed them with a combination between anarchistic and dictatorial style."

Despite the congenial work style, Warren decided to sell the Faire. "I was just getting eaten alive. I gained eight pounds per Faire. I went into this at 200 pounds and I've come out at 265," he says.

After near-deals and eventual misses with Sheldon Adelson of COMDEX Computer shows and Pat McGovern, Warren finally sold the West Coast Computer Faire to Prentice-Hall in 1983 for over $2 million.

The last Faire Warren operated attracted 47,000 attendees and 800 exhibitors (with 130 on the waiting list). Warren arrived in a coat and tie, not his usual plaid shirt and jeans. And he walked sedately about in shoes instead of wheeling around on skates.

Warren hasn't joined the ranks of the professional managers and conformists, however. He's retreated to his mountain top to hatch new plans for communitarianism and computers. In mid-1984 he was busy organizing the Peninsula Citizen Advocates to fight the local planning board. Seems he wants to build a community on his 40 acres, and the planning board wants to limit him to his one mansion. How can anyone start a utopian community with only one mansion?

THE R-RATED COMPUTER SHOW

North-East Expositions, which puts on Softcon, the New
Orleans software show, warned attendees in 1984 that no
person under the age of 16 would be admitted to the show
unless he or she be "president of other executive officer of
an exhibiting company."

HARDWARE WARS

David Bunnell, publisher of *PC World,* witnessed the following incident aboard a Delta flight on his way back to
San Francisco from New Orleans. Bunnell passed his
account on to columnist Herb Caen, who presented it to
his *San Francisco Chronicle* readers as follows: "Apple's Mike
Boich opening an overhead compartment in which to
store his new Macintosh—at which out dropped an
Osborne computer that hit a woman passenger on the
head. Not just *any* Osborne but one belonging to Adam
Osborne Himself, aboard the same flight. When last seen,
Boich and Osborne were at the Houston airport filling out
endless insurance forms. As for the lady, she may or may
not sue. She is still computing."

Jeffrey Wilkins

"When you're twenty-one and start a company, about all you know how to do is to knock on doors and ask for the order"

▶ **BEST-KNOWN VENTURE:** CompuServe

OTHER VENTURE: Meisner-Wilkins burglar alarms

BORN: 1944

RAISED: Rapid City, South Dakota

FATHER'S OCCUPATION: Car dealership, real estate

FIRST DOLLAR EARNED: Selling snow cones at public swimming pools

SCHOOLING: B.S. and M.S., electrical engineering, University of Arizona

ORIGINAL FINANCING: Father-in-law's company

PERSONAL NET WORTH: 46,301 shares of H & R Block, worth over $2 million in 1984

HOME: Suburb of Columbus, Ohio

FAMILY: Married; three children

PERSONAL TRANSPORTATION: Mercedes 500 SL

CompuServe

COMPUSERVE INC.: Foremost vendor of general information services by phone to home computer users.

YEAR FOUNDED: 1970

EMPLOYEES: 600

HEADQUARTERS: Columbus, Ohio

SALES: $52 million ($12 million for microcomputer information services in fiscal year 1984)

SUBSCRIBERS: 130,000

OWNERSHIP: Wholly-owned subsidiary of H & R Block

Once, Jeffrey Wilkins almost made a mistake. He was about to close a deal with Texas Instruments. But after the lawyers left, Wilkins couldn't sleep. Around three in the morning, he made a list of all the contract's pluses and minuses, and it came to him: "I wrote at the bottom of the page, 'They just want to put us on a shelf.' What that meant was, they weren't ready yet to go after the market. They just wanted to tie us up to an exclusive agreement that would prevent us from going anywhere." Wilkins nixed the TI deal.

That was probably the only close call CompuServe has had on its carefully worked-out path from its origin—processing data for a small Ohio life insurance company—to a place in the ranks of information-age pioneers selling a smorgasbord of services to individual consumers.

A CompuServe subscriber with a personal computer and a telephone modem can call in and use the service to make an airline reservation, read the *Washington Post,* scan the AP Wire Service, pick up some free software, check a stock portfolio, or browse a data bank or encyclopedia. There are also a number of popular "bulletin boards," which allow people to post messages for one another. One functions like a CB radio, allowing up to 40 users at a time to chew the fat. The basic fee is $12.50 an hour ($6 nights and weekends). Many of the special services cost extra, but an experienced subscriber can accomplish a lot while drinking a cup of coffee. It's also still possible to use CompuServe for its original purpose, time-sharing on a large computer.

CompuServe began with a phone call in 1969. Harry Gard was the head of Golden United Investment Company, a life insurance company in Columbus, Ohio. He wanted to go modern and computerize, but knew nothing about computers and was afraid an expert would take advantage of his ignorance. Then it occurred to him there was someone in the family who could help him out—his very smart son-in-law, Jeffrey Wilkins, who had studied electrical engineering at the University of Arizona.

Wilkins was no novice when it came to business. At 14 he persuaded the city council of Rapid City, South Dakota, to let him sell snow cones, soda, and popcorn at the public swimming pools. "It was what you call a highly leveraged business. Cost of materials was less than 10 percent of the retail price. Labor was inexpensive because there were always people around the pool who would work for what they could eat. I learned a lot from it." Wilkins started his first business as an adult shortly after receiving his bachelor's degree in 1967. He and a fellow graduate student teamed up to found Meisner-Wilkins, a company that manufactured and installed burglar alarm systems in crime-ridden areas of Tucson. After a couple of years, they sold the venture to a local corporation for $10,000. "Not a very big deal," but it turned out well for both sides: the alarm company (which had previously lost money) went on to flourish, and Wilkins got the chance to learn more about business from one of the new owners, Tom Brown, a Harvard M.B.A.

"When you're twenty-one years old and start a company," Wilkins recalls, "about all you know how to do is to knock on doors and ask for the order." Among other things, Brown taught Wilkins that two elements are essential for a successful business career: (1) Plan ahead and (2) Never stop educating yourself.

When Harry Gard called up for help, Wilkins at first failed to recognize the potential hidden in his father-in-law's request; he also didn't know much about data processing. Wilkins merely responded dutifully by recommending to Gard a co-worker at the university, an engineer named John Goltz. So it was Goltz who went to Columbus and realized that the great expense of installing and buying a data processing system could be absorbed by selling those same computer services to other companies. Better yet, Golden United might even make money on the deal. But Goltz was more interested in technology than management.

Gard was *almost* sold on the idea. There was one additional little requirement: he still wanted his son-in-law involved. And once Gard informed Wilkins of the $1.5 million Golden United was willing to invest in the new project, Wilkins looked back over his little burglar alarm company and decided to "give it a whirl."

But first Wilkins discussed the issue of control with his father-in-law. Wilkins's father had run his own business, and Wilkins had never planned to work for anyone but himself. So he and Gard reached an understanding: Wilkins could be completely in charge unless he got in over his head. If that happened, control would go back to Golden United. Gard agreed, even though Wilkins was then only 25 years old.

Wilkins then put together a business plan that showed the company losing half a million dollars its first two years. He expected Golden United to balk at that, since it had only $6 million in capital; but Gard approved. "I realized at that time that he had meant everything he said, that he was willing to take the risk and sit back and wait. He did exactly what he said he would do, and I did the same."

By doing the same, Wilkins means he lost $490,000 during CompuServe's first two years of operation, 1970 and '71, before earning $250,000 (on sales of $2 million) in 1972. But Wilkins wasn't sorry he'd lost the money. He congratulated himself on a "pretty accurate business plan." And, he now adds, "During that time I'd say probably 200 companies that were in our business failed."

At first the business offered time on a mainframe to insurance companies. But soon Wilkins sent salesmen to major corporations of all kinds around Columbus. Encouraged by the success of his projections, Wilkins whipped up plan after plan.

Through careful study of all the companies in the timesharing business, Wilkins discovered that all the successful ones used a particular computer—Digital Equipment's PDP-10. CompuServe bought one—even though, at $700,000, it cost almost half his working capital.

When large companies began to buy their own computers, Wilkins stayed a step ahead by offering companies like GM and Diamond Shamrock a different service. He developed software to take care of particular kinds of needs, such as financial planning.

In 1978, even though home computers were still at the hobbyist stage, Wilkins saw that it was just a matter of time before much of what CompuServe had been offering on its mainframe network would be available on personal computers. When others might have reacted defensively, Wilkins did some more planning. He calmly asked himself in what ways CompuServe was least likely to be supplanted by personal computers, and came up with two: the ability to offer access to large information banks and the development of its communications network for corporate businesses. That network is a very sophisticated system that controls the traffic of large amounts of data sent through the phone lines.

Wilkins tested the waters for his new service by setting up a network he called MicroNet for the Midwestern Association of Computer Clubs. Even then, in 1978, the computer buffs jumped at the opportunity to exchange information and use the storage capacity and communications power of CompuServe's computers.

Pleased with the experiment, Wilkins decided to sell computer time to personal computer owners during evening hours, when the big commercial users weren't on line anyway. The question was how to reach his new kind of customers.

For the next two years, Wilkins struggled with the problem of finding a company with an established distribution system to launch the new network. It was during this period that he almost made the potentially disastrous coupling with Texas Instruments.

Wilkins finally solved the problem in his usual way: more research. He came up with Tandy, the perfect partner because of its 8,000 Radio Shack stores. CompuServe's service is now sold in over 14,000 stores (mostly Radio Shacks and other retail computer stores), where new subscribers can purchase a "starter kit" consisting of a user I.D., a password, and a printed booklet, along with some free time to try out the services. There were over 130,000 subscribers by the summer of 1984, and according to Wilkins, well over half the people are busy exchanging information amongst themselves (as opposed to using the data banks and services). This means an entirely new world of communications is springing up on computer terminals across the country.

Wilkins professes not to worry about competition. He claims that The Source has many fewer subscribers, around 40,000, and Dow Jones News Retrieval is mostly a commercial and investors' service for which he sees a limited market. CompuServe can afford to charge a lower rate for its services because it has long owned its telecommunications network while others must lease theirs, according to Wilkins.

Besides confidence in his own business judgment, since 1980 Wilkins has had another reason to feel secure—that's the year mighty H & R Block, the tax preparers, purchased CompuServe for $22.7 million.

As usual, it's a story about planning. Wilkins took his company public in 1975, "to give it its own identity." But he calculated that CompuServe's sales would have to grow at a rate of at least 50 percent a year to make enough research money to stay competitive. As an alternative to this breakneck pace, Wilkins drew up a hypothetical profile of "Mr. Right," the ideal suitor for his company. After five years of turning down offers, he was quite pleased to be approached by Henry Block. Every aspect of the company matched the list he had squirreled away in a bottom drawer.

H & R Block, too, had every reason to be pleased with its new acquisition. CompuServe had sales of $12 million in fiscal 1984, and the personal computer services network, which barely existed at the time of the takeover, is currently bringing in over $25 million a year—almost 30 percent of CompuServe's projected sales for fiscal 1985.

At the time of the sale, Wilkins owned only 5 percent of CompuServe, which became 46,301 shares of H & R Block (worth over $2 million in mid-1984). His attitude about that is philosophical: "People today read all the stories and think, 'Just because I have the idea, I ought to have 40 percent of the company.' Well, there's a lot more to it than just the idea." After all, he points out, he originally brought so little capital to the project he'd had to borrow $1,500 just to move to Columbus.

Meanwhile, the stress on education continues. In 1984, Wilkins instituted a formal program of executive development for his 600 employees. He still participates enthusiastically in the Young Presidents' Organization, a group which offers continuing education in management to young chief executives (Wilkins turned 40 in 1984).

Wilkins doesn't appear to measure success by his lifestyle and dislikes being made the object of personal publicity. But he's happy to admit that his efficiency has gained him a 45-hour work week that gives him more time to spend with his family. He keeps in shape in the company gym, working out three mornings a week.

Wilkins tries to keep the spotlight on his company and to give his employees full credit. "Individuals don't create companies," he says. "There are an awful lot of people responsible for CompuServe." But you can bet that Wilkins will continue to guide CompuServe with plans in hand, ready to count the pluses and minuses before he makes a move.

HIGH-TECH IMMIGRANTS

	Country of Origin
John Ellenby (Grid Systems)	England
K. Philip Hwang (TeleVideo)	Korea
Adam Osborne (Osborne Computer)	Thailand
Go Sugiura (Amdek)	Japan
Jugi Tandon (Tandon Corp.)	India
Jack Tramiel (Commodore)	Poland
Camilo Wilson (Lifetree Software)	Chile
Ihor Wolosenko (Synapse Software)	Ukraine

CHAPTER 6

MONEYBAGS
& INDUSTRY GURUS

William Hambrecht

"I'm probably the only guy who went to Princeton because it was Norman Thomas's school"

▶ **BEST-KNOWN VENTURE:** Hambrecht & Quist

OTHER VENTURES: Wine Creek Ranch, Belvedere Winery

BORN: 1935

RAISED: Babylon and Baldwin, Long Island, New York

FATHER'S OCCUPATION: Mobil Oil manager

FIRST DOLLAR EARNED: Golf caddy

SCHOOLING: B.A., history, Princeton University

ORIGINAL FINANCING: $1 million from four wealthy San Franciscans, plus personal savings

PERSONAL NET WORTH: At least $50 million

HOME: San Francisco, California

FAMILY: Married; five children

PERSONAL TRANSPORTATION: Audi, Jaguar

HAMBRECHT & QUIST

HAMBRECHT & QUIST INC.: Investment bankers specializing in emerging high-growth technology companies.

▶ **BEST-KNOWN PRODUCTS:** Apple Computer, Convergent Technologies, People Express, Dreyer's Grand Ice Cream

YEAR FOUNDED: 1968

EMPLOYEES: 360

HEADQUARTERS: San Francisco, California

SALES: $120 million

PROFITS: $20 million

OWNERSHIP: Privately owned, Hambrecht being the largest investor

If you have an idea for a new computer or for elegant systems to run a computer, the next thing you will need is money. In the computer industry, one deep wellspring for such start-ups has been the San Francisco investment banking firm of Hambrecht & Quist, a company which, in backing entrepreneurs, has scored an entrepreneurial triumph of its own.

William Hambrecht and George Quist were not exactly impoverished when they started their business in 1968. Both came from modest backgrounds, but each by then had achieved a measure of success in the investment world, working for others. It was their vision (to set up a venture capital and investment banking firm that would bankroll high-technology outfits) that enabled them to steal a march on Morgan Stanley, Goldman Sachs, and other prestigious investment bankers on Wall Street. And one reason they scored is that they were in San Francisco, close to the cutting edge of new technologies. They saw what the Wall Streeters could not see, that this was the most explosive new industry on the horizon.

Quist, who died of a heart attack at the end of 1982, was a native of San Francisco. Co-founder Bill Hambrecht, a native of Long Island, is a convert to California. He once explained why:

"Looking back, I am still amazed at how easy it was to raise money to start Hambrecht & Quist. One evening in San Diego, my partner and I decided to start our firm. We wrote a brief, four-page business plan on the plane the next day. We visited four prominent San Francisco families that afternoon and by that evening we had raised a million dollars. I couldn't imagine doing that in New York, Boston, or Philadelphia. I knew that my cousin, a Philadelphia banker, wouldn't have made the loan. But here in California, our investors are only one generation removed from the risk-takers who created the capital in the first place. Their willingness to take risks has its cultural roots in the pioneer traditions of this state."

Happenstance plays a part in everyone's life, and it certainly did in Bill Hambrecht's. He was born in 1935 in Oceanside, Long Island, the younger of two sons. (His elder brother, George, was killed at age 28 in a plane crash.) Hambrecht's father was a manager for Mobil Oil. And Hambrecht grew up in two Long Island towns not noted for their chic—first Babylon and then Baldwin, where he went to high school. As a teenager he worked at caddying and landscaping. His grades were apparently not remarkable, and he showed no aptitude for science, but he was big and tough enough to play tackle on the high school football team (he also made the basketball team). It was his athletic prowess, he suggests, that got him into Princeton in 1953.

But there was more to Bill Hambrecht going to Princeton than just football. As a boy he had been greatly influenced by his grandfather, a Norman Thomas socialist. Norman Thomas, the great leader of the American Socialist Party, was a Princeton graduate. "I'm probably the only guy who ever went to Princeton because it was Norman Thomas's school," jokes Hambrecht today.

Hambrecht didn't see much action on the Princeton football field—he underwent three knee operations and spent much of his athletic time in the training room. He graduated *cum laude* in 1957, having majored in history and minored in economics. During the summers, thanks to his football connection, he drove a Pepsi-Cola truck.

He wasn't certain what he wanted to do after graduating, but, like many a Princeton graduate, he headed for Wall Street. Through a connection at Lehman Bros., he landed at American Metal, predecessor company to today's AMAX. Then a Princeton classmate, Dennis Delafield, invited him to come south to Florida to join his family's investment firm, Security Associates. In the fall of 1958, he did. For a variety of reasons, it was a significant move.

First, he found he liked the underwriting business, which is basically the business of raising money for companies.

Second, he was introduced to the world of high technology. Security Associates was located in Winter Park, near Orlando, and that central Florida area was becoming populated with new electronic firms serving the aerospace activities at Cape Canaveral. It was Bill Hambrecht's introduction to high-tech financing.

Third, he met his bride, Sally Pigman, who was then a student at Florida State University. She is the daughter of a scientist who had moved from Evanston, Illinois, to work at Cape Canaveral.

Hambrecht's next port of call was Chicago. Security Associates was acquired by an old-line Wall Street investment banking house, A.C. Allyn & Co., and in 1961 Hambrecht left Florida to join Allyn's Chicago office. It was a period of headlong expansion, numerous mergers, and utter chaos in the securities industry. Hambrecht was hardly ensconced in Chicago when Allyn sold out to Francis I. duPont & Co., then one of the major Wall Street brokerage houses. In 1965, duPont sent Hambrecht to the West Coast to head up its San Francisco office. And that's where he met George Quist, who in the mid-'60s was running the venture capital arm of Bank of America.

When the Hambrechts moved to California, they already had three children. They settled first in a large flat in San Francisco's Cow Hollow district; two more children were born while they lived there. In 1968 the Hambrechts moved across the Bay to Tiburon, from where Bill could take a ferry every morning to get to his office in the financial district.

The stories written about Bill Hambrecht usually have said that he started his company with Quist because duPont wanted to transfer him to New York. There's some truth to that, but there was probably another reason as well: Bill Hambrecht didn't like the attitude that prevailed at duPont. He told us that in 1962 he had persuaded Arthur Allyn to put $250,000 into a new company called Systems Engineering Laboratory, which eventually became part of Gould Inc. In return for his efforts, Hambrecht was given a 5 percent slice of the brokerage house's action. That 5 percent turned out to be worth a lot a few years later when duPont brought the company public. The $250,000 Allyn had put up was then worth $8.5 million—and young Bill Hambrecht's share was worth almost $450,000. When the duPont people in New York saw these figures in the offering prospectus, they weren't too happy, according to Hambrecht. "They saw this twenty-eight-year-old kid down for 450,000 dollars, and they made it clear that they didn't want this to happen in the future. They didn't bother to appreciate the millions they were making on the deal." So Hambrecht was more than ready to plot a new venture with Quist. Shortly after H&Q was formed, Francis I. duPont went down the drain in the back office debacle—the inability to keep up with the clerical load of the stock market boom—that buried many Wall Street houses.

Hambrecht and Quist always knew what they wanted to do: back high-tech firms with unique ideas. By getting in early and finding companies that didn't crash, H&Q made enormous amounts of money for themselves—and their investors. One high-tech firm after another was financed in its infancy by H&Q. It wasn't always easy. In the mid-'70s the stock market was in the doldrums and few private companies were going public. H&Q had to close its New York office, and both Hambrecht and Quist mortgaged their homes to borrow $2 million to pay some of their investors who wanted out.

H&Q is not infallible. It has financed companies that failed—Magnuson Computers, for example. And it has financed other companies—Diasonics, Eagle Computer, and Wicat Systems, for example—which have performed miserably in both the marketplace and the stock market. Eagle Computer is perhaps the quintessential boom-and-bust, high-tech story. H&Q brought it public in June 1983, pricing the stock at $13 a share; the offering raised $33 million for the fledgling microcomputer maker. On the opening day Eagle Computer closed at $15.50 a share. After celebrating the successful offering, Dennis R. Barnhart, the 40-year-old president of Eagle, was killed when his new Ferrari went off the road. The following day H&Q rescinded the offering, but a week later it brought the stock out again, this time at $12 a share. In a spurt that surprised all the experts, Eagle Computer soared to a high of $22 before closing at $17.25. A year later, Eagle Computer was selling at $1.50 a share.

H&Q also missed the first round at Apple Computer. Hambrecht told us that the reason they didn't invest in Apple at the start was that there was a highly regarded team of H&Q researchers who had correctly identified CB radios as fads that would quickly die out. H&Q saved a lot of money by staying out of that area. When this same team said that the personal computer was a fad of the same ilk, they were listened to, and H&Q turned its back on first-round financing for Apple. They did, however, come in on the second round—and they brought Apple public in 1980.

H&Q does more than just pump money into companies. It often provides management assistance, especially if an H&Q-financed firm gets into trouble. "We don't walk away as long as we think there's value," Hambrecht says. The chairman of H&Q in 1984 was Q.T. Wiles, known as the "Red Adair of investment banking." Adair is a world-class squelcher of oil-field fires. Wiles is a world-class squelcher of problems in high-tech start-ups. In 1984, he was serving as chairman of the board of four different companies: Silicon General, VLSI Technology, Granger Associates, and Zymed. Bill Hambrecht himself sits on 17 different boards of directors. When we asked him how they found time to meet all these commitments, he said, "Oh, well, some of these meetings are just held here in Q.T. Wiles's office."

H&Q can go through boom-and-bust cycles of its own. In 1983, it managed $2.2 billion of public offerings. Among these were 26 new issues for $1 billion—companies selling stock for the first time—Eagle and Wicat, for example. But that was 1983. In 1984, activity dried up—and H&Q co-managed only eight public offerings worth $96 million in the first eight months of the year. As a result, H&Q cut back its staff by 5 percent in the summer of 1984, bringing the number of employees down to 360. But H&Q's cachet is still such that any high-tech company going public for the first time wants to have this firm's imprimatur on its prospectus. It's the banker of choice for companies with unique ideas.

H&Q wears its crown with very little pomp and circumstance. The company's offices in the old Russ Building on Montgomery Street have a dowdy, "old-shoe" atmosphere. Hambrecht is very accessible, and everyone calls him Bill. In 1983, the company switched from being a partnership to being a corporation, to signal that it aimed to have some kind of permanence. In a partnership, all profits are paid out as they are made. A corporation retains earnings; it has a life of its own. Bill Hambrecht is the largest stockholder, but virtually everyone who works at Hambrecht & Quist owns stock—they can buy it at half the book value.

H&Q co-managed the initial public offering of Apple Computer with one of the Wall Street blue bloods, Morgan Stanley, and Bill Hambrecht likes to tell the story of how, during a meeting at Apple, one of the Apple people turned around and said: "Hey, you're more like us than them [Morgan Stanley]."

Bill Hambrecht likes companies which have an egalitarian feeling about them. It was H&Q that brought People Express Airlines public. "We didn't know anything about the airline business," Hambrecht told us, "but we liked the philosophy of insisting that all employees own stock in the company." H&Q also brought Dreyer's Grand Ice Cream public. Why? Because they were intrigued by a company that refused to sacrifice quality standards in making ice cream. "The consumer is smarter than most mass marketers think," says Hambrecht. "They will buy quality."

Hambrecht's political sympathies have remained Democratic, despite the many millions he has made. "I've been a lifelong Democrat," he once explained, "because I feel it's more a party of inclusion than exclusion. It's more in tune with a way of organizing and sharing the rewards of the economy."

Now that most of their children are in college, Hambrecht and his wife have moved back to San Francisco. The Hambrechts are avid wine connoisseurs, and the large vineyard they own in Sonoma produced a prizewinning Pinot Noir in 1984. Bill has invested in other wineries as well. One of them, Chalone, sold stock to the public in 1984; the major underwriter for the offering, needless to say, was H&Q.

What does it take to get backing from Hambrecht & Quist? Bill Hambrecht once spelled it out as follows:

—"First, you must be right in your initial concept. If you're wrong, you must recognize it and change very quickly.

—"Second, you need good people. They must possess an intellectual integrity in seeing things as they are, rather than as what they want to see. Most problems are solvable if you don't kid yourself about the problem.

—"Third, you must be able to get enough financing to give your idea time to prove itself.

—"Finally, you must motivate your people to extraordinary efforts. This is your competitive edge. It is not enough to just say the right things, you really have to live and believe them."

H&Q refuses most of the people who come to it for financing. Hambrecht once told *Fortune* magazine: "You can tell by the way a guy hires how he thinks. The guy who hires weak people is one you have to worry about."

But that doesn't mean H&Q is reluctant to see prospects. Bill Hambrecht has been known to speak at large meetings and issue this invitation: "If you know business, have that unique idea, and have the sense of commitment needed to pull it off, give me a call."

Portia Isaacson

"I'm not patient; you know what I mean. One of our rules is 'Never hesitate to think'"

▶ **BEST-KNOWN VENTURE:** Future Computing

OTHER VENTURE: The Micro Store

BORN: 1942

RAISED: Stratford, Oklahoma

PARENTS' OCCUPATION: Dairy farmers

FIRST DOLLAR EARNED: Carhop

SCHOOLING: B.S., physics and mathematics, East Central Oklahoma State University; M.S., computer science, North Texas State University; M.S., computer engineering, and Ph.D., computer science, Southern Methodist University

PERSONAL NET WORTH: $5 million

FAMILY: Married and divorced (four times); married to husband number five; three sons from first marriage

PERSONAL TRANSPORTATION: 1984 BMW

FUTURE COMPUTING INCORPORATED: Largest supplier of information about the personal computer industry.

▶ **BEST-KNOWN PRODUCT:** Portia Isaacson

YEAR FOUNDED: 1980

EMPLOYEES: 135

HEADQUARTERS: Richardson, Texas

SALES: $10 million (1984 projection)

PROFITS: $1.2 million (1984 projection)

OWNERSHIP: Wholly owned subsidiary of McGraw-Hill, Inc.

The scene is the Hyatt Regency Hotel on San Francisco Bay, June 21 and 22, 1984, five months after Apple introduced its new personal computer, the Macintosh. The occasion was MacForum, a conference focusing on the impact and market potential of this new piece of hardware. The conference featured a star-studded array of speakers. On hand were Steve Jobs and John Sculley, chairman and president of Apple, respectively; Trip Hawkins, president of Electronic Arts; Marty Alpert, president of Tecmar; Regis McKenna, the Silicon Valley public relations guru; and, not incidentally, Dr. Portia Isaacson, president and chief executive officer of Future Computing, and her husband, Dr. Egil Juliussen, then chairman of Future Computing. It was Future Computing that had put this conference together.

Gathered in the Hyatt ballroom to listen to these luminaries and to put questions to them were some 150 people. For this privilege, each paid an $895 registration fee, which did not cover their hotel room costs. This is a perfect example of the role played by Future Computing, the company founded by Portia Isaacson. The reason people are willing to part with

$895 to attend a two-day conference is that information about a new product like the Macintosh is vital. You need to know about it if you are in the retail business, selling computer equipment. You need to know about it if you are in the software business, designing programs to be used by the new computer. You need to know about it if you are manufacturing parts that can be used with this computer. And you naturally want to know about it if you are making and selling a competing product.

Information is the key to success—and information gathering and selling is what Future Computing is all about. It does more than just stage conferences. It issues newsletters and research reports, consults, and has various package deals for subscribers, which entitle you to a whole gamut of information. Future Computing's list of subscribers reads like a "Who's Who" of the computer industry. Some 330 subscribers pay $15,000 a year to get the whole range of services. Subscribers also get a discount on those conference fees—$716 instead of $895. And all of this information is related to the personal computer industry.

The founder of Future Computing is a dynamic woman who grew up as the eldest child on a 360-acre dairy farm in Oklahoma. Did she work as a kid? "Extremely so," is her answer, adding: "On a farm you bust your butt. You have to do everything. What I did a lot every day, twice a day, was what we called 'gathering up the cows.' You get on your horse and you go round up the cows. Bring them in to milk. Early in the morning and at night."

It was not a prosperous farm. Isaacson remembers that there were weeks when she didn't know if she would have money to buy lunch at school. She was the first person in her family to finish high school. And after she graduated, she hopped on a bus for Dallas, which was 200 miles away. She was a little short of 18 years old—and she had a total of $25. She landed a job right away as a carhop at a restaurant and then worked in a chemical laboratory. Science was always her strong suit. At the same time she started night school at Southern Methodist University but "didn't make it through the first semester because I started doing the arithmetic on how long it was going to take me to finish—and it was about 300 years. I'm not patient, you know what I mean."

So Portia Isaacson enlisted in the Army. "I thought, well, if you're never going to get out of college, the logical thing is to join the Army. That's the way an 18 year old thinks."

The two years she spent in the Army were, in her own words, "wonderful." They taught her something about the world. "Having grown up on a farm in Oklahoma, you really aren't experienced at all in the ways of the world. You barely even know how to catch a bus."

Discharged from the Army, she began to learn from the school of hard knocks. She married immediately, when she was 20 years old, and quickly had twin boys and then a third son. Her husband deserted her. She was living in Ada, a town in the south-central part of Oklahoma, not far from the Texas border. With the help of several welfare programs, she supported her kids, worked full time and went to school full time (at East Central Oklahoma State), all simultaneously.

"I had a lady live with me so at night I could work. I had some wonderful jobs. I worked in a bar. I worked in a hospital emergency room. It wasn't fun at all. On days when the tips weren't very good, I might have stolen some baby food."

She attended school during the day, majoring in physics and math, determined to get her degree because she reasoned the only way to support her children would be to get an education. After graduating she headed for Dallas with her three sons and got a job as a scientific computer programmer, not something that any respectable physicist would feel good about: "It's like taking a job typing," but "I was desperate. I was deeply in debt, you know. I was starving. I had three cute little boys, almost nothing to eat, and no clothes." It was in Dallas, at the end of the '60s and in the early '70s, that Isaacson drifted into computer work, continuing her triple-tier life: working, going to school, and taking care of her family. She learned computer programming on the job at Bell Helicopter, Lockheed, Computer Usage, and Xerox. She then began to do a little consulting, having learned a key skill: interfacing IBM mainframes with non-IBM equipment. She once told a reporter that she has had a hard time getting ahead in the corporate world because she is a woman. "At that time," she told Jo Vance, a reporter for the *Plano Texas Review,* "women were rare in the industry. My answer to that was to go back to school and get more degrees." She pursued her education at North Texas State and SMU, earning two master's degrees and a Ph.D. Meanwhile, she also found time to remarry— several times.

She and her fourth husband, David Wilson, opened a computer store in Dallas. That was in 1976. In a year, it was doing $1 million annually. It was called the Micro Store. It was the first retail computer store in Texas and one of the first in the country. Even though she was a co-owner, Isaacson didn't spend a lot of time in the store. She had become an evangelist for the computer industry. She taught at the University of Texas, she was active in professional societies, and she wrote and lectured widely on computers, so much so that in 1977 she chaired the National Computer Conference. She was 35 years old and was already one of the most well-known personalities in the emerging computer industry. "I had this platform and all this visibility. The press was calling me all the time. Everybody thought I was a little nuts—but entertaining. That fame, or whatever it was, was an important thing that caused me, in a way, to be where I am today. I guess I became tagged as a futurist, seeing some big wave of things coming long before anyone else. I'm still in the same business."

Portia Isaacson's next stop was with the fabled Ross Perot's Electronic Data Systems in Dallas. He made, as she says, "your basic offer you can't refuse." Isaacson had a shot there at starting a business from scratch. Perot wanted to go into the personal computer business, and he had his new vice president start a unit to produce broadcast quality video instructional materials for personal computers. It was a great idea, Isaacson told us, but "about three to five years too early. Really too early. We made the money back that we invested, but it wasn't viable at that time, particularly not in a company like EDS, which is in a totally different business (data processing). It would have been better off in a publishing company."

But Portia Isaacson benefited from the EDS stint. It gave her experience in starting a new business. She was also divorced again. (Her fourth husband now works for her.) She left EDS at the end of 1979 to start her own business, Future Computing, and she was married for the fifth time—to Egil Juliussen, a distinguished Norwegian-born engineer who was then a market-research executive and planner at Texas Instruments. They were married in January 1980. Future Computing was incorporated eight months later. A year later Juliussen left TI to join his wife's company. They built it into the eyes and ears of the computer industry. You want to know which computers are selling best? Call Future Computing. You want to know which stores are selling which products? Call Future Computing. You want to know what kind of computer equipment the Fortune 500 companies are buying, ask Future Computing.

Many people are impressed with Portia Isaacson's drive and sales ability. She knows how to sell herself. She's also tough. A 1984 *InfoWorld* profile of her began as follows: "Tough as nails. That's Portia Isaacson, no matter who you ask." But then Isaacson herself told the reporter she would suggest the term "bull-headed" to describe herself. "I'm very goal-oriented, and I have a lot of focus," she said, adding: "I always play to win."

Working at that pace can take its toll. Reporter Jo Vance had this to say about Portia Isaacson and Egil Juliussen: "The demands of a growing business require the bulk of their attention. Perhaps it is more accurate to say that the business is their social life." And Portia told another interviewer: "Egil and I work seven days a week; we even get calls during breakfast on Sunday mornings."

However, relief may be on the way. In July 1984 McGraw-Hill, the big New York-based publishing company, bought Future Computing for a reported $8 million—plus additional payouts based on profits. That was just a day after General Motors announced that it was buying Ross Perot's company. Neither of these developments was predicted by Future Computing.

Regis McKenna

"We are more part of the electronics industry than part of the PR industry. I've never studied public relations; I've studied technology"

▶ **BEST-KNOWN VENTURE:** Regis McKenna Public Relations

BORN: 1939

RAISED: Pittsburgh, Pennsylvania

FATHER'S OCCUPATION: Public utilities manager

FIRST DOLLAR EARNED: Photography lab assistant

SCHOOLING: St. Vincent College; Duquesne University; San Jose State University (no degree)

ORIGINAL FINANCING: $500 from savings

PERSONAL NET WORTH: $10 million

HOME: Sunnyvale, California

FAMILY: Married; two sons, one daughter

PERSONAL TRANSPORTATION: Mercedes

Regis McKenna

REGIS MCKENNA PUBLIC RELATIONS INC.: Public relations guru to Silicon Valley.

▶ **BEST-KNOWN CLIENTS:** Apple Computer, Convergent Technologies, Digital Research, Electronic Arts, Genentech, Intel, TeleVideo Systems

YEAR FOUNDED: 1970

EMPLOYEES: 115

HEADQUARTERS: Palo Alto, California

SALES: $10 million (1984 projection)

PROFITS: $1 million (estimate)

OWNERSHIP: Privately held by Regis McKenna (100 percent)

It's not too surprising that Regis McKenna emerged as the philosophical guru of Silicon Valley. He grew up in a devout Roman Catholic family, the second to last of seven sons. Four of his brothers became priests or monks. McKenna himself studied existential philosophy at Duquesne University, run by the Holy Ghost Fathers in Pittsburgh, his hometown. He brings to the business of public relations an analytical and dialectical turn of mind that has enabled him to communicate to the outside world—and the media in particular—the attributes of his clients, which are all high-technology companies.

The success of Regis McKenna Public Relations is still astounding. It will probably come as no news to the Public Relations Society of America that public relations does not rank high in esteem, either among business people who use it or among press and broadcast people who have to deal with the mountain of press releases, press conferences and other events pushing products and/or services. Business leaders show their disdain by placing public relations far down on the corporate totem pole; journalists show theirs by invidious references to "flacks."

Regis McKenna escapes such typecasting. Clients retain him for his conceptual thinking, and for his ability to help position a company. "The way we look at it here," McKenna told us, "is that public relations is the last thing you do anyway. The strategy development has to be in place before you can communicate about it." His work for the high-tech companies of Silicon Valley has been so effective that he is in the enviable position of being able to pick and choose his clients. *Fortune* summed it up in 1982: "Simply being a client of Regis McKenna Public Relations has become a kind of anointment for a high-tech business."

Among the companies basking in such anointment in 1984 were Apple Computer, Intel, TeleVideo, and Digital Research. When Apple introduced its Macintosh computer in the first month of 1984, Regis McKenna's hand was much in evidence. There seemed to be blanket coverage of the introduction—in the trade press, newspapers, magazines, radio and television. No fewer than 16 magazines ran cover stories on the Macintosh. Behind this avalanche of publicity were months of advance work by McKenna and his staff, patiently lining up one-on-one interviews with reporters who were given two-and three-hour briefings on the features of the new computer. The press kit announcing the Macintosh was also vintage McKenna. It contained releases that were crisply written, with no superlatives. It contained photographs that were sharp. The explanations were clear. It contained a T-shirt. And all the materials were packaged in a plastic container: if you have a high-tech public relations agency, why not act like a high-tech outfit yourself?

The man behind this PR company is the opposite of the image conjured up by the term "flack." He's quiet and soft-spoken, slight of build, and dresses conservatively. At the same time, he is an evangelist, at home selling ideas. McKenna never attends public relations industry events. Instead, he spends a fair amount of time on panels and commissions that deal with electronics, industrialization, and economics. He likes to articulate a philosophy, not only for clients, but for America's future. And he hires with the same anti-public relations bias, choosing people with backgrounds in high-tech companies, who will be able to understand, work with, and interpret the technologies they encounter.

What does a client get from Regis McKenna?

—In 1967, when he was 28 years old, McKenna was hired by National Semiconductor to be its marketing communications director, which included responsibility for public relations and advertising. National Semi was not then the giant it is today. It was, in fact, close to bankruptcy; annual sales were $7 million. McKenna's ideas, translated into ads and news releases, positioned National Semiconductor as more than just another manufacturer of semiconductors. Charles E. Sporck, founder of the company, said: "Regis spread the idea that we were a technological leader long before we actually were. His ads made people think everything new and good came only from National."

—McKenna left National Semiconductor in 1970 to set up his own advertising and PR firm. One of his first clients was Intel, where Marcian "Ted" Hoff had just invented the chip that later came to be called the microprocessor. McKenna's positioning played an important role in establishing this product and its maker, Intel, as technology leaders. His initial ad in a fall 1971 issue of *Electronic News* said boldly: "Announcing a new era in integrated electronics: a microprogrammable computer on a chip." Intel's co-founder, Robert Noyce, credited McKenna for helping to get the new technology accepted. "It was a battle of opinion," he said, "and Regis's marketing ploys had a lot to do with winning it." L.J. Sevin, founder of Mostek, an Intel competitor, said: "Regis clobbered us by positioning Intel as the technology leader. They had an easier time hiring engineers and getting through to their customers' executives. I didn't realize PR mattered so much until it was too late." (Mostek was later sold to United Technologies.)

—When he took on Apple in 1977 (before it was even incorporated, but after he'd tried to turn down the scruffy— and persistent—Steve Jobs a couple of times), McKenna again did more than just issue press releases. For one thing, his company designed the colorful Apple insignia that became the company's logo. And then he made a characteristically bold move. Instead of limiting ads for the Apple computer to industry publications, he decided to run a color page in *Playboy* magazine. McKenna explained the decision as follows: "It was done to get national attention, to popularize this idea of low-cost computers." He gave Apple a different kind of assistance as well, when he introduced Jobs to venture capitalist Don Valentine, who not only invested but also suggested Mike Markkula for Apple's first president—an example of the Silicon Valley "network" in action.

McKenna believes strongly in concentrating attention on the few people who are influential. "There are probably no more than 20 or 30 people in any one industry who have a major impact on trends, standards, opinion, and a company's image or character," he said. "Ninety percent of the world's views are controlled by the 10 percent who are opinion makers. A good job of public relations demands that you develop relationships with relatively few people."

McKenna was once asked how he makes a company successful. He replied: "I don't know that we make a company successful as much as we help a company articulate a strategy that most of the entrepreneurs know intuitively is there. What I mean is that in most of the companies that start out, the founders have a real intuitive knowledge of the market and the product business. That's not always explicit. By working with them, we help articulate that to a broader audience. We help them by being their conscience."

Regis McKenna came to California via an unusual route. He never graduated from Duquesne, or received any higher degree, though he kept attending colleges wherever he found himself until 1979. (He finally gave up with only three credits to go—in French literature—when he couldn't find a parking place at San Jose State on a rainy winter afternoon.) He married his childhood sweetheart, Dianne Page, when he was 20, and went to work immediately selling advertising space for four technical magazines published by a Pittsburgh company, Instruments Publishing. Twenty-five years later he can still rattle off their names: *Instruments & Control Systems, Instruments & Apparatus News, Medical Electronic News,* and *Military Systems*

Design.

Soon he was working closely with the publisher, Richard M. Rimbach, Sr., "an incredible individual. I sat at his elbow for a couple of years doing nothing but learning the business— he did market research, edited, rewrote press releases, proof-read. It was my education into the real business, I guess, that I'm in today." It was this company that transferred him to California. He then joined a small advertising agency, Jack Harrick Advertising, that did business with the early semiconductor makers. His big break came when he realized that there was a market for a coordinated set of public relations services for these companies. His boss disagreed, so McKenna accepted an offer from General Micro Electronics, "the first commercial MOS [metal oxide semiconductor] company, really the basis for all the technology you see today."

In 1967 he moved on to National Semiconductor.

There, "you did whatever you had to because there weren't enough people to go around. You had to sell products, you had to sweep the floors. I brought in the first purchasing agent. I sold wafers. I went all over the world helping them set up marketing. I was blessed by having those opportunities to be able to sit and observe and participate in the *total* company. And so I learned from everybody."

When McKenna left National Semiconductor to set up shop on his own, he had $500 in savings ("the first month's rent") and a typewriter. He got two accounts quickly, Electronic Arrays and Monolithic Memories, and then, in 1971, Intel, which is still an agency mainstay.

McKenna considers himself lucky to have been part of some of the most important innovations of the last 10 years: "the first microprocessor; the first personal computer; the first recombinant DNA product out of Genentech; the first retail computer store; those things really represent the major, major achievements. To us, at the time, they were just another product, I guess, we were hustling to get out and launch. They have become probably the most significant ones of the decade." Of course, some clients do get away. Bill Gates, for example, pulled Microsoft's account because he was irritated that Regis McKenna was also handling arch rival Digital Research.

But Regis McKenna Public Relations has been a skyrocket in recent years, doubling its business every two years. In mid-1984 it was handling 50 clients, all of them high-tech outfits, and it had a staff of 115 persons, two-thirds of them in the original office in Palo Alto, and the rest in branches in Portland, Oregon; Phoenix; Costa Mesa, California; and Paris. New offices were being planned for Boston, Munich, London, and Tokyo. Clients paid McKenna fees of $6 million in 1983. Billings for 1984 were expected to come in around $10 million, which should move the firm into the "Top 10" in the public relations industry. McKenna got out of the ad agency business in 1981, selling that part of his business to Chiat/Day for $1.5 million. (It was Chiat/Day that produced the anti-Big Blue ad for the Macintosh in early 1984.)

McKenna himself has fared well, with a personal worth estimated to be in the neighborhood of $10 million. In addition to the profits made by his firm, he has benefited from investments in Silicon Valley partnerships and from shares he bought in many of the fledgling companies he represented. He bought Apple stock, for example, at 50 cents a share.

McKenna is a diabetic (one of his brothers died from diabetes) and wears a portable insulin pump on his belt. But it doesn't appear to slow him down: he, his wife Dianne, and their three children all run and hike and go off on frequent backpacking trips. He tries to run at least four miles every day. And he's involved in politics. Dianne has been mayor of Sunnyvale twice, and McKenna, like some other computer industry leaders, is a Democrat. When the Democratic National Convention came to San Francisco in July 1984, McKenna was there as an active California delegate for Gary Hart. Needless to say, Hart carried the state, and won in Silicon Valley hands down.

$100 MILLION SALES CLUB

Sales

Don Estridge (IBM Entry Systems Division)	$4 billion (1983 est.)
William Millard (ComputerLand)	$1.8 billion (1984)
Jack Tramiel (Commodore)	$1.3 billion (1983)
Steve Jobs (Apple Computer)	$983 million (1983)
Jerry Sanders (Advanced Micro Devices)	$583 million (1984)
Jugi Tandon (Tandon Corp.)	$303 million (1983)
Sheldon Adelson (Interface Group)	$200 million (1983)
Pat McGovern (International Data Group)	$150 million (1984)
Takayoshi Shiina (Sord Computer)	$100 million (1983)

Thomas Perkins

"The entrepreneurs know that it doesn't always work. It's not uncommon to go through a couple of failures before you hit it"

▶ **BEST-KNOWN VENTURE:** Kleiner Perkins Caufield & Byers

OTHER VENTURE: University Laboratories

BORN: 1932

RAISED: Oak Park, Illinois, and White Plains, New York

FATHER'S OCCUPATION: Insurance adjuster

FIRST DOLLAR EARNED: Paper route

SCHOOLING: B.S., electrical engineering, Massachusetts Institute of Technology; M.B.A., Harvard Business School

ORIGINAL FINANCING: $8 million, half of which came from the Pittsburgh Coke fortune

HOME: Belvedere, California

FAMILY: Married; two children

PERSONAL TRANSPORTATION: Mercedes, large antique car collection

Kleiner Perkins Caufield & Byers

KLEINER PERKINS CAUFIELD & BYERS: Champion venture
capital partnership with a penchant for risky-
investment, pure start-up firms.

▶ **BEST-KNOWN PRODUCTS:** Tandem Computers, Vitalink
Communications, Sun Microsystems, Electronic Arts,
Genentech

YEAR FOUNDED: 1972

EMPLOYEES: 17

HEADQUARTERS: San Francisco, California

SALES: $230 million capital under management

OWNERSHIP: Approximately 45 limited partnerships

Tom Perkins has movie star quality, in a Gary Cooper kind
of way. He's tall and lean and has Cooper's laconic style.
In 1984, when he was 52 years old, he could pass for 40.
He's not a glad-hander, but is soft-spoken and tends to look
down when he talks. But, also like Gary Cooper, the deadpan
exterior masks intensity. You get the feeling that if there were a
shoot-out in Silicon Valley, Tom Perkins would win. It's a valley
where he has already won a lot of victories as a venture
capitalist of the first rank. Among the computer-linked companies that have been fertilized by Kleiner Perkins Caufield &
Byers, a San Francisco-based venture capital partnership, are
Tandem Computers, Vitalink Communications, Sun Microsystems, Imagic, Electronic Arts, Parallel Computers, Quantum, Plexus, DataFlow, and Cadlinc. Not all these companies
are in Silicon Valley. DataFlow is in Boston, Cadlinc in
Chicago. Perhaps the most celebrated company to emerge out
of Kleiner Perkins is Genentech, the Bay Area genetic engineering firm.

What does a venture capitalist do? He (and there are almost no female venture capitalists in the field) listens to ideas from people who want to start new companies. If he likes the idea—and the proposer—he will put money into it, his own as well as other people's. Then he will watch the fledgling company, perhaps even play a part in its management. Down the way he may have to pump in more money. If the company goes down the tubes, the venture capitalist loses his entire stake. On the other hand, if it hits, he—and the investors who came in with him—are bound to make a lot of money. The $1.5 million Kleiner Perkins put in to start Tandem grew to $220 million. The $200,000 invested in Genentech paid off in stock worth $40 million.

Not everyone loves venture capitalists. Reporter Joel Kotkin did an insightful piece for *Inc.* in the summer of 1984, concluding: "Venture capital today is becoming a victim of its own successes. Once a collection of small firms run by brilliant, if often idiosyncratic, individuals, the venture capital business is developing into a large-scale, highly institutionalized industry."

And if the venture capital business is becoming institutionalized, it's partly because of Kleiner Perkins. The partnership has been so successful—of the 100 companies it backed in its first 12 years, 80 were still operating in 1984—that everyone wants to invest in its start-ups. In late 1982, to accommodate new investors—insurance companies and pension funds, for example—Kleiner Perkins organized (together with Morgan Stanley) the first big venture capital fund. Investors put $150 million into it. These are investors willing to let Kleiner Perkins decide which companies to support; they just want to be in on the killing. And for the privilege, they will give Kleiner Perkins a full 30 percent of all profits.

Making a quick killing is clearly not Tom Perkins' motivation. He was a millionaire before he became a venture capitalist, having made it on a venture of his own. He's an engineer and a businessman, and obviously enjoys grappling with both technical ideas and corporate administrative problems. He doesn't just look around for places to park money. This is characteristic of the Kleiner Perkins approach. The partners like to be in the trenches with the companies they fund. A number of companies—Tandem and Genentech are the most notable examples—were hatched inside the walls of Kleiner Perkins. Robert Swanson, founder of Genentech, was a Kleiner Perkins partner, and so was James Treybig, founder of Tandem Computers. Treybig, in fact, worked for Perkins at Hewlett-Packard. Perkins himself sits on 15 different boards of directors and is chairman of the board at both Tandem and Genentech.

Perkins is the only child of a middle-class family. He was born in Oak Park, a western suburb of Chicago known for its many Frank Lloyd Wright homes and also for being the birthplace of Ernest Hemingway. His father was an insurance adjuster who, early in Tom's life, moved the family to White Plains, New York. As a teenager Tom worked in grocery stores, had paper routes, and also earned money tutoring other kids in mathematics and physics. The man who made a big difference in his life—"I owe everything to him," he says—was a physics teacher at White Plains High School, a Mr. Wilson. Perkins hadn't thought much about going to college, but Wilson not only insisted that he go but made him apply to MIT, which admitted him on a scholarship.

"My original plan was to be a physicist," Perkins told us. "But at MIT, I encountered *real* physicists. You know, geniuses. And I realized that I didn't have the mental equipment to do original work." So in his junior year Perkins switched from physics to electrical engineering; he graduated in 1953. He worked for a while at Sperry Gyroscope, designing radar-controlled gunsights, and then entered the Harvard Business School to get an M.B.A. He came out to California in 1957 to work for Hewlett-Packard, one of the first M.B.A.s ever hired there. He worked in marketing and engineering but his most important contribution was starting their computer operations. "I was the first general manager of what became a division of the company," he said. "I literally put them into computers. And part of that was running the research labs."

Perkins obviously did very well at Hewlett-Packard. He became William Hewlett's deputy when David Packard went to Washington in 1969 to become deputy defense secretary in the first Nixon administration.

Perkins also did well moonlighting (with the company's permission) as an inventor. He devised a method of putting mirrors inside laser tubes and established a company, University Laboratories, in Berkeley, California, to develop applications for his invention. It turned out there were many. Tom Perkins's invention converted the laser from an instrument for scientists into a dependable, relatively inexpensive tool for performing such practical tasks as laying sewer pipe. In 1970, Perkins merged his company into a publicly held firm, Spectra-Physics (one of the first companies brought public by Hambrecht & Quist), and he came away with $2 million. Two years later he left Hewlett-Packard and teamed up with Eugene Kleiner to start a venture capitalist firm.

Kleiner, like Perkins, is an engineer—and a celebrated one. He was one of the eight brilliant scientists who walked out of Shockley Laboratories in 1957 and, with funding secured by Arthur Rock, founded Fairchild Semiconductor. That event is considered by many people the birth of Silicon Valley.

Tom Perkins clearly has a zest for high-risk start-ups. He likes the challenge not only of investing but of helping shepherd a company through its early stages. He is known as a ruthless analyst of business plans, and associates have described him as "an almost compulsive perfectionist." Albert L. Horley, one entrepreneur (Vitalink Communications) who was backed by Kleiner Perkins, described him as follows: "Tom is the kind of guy who has to be the top of the top or he won't go for it."

Perkins exhibits the same kind of zeal in his hobby, which is collecting and restoring old cars, with the emphasis on *restoring*. He likes to work on them himself and exhibit them at antique car shows. His specialty is the supercharged sports car—Bugattis, Alfa Romeos, Ferraris—and his collection, which numbered 30 in 1984, is the largest in the world. He keeps three cars at a house he owns in England. He participates in car rallies in England and on the continent, and in 1984 he self-published a book, *Supercharged Sports Cars*. For everyday tooling around, Perkins drives a Mercedes diesel. When someone once asked him what he was going to do if he hadn't been planning on college, Perkins replied, jokingly, "be an auto mechanic."

Although he's a millionaire many times over (Kleiner Perkins oversees more than $300 million in investments), Perkins is still a Democrat. "I believe in the social goals of the Democrats," he said, "but I believe the way to get there is usually with the economic programs of the Republicans. So I'm really schizophrenic. I'm not nearly the Democrat that Bill Hambrecht is." What he does share with Hambrecht is a strong belief in employee ownership of companies. "Just about every company I'm involved with, every employee is a shareholder," he said. Tandem Computers offers stock options to all employees, a rarity in U.S. business. James Treybig, president of Tandem (Perkins is chairman), once told a *Life* magazine reporter: "Capitalism and humanism are converging. You can no longer optimize profits and screw people. Tandem's a socialist company."

There's nothing socialist about the way Kleiner Perkins organizes partnerships. Here's how Perkins explained the setup: "It's a series of partnerships. As a matter of policy, we never reinvest profits. We distribute all profits back to our limited partners. So we're always running out of money, and that's why we keep forming new partnerships. We just think that investors like to get their money back and then decide whether they want to reinvest in yet another partnership. They always do, but at least they have the freedom of choice."

Kleiner Perkins had about 45 limited partners (the outside investors) in mid-1984. According to Perkins, they've never lost a partner. Is there something about California that makes an especially hospitable environment for entrepreneurs and venture capitalists? Hambrecht thinks so, and Perkins agrees. He told us:

"There is something unique about California. A lot of things are in place here. The banks understand it more than anywhere else. You've got universities that are feeding out ideas more than anywhere else. You've got realtors who understand how it all works and are willing to speculate and gamble with small companies where they won't elsewhere. And then, most important, you've got the entrepreneurs here. The point is, there's almost nobody in Silicon Valley who doesn't know somebody else that's made a million dollars. At least! Whereas there is almost nobody in Chicago who knows anybody that has ever come remotely close to making a million dollars. And that's all the difference. Out here, they know it can be done. In Chicago, it doesn't even occur to them."

Perkins found more than gold in California—he found his wife, the former Gerd Thune-Ellifsen, who was born in Norway. They live in one of the most posh suburbs in the Bay Area, the Belvedere enclave in Marin County, where residents enjoy spectacular views of San Francisco, the Golden Gate Bridge, and the Bay Bridge. They were married in 1961 and have two children: a son, Tor, who, in 1984, was majoring in physics at Pomona College in Claremont and wants to be a venture capitalist, and a daughter, Elizabeth, who entered Sarah Lawrence College in the fall of 1984 and intends to major in French.

WHAT GOES UP WILL COME DOWN

Because of Wall Street's fickle attitude towards high-technology stocks, for each of these entrepreneurs there were two days in 1983 or 1984 when they could have checked the price of their stocks in the newspaper and computed the value of their holdings as follows:

High/Low

K. Philip Hwang (TeleVideo)	$1.14 billion/$102 million
Steve Jobs (Apple Computer)	$437 million/$119 million
Andrew Kay (Kaypro)	$248 million/$65 million
Reid Anderson (Verbatim)	$133 million/$31 million
James Toreson (Xebec)	$126 million/$33 million
Jack Tramiel (Commodore)	$126 million/$39 million
Mitch Kapor (Lotus)	$112 million/$42 million
Jugi Tandon (Tandon Corp.)	$106 million/$19 million
Lorraine Mecca (Micro D)	$54 million/$15 million
George Tate (Ashton-Tate)	$48 million/$20 million

Arthur Rock

"Nearly every mistake I've made has been because I picked the wrong people, not the wrong idea"

▶ **BEST-KNOWN VENTURE:** Arthur Rock & Company

OTHER VENTURES: Apple Computer, Intel, Diasonics, Scientific Data Systems, Fairchild Semiconductor, Teledyne

BORN: 1926

RAISED: Rochester, New York

FATHER'S OCCUPATION: Candy store proprietor

FIRST DOLLAR EARNED: Selling candy

SCHOOLING: B.S., Syracuse University; M.B.A., Harvard Business School

PERSONAL NET WORTH: $200 million

HOME: San Francisco, California

FAMILY: Married; no children

PERSONAL TRANSPORTATION: 1963 Porsche 1600

ARTHUR ROCK & CO

ARTHUR ROCK & COMPANY: Premier venture capitalist; best
of the risk-taking, high-tech high rollers.

▶ **BEST-KNOWN PRODUCT:** Money

YEAR FOUNDED: 1961

EMPLOYEES: 1

HEADQUARTERS: San Francisco, California

MINIMUM INVESTMENT: $100,000

PREFERRED DEAL: $600,000 and over

OWNERSHIP: Private

I f you have what you think is a good idea for a new product
or new technological process, and if you happen to be a first-
born child, take it to Arthur Rock, the *ne plus ultra* of venture
capitalists. He has demonstrated an uncanny sense of the market potential for new computer start-ups—and he has noted
that the most successful entrepreneurs are often the first children born in their families. This counts for a lot in his book—
and his book today can unleash millions. Robert Noyce, co-
founder of Intel, is a first-born child. So were the founders of
several other Rock-financed companies. And come to think of
it, Rock himself is the eldest child in his family.

That family was headed by a Russian-Jewish immigrant
who came to this country around World War I—"somewhere
between 1915 and 1920," says Rock, "I'm not sure." His
mother was a Cohen, one of the two great rabbinical families
in Jewish history. Rock's father operated a candy store in
Rochester, New York, and young Arthur worked in the store as
a child and teenager. So he developed an early instinct for
business. He was not a particularly good student, although he
improved as the classes got tougher. As a youngster he seemed

to be a loner. His time was taken up entirely by school and working in stores, and not just his father's store. He had one uncle who had a dairy, another uncle who had a grocery. He worked on Saturdays and Sundays. And during the summer, he worked for others—in drugstores. Looking back today, he can say, "I enjoyed the commerce end of it."

After graduating from Harvard Business School in 1951, he went to Wall Street but not as a broker. He chose the investment banking side of the business—in other words, deal-making. From the start he had a strong interest in scientific companies. In one of his first deals, he helped finance General Transistor, the first independent company in the nation organized around the manufacture of transistors.

Accidents have a way of shaping our lives. Rock was at Hayden Stone in New York, working in the corporate department, when a letter arrived from the West Coast. It was from a scientist who had been working at the Shockley Laboratory Division of Beckman Instruments in Mountain View, California, just south of Palo Alto and Stanford University. The scientist wrote at the suggestion of his father, who had an account at Hayden Stone. It seems that eight distinguished scientists were unhappy working with the famed Nobel laureate, William Shockley, and they wanted to leave. "They thought they were stronger together than separate," Rock recalled for us in an interview. "So I came out to talk to them." The eight scientists were Robert Noyce and Gordon Moore (who later founded Intel), Jean Hoerni (now chairman of Telemos), Eugene Kleiner (now a venture capitalist), Jay T. Last, Victor Grinich, C. Sheldon Roberts, and Julius Blank.

Rock came west with another Hayden Stone man. "We talked to these eight scientists and decided that we ought to agree to form a company and then try to raise some money for them. In those days there were no venture capitalists. Nothing called a venture capital firm. We went around looking for a million-and-a-half dollars for them. We went to twenty-five or thirty companies and none of them had ever thought about investing in a new business." The eight scientists had not yet chosen a leader, so all of them came along to the meetings. "They had a lot of questions," says Rock in his wry way. "But we finally located Sherman Fairchild. He was a very interesting man. He was, when he died, the largest shareholder in IBM—and a scientist in his own right." Thinking back on that moment, Rock said: "We didn't have any money. Nobody else I knew did. They just weren't doing deals like they're doing today. This was 1957."

For investing $1.5 million in these scientific whiz kids, Fairchild was given an option to purchase at a later date all the stock in the newly formed company, Fairchild Semiconductor. The stock was divided as follows: each of the eight scientists had 10 percent, and the remaining 20 percent went to Hayden Stone. In 1959, two years later, Fairchild exercised all its options for a total of $3 million, which meant that each of the scientists received $300,000 and Hayden Stone, $600,000.

Two years after that, in 1961, Arthur Rock left Wall Street to come to San Francisco and team up with Tommy Davis, who had been with Kern County Land Company, in a venture capital firm named Davis & Rock. It was a new-fangled concept for the United States, but it was something the Rothschilds and other European merchant bankers had been doing for centuries: backing promising ventures with seed capital. You make out well if the company makes out well; otherwise you lose. You need to have very good judgment. Arthur Rock does.

One of his first deals was with Scientific Data Systems, founded by Max Palevsky. Rock put up $280,000 to help start SDS, cashing in eight years later, in 1969, when Xerox bought the company for $950 million. Once it became part of Xerox, SDS disappeared into oblivion. Rock's explanation: "Xerox didn't do it right. The only thing I can tell you is that when we sold SDS, it was a one-hundred-million-dollar business making ten million dollars after taxes. At the same time Digital Equipment did fifty million dollars and four million dollars after taxes. And we were direct competitors [in minicomputers]. Same business. I personally feel that Xerox just didn't do it right. Mismanagement, yes sir."

Management is something Arthur Rock deeply cares about. He just doesn't put his money into a deal and then walk away. He usually goes on the board of companies he has backed. He spends time with them, trying to solve their problems. He clearly wants to be known as more than just a money man.

Laconic is one way to characterize Rock. He has a detached air about him—clinical and analytical are words that have been used to describe him. He put his feet up on a sofa while talking to us, but he didn't relax much. The one time his eyes did light up was when he talked about his wife, Toni Rembi. They were married in 1975. She is a managing partner in San Francisco's largest corporate law firm, Pillsbury, Madison & Sutro. Asked who has influenced him the most outside of business, he said, unhesitatingly, "my wife."

In 1984, Rock was serving on the boards of several companies in which he had put money—his own and money from friends who trust his judgment. Half of them are public: Intel, Apple, Teledye, and Diasonics. The other four are private startups: Rational Machines, Ridge Computers, Elxsi Internatonal, and Dialogic. All make computers, in one form or another—but they are not in direct competition with each other. Rock also serves on the board of Hambrecht & Quist, another venture capitalist outfit.

Everyone who has met Rock talks about his ability to read people. Max Palevsky once said of him, "He has an incredible intuition. His nose never ceases to amaze me."

Thomas Davis, his former partner (the company is now just Arthur Rock & Co.), said, "He only wants right answers."

Time writer Michael Moritz said: "Rock's quiet manner often intimidates strangers and can daunt even close friends. Says one associate, 'I was scared to death of him for the first ten years I knew him.'"

We asked Arthur Rock what it takes to start a new company. He had a ready answer: "A very great desire to do this. Burning, crazy desire. Absolute crazy desire to build a company and make it succeed. A person has to be very, very honest. I don't mean taking money out of your pocket or cheating on his income tax. I mean honest with himself. That he can recognize problems. Admit mistakes, foresee the problems, realize his own shortcomings if he has any."

Talking about Bob Noyce, Rock said: "I consider myself lucky to know him. I don't think there are ten people like that in the United States."

Rock's office is in the same place it was when he opened for business in 1961: San Francisco's Russ Building. While he has helped to found companies with total sales running in the billions and his personal fortune is now estimated at $200 million, he has not expanded his own office one whit. As a matter of fact, it doesn't seem he has purchased any new furniture. He has one employee, his secretary and office manager, Marie Getchel, who has been with him since 1966.

"I'm not an administrator," Rock concedes. "I have a tough time running one secretary, I don't run people. I don't have to organize people."

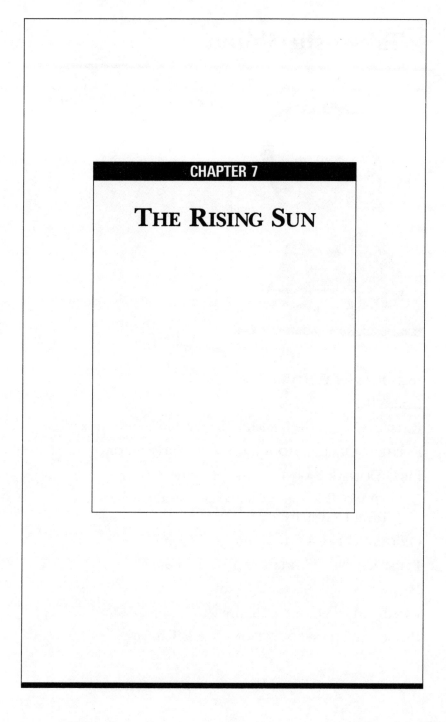

CHAPTER 7

THE RISING SUN

Takayoshi Shiina

"Zero is a zen number and, like Sord, has no limitations"

▶ **BEST-KNOWN VENTURE:** Sord

BORN: 1943

RAISED: On a chicken farm in Chiba Prefecture, Japan

FATHER'S OCCUPATION: Journalist, chicken farmer

FIRST DOLLAR EARNED: Stealing watermelons

SCHOOLING: B.S. (equivalent), electrical engineering, Tokai University

ORIGINAL FINANCING: Family and friends

PERSONAL NET WORTH: 39 percent of Sord

HOME: Chiba Prefecture, Japan

FAMILY: Married; three children

PERSONAL TRANSPORTATION: Toyota Crown

SORD COMPUTER COMPANY: One of the few truly
entrepreneurial Japanese companies—introduced the
world's first microcomputer with an operating system in
April 1974.

▶ **BEST-KNOWN PRODUCTS:** PIPS software and the M Series of
microcomputers

YEAR FOUNDED: 1970

EMPLOYEES: 1,000

HEADQUARTERS: Tokyo, Japan

SALES: $85 million (1983); $125 million (1984 projection)

PROFITS: $8 million

OWNERSHIP: Privately held; Shiina, family, and employees
own 70 percent, outside investors (banks and security
companies) own 30 percent

At seven in the evening, the end of every exhausting six-
day work week, another group of a dozen or so Sord
employees settles in for an eight-hour lecture by the
founder, Takayoshi Shiina. One shouldn't count on being able
to leave by three a.m. either, because, Shiina admits, he sometimes continues until dawn.

It is difficult to imagine what Shiina talks about week after
week, but some clues are offered in a paperback book with a
bright orange cover entitled *The Flame from Japan*, written by
Takeo Miyauchi and copyrighted by Sord. This Japanese
Horatio Alger story of Shiina's rise reveals a great deal about
how its maverick hero would like to be seen. When he became
an entrepreneur, the concept still ran completely against the
grain of Japanese society, but Miyauchi's book—a best-seller
in Japan—weaves a kind of romantic legend around Shiina's
eccentric path.

Shiina likes references to his samurai ancestors and, although it's never quite spelled out, the association of the entrepreneur with that fearless, honorable, and extinct figure from Japan's past is a brilliant piece of public relations. *The Flame from Japan* tells us that Shiina was born in 1943 in Manchuria, where his whole family, including uncles and cousins, had gone as part of the Japanese occupation. Repatriated to a defeated Japan in 1946, having lost all his possessions, Shiina's journalist father had to become a humble chicken farmer. Young Takayoshi did not like farming.

He became a "gang leader" in a small town in Chiba Prefecture, about 50 miles from Tokyo. In the scarcity of the postwar years, the enterprising lad became deft at watermelon-stealing—a skill at which he attained "superior ranking." When he reached the age of 13 his mother insisted that he go live with her brother in Tokyo and attend the sorts of schools that would get him into a good university. Shiina protested but eventually acquiesced.

Uncle Wakamatsu Ono ran a camera shop after the war; before that he had been a railway man for many years in Manchuria. But his real passions were thinking and teaching, and he soon became Takayoshi's guru. They developed a very unusual routine. After finishing with school and homework, the boy helped in the camera store until 10 o'clock at night. Then, at the back of the store, Uncle Ono lectured for one to four hours. On religion, philosophy, history, and literature. On salesmanship and politics. On Buddha and Christ. When the lecture was over they sang a song. Not a popular ditty, but a classical Chinese poem. This arrangement continued for five years, and Uncle Ono remained a fixed star in Takayoshi's universe for as long as the older man lived.

Mrs. Shiina's hope of getting her son into a top university was fulfilled. After a year's cramming, he successfully passed the entrance examination for the Self-Defense Force Academy—a kind of Japanese West Point. But two weeks after entering, Shiina quit. He gives two reasons now: the Japanese military had "no budget, no new weapons, no dreams." And, without proper family connections, Shiina stood little chance of rising to what he felt would be an appropriate rank.

Sometime before his brief tenure at military school, Shiina had decided that he would make his mark either as a warrior or a business tycoon. In his way of thinking, the two paths were philosophically very close. Returning home to the ridicule of his village after dropping out of the Self-Defense Force Academy, Shiina had only one alternative left. But before embarking on a business empire, he felt he needed a credo. The 20-year-old Shiina dreamed up "The Eleven Commandments for a Successful Business"—a list still prominently displayed at Sord.

The list contains a number of general ideals about serving humanity, combined with typical Japanese corporate principles: the company is a family; employees must be fully dedicated to the common task; individuals must have initiative, setting and meeting their own goals; labor and management must respect and cooperate with each other. But it also bears distinctive Shiina marks. He urges the value of youthfulness and fresh ideas. And, in the eleventh commandment, he reveals an expansionist gleam in his eye: "The company must expand internationally. An international outlook must be fostered among all employees."

With his new-found sense of mission, Shiina gave himself permission to break one Japanese rule after another. After giving up the military alternative, the reasonable course was to prepare for the equally difficult university entrance examinations by attending a Tokyo school dedicated to that purpose. He went—for two days—but decided that the commute wasted too much time and that he'd learn faster on his own at the local library. The Scornful Observers (who are depicted throughout *The Flame from Japan* as watching every move Shiina makes) labeled him a dropout and a dreamer, but Shiina was confident he'd get into a top university.

He didn't. Rejection notices piled up. Finally, at the last possible second, he slid into mediocre Tokai University. The place offered was not in the business school, where he wanted to be, but in electrical engineering. "Take it," said Uncle Ono. "Someday electronics will rule the world." Shiina took it.

As a student he expressed contempt for both classroom and lab. A waste of time. "Why should I learn to run those machines? I'll be hiring people to run them for me!" He sat in coffee shops, holding forth on his ideas and ambitions, and gathering disciples.

After graduation, Shiina looked for a job, just to get some experience before starting his own company. He applied to an unnamed foreign employer, thinking he might learn more interesting things there, and was shocked when told he was hired after an interview that lasted a few minutes. In Japan, employment, like marriage, is usually a lifetime proposition. There are batteries of tests, investigations of the candidate's family, and long interviews. Shaken by the brusque hiring procedure, Shiina went on to the company's training program. There he was bombarded with rules and regulations—they even outlined a procedure for going to the toilet. At the end of the first day he approached the personnel manager, handed back the training materials, and announced, "There's no way I can work for you. I've never heard of so many rules, even in the military. You know absolutely nothing about human beings." With that, he marched out.

By this time Shiina's classmates had all trooped off to their new jobs. He confided his worries to a trusted professor who sent him to meet the head of a new electronics company. The preliminary examinations at Rikei Industries went well and Shiina found himself in the office of the president, about to sign a contract. Suddenly he blurted, "To be honest, I don't expect to stay here more than three years. I want to be independent." Nobody says that in Japan. "Either this fellow is crazy," the president mused, "or he's the most honest man I've ever met." Shiina was hired.

The three years turned to seven—1963 to '70. Assigned by Rikei to sell Digital Equipment Corporation (DEC) minicomputers imported from America, he boosted the account phenomenally. While still a trainee he translated the DEC catalogs and manual into Japanese, on his own time. Then he managed to get sent to DEC headquarters in Massachusetts for a month. After that he was Rikei's self-appointed "expert" and chief enthusiast on minicomputers. As the DEC account leaped forward, executives from other companies started calling Shiina for advice, and organizations invited him as a speaker. He was somebody.

Within a few years Shiina convinced his bosses to set up a fully staffed Computer Center, which would focus on developing Japanese software to make the imported hardware more useful. But none of Rikei's engineers understood computer systems—least of all Shiina, who had scorned to get his hands dirty in college.

An important theme of Shiina's story begins here: headhunting. That commonplace element of the Western corporate scene is a near sacrilege in Japan, where employees usually spend their entire careers with one company. But Shiina gives his recruitment stories the romantic tint of those scenes in samurai movies in which a *ronin,* or renegade samurai, lures others away from their lords, usually in the smoky haze of a rural inn.

Shiina's college pal Nobuhiro Sato had a fine job at Burroughs, a large American electronics company. He was good at hardware, brilliant at software, and expected to rise to the top of his field. At one of their get-togethers after work, Shiina bluntly asked him to quit Burroughs and join Rikei. Sato nearly choked. But several hours later, in the glow of Shiina's persuasive powers, and aided by a huge quantity of Japanese beer, Sato toasted on it.

It took a few months to make the transition. When he did—going from a huge international firm to a relative nonentity—Sato was disappointed. Things at Rikei were not quite as Shiina had said they would be. Shiina was disappointed, too, since the company failed to put him in charge of the Center. One day in the spring of 1969, Shiina said to his somewhat depressed friend, "Let's quit Rikei and start our own company." "Why not?" was Sato's glum reply.

Shiina, his mother, Uncle Ono, Sato, and a few other friends passed the hat and raised $1,800. They formed the name, Sord, by taking the first two letters from "soft" and the last two from "hard." In lieu of a product, Shiina had a dream, which at once both enticed and appalled the practical Sato. Shiina wanted to build a small personal computer (with compatible software) that would sell for $2,000—one-twentieth the price of the cheapest DEC computer then available. This was in 1969—five years before the first appearance of the Altair, generally considered to be the first personal computer in the United States. But at that time it was just an idea of Shiina's. For now he and Sato had to keep working at Rikei. A third henchman, classmate Takeshi Sakuma, enthusiastically schemed with them in secret, but he too held on to his very desirable job at Sharp Electronics.

At the end of 1969, Shiina left Rikei to devote himself to Sord. After some months of floundering and being supported by his sisters, he landed a contract to develop a software system for a former Rikei customer. Sato joined him in May 1970, along with another college friend, Yukio Hata. The team worked feverishly on a leased Hitachi minicomputer worth hundreds of times Sord's assets.

One day they arrived at their office to find that it had been burglarized. There existed only a single copy of all the work they had done—if that copy or the precious computer was gone, they were finished. It took a while to ascertain that the machine was still in place and undamaged. But the papers? Further rummaging revealed that they were there, with an unpleasant addition. The thief, disgusted at not finding anything he considered valuable, had left a pile of excrement on them. The young engineers gazed aghast at the rank omen. Shiina broke the silence: "Good fortune: our work has been fertilized."

His divination proved accurate. Sord's software business thrived in the next year; still the company remained deep in the red. In May 1971, they got a big hardware order and Shiina accepted it, though he had no hardware engineer. The solution: more headhunting. This time the target was Takeshi Sakuma, happily living in Osaka (he didn't like Tokyo) and "married" to Sharp.

Sato and Shiina went down to Osaka for a friendly visit. This time the lubricant was *sake*. At a carefully timed moment in the wee hours of the morning, after much talk about Sord's dreams and attainments, Shiina fired: "Why not quit Sharp and join us?" While Sakuma sputtered, Shiina poured forth his eloquence. Autonomy! Creativity! Pioneers at the dawn of a new age! A little before daybreak Sakuma succumbed, and shortly afterward he moved to Tokyo. With the acquisition of Sato and Sakuma, Sord's two pillars, software and hardware, had been firmly planted.

The next three years were a story of 16-hour days (and sometimes 24-hour days, as the pioneers took to sleeping in their offices), minute salaries, and growing reputation. At the end of 1972, there were 10 men at Sord. If the year's profits had been distributed equally, each would have made about half of what his former job paid per month. But they weren't distributed equally; Shiina's two sisters went on supporting the would-be tycoon so that he could pay the others. But expansion continued. Headhunting continued. Shiina found a bride in 1971, and the bride had a brother—Hiroaki Kaneko—who took an instant dislike to the entrepreneur with the "cold eyes" and boastful ways. They clashed, but Shiina admired his spirit. A year later Kaneko was on the Sord team. Then Sakuma went headhunting at Sharp and brought back a prize, Akihiko Hiroishi, who had previously opined that Sakuma was committing professional suicide by moving to the new company. Hiroishi became chief of hardware at Sord. He also married one of Shiina's sisters.

The years between 1972 and '75, during which Sord became a really viable and robust business, were consumed with the effort to build a computer for "everyman." Shiina looked to American technology, which he knew was years ahead of Japanese. But he also criticized it for two fundamental weaknesses: the machines were too expenses and too hard to use. When Intel announced its 8008 microprocessor chip, Shiina was sure they'd found the answer. The Sord team worked feverishly for 10 months to produce a prototype machine based on the Intel chip. They unveiled it amid high expectations in 1973, but it proved to be a bitter disappointment. The world's first microcomputer (completed two years before the American Altair) took 10 minutes to produce results that could be obtained in seconds on an abacus.

As they debated whether to carry on the extravagantly expensive effort to develop their own machine, news came of a new microchip from Intel (the 8080), many times more powerful than the old. Once they got their hands on the new chip, they flew. Their prototype was a hit at the 1974 electronics show in Tokyo. A few more kinks were ironed out (like switching from the "delicate" Intel chip to a rugged one from Texas Instruments), and mass production commenced with a roaring backlog of orders. The price of Sord's system 80 was one-half to one-third that of the competition that began to emerge from the Japanese electronics giants.

Sord's progress from this point on is best described in Shiina's own words: "In 1974 we succeeded in the micro-computers with floppy disk drives; in 1975 we succeeded with high-capacity floppy disk drives; that was a huge success in my company. In 1976 we announced the desktop personal com-puter. Every year we grew twice, three times."

Just before he turned 30, Shiina wrote in his diary: "My goals will now be in threes. By thirty-three I will achieve 300 million yen in sales." The year of Shiina's thirty-third birthday, Sord's sales were more than 700 million yen (about $3 million at the current exchange rate).

In the same year, 1977, Uncle Ono died. He had served as president of Sord, as well as being Shiina's personal mentor. During his uncle's illness, Shiina continued to consult with him while embarking on his boldest headhunting expedition yet: the search for an older and highly respected man to be the titular head of Sord. Repeatedly his advances to top executives were rebuffed. Finally, at a joking suggestion from a friend, he went to Jiro Miyazawa, the president of a joint Japanese-American firm called Toppan-Moore, which had annual sales of about 20 billion yen ($80 million). Miyazawa was another samurai: at 73 he still worked out regularly at *kendo,* the Japanese art of fencing. After some weeks of thrusting and parrying, they struck an agreement. Miyazawa would be Chairman of the Board and Toppan-Moore would get 20 percent of Sord's stock. Shiina remained Sord's president.

In 1980 a survey of 600,000 companies over the preceding five years declared Sord to be the fastest-growing company in Japan.

Around the same time Sord introduced the Pan Informa-tion Processing System (PIPS), a software operating system for which revolutionary claims were made. It was touted as incomparably simple and versatile, a computer language that "does away with programming forever." By 1983 PIPS outsold all other software in Japan. Looking forward to a global empire, Sord has translated it (so far) into Chinese, Korean, Arabic, English, and several European languages.

The next grand concept was the PIPS Inn, which fulfilled Shiina's desire to open a network of franchised computer stores. These svelte establishments, with carpets, curving tables, and potted plants, look more like a cross between an executive office and a living room than a store. Customers can practice, observe, get training, and, of course, buy. At the first PIPS Inn opening in late 1980, Shiina raised his glass and toasted: "Now only nine hundred and ninety-nine more to go!"

Sord now has factories in Ireland and Singapore. The next frontier is America. An attempt to start a U.S. subsidiary in 1975 aborted when a tall Nevadan whom Shiina trusted implicitly decided to take the money and run. The campaign in the '80s is much better planned: "Other Japanese companies are sleeping like rabbits," Shiina told an interviewer in 1983. Sord, in contrast, is poised like a hawk, its eye fixed on the American market. The company has opened offices in New York and Los Angeles.

The master plan runs something like this. First, market dominance in Japan, along with powerful affiliates in Europe, North America, and other parts of Asia. Then, from computers, Shiina wants to branch off into related fields; he has set the seemingly incredible goal of establishing 50 entirely new companies over the next several years. This kind of expansion is imaginable because "the computer society is still in its infancy." Shiina's "final goal," to the extent that it can be encapsulated, "would be the establishment of a worldwide Sord 'family,' all of whose members share similar goals and a similar dedication to excellence, service, and society."

In a different mood, talking to a British journalist in 1981, Shiina said simply, "My ambition is to become another Mr. Matsushita." (Matsushita is the richest industrialist in Japan, having founded an electronics company that sells Panasonic, Quasar, and other brands.)

Despite his grandiose personal ambitions, Shiina has always emphasized an egalitarian spirit among employees and managers. This is one of the reasons he is described as a "maverick," or "un-Japanese." Other reasons include his taste for adventurous risk-taking; his readiness to delegate authority; and his insistence that workers be given plenty of independence and trust to exercise their creativity. When we talked with him he was cheerfully mixing with co-workers, customers, and passers-by on the floor of COMDEX, the computer trade show, in Los Angeles. The mild-mannered warrior said he enjoyed "making the mixtures" between the old-fashioned values his uncle taught him and the fresh, new ideas he is always seeking out.

With our American expectations, we asked if his wealth had enabled him to acquire fancy houses and cars. "No," he said, "not yet." It seems that in Japan it's very bad form to display your wealth. While it's perfectly normal, Shiina realizes, for a rich American to have a big house, car, and yacht, a Japanese is supposed to stick to "small house, ungorgeous food, small car."

But he hopes soon to be liberated from this constriction. "In some sense I don't care about Japanese standard," he smiles. "I am already international."

INDEX

Cadlinc, 447
Calsoft, 236
Campbell, James S., 33
Carlson, Ed, 173
Carlston, Cathy, 151
Carlston, Don, 150
Carlston, Doug, 144-153, 117
Carlston, Gary, 145
cars, entrepreneurs', 213
Cary, Frank T., 21
Catalyst Technology, 8
CCTC, 315
Chapman, Gene, 187
Chiat/Day, 444
Chomsky, Naom, 250
Choplifter!, 152
Chuck E. Cheese, 8
Citicorp Venture Capital, 16
Cole, David, 234
colleges attended, 97
Colossal Cave, 239
COMDEX, 363, 412
Commbat, 115
Commodore International, 104
Compaq, 143
Compass, GRiD, 13
CompuPro, 42, 82
CompuServe, 414
ComputerLand, 246, 340
Computer Playground, 336
Computer Showcase Expos, 363
Computer Space, 5
Computerworld, 383, 387, 411
Computers and Automation, 385
Computers for Everybody, 395
Connector Distribution Corp., 335
Control Data, 398
Convergent Technologies, 70, 425, 439
Cosmic Tunnels, 171
Cousteau, Jacques, 250
CP/M, 208, 218
CPU Computer Corp., 380
Crane, Dave, 7
Creative Strategies International, 179
Cromemco, 36
Crowley, Mary, 153
Csige, Geza, 336
Currie, Ed, 375
Cutler, Scott, 122
CW Communications, 371

Dark Crystal, 237
Data Communications User, 367

DataFlow, 447
Datalife, 268
Datatronic A.B., 102
David's Midnight Magic, 152
Davidson, Tom, 279
Davis, Tommy, 457
Dazzler, 39
DB Master, 380
dBase II User's Guide, 380
dBase II, 166, 229, 379
dBase III, 234
Deadline, 123
DEC 2060, 125
DEC PDP-10 computer, 158, 418
Dialcom, 402
Dialogic, 458
Diasonics, 428, 458
Didday, Rich, 394
Digital Broadcasting Corp, 402
Digital Equipment Corporation
    (DEC), 50, 72, 131, 457, 466
Digital Music Company, 403
Digital Research, 92, 204, 440, 443
dilithium Press, 392
Dilworth, Robert, 84
Disney, Walt, 6
doctorates, entrepreneurs with, 41
Dodge Racer, 251
Dornbrook, Michael, 123
Dortch, Michael, 67
Douglas Aircraft, 301
Dow Jones News Retrieval, 419
Dozoretz, Ronald, 186
*Dr. Dobb's Journal of Computer
    Calisthenics and Orthodontia,* 407
Dr. J and Larry Bird Go One-On-One,
    177
DR Logo, 210
Dunn, Homer, 32

Eagle Computer, 428
Easywriter, 246
Edlin, Jim, 374
education, least formal, 333
Edu-Ware Services, 222
Egan, Jim, 35
Electronic Arts, 176, 433, 439, 447
Electronic Data Systems, 436
Ellenby, John, 12-18
Elxsi Internatonal, 458
ENIAC, 130
Enigma, 254
Erhard, Werner, 342
Erickson, Milton, 250
est, 342